GOOD NIGHT
GOD & BLESS

GOOD,
GOD

NIGHT BLESS

A GUIDE TO **CONVENT**
AND **MONASTERY**
ACCOMMODATION
IN EUROPE

VOLUME TWO
FRANCE
UNITED KINGDOM
IRELAND

BY **TRISH CLARK**

HiddenSpring

GOOD NIGHT GOD & BLESS

www.goodnightandgodbless.com
info@goodnightandgodbless.com

Text copyright © 2010 by Trish Clark 2010
First published 2010.
10 9 8 7 6 5 4 3 2 1

LIBRARY OF CONGRESS
    CONTROL NUMBER 2009938879
Clark, Patricia Maureen, 1946–
Good Night and God Bless: a guide to convent
    and monastery accommodation in Europe
Volume Two: France, England & Ireland

Published by **HiddenSpring**
An imprint of **Paulist Press**
997 Macarthur Boulevard
Mahwah, New Jersey 07430

www.hiddenspringbooks.com

Printed and bound in China

ISBN 978–1–58768–057–1

NOTE ✦ While every care has been taken to
provide accurate information in this book,
it's inevitable that in some cases prices, the
availability and style of accommodation,
directions, opening times, transport
times and routes and other details will
have changed by the time you travel. It's
essential that you check all important
details before travelling. Please help us
prepare future editions by emailing your
advice to *info@goodnightandgodbless.com*

❡ Similar accommodations are available
throughout Europe, as described in:
VOL I   Austria, Czech Republic & Italy
            Out now
VOL III Germany, Spain & Eastern Europe
            Available soon

AUTHOR Trish Clark
EDITOR Janet Hutchinson
PROOFREADER Annabel Adair
INDEXER Teresa Burnett
DESIGNER Stuart Gibson
    for Book Design Australia Pty Ltd
ORIGINAL ILLUSTRATIONS
    Nathan Peter Wong
MAPS Kathi Klinger
AUTHOR IMAGE Ian Barnes Photography
ADDITIONAL IMAGES *courtesy of* iStockPhoto
PRODUCTION Theresa Sparacio

HiddenSpring

Contents

Foreword

ROM THE COMMANDING MONASTERY of Monte Cassino between Naples and Rome, to the eerie Mont St Michel on the tidal flats of northern France, the Roman Catholic Church has left its mark—architectural as well as spiritual—across continental Europe. In addition, on the other side of the English Channel are numerous convents and monasteries, all extraordinary buildings and well worth a visit.

These religious establishments represent the remarkable history of the development of Christianity in this part of the world. Why is this so, you may ask. Well, from the time Jesus Christ was on Earth, Christianity spread rapidly eastward from Jerusalem. Within 100 years, there was a Bishop of Lyons in France, and by then St Peter had well and truly made it to Rome and laid the foundations for the Catholic Church. From there Christ's message was relayed in all directions.

In fact, by 432 AD, St Patrick had been ordained a Bishop in Rome and despatched to Ireland. And only one hundred and fifty or so years later, after informal links had emerged in what is now known as the United Kingdom, an official Church mission was despatched there from Rome.

The many priests and monks and nuns undertaking the early work of the Church needed a safe place to sleep and chant and pray. Moreover, they required somewhere to record the learnings of the period and build the now vast libraries of religious knowledge. As a result, an extensive network of monasteries and convents developed across Europe. These stretched from Rome to Paris, to London and Dublin, and well beyond.

❡ For centuries these were the living and working places of thousands of devoted nuns and monks. But times have changed, and today many of these beautiful buildings have opened their doors to overnight guests. For a modest sum, you can get bed and breakfast—and for no extra cost avail yourself of the unique ambience and the often-superb vistas on offer.

❡ Volume One of *Good Night and God Bless* provides meticulously researched, easily accessed, up-to-date information on exactly where you can stay in an old monastery or convent across much of Europe. Volume Two is an equally invaluable guide. I commend Trish Clark, the author of this remarkable travel and accommodation guide. The details she includes in both these books allow us to step back for a while into the rich religious history of so much of Christian Europe. She takes us into the revamped cells and refectories that now provide the creature comforts for 21st-century travellers and pilgrims yet still retain a lingering sense of the presence of the Holy Spirit.

❡ In offering this commendation, I hasten to add that I am not in a position to endorse any one convent or monastery over another. But may I suggest a way of benchmarking your European experiences. Either before or after a stay in the religious accommodations of Europe, please consider visiting Australia's only 'Monastic Town', New Norcia in Western Australia. The monastery here was established way back in the first half of the 19th century by two Spanish Benedictine monks and these days it too offers various types of accommodation.

❡ I hope you are able to stay in at least some of the accommodations that Trish Clark so comprehensively details in this book, especially as many of these blessed bedrooms are in fact available for all, the holy and unholy alike. Who knows, but from sleeping in these locations, the unholy might become holy! Armed with *Good Night and God Bless* it is over to you.

Tim Fischer

TIM FISCHER, AC
Former Deputy Prime Minister
of Australia
Resident Australian Ambassador to
the Holy See—January 2009

image ❡ Cloisters, Mont Saint-Michel.
photo Drosera.

main image ◀ Historic carousel near
the Basilica du Sacre-Coeur, Paris.
William Fawcett.

opposite, top left to bottom
❧ Abbaye St-Pierre, Solesmes.
❧ Abbaye Notre-Dame de Sénanque,
Provence. *Jan Tyler.*
❧ Gargoyle on the roof of the Cathédrale
Notre-Dame de Paris. *S. Greg Panosian.*
❧ Abbaye Ste-Cécile, Solesmes.

this page, top to bottom ❧ Abbaye St-Joseph
a Flavigny, Favigny-sur-Ozerain.
Father Mary Pius OSB.
❧ L'Abbaye-aux-Hommes, Caen.
Claudio Giovanni Colombo.

main image ❧ Gunnerside, Swaledale, North Yorkshire, *John Woodworth.*

far left, top to bottom
❧ Adorices Convent, Kensington, London.
❧ Caldey Abbey, Wales, *gsanders.co.uk*
❧ Bar Convent near city walls, York. *Stuart Gibson.*

near left, top to bottom
❧ Abbey Church, Iona. *John Butterfield.*
❧ Author at Buckfast Abbey, Buckfastleigh, Devon. *Lucy Clark.*

main image ❮ Mountains at Bray. *Steeve Roche.*
left, top to bottom
❮ Kylemore Abbey, Co Galway.
❮ Glenstal Abbey, Murroe, Co Limerick.

near right, top to bottom
❮ Trinity College, Dublin. *Gail A Johnson.*
❮ St Patrick's Seminary, Maynooth, Co Dublin.

far right, top to bottom
❮ St Colman's Cathedral, Cobh, Co Cork.
Alan Tobey.
❮ Monastic settlement on Holy Island,
Lough Derg, Co Clare.

UK *below, top to bottom*
❮ Convent of the Franciscan Sisters of Malta, Pimlico, London.
❮ The Friars, Aylesford, Kent.
❮ More House, London.
❮ Tyburn Convent, London.

IRELAND
above, top to bottom
❮ Monastery of St Alphonsus, Dublin.
❮ Mt Melleray Abbey, Co Waterford.
❮ Kenmare, Co Kerry.
© *Tourism Ireland.*

FRANCE
above, top to bottom
❮ Notre Dame de Lerins, Île St-Honorat, Cannes.
❮ Abbaye Ste-Cécile, Solesmes.
❮ Maison d'Accueil Lacordaire, Vence.
❮ Maison St-Pierre, Paris.

❮ *All images courtesy of iStockPhoto or Trish Clark, if not otherwise credited.*

Introduction

 **G**OODNIGHT AND GOD BLESS is a guide to cheap, safe, clean and well-located accommodation for tourists, travellers and pilgrims in Europe. This book is the second in a series of three which provides details of guesthouse accommodation in over 500 convents, abbeys, monasteries and other religious establishments in Europe.

❧ **Volume I** is a guide to the religious guesthouses of Italy, Austria and the Czech Republic.

❧ **Volume II** covers the convents and monasteries of France, England, Ireland, Scotland and Wales.

❧ **Volume III** will include Spain, Germany and several smaller Eastern European countries.

❧ Tourists, travellers and pilgrims—be they men, women, children, individuals, families or larger groups—are welcome to stay in these convent and monastery guesthouses. And the warm hospitality is extended to non-Catholics as well as those of no religious beliefs. Any exceptions are noted in the individual entries.

❧ Hospitality has long been a tradition of religious orders and these days, with religious communities struggling under the weight of the maintenance costs of ancient buildings and the sad decline in the number of monks, priest and nuns, the only winners are the travelling public. Throughout Europe unused monks and nuns' cells are being quietly refurbished, some with added en suites, and opening up as general accommodation. Many once-dour refectories, where simple repasts were eaten either in silence or to the sombre tones of a monk or nun reading from the scriptures, have become lively places of conversation—and some surprisingly good dining.

❡ Location has always been important when establishing a religious settlement. Peaceful surroundings were considered essential to a monk's simple, contemplative lifestyle. But sadly, on account of the often panoramic views afforded by their settings—to say nothing of the history, architectural splendour and sheer size of these religious establishments—many of these magnificent estates are now easy pickings for the major hotel chains and property developers.

❡ Even so, beautiful rural monasteries are still to be found scattered throughout France, Ireland and the UK. Some have been built on idyllic islands or on the foreshores of lakes and rivers. Others stand on sprawling country estates. Kylemore Abbey, on the banks of a tranquil lake in Galway, must surely be one of the most picturesque abbeys in all Ireland. Aylesford Priory, so close to London but still in splendid rural isolation, and the Cistercian Abbey of Sénanque, becalmed on a fragrant sea of purple lavender each Provençale summer, are both postcard perfect.

❡ In times past many such an isolated monastery was sought out by the common people. They brought their children to be educated by the scholarly monks, or they came to participate in religious ceremonies or in search of employment. The grateful villagers' debts to the monks were paid in kind and over the centuries these once-remote monasteries expanded, all the while accumulating the now precious works of art, rare books and exquisite pieces of hand-crafted furniture.

❡ Today these same monasteries are in the centres of the villages and towns which, over the centuries, have slowly grown around them. Tyburn Convent, next to London's Oxford Street shopping district, stands in the shadows of Marble Arch overlooking Hyde Park. More House, run by the Catholic Canonesses of St Augustine, is in trendy (and royal) Kensington. A monastery of the Blessed Sacrament Fathers is just metres from the Avenue Champs-Elysées and Napoleon Bonaparte's monument the Arc de Triomphe in Paris. Across the sea in Ireland, near what is nowadays the thriving CBD of Dublin, a life-sized statue of Mother Catherine MacCauley, believed to be a future Irish saint, greets visitors to the convent she established which was the foundation of the now-international religious order of the Sisters of Mercy.

❡ As a part of my research for this book, and with two of my children in tow, I travelled by regional train, local bus and monks' delivery van to an abbey located high amidst the French Alps. Here I discovered not only a spiritual refuge but a restful, scenic place that was also much frequented by travellers and bushwalkers in the know who'd collected their substantial (and delicious) French picnic from the abbey kitchen and set out for a day's hiking in the mountains. Other favourites of mine include a disused seminary (the remaining monks have moved to a smaller building next door) on the waterfront in Nice—a handy and picturesque base for exploring the French Riviera. And I adore the gracious, hospitable French convent in the hills of the Côtes d'Azur where for many years Henri Matisse painted. Amidst much controversy, the famous French artist designed and built the nuns' chapel with the assistance of his very good friend and fellow artist, Sister Jacques-Marie. A local Dominican nun, Sister Jacques-Marie was once Matisse's former nurse as well as being a model for some of his paintings.

❡ During World War II and the Nazi occupation of France a medieval abbey situated close to Paris provided a safe hideaway for American nun Mother Benedict Duss OSB, and the inspiration for the founding of the Regina Laudis Abbey in Bethlehem, Connecticut, the first contemplative Benedictine abbey for women in the USA. A convent in Yorkshire, established in the 17th century, is the oldest, still-operating convent in England. It offers a comfy bed to the weary traveller along with a genuine welcome. And the sustenance provided from the sisters' on-site café is a blessing after a long day exploring the countryside.

❡ In Maynooth on the outskirts of Dublin, close by the sizable ruins of the town castle, an ancient Irish seminary offers accommodation to tourists all year round. Set among vast landscaped gardens and expansive emerald green lawns, this place is surely one of Ireland's best-kept secrets. And Trinity College, in the heart of Dublin city, is not only renown as the county's oldest university but also as a comfortable— and affordable—place to stay.

The accommodations in this book have been divided into two sections.

OPEN HOUSES ❧ The Open House section reviews those convents that accommodate the tourist and the general traveller. These accommodations come in varying standards of comfort. A basic convent guesthouse might consist of a few former nuns' cells which have been refurbished for the traveller and bathrooms may be shared. A simple breakfast may be the only meal available and there could be a curfew. Other convents have been offering accommodation to tourists for years and are well practised in the art of providing for 21st-century guests. These type of guesthouses are often run by the sisters themselves, sometimes with outside help; en suite bathrooms have been added and meals are available. Then there are the convent guesthouses where, sometimes on account of declining numbers, the sisters have chosen to employ friends or outsiders to run their business. The sisters will still be around but you generally find that you get more of a hotel (not usually 5-star!) type of experience here. However, the cheap, clean, safe and well-located rule still applies.

SPIRITUAL RETREATS ❧ Spiritual Retreats, on the other hand, provide temporary refuge for those wishing to undertake retreats, pilgrimages or other religious activities. It is important to realise that a house of Spiritual Retreat is not in any way suitable for the tourist or the general traveller as a place of overnight accommodation. The only thing the two different types of religious accommodation have in common is a warm welcome!

❧ *Good Night and God Bless* provides detailed descriptions of each of the facilities featured. There are directions on how to get there, along with general tourist information and some ideas for things to do and see in the surrounding area. It also lists places to eat (and drink). And there are a few curious titbits of trivia and some amusing anecdotes as well.

❧ In a separate part of the book the details of hundreds of additional convents, abbeys and monasteries which are open to tourists, travellers and pilgrims are listed. Another section is devoted to pilgrimages and significant religious celebrations in the countries included in the book.

❧ I hope you find Volume II of *Good Night and God Bless* a useful guide in the planning of your journey, whatever its purpose. Finally, here are some hints for booking religious accommodation:

❧ Book early and don't necessarily expect to hear back immediately. Monks and nuns have other important things to do which take priority.

❧ Don't write as you would if booking a room in a luxury chain hotel. Write as though you are requesting to stay in someone's house.

❧ Book via e-mail if possible, and with the help of a free Internet language translator (not perfect, but workable) translate the text into the local language and send it off in English as well.

❧ If curfews are a concern please enquire before making a booking.

❧ And most importantly—be happy and enjoy this unique experience.

TRISH CLARK
Sydney, Australia

How to use this book

ACCOMMODATION ⟨ The book describes *two different categories of accommodation*; **Open Houses** and **Spiritual Retreats**. Lists of **Additional Accommodation** covering both categories are also included.

⟨ **Open Houses** include convents, monasteries and Christian hotels which are open to tourists and holidaymakers. Men, women, children, couples and individuals of any religious persuasion can use this accommodation (except where otherwise specified). Christian hotels are linked to Protestant churches and are run in an atmosphere of cordial hospitality and Christian spirit.

⟨ **Spiritual Retreats** are suitable only for those men and women who wish to embrace a spiritual dimension in the course of their holiday—a day of meditation, a period of quiet reflection, a religious retreat, or a pilgrimage.

⟨ **Additional Accommodation** includes suitable establishments for tourists or for those on a spiritual journey. Pilgrims are also welcome to stay in accommodation available to tourists.

⟨ Simple **maps** (not to scale) show the location of the accommodation. Detailed maps are available from tourist offices or may be found on the Internet.

4

Paris / Centre / Île-de-France

ONGWRITER COLE PORTER loved Paris 'when it sizzle while crooner Frank Sinatra loved the city 'every moment of the year'. The millions who have headed t France's romantic, free-spirited capital to launch a lo affair of their own would surely agree. Take a leisurel stroll along the Seine. Or get a bird's eye view of the trademark *arrondissements* of this thrilling, sophisticated city from the top of t Eiffel Tower; the panorama is even more spectacular by night. And while there are plenty of places to dine in style and elegance you can just as easily—and much more cheaply—mingle with the locals for a breakfast *café crème* at any pavement café.

Many roads out of Paris meander through the Île-de-France, som leading to a bevy of extravagant palaces in the Loire, elegantly landscaped parks and magnificent châteaux that for centuries have been the lavish playgrounds of kings, queens and latterday presidents.

Regional France is one of the oldest wine-producing areas in the world. Less well known perhaps is the fact that monks played a leading role in the early stages of the French wine industry. They planted vineyards around their newly established monasteries, and viticulture continues to be widely carried out by religious orders today.

Regardless of wars, revolution and a bubonic plague which decimated religious communities, Christianity survived in Paris. And whether you are religious or not, it's easy to immerse yourself in the wonders of this majestic city and explore its magnetic charm from the base of a safe, inexpensive, hospitable religious guesthous

But for a complete change of pace, let the kids persuade you to ta them to Paris Disneyland.

⟨ Some accommodation offers **accessibility** for the mobility disabled; this is indicated with an icon.

⟨ **Restrictions** may apply to certain accommodation such as female-only or male-only access; these are shown in each entry.

⟨ **Prices** shown are approximate, and are based on a twin share, per person per night basis for the low season. Prices for accommodation at Spiritual Retreats usually need to be negotiated on enquiry.

FRANCE
Open Houses
Paris / Centre / Île-de-France Paris

01

FIAP Jean Monnet

FIAP, Foyer International d'Accueil de Paris (*Paris House of Welcome*), was established in 1968 as an international, non-profit organisation offering accommodation to young people from all over the world. Accommodation can be arranged on a short- or long-term basis, with special prices applying to groups and longer stays.

¶ The hostel is situated in the **14th arrondissement** on the city's left bank and has around 500 beds available in 200 single, double and multiple rooms. Each guestroom is quite spacious and comfortably furnished, and has an en suite bathroom and telephone. All rooms are serviced daily and sheets and towels are provided. There is a laundry for the use of guests and 11 of the guestrooms have wheelchair access.

¶ The centre offers an attractive **choice of eating options**, including a large, glass-roofed bar area, *Le Parisien*, which has an outdoor terrace; *Le Francilien*, a traditional French restaurant; and *L'Européen*, a self-service cafeteria. The restaurants cater for all meals and offer a take-away packed lunch service. Facilities include a **discotheque** and concerts held several times each week, table tennis rooms, a television/video room and music rooms. Guests can book tours and sightseeing excursions at the FIAP tourist information office and a **French language school** operates on the premises. The reception desk is open 24 hours per day. Security is provided and credit cards are accepted. The centre has a large garden area but no parking facilities. It is a 20-minute train ride (with one change) into the centre of Paris.

✉ 30, Rue Cabanis
F-75014 Paris
☎ +33(0) 1 43 13 17 17
✆ +33(0) 1 45 81 63 91
✉ fiap@fiap-paris.org
🖰 www.fiap.asso.fr
🛏 From €40.00 pp, including breakfast.
☞ Take the train to Métro Station Glacière (Line 6), 1km is 400 metres from the station.
† Sunday Mass 0900, 1030, 1205 & 1845
l'Église St-Sulpice
2, Rue Palatine, Paris (entrance is on Rue Garancière).
🕮 Open to men, women & groups

FRANCE
Open Houses
Paris / Centre / Île-de-France Paris

✉	Address
🖼	Accommodation price
☎	Telephone
✆	Fax
✉	Email or website
☞	Directions
🛏	Opening seasons
†	Church services
♿	Accessibility
€/£	Meal price range

	low price	€ / £
	mid price	€€€ / £££
	high price	€€€€€ / £££££

🕮	Open to both men & women
👤	Open to women only
👤	Open to men only
👥	Open to groups only
👤	Open to Priests only
T	Tourist Accommodation
S	Spiritual Retreat
ST	Tourist Accommodation with Spiritual Retreat Option

PILGRIMAGES ↙ A section at the end of each geographical region provides information about the most popular pilgrimages in each area.

PLACES OF INTEREST ↙ in the local area and surrounds are listed under each reviewed property, and include sightseeing and day trips.

FOOD AND DRINK ↙ comprises a small listing of popular and distinctive local restaurants and cafés.

HEARING MASS is the ceremony
I most favour during my travels.
Church is the only place where
someone speaks to me and I do
not have to answer back.

GENERAL CHARLES DE GAULLE
(1890–1970),
FORMER PRESIDENT OF FRANCE

FRANCE

ACH YEAR, VISITORS FLOCK TO FRANCE in such numbers that the country is consistently rated the world's number one travel destination. So why not follow in their footsteps and discover for yourself all that the fascinating Gallic lifestyle has to offer. Culture vultures can bask in a scintillating array of temptations—from leading galleries and museums to eminent opera houses, from ruined island abbeys to towering medieval cathedrals, from the vast gardens of opulent estates to castles replete with tales of romance and chivalry.

History enthusiasts can seek out the extensive Roman ruins scattered across the country's south, or retreat to the north to the renowned battlefields of two world wars. The hedonistic opt for the glorious beaches along the Provencale coastline and to the glistening white wonderland of the French ski country. And gastronomes are bound to relish the soul-satisfying French cuisine and the country's luscious, velvety wines.

France has long been a largely Catholic country, Avignon being the controversial seat of the Papacy in the 14th century. Today, France's monasteries and abbeys stand as reminders of an enduring Christian heritage. Many open their doors to tourists, while others offer more serious pursuits to those seeking spiritual solace. And when you step outside the cloisters the Gallic way of life beckons. All you need do is join in.

Paris / Centre / Île-de-France

ONGWRITER COLE PORTER loved Paris 'when it sizzles' while crooner Frank Sinatra loved the city 'every moment of the year'. The millions who have headed to France's romantic, free-spirited capital to launch a love affair of their own would surely agree. Take a leisurely stroll along the Seine. Or get a bird's eye view of the trademark *arrondissements* of this thrilling, sophisticated city from the top of the Eiffel Tower; the panorama is even more spectacular by night. And while there are plenty of places to dine in style and elegance you can just as easily—and much more cheaply—mingle with the locals for a breakfast *café crème* at any pavement café.

Many roads out of Paris meander through the Île-de-France, some leading to a bevy of extravagant palaces in the Loire, elegantly landscaped parks and magnificent châteaux that for centuries have been the lavish playgrounds of kings, queens and latterday presidents.

Regional France is one of the oldest wine-producing areas in the world. Less well known perhaps is the fact that monks played a leading role in the early stages of the French wine industry. They planted vineyards around their newly established monasteries, and viticulture continues to be widely carried out by religious orders today.

Regardless of wars, revolution and a bubonic plague which decimated religious communities, Christianity survived in Paris. And whether you are religious or not, it's easy to immerse yourself in the wonders of this majestic city and explore its magnetic charms from the base of a safe, inexpensive, hospitable religious guesthouse.

But for a complete change of pace, let the kids persuade you to take them to Paris Disneyland.

01

FIAP Jean Monnet

FIAP, Foyer International d'Accueil de Paris (*Paris House of Welcome*), was established in 1968 as an international, non-profit organisation offering accommodation to young people from all over the world. Accommodation can be arranged on a short- or long-term basis, with special prices applying to groups and longer stays.

❡ The hostel is situated in the **14th arrondissement** on the city's left bank and has around 500 beds available in 200 single, double and multiple rooms. Each guestroom is quite spacious and comfortably furnished, and has an en suite bathroom and telephone. All rooms are serviced daily and sheets and towels are provided. There is a laundry for the use of guests and 11 of the guestrooms have wheelchair access.

❡ The centre offers an attractive **choice of eating options,** including a large, glass-roofed bar area, *Le Parisien*, which has an outdoor terrace; *Le Francilien*, a traditional French restaurant; and *L'Européen*, a self-service cafeteria. The restaurants cater for all meals and offer a take-away packed lunch service. Facilities include a **discotheque** and **concerts** held several times each week, table tennis rooms, a television/video room and music rooms. Guests can book tours and sightseeing excursions at the FIAP tourist information office and a **French language school** operates on the premises. The reception desk is open 24 hours per day. Security is provided and credit cards are accepted. The centre has a large garden area but no parking facilities. It is a 20-minute train ride (with one change) into the centre of Paris.

✉ 30, Rue Cabanis
F-75014 Paris

✆ +33 (0) 1 43 13 17 17
✆ +33 (0) 1 45 81 63 91

✎ fiap@fiap-paris.org

✎ www.fiap.asso.fr

🚇 from €40.00 pp, including breakfast.

☞ Take the train to Métro Station Glacière (Line 6). FIAP is 400 metres from the station.

✝ Sunday Mass
0900, 1030, 1205 & 1845
l'Église St-Sulpice
2, Rue Palatine, Paris (entrance is on Rue Garancière).

❧ Open to men, women & groups

Open Houses
Paris / Centre / Île-de-France Paris

PLACES OF INTEREST ❧ **The Montparnasse Tower** in the Avenue du Maine, less than 2 kilometres from FIAP, boasts the fastest lift in Europe. The ear-popping ascent takes just 38 seconds to reach the 56th floor. From there, stairs lead up to an outdoor viewing area on the roof of the building from where awesome, panoramic views of Paris can be enjoyed. The closest Metro station is Montparnasse-Bienvenue.

❧ Opposite the Montparnasse train station is the **Cimetière du Montparnasse** where many of the city's past literary and artistic elite are buried in sectioned-off 'old' and 'new' areas. French sculptor and architect of the Statue of Liberty, Frédéric Bartholdi (1834–1904), American novelist and philosopher Susan Sontag (1933–2004), Bernard Lacoste (1931–2006), head of the clothing empire, to name but a few, are among those entombed here. Most of the gravestones are true works of art and tree-lined pathways make it easy to negotiate the cemetery. Maps are available at the entrance and the surroundings are so lovely that it is not unusual to see people picnicking.

❧ The French department store **Galeries Lafayette** has a branch in Montparnasse near the Montparnasse Metro Station. An artists' market is held on the Boulevard Edgar Quinet (Métro Edgar Quinet) every Sunday. Artists, sculptors, jewellers and all manner of craftworkers exhibit here. And if you can't make it to the cloisters you could always visit **l'Artisanat Monastique** at 68, Avenue Denfert Rochereau which is packed with all sorts of beautiful items made by monks and nuns in hundreds of monasteries throughout France—towels, table linen, lace, embroidery, even pyjamas and dressing gowns.

❧ Marie de'Medici, Regent of France (1573–1642) to her son King Louis XIII (1601–1643), had a taste for large gardens and the **Palais du Luxembourg**, on the Rue de Vaugirard was established for her in the grounds of what is now the 23-hectare **Luxembourg Gardens**. The palace itself is now home to the French Senate but the gardens, one of the city's most popular green spaces, are open for all to enjoy.

❧ The Chapel of the Catholic University in Rue de Vaurigard was once the **Church of St-Joseph-des-Carmes** and part of a Carmelite convent. An historic religious site, scores of priests and religious were murdered here in 1792 during the French Revolution in what is known as the September Massacre. Many of the victims' relics are in the crypt of the chapel.

✝ Sunday Mass 1000 & 1100

❧ Meanwhile, of interest to the morbidly curious, across the Seine, between a brasserie and a *boulangerie* (bakery) at number 8, Rue des Halles is a shop called the **Destruction des Animaux Nuisibles** (*pest exterminators*) which was featured in the 2007 animated movie *Ratatouille* about a rampaging Parisian rat, bent on destroying the city. The 'boutique' is run by a family of rodent killers who hang their conquests in the front display window. Inside is all manner of rat-ridding paraphernalia.

FOOD AND DRINK ❧ If you're keen to join Paris café society, make sure to check the prices before taking a seat at an outdoor table. Depending on the location, it could be a lot cheaper to have that *café au lait* indoors.

❧ The district behind **The Pantheon** (in the Rue St Jacques) is a bustling, colourful quarter for numerous well-priced cafés and bistros which open in the evening. Most have *à prix fix* (fixed-price) menus as well as à la carte, and the area is a fascinating place to pull up a chair and people watch.

❧ The restaurant **Le Christine** must be one of the most charming places to eat in the city. This warm, cosy, softly lit hideaway is open until late and the food is always freshly prepared and served with typical French flair. The fixed-price menu delivers a pleasant surprise, cost-wise.

✉ 1, Rue Christine

☎ +33 (0) 1 40 51 71 64   €€€

❧ Dine with an eagle's eye view at the 56th-floor restaurant in the **Montparnasse**, which wasn't named **Le 360° Café** for nothing. Drinks and light meals are served—and on a clear day the views extend to almost 40 kilometres.

✉ 56th floor, Montparnasse Tower

☎ +33 (0) 1 45 38 52 56   €€€

Open Houses
Paris / Centre / Île-de-France Paris

02

Foyer Saint-Jean Eudes

The Foyer St-Jean Eudes is named after John Eudes (1601–1670), the 17th-century saint and founder of the French Catholic ecclesiastical society, *La Congrégation de Jésus et Marie* (The Congregation of Jesus and Mary), also known as the Eudists. The organisation is made up of various communities of Catholic priests and lay brothers, some of whom are attached to the house in Paris. The complex is quite near FIAP (see previous entry), on the other side of the main boulevard and close to the train station. St-Jean Eudes also founded the female institute of the Sisters of Our Lady of Charity of the Refuge.

❡ The Foyer accommodates students during term time but some guestrooms are kept aside for members of the clergy. However, lay people who share similar Christian values as the religious people who live here are also made welcome throughout the year. The complex stands like a modern block of apartments on a street corner and has undergone **extensive renovations** (2007). Some guestrooms have a private shower and wash basin and others share a bathroom on the same floor. Breakfast is the only meal served but cafés and restaurants are scattered throughout the surrounding area. The centre has a small garden and a television room. Internet access is provided. No on-site car parking is available and credit cards are not accepted. It is a 20-minute train ride (with one change) into the centre of Paris.

✉ 1, Rue Dolent
F-75014 Paris

☏ +33 (0) 1 44 08 70 00
☏ +33 (0) 1 43 36 72 03

✉ foyer-saint-jean-eudes@wanadoo.fr
✉ fosjeaneudes@yahoo.fr
✉ www.eudistes-france.com

€40.00 pp, including breakfast.

☞ Take the train to Métro Station Glacière (Line 6). The Foyer is 400 metres from the station.

✝ Sunday Mass
0800
Chapelle St-Jean Eudes, 1, Rue Dolent.

Open to both men & women

PLACES OF INTEREST ❧ An entrance to **Les Catacombes de Paris** (*Catacombs of Paris*) at 1, Avenue du Colonel Henri Rol-Tanguy, near the Place Denfert-Rochereau train station, is in the same arrondissement as the Foyer. The catacombs comprise a web of tunnels and caves where millions of bones of former Parisians are stacked in what were once quarries dating back to Roman times. In the 18th century the tunnels were the answer to the city's overcrowded cemeteries. A vertiginous spiral staircase leads down to where each tunnel is marked with the name of the street above. Some tunnels are burrowed under the city's infamous **La Santé Prison**, once home to convicted murderer and Catholic convert Jacques Fesch (1930–1957). In 1987, the Archbishop of Paris, Cardinal Jean-Marie Lustiger, opened a diocesan inquiry into Fesch's life and conversion; as a result the controversial case for declaring him a saint of the Roman Catholic Church formally opened in 1993. As of 2010, no decision has been made.

❧ The city's other famous burial ground is the **Cimetière du Père-Lachaise** in the 20th arrondissement where American-born rock music icon Jim Morrison (1943–1971) was laid to rest. The ashes of Maria Kalogeropoulos, also known as opera singer Maria Callas (1923–1977), were stolen from here, Irish writer Oscar Wilde (1854–1900) is entombed here, and American writer and art collector Gertrude Stein (1874–1946) lies here beside her close companion, author Alice B. Toklas (1877–1967).

❧ **Le Louvre** and the **Musée d'Orsay** are 'must sees', but if the kids are with you they will love the **Museum of Magic** at 11, Rue St Paul in the Marais district, which is a great place for lots of family fun and entertainment, with magic shows, a few ghosts and magic lessons for up-and-coming wizards. **The Cirque de Paris** in Villeneuve la Garenne, a suburb in the north of Paris, is a training ground for would-be circus stars who can learn the tricks of the trade under the big top with the stars.

Open Houses
Paris / Centre / Île-de-France Paris

❡ The 12th-century **Church of St-Germain l'Auxerrois**, next to Le Louvre, is famous for Louis XVI's church organ. More recently its name has been linked to American basketball star Tony Parker and Eva Longoria, an actress in the television series *Desperate Housewives*, who married in the church in July 2008.

✝ Sunday Mass 0945, 1130 & 1900

❡ The **Memorial of the Liberation of Paris** and the **Musée Jean Moulin,** in the **Jardin Atlantique** (*Atlantic Garden*) near Gare Montparnasse, are separate museums dedicated to two heroes of the French Resistance, Jean Moulin (1899–1943) and Maréchal Philippe Leclerc (1902–1947). Items connected with the French Liberation and the achievements of Moulin and Leclerc are on display here.

❡ Those who wear glasses can dare to be different with a pair of unique spectacle frames from the studio of **Francis Klein** at 30, Rue Bonaparte. Francis Klein's striking *lunettes* are based on styles that were all the rage decades ago.

FOOD AND DRINK ✦ In a street which is lined with unique shops and boutiques, **Monastica**, run by the sisters of the Monastic Fraternity of Jerusalem, sells the edible side of monastic produce in France—tea, honey, biscuits, jams, chocolate and heavenly *gateaux* (cakes) all made by monks and nuns.

✉ 11, Rue du Pont Louis-Philippe

☎ +33 (0) 1 48 87 85 13

❡ You will literally feel 'on top of the world' dining in the evening at **58 Tour Eiffel** in the Eiffel Tower on the Rue du Champ de Mars. Up a little higher, the exclusive and more expensive **Jules Vernes Restaurant** has been awarded a coveted Michelin Star rating. The chefs here have all trained under legendary French master Alain Ducasse (b. 1956).

✉ 58 Tour Eiffel

☎ +33 (0) 1 72 76 18 46   €€€€

✉ Jules Verne

☎ +33 (0) 1 45 55 61 44   €€€€€

❡ Not your typical French bistro, **La Mère Agitée** (*The Restless Mother*) publicises itself as *'non conformiste'*—the menu (tiny with few choices) changes daily according to the mood of Valérie, the female chef/owner.
It can't be easy cooking up a storm in this frantic, somewhat dishevelled, family restaurant but the end result attracts a regular crowd of loyal locals.

✉ 21, Rue Campagne Première

☎ +33 (0) 1 43 35 56 64   €€–€€€

03

Maison Saint-Yves

Dominated by its stupendous **Gothic cathedral**, the town of **Chartres** is only 80 kilometres south-west of Paris, a pleasant day trip from the capital. Chartres refers to itself as 'the capital of light and perfume'— although Grasse in Provence might not agree. The town relies heavily on religious tourism and the majestic cathedral is a treasure trove of stained-glass windows and detailed ornamental stone sculptures, some dating from the 12th century; it is replete with enough wonders to keep the most jaded traveller inspired all day.

❧ Behind the cathedral and across the road, the 17th-century Maison Saint-Yves, a former monastery and later a seminary, is now run by the local diocese. It offers simple but comfortable accommodation to tourists and pilgrims all year round. The guestrooms come in twin, single or triple configurations and all have en suite bathrooms. Breakfast and all other meals can be arranged; the food is good, basic, French-style home cooking. The centre is approximately 10 minutes' walk to the old town; there are cafés and restaurants in the vicinity.

❧ Parking in Chartres is limited and a maze of pedestrian streets and bollards (near the Maison Saint-Yves) can make driving here a bit of a nightmare, but the property has a large, tree-lined, courtyard parking area for the use of guests. Some of the guestrooms overlook this courtyard and can be a little noisy. You could ask for one of the garden rooms, some of which have lovely views over the town and countryside.

✉ 1, Rue Saint-Eman
F-28000 Chartres
Eure-et-Loir

✆ +33 (0) 2 37 88 37 40
✆ +33 (0) 2 37 88 37 49

✉ hotellerie@maison-st-yves.com

🖰 www.maison-st-yves.com

🛏 from €30.00 pp

☞ Maison Saint-Yves is approximately 1 kilometre from Chartres train station.

♱ **Sunday Mass**
0915, 1100 & 1800.
Cathédrale de Chartres.

♿ Discuss your needs in advance of arriving, ideally when booking.

⚭ Open to men, women & groups

Open Houses
Paris / Centre / Île-de-France Chartres

PLACES OF INTEREST ❦ The monumental **Cathédrale Notre-Dame de Chartres** (*Cathedral of Our Lady of Chartres*) is the town's premier drawcard, and hours could be spent exploring a bounty of riches. The cathedral has been an important pilgrimage site since medieval times. French king and devout Catholic, Henry III (1551–1589) made eighteen pilgrimages to Chartres; these days rows of visitors sit with their heads uplifted 'reading' the story of the 4,000 figures depicted in the stained-glass windows. Others come to see the veil which is said to have been worn by the Blessed Virgin. Laid into the floor of the nave is an 11-circuit labyrinth, built around 1200, which on Fridays (except Good Friday) between the first Sunday in Lent and All Saints' Day, pilgrims still walk (some on their knees, as in medieval times) in a symbolic pilgrimage. At most other times the labyrinth is covered with chairs for use during services.

❧ The amusing Englishman **Malcolm Miller** is a scholarly expert on the cathedral. He conducts entertaining lecture tours twice a day between Easter and November.

❧ If travelling by train or motoring between Paris and Chartres, you could stop off at **Versailles** and the grandiose home of Louis XVI (1754–1793) and his Austrian princess, Marie Antoinette (1755–1793). Conveniently, the train station is situated close to the Château de Versailles. Tour the sumptuous interiors including the king's bedchamber and private apartments, and maybe take home a bottle (expensive!) of Marie Antoinette's perfume, M. A. Sillage de la Reine (*In the Wake of The Queen*) made by French perfumer Francis Kurkdjian. It is on sale in the palace gift shop; sadly, no free samples are available. Prices range between $450 and $10,500 USD.

❧ **Le Hameau de Marie-Antoinette** (*Village of Marie-Antoinette*) is at the far end of the estate and was built especially for Marie-Antoinette by her husband so she could escape the rigours and constraints of royal life in the main château. Being so close to Paris, Versailles is a popular weekend getaway for Parisians. The easiest way to explore the enormous park surrounding the château is to hire a bicycle or take the tourist train.

❧ The **Musée Lambine** at 54, Boulevard de la Reine was established in a restored 18th-century mansion and recounts the history of the city of Versailles.

❧ **The Versailles Baroque Music Centre** conducts a series of classical concerts at the Château de Versailles between September and January. The concerts are a showcase for 17th- and 18th-century French music and bookings are essential.

❧ The town of **Conflans Ste-Honorine**, 25 kilometres north of Versailles, is established around the junction of the Seine and Oise rivers. It is known as the barge capital of France and boats and craft of all shapes and sizes continually ply the busy waterways. The town is one of the stops on the cruise route from Paris, thereby ensuring a constant flow of visitors eager to leave tourist dollars behind. Many visit the **Museum of Shipping**; others opt to relax in the waterside cafés.

FOOD AND DRINK ❧ Close to the Maison St-Yves, **Le Bistrot de la Cathédrale** is a typical neighbourhood bistro with a warm and charming ambience, and eager-to-please staff. The menu generally includes game terrine, duck confit, steak tartare, frites and a delicious selection of desserts. A fixed-price menu is usually available. Busy at weekends.

✉ 1, Cloître Notre Dame

☎ +33 (0) 2 37 36 59 60　　　　€€€-€€€€

❧ **Le Pichet** is another good, traditional French restaurant. On Sundays only, the favourite dish of King Henri IV (1553–1610)—*la poule au pot du bon roi Henri IV* (a thick, soupy chicken stew)—is served, sometimes by the man himself!

✉ 19, Rue de Cheval Blanc

☎ +33 (0) 2 37 21 08 35　　　　€€€

❧ Tourists are well catered for in Chartres and a good number of cafés and restaurants can be found in the vicinity of the cathedral. If you are simply looking to rest your legs and satisfy a sweet tooth, look no further than the **Pâtisserie Migeon** at 2, Rue du Soleil d'Or.

04

Le Maison de la Mission

One of the best things about staying at Le Maison de la Mission is that Paris can be accessed in a day trip from here. In fact, it is only a 45-minute train journey away and the local La Ferté train station is just a few minutes' walk from the convent. **The Loire Valley**, the **Champagne** area and **Disneyland Paris** are all within easy reach.

❡ The guesthouse is in a quiet location, set in large grounds in a small riverside community and within close walking distance of the town centre. Le Maison de la Mission is large, well run, and has been managed by an order of Polish nuns, the Sisters of the Congregation of the Daughters of Mary Immaculate, since 1991; it is owned by the Polish Catholic Mission which has established centres throughout Europe to minister to the needs of Polish people living away from home. Tourists, groups, families and pilgrims are welcome for overnight or more extensive stays. Most of the guestrooms are doubles and triples, with some extra large rooms available for families. All guestrooms are comfortably furnished and have en suite bathrooms.

❡ The sisters offer a variety of accommodation options. There is a **camp site** in the park surrounding the convent; this cheaper option is popular with young people during the warmer weather. The sisters cater for all meals if required, with a choice of **Polish or French cuisine**. Meals are reasonably priced. A laundry is available for the use of guests and there is plenty of parking. People of all nationalities are welcome to stay here.

❡ Conference groups are welcome.

✉ 31, Rue d'Hugny F-77260 La Ferté sous Jouarre Seine-et-Marne

☎ +33 (0) 1 60 22 03 76
☎ +33 (0) 1 60 22 03 76

✉ e-mail: pmk.laferte@free.fr

🔗 www.mission-catholique-polonaise.net

🛏 from €24.00 pp, including French or Polish breakfast. Camp site from €7.00 pp.

☞ From Paris Gare de l'Est take the Chateau Thierry regional line to La Ferté sous Jouarre. The convent is close to the train station.

✝ **Sunday Mass** 0915. Abbaye Notre-Dame de Jouarre, La Ferté sous Jouarre.

🕮 Open to men, women & groups

PLACES OF INTEREST ❧ **The Benedictine Abbaye Notre-Dame de Jouarre** (*Abbey of Our Lady of Jouarre*) situated 2 kilometres south of La Ferté sous Jouarre, was founded around 630AD. Beneath it are some of the oldest crypts in Europe. The abbey bell-tower, where nuns hid during the Nazi occupation, was built during the 13th century. At the end of World War II, the abbey was liberated by American **General George S. Patton Jr** (1885–1945). Among those rescued was a remarkable young nun, **Sister Benedict** OSB, born Vera Duss (1920–2005) in Pittsburgh, Pennsylvania. Sister Benedict gained a medical degree from the Sorbonne in Paris and in 1946, in gratitude to her American saviours, established the Abbey of Regina Laudis in Bethlehem, Connecticut. She remained abbess until she stepped down in 1995 while briefly under a cloud during Vatican investigations into allegations (later disproven) that the convent was run in a 'cultlike' manner.

❧ Mother Benedict's life is the subject of a fascinating memoir, *Mother Benedict: Foundress of the Abbey of Regina Laudis*, by Antoinette Bosco (Ignatius Press). The current prioress of Regina Laudis is **Mother Dolores Hart** (b. 1938), former actor and **Elvis Presley**'s (1935–1977) co-star (*Loving You*, *Where the Boys Are* and *King Creole*, in which she and Elvis shared an on-screen kiss) who forsook Hollywood to become a contemplative Benedictine nun. The grand-daughter of **General George S. Patton Jr**, **Mother Margaret Georgina Patton** OSB, joined the Regina Laudis community in 1982.

❧ Meanwhile, back in France the town of **Provins**, some 47 kilometres south of La Ferté is a listed World Heritage site once known for its medieval trade fairs. A Medieval Festival is held here each year in June. If you are short of time take the tourist train around the 'old town', a return journey of 30 minutes.

❧ A former Bishop of Meaux (*Metz*), Jacques Bossuet (1627–1704), lies buried in the town's Gothic **Cathédrale St-Étienne**, a French national monument. Nearby is the former episcopal palace and gardens, now a museum. Each week, between June and September, the town hosts a spectacular *son et lumière* with costumed locals re-enacting the history of the area. Performances take place in front of the cathedral.

Open Houses
Paris / Centre / Île-de-France

La Ferté sous Jouarre

❦ The dizzyingly extravagant **Château de Fontainebleau**, south of La Ferté, was once home to Napoléon Bonaparte (1769–1821) and Empress Joséphine (1763–1814). It is not known if they found time to practise on the *jeu de paume* 'real tennis' court installed by Henry IV (1553–1610). However, the indoor court has been preserved and guides willingly demonstrate how royalty played the game.

❦ **Barbizon**, the 'village of painters' near Fontainbleau, was the home of the 19th-century landscape artists of the Barbizon School; the town still has a multitude of artists' studios and galleries to which curious art lovers flock.

❦ **La Vallee** discount shopping outlet, where major French and international designer labels are represented, is in the **Disneyland** complex, at Marne-la-Vallée, 35 minutes east of Paris by train from Gare d'Lyon and approximately the same distance from La Ferté.

FOOD AND DRINK ❦ From La Ferté you could hire a canal boat and sail to the vineyards of **Epernay** in Champagne where dozens of stately Champagne houses line the Avenue de Champagne and many, like **Moet and Chandon**, welcome drop-in visitors.

❦ Historical **Meaux**, 19 kilometres west of La Ferté sous Jouarre, is sometimes referred to as the Brie capital of France on account of the Brie de Meaux cheese produced here. Load up the picnic basket with a thick, creamy wedge, a crunchy baguette and maybe a bottle of Champagne from a local vineyard for some al fresco dining on the banks of the River Marne. Meaux, like Dijon, is also known for its locally made mustard.

❦ There are a number of cafés, restaurants and tea rooms in La Ferté and its surrounding area. One of the nicest and most typically French is **Le Bec Fin** where a simple menu with an emphasis on seafood keeps the locals well fed and coming back for more. And if cholesterol isn't a problem, 'proper' French tripe is often featured on the menu.

✉ 1, Quai des Anglais

☎ +33 (0)1 60 22 01 27   €€€

Alsace

 KNOWN FOR ITS FINE WINES and gastronomic flair, tiny Alsace (8,280 square kilometres) lies on the borders of Germany and Switzerland. A long chain of mountainous ranges stretches through central Europe. Each winter they are blanketed in snow. However, in the Alsace region the Alps act as a buffer against harsh summer weather, creating a warm, dry climate—perfect for comfortable, relaxed touring.

Alsace has more restaurants with Michelin stars than any other area in France but thousands of fine, authentic, albeit less acclaimed eateries serve up the best of both worlds—French food and wine, and German beer. Make sure you try the regional specialities such as *Flammeküeche* (a thin crusted bacon and onion pizza) and *Kugelhopf* (a traditional Alsatian pastry). If you are ravenous, consider a whole pork knuckle (*jambonneau*)—there are plenty of places to walk off any excesses. And most Alsatian walking routes invariably lead to a ruined castle, a charming, romantic village or at least a hospitable, family-owned vineyard.

From the 9th century until the end of World War II Alsace had been occupied by Germany on and off and a strong German influence remains, most noticable in cuisine, language and architecture. If you find yourself in the north of the region, the monasteries of Germany's Black Forest are just over the border and in a move emulating their Alsatian counterparts, many have now turned their hand to the ministry of hospitality.

05

Le Liebfrauenberg

Once a place of pilgrimage and occupied by Catholic Franciscan monks, **Le Liebfrauenberg** is now owned and run by the Members of the Community of Protestant Churches of Alsace and Moselle as a conference and accommodation facility for groups (particularly school groups) of all sizes. Individuals are also welcome here. The Community has owned Le Liebrauenberg since 1954.

⁌ The complex is situated in a rural area within the North Vosges Regional Nature Park on the outskirts of the village of **Goersdorf** and provides a number of accommodation options. The main house offers accommodation for up to 80 people, while the hostel section caters for young people in another 10 guestrooms of varying sizes. Family rooms sleeping up to six people are also available. 'The Pavilion', another house on the property, accommodates small groups and families (12 persons maximum); it is self-contained with four bedrooms and a kitchen.

⁌ All meals are served in the dining rooms in the main building of Le Liebfrauenberg. Packed lunches can be arranged. The house speciality is *tarte-flambée*, a delicious thin-crusted Alsatian pizza. The main building also has a bar, a lift and a small convenience shop. Other facilities include Internet access, a television room, wheelchair access and a large parking area. Conference facilities are available.

✉ 220, Rue du Château
F-67360 Goersdorf
Bas-Rhin

☎ +33 (0) 3 88 09 31 21
📠 +33 (0) 3 88 09 46 49

✉ contact@liebfrauenberg.com

🖱 www.liebfrauenberg.com

🛏 from €45.00 pp, including breakfast.

☞ Take the train from Strasbourg to Haguenau which is 17 kilometres south of Goersdorf. From Haguenau take a taxi to Le Liebfrauenberg.

✝ **Sunday Service** 1000.
l'Église Luthérienne Place Albert Schweitzer, Haguenau.

♿ Discuss your needs in advance of arriving, ideally when booking.

⚭ Open to men, women & groups

PLACES OF INTEREST ❧ The hills behind Goersdorf are crossed with a network of walking trails as well as some flatter areas well suited to cycling. More hiking and biking prospects can be found near **Haguenau** which lies in the centre of the **Forêt de Haguenau**, sometimes called the Holy Forest because of the number of religious houses which were established here. Most have been abolished, demolished or converted into 5-star hotels. However, the Carmelite Convent in **Marienthal** is still operative.

❧ From Goersdorf there is easy motoring access to **Germany** and **Luxembourg**. The German border is only 15 kilometres north of the town and the town of **Fischbach bei Dahn**, in 'moselle' country, is 3 kilometres further on. Underground tours can be taken of the medieval copper mine at Fischbach which is the start of the 125-kilometre German gemstone motoring route leading to gemstone shops, cutters and jewellery design studios and to the town of **Veitsrodt** in the German state of Rheinland-Pfalz (*Rhineland-Palatinate.*)

❧ **Soufflenheim**, 25 kilometres south-east of Goersdorf and close to the German border, is known for its pottery shops and artists' studios. The town is on the Alsatian pottery motoring route along with the villages of **Betschdorf** and **Haguenau**. North of Betschdorf is the village of **Hunspach**, often referred to 'as the most beautiful village in France'. And it's easy to see why, with its unique Alsatian heritage still very much intact.

❧ Take the kids to **Didiland**, the Alsatian version of Disneyland, and recuperate afterwards in the mineral springs and spas at **Morsbronn-les-Bains**, 7 kilometres south of Goersdorf. The **Nautiland Water Park** in Rue des Dominicains, Haguenau is another favourite with youngsters.

❧ The **Lembach Walking Trails** commence from the village of Lembach on the fringe of the Vosges Forest in Alsace and close to the Pfälzerwald forest in Germany. From Lembach numerous paths branch off through farmland, tiny villages and hamlets and past wartime relics and the ruins of a dozen medieval castles. The trails are maintained by volunteer members of the Vosgean Club, an Alsatian organisation dedicated to pedestrian tourism.

Open Houses
Alsace Goersdorf

❡ In 1870 during the Franco-Prussian War, a tragic battle took place on the fields outside **Wörth**, two kilometres south of Goersdorf, when 20,000 French and German troops were killed in the Battle of Fröschwiller. **The Musée de La Bataille du 6 Août**, (*Museum of the Battle of the 6th of August*) at 2, Rue du Moulin in Wörth, honours the thousands of French soldiers who lost their lives.

❡ Take a fascinating journey into the past at the outdoor **Ecomuseum** in **Ungersheim**, in the district of Mullhouse in the south of Alsace. The outdoor museum is a collection of 70 authentic Alsatian houses which form an ancient village complete with sporting fields, gardens and village shops, the oldest dating from the 15th century. The museum's houses and workshops are manned by locals who offer glimpses into what village life was like several centuries ago.

FOOD AND DRINK ❡ Dedicated gourmets who like to work off their indulgences might be interested in a hike through the meadows, woods and rural villages of the upper **Bruche Valley** in central Alsace, with numerous stopovers en route to sample the local specialities. The hike usually takes 4 days and full details are available from local tourist offices in Strasbourg.

❡ Although the population of Goersdorf is under 1,000, there are a few cosy little *winstubs* (a wine bar usually attached to a dining area) and a couple of traditional French restaurants serving Alsatian favourites, including *Choucroute* (sausages with pickled cabbage), *bäckeoff* (a three-meat casserole of pork, lamb and beef) and the ever-popular classic *crêpes d'Alsace*.

✉ Restaurant Couronne, 84, Rue Principale.
📞+33 (0) 3 88 09 33 56   €€€

✉ Le Palais Gourmand,
   220, Rue Moulin Liebfrauenthal.
📞+33 (0) 3 88 09 42 74   €€€

❡ Release those 'happy' endorphins with the help of talented chocolatier Daniel Stoffel and his sublime creations which are on sale at the **Chocolate Factory**, 50, Route de Bitche, Haguenau.

❡ A morning produce market is held in the **Halle aux Houblons** in Haguenau every Tuesday and Friday.

06

Le Grand Hôtel

During the 7th century Irish Benedictine monks founded a monastery in the **Vosges Mountains** overlooking the Munster Valley and where the first Munster cheese was created. The recipe was once a secret known only to the monks. However, over time, the way they made the cheese became known to the local villagers who still produce it according to the original method. Munster might be the smelliest cheese in Alsace but it is the perfect partner for a glass of aromatic, spicy Alsatian Gewurztraminer. The cheese can often be tasted in the restaurant of the Grand Hotel which is situated in the heart of Munster.

❡ **The Grand Hotel** is run by a Christian, diocesan non-profit organisation and is not in any way 'grand'. Its days of glory are long gone, but it is clean, modestly furnished and quite adequate for those looking for somewhere cheap and cheerful to spend the night. Groups are preferred here though smaller numbers of guests are welcome if a room is available. The guestrooms are located on three floors and most have fully equipped kitchenettes. All rooms have a television, telephone and an en suite bathroom. Facilities include a lounge room, bar, games room, gym and guest laundry. There is an outdoor terrace, attractive gardens and a swimming pool. Babysitting can be arranged, and there is a lift to all floors. All meals are served. Sporting activities in the area include cross-country skiing in winter and fishing, cycling and *petanque* (similar to bowls) in the summer. The hotel has access for the disabled and car parking is available. Pets are welcome.

✉ 1, Rue de la Gare
F-68140 Munster
Haut-Rhin

✆ +33 (0) 3 89 77 30 37
✆ +33 (0) 3 89 77 30 06

✍ grandhotelmunster68@
yahoo.fr

✍ www.grandhotel.free.fr

💶 from €30.00 pp

☞ Take the train to the main Munster train station. The hotel is approximately 200 metres from here.

✝ **Sunday Mass**
1030.
l'Église St Léger,
6, Rue de L'église,
Munster.

♿ Discuss your needs in advance of arriving, ideally when booking.

👥 Open to men, women & groups

Open Houses
Alsace Munster

PLACES OF INTEREST ⸭ Once the home of doctor, philosopher and theologian **Albert Schweitzer** (1875–1965), the Schweitzer Museum in **Gunsbach**, near Munster, is dedicated to his life and works. A kilometre-long path leads around Gunsbach, commencing at the old presbytery where the family once lived and ending at the museum, located in the home Schweitzer built in 1928 for himself and his German wife Hélène (1879–1957).

⸭ A vineyard is never far away in Alsace and the **Museum of the Vineyard**, located within the **Château de la Confrérie St-Etienne** in Kíentzheim 20 kilometres north-east of Munster, interprets the history of the wine industry in the region. The castle is the headquarters of the exclusive Brotherhood of St Stephen, a wine society dating back to the 14th century, which carefully controls the quality of the local vintages. The society's high-ranking members look most impressive in ankle-length scarlet capes, broad black berets and official chains of office.

⸭ From a distance the picture-postcard little village of **Mittelwihr**, near **Kíentzheim**, appears like an illustration in a travel brochure. Mittelwihr's perfectly preserved and possibly even more beautiful sister village, **Riquewihr**, known locally as the 'pearl of the vineyards', is encircled by thick, rough-hewn stone ramparts dating back to the 13th century. Riquewihr and its neighbouring village **Ribeauvillé** are surrounded by *grand cru* vineyards and connoisseurs can follow the *grand cru* vineyard trail which leads to over 50 wineries, some of which have been producing fine wine for centuries.

⸭ The 25-kilometre-long **Castles Driving Route** commences at the village of **Wintzenheim**. Near to Wintzenheim, in the enclave of Logelbach stands the unique **Chapelle Sainte-Thérèse-de-Lisieux** (*Chapel of St Therese of Lisieux*) which was built by the local Herzog family in 1862 as a modest replica of the Sainte-Chapelle in Paris. A relic of Sainte-Thérèse-de-Lisieux is kept in the chapel.

† Sunday Mass 0900

❡ The medieval town of **Wettolsheim** lies between Munster and Colmar and is a stop on the Alsatian wine road. In the centre of the town stands a replica of the **Massabielle Grotto** in Lourdes in the Hautes-Pyrénées, where Our Lady is said to have appeared to Bernadette Soubirous in 1858. The focus of numerous religious events, the shrine was established by Bishop François-Xavier Schoepfer, Bishop of Tarbes and Lourdes between 1899 and 1927.

❡ During the summer months the Nightwatchman of **Turckheim**, an ancient wine town north-east of Munster, makes the rounds of the village at 2200 each evening. Fairytales and a little singing are all part of the tour which departs from in front of the tourist office.

❡ The **Staub Factory Outlet** at 2, Rue St-Gilles, in Turckheim, has a shop selling this renowned brand of enamelled cast iron French cookware at factory prices. If you are seeking locally made souvenirs the easy-to-pack Alsatian table linen is a speciality of the **Beauvillé** factory shop at 19, Route de Sainte-Marie-aux-Mines in Ribeauvillé, 14 kilometres north.

FOOD AND DRINK ❧ **Cheese** connoisseurs will take great delight in the 'cheese road' leading out of Munster, calling in at the local dairy farms along the way for samples and tastings. Maps are available at the local tourist office.

❡ It would be hard to find a more charming restaurant than **Au Dolder** in the Hotel Au Dolder in the fairytale village of Riquewihr. Inside or in the casual country garden, diners can choose from a menu which may include *râler la langue et pommes de terres gratinées au Munster* (beef tongue with fried potato topped with Munster cheese), *les cuisses de grenouilles au riesling* (frogs' legs), and the ever-popular *la quiche lorraine maison* (traditional quiche).

✉ 52, Avenue du Général de Gaulle, Riquewihr.
☎ +33 (0) 3 89 47 92 56   €€€€

❡ And there is a little treasure of a restaurant in the village of **Eguisheim**, 20 kilometres east of Munster. Situated in a gorgeous, 17th-century Alsatian house, *Le Pavillon Gourmand* is run by the local Schubnel family, who have trained under some of the country's top chefs. The menu focuses on local, seasonal produce combined in various fixed-price menus.

✉ 101, Rue du Rempart Sud, Eguisheim.
☎ +33 (0) 3 89 24 36 88   €€€-€€€€

07

Hostellerie du Mont Ste-Odile

Perched above the village of **Otrott**, the **Hostellerie du Mont Ste-Odile** is situated in what was once a flourishing monastery. The hostel is run jointly by parish priests and sisters of the order of *Les Soeurs de la Croix* (Sisters of the Cross) along with lay supporters from the local diocese. The order was founded in Alsace in 1848 and has six convents in the region.

⚜ Events such as concerts, plays and musicals are often held here and are well supported by appreciative locals. The view from the mountain can only be described as spectacular—and on a clear day the **Black Forest** in Germany's south can be seen in the distance.

⚜ The complex is now a tourist destination as well as a place of pilgrimage with 120 guestrooms available in single, twin and triple configurations. Many of the guestrooms have en suites attached; others share a bathroom on the same floor. There are a number of dining areas offering a mix of a la carte and self-service menus.

⚜ It is possible to drive up the mountain and parking is available.

⚜ Short pilgrimages for those who may be just passing through the town can be arranged. A visit to the grotto where **Ste-Odile** used to rest is a stop on the pilgrimage trail, along with the saint's 'miraculous' spring. Odile was born blind and recovered her sight when she was baptised in the waters of the spring at the age of 12. Odile is the Patron Saint of Alsace.

✉ Mont-Ste-Odile
F-67530
Ottrott Bas-Rhin

☎ +33 (0) 3 88 95 80 53
📠 +33 (0) 3 88 95 82 96

✆ info@mont-sainte-odile.com

🖥 www.mont-sainte-odile.com

🛏 from €35.00 pp, including breakfast.

☞ Obernai train station is 14 kilometres from Mont Ste-Odile; a taxi is available. From Strasbourg bus station, bus 210 travels to Ottrott.

✝ **Sunday Mass**
1000, 1130 & 1700.
l'Église du Mont Ste-Odile, Ottrott.

♿ Discuss your needs in advance of arriving, ideally when booking.

👥 Open to men, women & groups

PLACES OF INTEREST ⟡ **Ottrott** is a charming medieval village nestled at the foot of Mont Ste-Odile. In the clouds above, the **Sanctuary of Mont Ste-Odile** sits poised on a rocky ledge as it has done for the past 1,300 years. Ste-Odile established the first monastery on the site in the mid-700s. Now owned and managed by the Strasbourg Archdiocese, Mont St-Odile is a place of pilgrimage, rest and welcome for the traveller, the devout and the curious alike, with much to interest all.

⟡ The mountain is a haven for walkers and more than 100 kilometres of marked walking paths zigzag from the property, some leading to awe-inspiring medieval treasures. A 10-kilometre-long **Pagan Wall**, parts of which still stand, was established here, possibly before 1,000 BC. A Way of the Cross, lined with hand-crafted ceramic stations studded into ancient stone walls, takes you to Odile's spring which has been flowing for 1,300 years. The chapel where Ste-Odile is buried in an 8th-century stone sarcophagus is in the main complex. A monastery shop sells books, postcards and religious items. Pope John Paul II visited Mont Ste-Odile in 1988.

⟡ The people of Ottrott are called *Ottrottois* and the village's award-winning red wine '*le rouge de Ottrott*'. The Alsace **route des vins** (*wine route*) passes through the Ottrott vineyards. There are walking paths in the area, *winestubs* and the ruins of a handful of medieval castles. The Ottrotter Red Wine Festival is held annually in August.

⟡ **Obernai**, 14 kilometres east of Ottrott, is one of Alsace's most visited towns. Larger than Ottrott, its narrow cobbled streets, shuttered half-timbered buildings, church spires and belfries create a romantic medieval atmosphere. Summer time is festival time in Obernai when each week concerts and musical events take place in the town's historic sites. A circus festival is held at the end of each April and a wine fair in mid-August. The Obernai grape harvest is celebrated with a spirited wine festival in October, the highlight being the new wine flowing from the Ste-Odile fountain in the town's picturesque marketplace.

Open Houses
Alsace Ottrott

❦ Local wood artists create decorative pictures, mosaics and household accessories in natural wood at the workshop of the **Marqueterie d'Art Spindler** in the hamlet of St-Leonard near Boersch, between Ottrott and Rosheim. The workshop has been operating out of the former 12th-century Benedictine **Abbey of St Leonard** for almost 100 years. Local artist **Charles Spindler** (1865–1938), whose works are displayed in the Victoria & Albert Museum in London, established the workshop.

❦ A **Tourist Steam Train** runs a circular route from **Rosheim** SNCF railway station, along the wine route and through Ottrott on Sundays and public holidays.

❦ The **Europa Theme Park**, a mini Disneyland, is located in **Rust** in Germany near the French border. The kids won't be bored; the park has over 100 rides, including a state-of-the-art rollercoaster.

FOOD AND DRINK ❦ Ottrott is just 40 kilometres from **Strasbourg's** Michelin-starred restaurants, among which are Emile Jung's legendary **Au Crocodile** and the romantic **Buerehiesel**. The no less 'haute cuisine' **Le Beau Site** in the Place de l'Église in Ottrott is in a restored, traditional, half-timbered building, where a modern version of traditional Alsatian cuisine is served.

✉ Au Crocodile, 10, Rue de l'Outre, Strasbourg.
☎ +33(0)3 88 32 13 02   €€€€€

✉ Buerehiesel, 4, Parc de l'Orangerie, Strasbourg.
☎ +33(0)3 88 45 56 65   €€€€€

✉ Le Beau Site, Place de l'Église, Ottrott.
☎ +33(0)3 88 48 14 30   €€€€€

❦ Back at the convent, the **Mont St-Odile Restaurant** is another agreeable (and easier on the pocket) place to sample some of the local cuisine while enjoying the superb views. The complex has a number of dining options as well as a delicatessen selling local picnic-type food and wine. Together with the famous Ottrotter red wine, the restaurants serve a variety of regional specialties such as goose liver pâté, Alsatian sauerkraut, chicken in Ottrotter red wine or fish in Ottrotter sauce.

❦ The **Vineyard of Robert Blanck** on the Route d'Ottrott near Obernai is situated at the foot of Mount St-Odile, where the Blanck family produces the rich, fruity wines the area is famous for. A casual cellar door restaurant opens most days.

08

FEC Association

The Strasbourg headquarters of the **FEC Association** (*Foyer de l'Étudiant Catholique*) is in a large, gracious mansion of typical Alsatian architecture situated near the centre of the city in an historical neighbourhood, just 200 metres from the famous cathedral. The building dates from the 16th century and was once a large family home. The FEC centre was established in 1925 by Frère Médard (1899–1998), a member of the teaching order the *Congrégation des frères de Matzenheim* (the Brothers of Matzenheim, more formally known as the Brothers of Christian Doctrine.) The order was founded in Nancy in 1922 by French Benedictine monk, Dom Joseph Fréchard of the Abbaye de Senones (Senones Abbey) in the Lorraine region.

¶ During the academic year the house is open to students studying at the university in Strasbourg. However, during the holiday period, 1 July to 30 September, the centre is open to tourists and visitors; it can accommodate men and women of all ages. The single and twin guestrooms are furnished in student style with a simple desk, bed and cupboard. Each room has a telephone, a small refrigerator and an en suite bathroom. The centre has a television room, a guest laundry and a lift to all floors. There is a large restaurant which is closed in August and on weekends. However, the residence is conveniently located with easy access to shops and cafés in the surrounding area.

✉ 17, Place Saint-Étienne
F-67081 Strasbourg
Bas-Rhin

🛏 Open 1 July–
30 September annually.

📞 +33 (0) 3 88 35 36 20
📠 +33 (0) 3 88 37 99 83

✉ fec.strasbourg@fec-asso.org

🌐 www.fec-asso.org

💶 from €32.00 pp

☛ Take the train to Gare de Strasbourg. From there, go by taxi or walk to the Foyer which is near the Strasbourg Cathedral, approximately 1 kilometre from the station. From the Gare de Strasbourg there are direct links to Paris, Lyon, Marseille, Nice, Montpellier, Toulouse, Bordeaux, Lille and Nantes.

✝ **Sunday Mass**
0800, 0930, 1100 & 1830.
Cathédrale Notre-Dame-de-Strasbourg, Place de la Cathédral, Strasbourg.

♿ Discuss your needs in advance of arriving, ideally when booking.

⚤ Open to men, women & groups

Open Houses

Alsace Strasbourg

PLACES OF INTEREST ⟋ The university city of **Strasbourg** is on the western side of the German border and has the distinction of being the location of the headquarters of the **European Parliament**. **The River Île** threads its way through this ancient capital of Alsace, a city of history, arts and culture. The old town area is a venue for opera, concerts, theatre and arts festivals which are held all year round.

⟨ Cross the **Passerelle Mimram** (a pedestrian bridge separating France from Germany) and you will be in the town of **Kehl am Rhein**, once a suburb of Strasbourg but now a German frontier town situated on the edge of the **Black Forest**. Both Kehl and Strasbourg have numerous pedestrian-only areas lined with cafés, restaurants and speciality shops—well suited for exploration on foot. Being so close to the German border, why not go and see the Black Forest? Tours can be arranged in either town.

⟨ Strasbourg's old town is known as **La Petite France**, a very pretty area of winding canals and narrow, cobbled alleyways lined with neat, almost ornamental, half-timbered houses whose window boxes flush with blushing geraniums. River cruises down the Rhine can be arranged from here and canals and waterways branch off in all directions.

⟨ For a grand view over Strasbourg, climb the 300 plus steps of the local cathedral's towering spire. Inside, at 1230 every day, the Twelve Apostles emerge from their private sanctuary to parade around the cathedral's Renaissance astronomical clock. Strasbourg's celebrated Gothic cathedral, the **Cathédrale Notre-Dame**, once the world's tallest building, was established during the 12th century on the **Grand Île** (the *Main Island*) in the River Île.

⟨ Sunday Mass 0800, 0930, 1100 & 1830

⟨ The **Musée Alsacien** (*Museum of Alsace*) on the Quai St-Nicholas is a tribute to the traditional Alsatian lifestyle and occupies the restored dwellings of former local residents.

One of the most popular tourist attractions in Alsace is the 12th-century **Château du Haut-Kœnigsbourg** near **Selestat** on the outskirts of Strasbourg. The castle sprawls grandly above the wine village of **Orschwiller** and early in the 20th century was completely rebuilt with turreted towers, ramparts, a moat and drawbridge; 16th-century furniture was installed, along with a collection of old weapons from its days as a massive medieval stronghold. Festivals, concerts and cultural events are held here on a regular basis. During summer weekends a shuttle bus runs between the train station in Sélestat and the castle.

The Strasbourg **flea market** takes place each Wednesday and Saturday on Rue de Vieil-Hôpital. The square in front of the cathedral is decked out with thousands of twinkling lights and lanterns each Christmas and is the fairytale setting for Strasbourg's annual **marché de Noël** (*Christmas market*). Stuffed storks (a good-luck emblem of Alsace) and cuckoo clocks are always on sale.

Galeries Lafayette and **Printemps**, the iconic French department stores, are located in Strasbourg.

FOOD AND DRINK Eat out on Strasbourg's lovely cathedral square, lined with souvenir stores for every taste and budget, and enough chocolate shops to satisfy the sweetest of souls. Further cravings can be satisfied at the museum of **Les Secrets du Chocolat** in the village of **Geispolsheim**, 15 kilometres south of the town.

The local restaurants in Strasbourg reflect the history and culture of France and Germany, with both Alsatian wines and German beers appearing on restaurant menus alongside the city's famous sausage.

La Cloche à Fromage near the Quai St-Nicolas is a cheeselover's paradise; it once made the *Guinness Book of Records* for the world's largest cheese platter. Try a chunk (200 varieties to choose from) on a home-made bread roll, or maybe share a fondue or raclette in the restaurant.

✉ 27, Rue des Tonneliers.

✆ +33 (0) 3 88 23 13 19   €€€

With its unique 14th-century architecture, the **Maison Kammerzell** in the Place de la Cathédrale is not easily missed; it's the ideal place to sit, relax and catch your breath after touring the massive cathedral. Inside are a number of unique dining rooms, all with different themes and cuisines.

✉ 16, Place de la Cathédrale.

✆ +33 (0) 3 88 32 42 14   €€€–€€€€

Auvergne

AUVERGNE IS THE PERFECT DESTINATION for nature lovers and outdoorsy types. The Volcans d'Auvergne National Park in the west of Auvergne covers much of the Cantal and Puy de Dome departments and is dominated by a chain of rocky troughs and craters, glacier-sculpted canyons, mineral springs and extinct volcanic ridges. A web of hiking trails threads through isolated highland villages constructed entirely of lava stones.

The Ancient Romans were no strangers to Auvergne. In 52 BC, when they discovered the waters of what is now the gracious old spa town of Vichy on the shores of the River d'Allier, Julius Caesar set about building Auvergne's first health and spa retreat. Much later, the fashionable spa towns of Volvic, St-Nectaire and Néris les Bains sprung up in his footsteps.

The geography of Auvergne has influenced *les produits des terroir* (the produce of the soil), particularly mineral water from the area's volcanic springs (Volvic is probably the best known brand) and cheese produced in the lush, fragrant, fertile high pastures. The Cantal is especially famous for St-Nectaire, a creamy, salty cheese, and for its superior Puy lentils. If you're looking for souvenirs, lace and umbrellas are traditional local products.

Auvergne's Romanesque churches are filled with religious art and relics, and a visit to the region's sacred shrines and pilgrimage sites is bound to sustain the spirit. Travellers and pilgrims alike can usually find accommodation in one of the region's religious houses.

OPEN HOUSE

09

Domaine de Chadenac

Ceyssac is a small enclave 6 kilometres west of the historical town of **Le Puy-en-Velay** which is on an ancient **pilgrimage route** leading to the shrine of St James (Santiago de Compostela) in Spain where the Apostle is believed to be buried. A section of the French route commences at the 12th-century Cathédrale Notre-Dame du Puy (*Puy Cathedral*) and proceeds through the rugged Auvergne countryside down to the border town of **St-Jean-Pied-de-Port** at the foot of the Pyrénées almost 700 kilometres away.

❧ The **Domaine-de-Chadenac** is run by an organisation known as the Catholic Outdoor Vacation Centre and for much of the year operates as a Christian meeting place for groups of young people. However, each year during July and August the complex opens as a holiday house where groups, and especially families, are welcome. The place is always a hive of activity with a multitude of sports on offer. As the complex is rurally located on hectares of farmland, walking and hiking opportunities abound. Over 120 beds are available and all guestrooms, although sparsely furnished, have en suites. Choose from single, double, triple or quad rooms, or a dormitory section which is set aside for large groups. There is a guest laundry, indoor and outdoor dining rooms, a bar, a communal lounge and a games room. Groups can take advantage of the football field and there is a large children's playground, a heated swimming pool and tennis courts on site.

✉ F-43000 Ceyssac Haute-Loire.

Open to travellers in July and August.

☎ +33 (0) 4 71 09 27 62
✆ +33 (0) 4 71 02 87 45

✉ domainedechadenac@orange.fr

🌐 www.chadenac43.free.fr

from €280.00 pp for 7 days, including breakfast and dinner. The tariff for shorter stays can be negotiated.

☞ Take the train to the Le Puy-en-Velay main station. From here take a taxi to the Domaine de Chadenac which is 6 kilometres away.

✝ **Sunday Mass 0700 & 1100.** Cathédrale Notre-Dame le Puy, Le Puy-en-Velay.

♿ Discuss your needs in advance of arriving, ideally when booking.

Open to men, women & groups

Open Houses
Auvergne Ceyssac

PLACES OF INTEREST ❧ You can't miss the **St-Michel d'Aiguilhe** (chapel), which around the 10th century was somewhat daringly established on the summit of a lofty volcanic outcrop. Almost 270 steps lead to the chapel with its simple altar, a shrine to St-Michel, some ancient frescoes and the best views in town.

☦ Thursday Mass 1830

◖ **Le Puy-en-Velay** is known for its locally grown lentils and for the verbena-flavoured liqueur which has been produced here since 1859. Both are sold in shops all over town.

◖ The town is also the historic headquarters of the French **lace-making** industry. When buying lace check that it carries the registered label with the *Dentelle du Puy Certification of Genuine Origin* which indicates authenticity. Most of the lace shops in the town sell genuine Puy lace and lace-making demonstrations and classes are carried out in many of them. Some of the town's patternmakers satisfy tourist curiosity and set up work on the footpaths.

◖ In the village of **La Chaise-Dieu**, 40 kilometres north of Le Puy, the unusual **L'Église Abbatiale St-Robert** (*Abbey Church of St Robert*) has a specially designed 'echo room' where centuries ago priests could safely hear the confessions of lepers. The acoustics are still such that if two people were to stand in the two farthest corners of the room, facing into the wall, the whispers of one could be clearly heard by the other. Pope Clement v, the renegade Pope who moved the seat of the Papacy to Avignon in the 14th century, is buried here.

☦ Sunday Mass 1100

◖ Le **Festival de La Chaise-Dieu**, an internationally recognised festival of **sacred music**, is held in the historic grandeur of the town's 11th-century Benedictine Abbey. The festival is usually held over a 2-week period each August.

◖ Tiny **Lavaudieu** (*Valley of God*) is 50 kilometres north-west of Le Puy. This lovely village grew around another former 11th-century abbey for Benedictine nuns and has won accolades for its beauty and charm. The abbey is still quite well preserved and in recent times frescoes dating back to the 14th century have been uncovered in the abbey church.

❦ The **Musée de la Résistance** (*Museum of the Resistance*) in Frugiéres le Pin, 50 kilometres north-west of Le Puy, is the memory bank of the French Resistance in Auvergne during World War II. Australian-born heroine of the Resistance, **Nancy Wake** (b. 1912, aka 'The White Mouse'), was based in Vichy after being parachuted into Auvergne where she worked covertly to evacuate escaped POWs.

❦ If lace-making doesn't appeal, you could try your hand at **sculpting**. Atelier **Pierre Rosseau** conducts lessons for children and adults from his studio at 31, Rue St-François Régis in Le Puy. Near **Monlet**, 30 kilometres north, weekend introductory courses in the art of **stained glass** are conducted by artist **Jacqueline Zwikel** from her workshop in La Ferme St-Antoine in the hamlet of Les Arbres. All materials are provided and English is spoken.

FOOD AND DRINK ❦ Most cafés and bistros in **Le Puy-en-Velay** serve a version of the famous superior green **lentils**. Local produce is available at a **market** held in Le Puy-en-Velay every Saturday in the old town on Rue Pannessac.

❦ If you're heading north, sample traditional Auvergne cheese in the cellars of the local producers in **St-Nectaire**. This cheese was reputedly the favourite of Louis XIV (1638–1715) and can often be found on the menu of the reasonably priced restaurant **La Parenthèse**, a tiny, cluttered little cubbyhole much favoured by the locals who know to book early.

✉ 8, Avenue de la Cathédrale.
☎ +33 (0) 4 71 02 83 00   €€–€€€

❦ If travelling north to **Clermont Ferrand**, you could stop for a bite at **La Petite Ecole**. This rather amusing restaurant has been designed and furnished as a classroom, complete with wooden desks and inkwells. Old slates serve as tablemats and the menu is on the blackboard. However, tea room food has never tasted this good! Eat inside or out of doors in the playground.

✉ Rilhac near Vergongheon.
☎ +33 (0) 4 71 76 97 43   €€€

10

La Maison des Planchettes

The medieval architecture and quaint, cobbled streets of the village of **St-Flour** (pronounced '*san-floor*') provide the historical setting for **La Maison des Planchettes** which was once a thriving Catholic seminary, the Grand Séminaire de St-Flour. The town was established around a church built by the 5th-century theologian and writer St Florus, who was later buried here. The 14th century **Cathédrale St-Pierre-et-St-Flour** (*Cathedral of St Peter and St Florus*) now stands on the site of the original church.

‖ La Maison des Planchettes is situated between the medieval 'high' town and the more modern 'low' town, within walking distance of shops and cafés. The complex is still owned by the local diocese and is now a traditional hostellerie where home cooking and a friendly, welcoming atmosphere contribute to its charm.

‖ Each of the 73 guestrooms is simply decorated and most are furnished with two beds. However, rooms are available to solo travellers. Many of the guestrooms have en suite bathrooms. Those without have a wash basin and some have a shower installed, though not all have toilets. Share bathrooms are located on each floor. Some rooms have views over rural St-Flour. All meals are available in the restaurant located within the complex and wine is served. Take-away lunches can be arranged. The house has wheelchair access with a lift to each floor. There is a large private parking area. Credit cards are accepted.

✉ 7, Rue de Planchettes F-15100 St-Flour Cantal.

☎ +33 (0) 4 71 60 10 08
℻ +33 (0) 4 71 60 22 44

✉ info@maison-des-planchettes.com

🖰 www.maison-des-planchettes.com

💶 from €33.00 pp, including breakfast.

☞ Take the train to St-Flour's Chaudes-Aigues station. La Maison des Planchettes is approximately 2 kilometres from the station; a pick-up can be arranged in advance.

✝ **Sunday Mass 1030.** Cathédrale St-Pierre, St-Flour.

♿ Discuss your needs in advance of arriving, ideally when booking.

👥 Open to men, women & groups

PLACES OF INTEREST ✦ The medieval town of **St-Flour** is spread across a volcanic hilltop from where a pedestrian path leads to another section of the town at the foot of the hill. St-Flour was once Auvergne's religious capital and most walking routes pass by the 14th-century Gothic edifice the Cathédrale St-Pierre, the permanent custodian of precious frescoes, murals, a 15th-century pieta and a rare, carved statue of a Black Christ.

❡ **Auvergne** is situated in the centre of France and is one of the country's most rural regions with a quarter of the population living in **Clermont Ferrand**. Even though Auvergne is off the usual, well-trodden tourist trail the areas around St-Flour have much of interest. A *son et lumière* theatrical and musical spectacular is presented among the hilltop ruins of the **Château d'Alleuze**, 10 kilometres south of St-Flour, every 2 years (in even-numbered years) during August. Mass is sometimes celebrated for the villagers of **Alleuze** in a tiny, grey stone church, the **Chapel of St-Illide**, situated near the château.

❡ The aptly named **Volcanic Rock Music Festival** is held each March in Clermont-Ferrand.

❡ The **European Park of Volcanism**, near the village of **St-Ours-les-Roches**, is 90 kilometres north of St-Flour. Visitors to **Vulcania** can tour the excavated depths of a volcano and maybe even survive an eruption. It was the idea of former French President **Giscard d'Estaing** (b. 1926) to build this theme park to attract more visitors to Auvergne, his home region. He now lives in the village of **Orcival**, near the town of Clermont Ferrand.

❡ A tourist train, the **Train Touristique des Gorges de l'Allier**, travels 66 kilometres on a round trip through the wild, volcanic landscape between the lovely medieval village of **Langeac** on the River Allier and **Langogne** in the Lozère department. It is said to be one of the most scenic rail journeys in the country. If you travel on a Tuesday or Thursday you will have time to browse around the bustling **Langeac market**. Langeac is 50 kilometres east of St-Flour.

Open Houses
Auvergne St-Flour

❧ A statue of a Black Madonna and Child stands above the main altar of the **La Basilique Notre-Dame-des-Miracles** (*Basilica of Our Lady of Miracles*) in the market town of **Mauriac**, 90 kilometres west of St-Flour. This Romanesque basilica has its origins in the 12th century. The original wooden statue was believed to have had miraculous properties but was destroyed some centuries ago and later re-carved.

✝ Sunday Mass 1030

❧ If travelling north, a stop at the 15th century **Abbaye St-Vincent-de-Chantelle** near the town of **St-Pourçain** could be worthwhile. The sisters here manufacture all manner of natural shampoos, cosmetics, fragrances and soaps, all of which are on sale in their shop at the monastery. Their beauty advice is free.

❧ A prodigious selection of **umbrellas** is available from shops in the 1,000-year-old town of **Aurillac**, known as the umbrella capital of France.

FOOD AND DRINK ❧ The Russian Orthodox **Monastére de la Mére de Dieu du Signe** (*Mother of God Monastery*) is situated in **Marcenat**, 60 kilometres north of St-Flour. The resident nuns built much of the monastery themselves and conduct tours; the highlight is the interior of the chapel. The nuns' home-made breads and cakes are on sale in their shop along with their sweet, scented honey.

✉ La Traverse.

☎ +33 (0) 4 71 78 84 68   €

❧ The reasonably priced, all-inclusive menu offered at the **Restaurant Le Médieval** in St-Flour usually includes at least one of the local specialities: *tripoux*, a dish of slow-cooked sheep tripe, with feet and other delicate morsels thrown in (nothing is wasted) along with onion and vegetables; or *gigot brayaude*, a leg of lamb cooked in white wine with onions and potatoes.

✉ 4, Rue des Agials.

☎ +33 (0) 4 71 60 30 86   €€€

❧ There is nowhere better to order a tangy ham and mustard baguette than in the gorgeous medieval village of **Charroux** where centuries ago monks first created zesty Charroux mustard using the local St-Pourçain white wine.

❧ **Markets** are held in St-Flour on Tuesdays and Saturdays and in Le Puy on Saturdays.

Burgundy

 URGUNDY AND WINE are well-suited partners if the prized vintages produced in the region are anything to go by. Throughout the province, walking and motoring routes thread through tiny, family-run, boutique vineyards as well as the distinguished *grand cru* estates of Château d'Yquem, Mouton Rothschild and Château Margaux.

Those on two wheels could follow the Voie Verte or Green Way, a 44-kilometre cycle path which winds through historical towns, villages and vineyards. Another fascinating way to explore the region is by barge; sheltered behind the meandering curves and bends along the 200-kilometre length of the Burgundy Canal are welcoming waterside bars and restaurants where you can enjoy a glass of one of the region's famous wines and sample Burgundy's renowned cuisine.

Choosing a mode of transport might be difficult, but eating and drinking well won't be a problem in Burgundy. You will find locally grown escargots, Bresse chicken and beef from Charolais on most menus. The delicious, soft Cîteaux cheese, produced by the Trappist monks of L'Abbaye Notre-Dame de Cîteaux, is a perfect match for a velvety Burgundy red. Napoleon downed his share of the monks' cheese with a drop of Domaine Moillard Le Chambertin, a label possibly not on the menu in the dining rooms of the region's convents and monasteries.

Open Houses
Burgundy La Bussière-sur Oche

11

Abbaye de la Bussière

In a sweeping valley between **Dijon** and **Beaune**, the tiny hamlet of **La Bussière** lies concealed beyond a gentle twist of the River Ouche in rural Cote d'Or. Founded around 1130 AD, the local abbey was established by Cistercian monks for whom the idyllic setting and rural tranquillity provided a haven of silence and solitude. However, the monks lost ownership of the abbey during the French Revolution and in later years it was taken over by religious sisters who offered hospitality to travellers.

In 2005 a public outcry erupted when the local Bishop sold the abbey to hoteliers, but things calmed down somewhat after a most sympathetic restoration was carried out with minimal structural change.

Today the abbey, painstakingly and sensitively restored to its original splendour, is set in landscaped formal gardens and acres of luxuriant lakeside grounds. The nuns' spartan cells have been enlarged and converted into exquisite guestrooms with en suite bathrooms and all modern conveniences. However, the medieval cloisters and the accoutrements of the previous monastic fraternity are much in evidence. According to reports the nuns who previously lived here fully approve.

The old refectory is now an epicurean and Michelin-starred restaurant serving the finest French cuisine, a world away from the simple platters partaken of by the previous occupants. A smaller, more casual dining room is used during the day. The village is a stop on the Burgundy canal cruise route and it is just a short walk to the abbey from where the barges moor.

✉ F-21360 La Bussière-sur-Ouche, Cote-d'Or.

📞 +33 (0) 3 80 49 02 29
📠 +33 (0) 3 80 49 05 23

✍ info@
abbayedelabussiere.fr
www.abbaye-dela-bussiere.com

💶 Please contact property direct for rates. Specials are available from time to time.

☞ The abbey is approximately 30 kilometres south of Dijon and 26 kilometres west of Nuit St-Georges. Transfers from Dijon train station can be arranged by the abbey. The village of La Bussière is on the canal route but land access is by car.

✝ **Sunday Mass** 1100. L'Église de Bligny-sur-Ouche, Bligny-sur-Ouche.

PLACES OF INTEREST ❧ The magnificent **Abbaye de la Bussière**, a classic of Cistercian architecture, has recently been sold and developed as a boutique hotel. The restoration has recaptured the grandeur of the original abbey and the entry has been retained to provide readers with a unique alternative and because this tucked-away corner of Burgundy is sometimes overlooked by tourists.

❡ The graveyard of the **La Bussière parish church** (the church belonged to the abbey when it was occupied by the Cistercians) is the final resting place of the crew members of the RAF bomber *Short Stirling* which was shot down over the village of St-Jean-de-Bœuf, near La Bussière-sur-Ouche on 13 August 1943 by a German Messerchmitt. The airmen—two New Zealanders, two Australians and four Englishmen—were on their way back to England after a bombing raid over Italy and, already damaged, strayed from the returning formation of aircraft. The graves are taken care of by local villagers who leave fresh flowers on them throughout the year. An anniversary service is held in the church each year.

❡ The magnificent 8-hectare garden estate of **Château Barbirey-sur-Ouche** is just 5 kilometres north of La Bussière. The semi-formal 19th-century designed gardens are a true work of art with the creations of French artists, sculptors and craftspeople displayed throughout. The gardens are open from April to October.

❡ At not exactly bullet train pace, **L'Escargot de la Côte** (a tourist train known locally as the *Côte Snail*) crawls along the tourist route through some of Burgundy's *grand cru* vineyards and nearby villages. During the summer months it departs from the church at Chambolle-Musigny, near the wine centre of **Nuits St-Georges**. A similar train departs from the village of **St-Emilion**, and another departs from the village of **Bligny-sur-Ouche** between May and October on a 10-kilometre circular route through the scenic Valley of Ouche. The journey takes approximately 1 hour and the train makes a stop for photo opportunities and to allow passengers to stretch their legs. Maps of the motoring route through the vineyards are available at the tourist office in **Nuits St-Georges**.

Open Houses
Burgundy La Bussière-sur Oche

❧ The medieval village of **Châteauneuf** (en Auxois) is 7 kilometres west of La Bussière; it has been nominated as one of the most beautiful villages in France. Guided tours can be taken of the 12th-century **Château de Châteauneuf en Auxois**, a well-preserved, restored and turreted castle with an interior chapel adorned with medieval frescoes of Christ and the Apostles. The village's namesake, Châteauneuf de Pape in the Vaucluse department in Provence, is a wine centre made famous by the Avignon Popes who fancied the local red wine. Under the French Pope John XXII (ruled 1316 to 1334) the wine became known under the label *vin du Pape* (wine of the Pope).

❧ The **Museum of Hemp** at 14, Rue de l'église in Bligny sur Ouche is the only hemp museum in France. The town was once a centre for weaving mills and textile factories and the museum provides a glimpse into the history of hemp manufacture in the area.

❧ Visitors to La Bussière could arrive via a barge cruising along the **Burgundy Canal** (*Canal de Bourgogne*) and there is usually plenty of time to browse the paintings and pottery offered by the local artists living and working along the shoreline.

FOOD AND DRINK ❧ If spices and condiments are of interest you could visit any of the dozens of mustard shops in **Dijon** or buy freshly made mustard more cheaply from a stall at the local markets. Market days in Dijon are Tuesday, Thursday, Friday and Saturday.

❧ You could motor down the 29-kilometre-long **Côte de Nuits Grand Cru Wine Road** from Dijon south to Corgoloin, near Beaune; stop at the prestigious vineyards of **Gevre-Chambertin**, **Vougeot** and **Nuits St-Georges** along the way and taste some exquisite drops. Each October, the wine-growing villages in Burgundy celebrate the year's harvest with festivals, parades and perhaps more than just a little *joie-de-vivre*. Everyone can join in.

❧ Savour every delicious mouthful of the sumptuous seven-course degustation menu of the 1-Michelin star **Gastronomic Restaurant**, in the Abbey of La Bussière. The best of Burgundian wines complement the exquisite cuisine. Deliciously expensive! However, the abbey's **Bistro Restaurant** is a little more laid back, with outdoor seating and a less formal menu. Perfect for a long lunch.

✉ Gastronomic Restaurant.
☏ +33 (0) 3 80 49 02 29   €€€€€

✉ Bistro Restaurant.
☏ +33 (0) 3 80 49 02 29   €€€-€€€€

12

Foyer du Sacré-Coeur

Paray-Le Monial is a monastic town in the **Saône et Loire** department of the Burgundy region. Each year the town attracts throngs of pilgrims who come to pray in the tiny church known as the **Chapel of the Visitations**, the most sacred place in the town, where it is said that in 1673 Christ appeared to the Blessed Margaret Mary Alacoque (1647–1690) who is buried here. Also popular with pilgrims is the town's 12th-century basilica which now serves as the local parish church.

❧ The town is well endowed with churches and the **Chapel of the Apparitions**, next to the convent of the Sisters of The Visitation of Mary, houses the bronze and glass reliquary containing the body of St Margaret-Mary, who was a member of the Visitation Order.

❧ The **Foyer du Sacré-Coeur**, a quiet establishment in the centre of this monastic town, is run by the Vistation sisters and is regularly filled with pilgrims and tourists. The order was founded in 1610 by St Francis de Sales and French saint Jane Frances de Chantal who established a monastery in Annecy in the Rhône-Alpes. The Foyer is situated across the street from la Chapelle des Apparitions (*Chapel of the Apparitions*). The guestrooms here are simply furnished but provide adequate accommodation in single, double and triple configurations. None of the guestrooms have en suites; shared bathroom facilities are on all floors. Meals are generally only available to groups, but cafés and restaurants are just steps away.

❧ The centre is closed during January.

✉ 14, Rue de la Visitation
F-71600 Paray-le-Monial Saône et Loire.

🗓 Closed during January.

📞 +33 (0) 3 85 81 11 01
📠 +33 (0) 3 85 81 26 83

✉ foyersc@club.fr

🖥 www.foyersc.club.fr

💶 from €20.00 pp

🚂 Take the train to Paray-le-Monial main station which is 2 kilometres from the Foyer du Sacré-Coeur.

✝ **Sunday Mass**
1100.
Basilique du Sacré-Coeur, Ave Jean Paul II, Paray-le-Monial.
0900.
Monastère de La Visitation.

👥 Open to men, women & groups

Open Houses
Burgundy Paray-Le-Monial

PLACES OF INTEREST **Paray-le-Monial** is the second most visited pilgrimage site in France (after **Lourdes**) and almost a million visitors arrive here each year. Both pilgrims and tourists will find much to do in this area. Pilgrims will most likely want to include a visit to the **Basilica of the Sacred Heart**, a major French pilgrimage site visited by Pope John Paul II in 1986.

Blessed Margaret Mary's confessor, **Father Claude de la Colombiere** (1641–1682), since 1992 St-Claude, has been honoured by his Jesuit counterparts with a dedicated chapel, **La Chapelle Colombière**, established close to the Chapel of the Apparitions. During a period working in London, Father Claude was appointed the spiritual advisor to the Italian-born Duchess of York, Maria Beatrice d'Este (1658–1718), Princess of Modena and wife of King James II (1633–1701).

The waterside town of **Digoin**, famous for its ceramics and 3 kilometres west of Le Paray le Monial, is situated at the junction of three of the Burgundy Canals. One leads to **Paray-le-Monial**; another to **Roanne** in the south; yet another canal leads to the island town of **Decize** and on to **Nevers**, a pottery town in the north-west. Cruises can be organised from here as well as fishing and boat hire. Barges cross the Loire overhead, on an unusual canal-bridge.

If you haven't yet overdosed on castles, consider motoring along the **Southern Burgundy Route du Château** (*Castle Route*). The route can commence from any of 17 historic, stately, romantic châteaux most with rambling interiors and hectares of formal gardens which have been lovingly restored. The medieval village of **Semur-en-Brionnais** 28 kilometres south of Paray-le-Monial is one of the most beautiful villages in Burgundy and home to the region's oldest castle, the 9th-century **Château St-Hugues**, the childhood home of Hugues de Semur (*St-Hugh the Great*, 1024—1109), the 6th Abbot of the medieval monastic centre in **Cluny**, east of Paray.

❧ If you prefer **wine** to castles, the **Burgundy** *Grand Cru* **wine route** commences in Dijon and weaves through 150 kilometres of picture postcard scenery and gastronomic paradise ending at **Georges Duboeuf**, Le Hameau du Vin (*The Hamlet of Wine*) in **Romanèche-Thorins**, south of Mâcon. The Duboeuf complex is an unusual and entertaining amusement park totally devoted to wine.

❧ The gardens and museum of the historical **Château de la Verrerie** in **Le Creusot** are 50 kilometres north of Paray. During the 18th century the château was a glass factory; Marie-Antoinette's crystal was specially made here. Today, the château is a museum of the history of the steel industry in Le Creusot.

❧ The **Musée de la Faïence** (*Museum of Earthenware*) within the Paray-le-Monial basilica complex displays ceramics from Charolles and Nevers, which for centuries were leading centres of china and ceramic production. The **Faïencerie de Charolles Earthenware Factory** in Charolles, 12 kilometres east of Paray, supplied hundreds of gold dishes for the banquet scenes in the *Harry Potter* films.

FOOD AND DRINK ❦ A motoring route following the region's **Romanesque churches** begins in **Paray-le-Monial**. Maps can be obtained at the local tourist office where directions to pottery studios and leather, wood and metal workshops can also be obtained. Goat farms, cheese dairies and snail farms are along the way; most are open to visitors.

❧ **La Maison du Charolais** (*Charolais Institute*), in the lovely market town of **Charolles**, is a bustling centre for the promotion of Charolais beef. A small charge is made for the institute's ever-popular guided tour which includes a 'beef tasting' complemented with a glass of local red wine. No faux-meat pies or vegetarian alternatives available!

✉ Molaize, (off the Route de Mâcon) Charolles.
☎ +33 (0) 3 85 24 00 46 **€€€–€€€€**

❧ **Roanne**, 50 kilometres south of Paray, is the location of the Troisgros family's illustrious restaurant **Maison Troisgros**, considered by reviewers as one of the best restaurants in the world.

✉ Place Jean Troisgros.
☎ +33 (0) 4 77 71 66 97 **€€€€€**

❧ Barges sail from **Chalon-sur-Saône**, north of Le Paray, to Arles and Avignon (around 7 days) making stops on the way for guests to wander through villages and sample the local delicacies. Shorter dinner cruises are also available.

Corsica

SO WELL INSTILLED IS ITALIAN CULTURE in Corsica that sometimes it is difficult to tell if the island is really French. Either way, it's an ideal place to laze on a sandy beach, chat over a glass of wine, sit idly in an oceanfront café or simply watch the sun sink below the Mediterranean horizon. Corsica is also a foodie's paradise. The hills are wild with fragrant herbs, olive groves, vineyards, citrus orchards and chestnut trees. Food is prepared in both Italian and French style and local wild boar, lamb and rabbit are usually on the menu along with pizza—prepared either the Italian way or the French.

The largest port towns on the island are Bastia and Ajaccio. The Place de St-Nicholas is the centre of Ajaccio, where under colourful café umbrellas locals and tourists alike can relax along the buzzy waterfront and ogle the cruise boats moored in the harbour. Being the birthplace of Napoleon Bonaparte (1769–1821), Ajaccio has a preoccupation with the former Emperor and every year hosts festivals of theatre and film as well as street parades in his honour.

Catholicism is deeply rooted in Corsica. During the 13th century brotherhoods of lay Catholics (called *confrères*) were established. The brotherhoods flourished and today they have their own churches, culture and religious practices, in line with the Catholic Church, although remaining independent. With the numbers of priests and nuns dwindling, these days the *confrères* and other lay people actively assist the religious orders in the running of those convent guesthouses that remain on the island.

OPEN HOUSE

13

La Maison Ste-Hyacinthe

The House of Hyacinth is situated near **Santa Maria di Lota**, a tiny village 10 kilometres north of the port town of Bastia, at the mountainous gateway to the Cap Corse further north.

❦ The convent is surrounded by acres of olive groves and palm trees, and has views over the surrounding hills. From the early 17th century until the French revolution the convent was occupied by Dominican monks. Post-revolution, sisters of the Franciscan Order made it their home until the 1980s. When the Franciscans left, the convent was vacant for ten years until in 1999 the Bishop of Ajaccio, André Jean René Lacrampe (1995–2003) invited the sisters of the Polish Catholic Mission to come and live here.

❦ The convent guesthouse consists of 45 guestrooms and a dormitory for those looking for cheaper accommodation. Some guestrooms have en suite facilities; others have just a wash basin, with share bathrooms on the same floor. Rooms are available on either a bed and breakfast basis or with all meals included. A number of cafés and restaurants are in the area and are accessible by car. Facilities include a communal television lounge room, wheelchair access and plenty of room for car parking. Most of the year the nuns run a shuttle bus service to the beach.

❦ Colour-coded, marked walking and hiking routes cross the whole island and some loop past the convent, hence the house is a favourite base for bushwalkers and hikers.

✉ 7, Rue de Plan Lieu Dit Miomo F-20200 Santa Maria di Lota Bastia.

📞 +33 (0) 4 95 33 28 29
📠 +33 (0) 4 95 33 28 29

✍ contact@maison-saint-hyacinthe.com

🖥 www.maison-saint-hyacinthe.com

🛏 from €33.00 pp (single), including breakfast.

☞ Take the train to Bastia which is in the north of the island. Guests can pre-arrange with the nuns to be picked up from the station on their arrival. Transfers can also be arranged from the ferry terminals. Buses run from Ajaccio to Bastia and depart from the Gare Routière, the main bus station in Ajaccio.

✝ **Sunday Mass** **0730, 1700 & 1900.** Centre Spirituel St-Hyacinthe, Santa Maria di Lota.

♿ Discuss your needs in advance of arriving, ideally when booking.

⚤ Open to men, women & groups

Open Houses

Corsica Santa Maria di Lota

PLACES OF INTEREST ❦ Much of **Bastia** was destroyed during World War II. However, its harbour and the older areas of the town were relatively unscathed. Bastia's 'old town' is a mixing pot of alleyways, 17th-century houses and stone buildings of somewhat faded elegance.

❦ Near the entrance to the old port in the district of **Terra Nuova** (or '*New Town*') stands **The Citadel** where the first settlement on the island was established by the Genoese, who occupied Corsica in the 14th century. Much of this area has been restored.

❦ In 1428 a boatload of local fishermen happened across a large oak crucifix of a black Christ floating in the sea off the island. This icon was later erected in the **Chapelle Ste-Croix** in Bastia and every Good Friday is at the forefront of a religious procession around The Citadel. Not to be outdone, the 15th-century Église Ste-Marie parades its precious silver statue of the Virgin Mary around the town on 15 August, the Feast of the Assumption.

❦ Bastia's shady **St-Nicholas beach** separates the old port from the new one, but the most popular beach on the peninsula is the **Plage de Tamarone**, near the harbour town of Macinaggio in the Cap Corse to the north of the island. **Macinaggio** is at the start of a 40-kilometre coastal walking trail called the **Sentier du Douanier** (*Route of the Customs Officers*) which tracks along the northern coastline to **Centuri** in Corsica's west.

❦ West of Bastia the **route des artisans** trails between the little villages of **l'Ile Rousse** and **Lumio**, and through tiny **Pigna** where you can visit the workshops and galleries of local ceramic artists and painters and observe woodcarvers hand-shaping musical instruments. Pigna and the surrounding villages become centres for traditional music each July when the '**Festivoce**', a fortnight-long festival of traditional Corsican music, is held.

❦ The 17 acres of the **Parc de Saleccia** on the northern outskirts of the village of l'Île Rousse are abundant with native Corsican trees, herbs and shrubs; this is a shady (and fragrant) place to stroll around on a scorching hot day.

The local tourist office in Bastia has maps of walking routes to many of the local villages. It is a 6-kilometre walk from the town to the mountain communities of **Ville di Pietrabugno** and **San Martino di Lota** and back to Bastia via the coast and the villages of **Miomo**, **Grigione** and **Pietranera**. Or visit the **Museum of Ethnography** in Bastia and uncover Corsica's past.

A circular motoring and hiking route begins at the medieval village of **Lama**, south-west of Bastia, which hosts a European film festival each August. The route passes through a rugged landscape to the neat and tidy little village of **Urtaca**, to the panoramic views of **Novella**, the hamlet of **Pedano** and on to the terraced village of **Pietralba**, a journey of almost 35 kilometres.

For more relaxed sight-seeing jump aboard the **U Trinighellu**, a widely-used tourist train which is also popular with the locals. The train travels through dozens of tunnels and across numerous suspension bridges and is something of an engineering marvel. The route runs between **Ajaccio** and **Bastia** via Corte and Ponte Leccia, and between **Ajaccio** and **Calvi** via l'Ile Rousse.

FOOD AND DRINK There are **markets** in Bastia every Saturday and Sunday morning in the Place de l'Hôtel de Ville and in the Place de St-Nicholas every Sunday morning. Check out the fashionable shops on the boulevard Paoli, or find a seat in one of the cafés on the square, soak up the sun and just watch the world go by.

Every second café seems to sell pizza but down by the old port the restaurant **A Casarella** is an excellent choice for sampling dishes from a traditional Corsican kitchen. At various times guests are treated to *Marinade de Sardines Fraîches à l'Huile d'Olive* (sardines in olive oil), *Filet d'Agneau en Croute d'Herbes* (lamb with herbs), *pulenta* (polenta), *Figatellu* (local sausage) and a zesty dessert by the name of *Tarte aux Citrons Corses du Couvent de St-Antoine*, with its possible connections to the local convent.

✉ 6, Rue Sainte-Croix.

☎ +33 (0) 4 95 32 02 32 €€–€€€

Florent on the west coast of **Cap Corse** is a seaside resort town which some say resembles St-Tropez on the mainland, mainly on account of its waterfront cafés and restaurants which are abuzz with tourists during summer.

14

Maison St-François

In 1835 Bishop Raphaël Casanelli d'Istria, Bishop of
Ajaccio (1833–1869), bestowed on the monks of the order
of the Oblates of Mary Immaculate the gift of this 17th
century monastery, which was formerly owned by the
Franciscan Order. The founder of the Oblates of Mary
Immaculate, Father Charles-Dominique Albini (1790–
1839), moved to Corsica from Aix-en-Provence in France
in 1936, to establish a seminary for trainee priests in
the newly acquired monastery. During his time in
Corsica he worked tirelessly, educating novice priests
and spreading the word of Christianity, travelling on
horseback throughout the island. Father Albini, known
as 'The Apostle of Corsica', died 3 years later and is
buried in a memorial chapel in the monastery.

❧ The **Maison St-François** is situated 50 kilometres
north of **Ajaccio** in the hills of the forested Deux
Sorru area on the outskirts of the village of **Vico**. The
accommodation section of the complex is run by a
group of lay friends of the convent who assist the monks
who reside here. The convent has a number of simple
single, twin and multiple guestrooms available for solo
travellers, couples and families with a maximum stay
of 2 weeks. Most rooms are on a share bathroom basis.
Cultural and artistic events, even cooking classes are
hosted in the cloisters throughout the year.

❧ A tour of the lovely old convent is most worthwhile as
the building contains artefacts and mementos from the
Franciscan era. Walking and hiking trails lead through
the surrounding hill country.

✉ Route d'Arbori
 F-20160 Vico, Corsica.

☎ +33 (0) 4 95 26 83 83
✆ +33 (0) 4 95 26 64 09

🛏 from €25.00 pp

☞ From the Gare
 Routière in Ajaccio,
 take the bus to Vico,
 almost 50 kilometres
 north. The ideal way
 to reach the Maison
 St-François is by car,
 which also allows for
 easy sightseeing in the
 surrounding areas.

✝ **Sunday Mass**
 1030.
 Maison St-François,
 Vico.

⚭ Open to both men &
 women

PLACES OF INTEREST ❧ The village of **Vico** is situated in the mountainous region of **Cinarca**, 15 kilometres inland from the beaches of the Gulf of Sagone on the western coast. From Vico there is easy access by car to lakes, beaches, walking trails and numerous Corsican villages. One of the most spectacular walking routes is the GR20, a 180-kilometre marked trail from **Calinzana** in the north to **Conca** in the south; it can also be walked in shorter sections. The hike, over rugged mountainous territory, is one of Europe's most difficult—for experienced and well-prepared trekkers only.

❧ Rejuvenate at the **thermal springs** in **Guagno les Bains**, 11 kilometres from Vico; the springs were once favoured by the Empress Eugénie (1826–1920), the wife of Napoleon III (1808–1873) and the last Empress of France, who would visit the area for beauty treatments.

❧ The tourist office in **Ajaccio** is in the Boulevard du Roi Jérôme; maps of 'Napoleon walks' are available here. The popular **Imperial Route** takes in the cathedral where the former Emperor was baptised, the **Bonaparte house** which is now a museum, and fountains and statues built to commemorate Napoleon's life. The trail continues for some way out of Ajaccio proper.

❧ During the summer months the shops and **markets** in Ajaccio remain open each Friday evening for late night shopping. For many of the locals this doubles as a night out and the atmosphere is lively and convivial. A colourful produce market is held in the Place César Campinchi in Ajaccio each day until 1300 (not on Sundays.) A bric-a-brac market is held on the boulevard Pascal Rossini each Sunday from 0700 until 1200.

❧ On the UNESCO World Heritage List, the **Calanches de Piana**, a wall of sheer, pinkish granite cliffs tower above a lapping, ink-blue sea. They are part of **Corsica's Regional National Park** which can be explored via numerous walking trails or by motoring through on the narrow, winding roads. However, the immensity of the cliffs can be better appreciated from the ocean and numerous cruise boats sail past. The Calanches form part of Corsica's western coastline between **Porto** to the north and **Piana**, 10 kilometres south.

Open Houses
Corsica Vico

❡ The **Chapelle de Notre-Dame de la Serra** is a spectacular observation point high above the Mediterranean. Next to the 15th-century chapel, a luminous white statue of the Madonna stands high on a rocky pinnacle (220 metres) overlooking the town of **Calvi**, the gulf and the ocean beyond. Mass is sometimes celebrated on a small, covered altar out of doors where the view must be a serious distraction. Drive up from Calvi or take the signposted, circular walk (approx. 2½ hours round trip).

❡ The **Plage de Calvi** (*Calvi beach*) follows the curve of the bay for some kilometres, and its long sweep of white sand is usually dotted with sunlounges and sunlovers who don't have to struggle too far for a cold drink or snack in a beachside café. And you can feel safe here—one of the Regiments of the **French Foreign Legion** is based in Calvi.

FOOD AND DRINK ❡ The sloping, sunkissed vineyards around **Ajaccio** produce some of Corsica's best wines. A *route de vin* can be taken from almost anywhere on the island by simply following the signs. However, the twisting, cliff-hanging roads are probably best navigated by a teetotaller.

❡ The **Clos Capitoro** vineyard is situated in the hills of **Pisciatella** behind the Gulf of Ajaccio. The family-run vineyard is a highly respected producer of a range of high-quality red, rosé and white wines. If you can't find this label in local restaurants the vineyard's sales and tasting room is open Monday to Friday (closed for lunch).
☎ +33 (0) 4 95 25 19 61

❡ Dine in any of the local restaurants in the **La Balagne** area in the north-west corner of the province and you will most likely be eating herbs and vegetables grown by the friars of the **Franciscan Monastery** in Corbara, who supply the local restaurants with their produce. **Corbara** is a tiny hilltop village near l'Île-Rousse.

❡ The restaurant **Auberge de la Restonica** on the Route de Restonica in the **Restonica Valley**, offers sustenance and relaxation for hikers and bushwalkers at its pine forest location on the picturesque, southern outskirts of **Corte** near **Pont-de-Trogone**.
☎ +33 (0) 4 95 46 09 58   €€

Languedoc-Roussillon

THE SPANISH, NEAR NEIGHBOURS OF LANGUEDOC, as well as the Romans have both left their mark on the region. Extensive Roman ruins can be seen in such towns as Arles, Carcassonne and Montpellier, and the Roman conquerers drank from a freshwater spring in Vergèze, still the source of Perrier water's bubbles.

Languedoc's sun-soaked beaches extend for 200 kilometres alongside the fashionable resorts that stretch to the Spanish border. Inspired by the clarity of light and its intense radiance, hordes of would-be Picassos sell their works on the seaside footpaths and in local cafés.

In winter, skiers and snowboarders make the most of the slopes and trails of the Cévennes National Park; year round, nature lovers and hikers head for the glorious forests and spectacular mountain scenery of the nearby Pyrenées.

The Romans established the first vineyards in this region. Their efforts were followed by those of the monasteries whose viticulture assisted the expanding industry. The Cistercian monks of Fontfroide Abbey near Narbonne produced wine, which along with the Châteauneuf-du-Pape appellation was once served in the papal dining room in Avignon. These days mere mortals can sample the 'Pope's wine' which is still produced on the abbey estate (the monks left in 1901) under the original AOC Corbières label.

And with truffle prices being what they are, November to March is a good time to try your hand at truffle hunting. Learn the tricks of the trade at the annual truffle fair held in Uzès at the end of January before retiring to the peace and quiet of one of the monasteries or convents of the region that offers accommodation.

Open Houses
Languedoc-Roussillon Nîmes

15

Château Maison Diocésaine de Nîmes

Close to the centre of **Nîmes**, the **Maison Diocésaine** is a former seminary for trainee priests; it is now owned and run by the local Catholic Diocese and used as a retreat and vacation centre. The château is situated in extensive, manicured grounds and a long line of arched, covered cloisters border an expanse of central, sheltered gardens. With lots of space and numerous rooms, Maison Diocésaine is ideally suited to accommodate large groups. However, tourists (either alone or in a group) and families can also stay overnight here. The centre is well set up for meetings and conferences and can cater for up to 180 day guests.

¶ Various room set-ups are available with the majority of guestrooms appointed with twin beds and en suite bathrooms. The château has a number of triple rooms, large family rooms and self-contained studio apartments which sleep up to eight guests. Rooms are clean and simply furnished and more than adequate for a short stay.

¶ Shared facilities include a television room and a dining room. All meals are available if required. There is an on-site chapel, a lift, wheelchair access and plenty of parking. The château is open all the year and is just 1 kilometre from the Rue de la Madeleine, the main shopping street of Nîmes. The centre is within walking distance of the main train station.

✉ 6, Rue Salomon Reinach
F-30000 Nîmes Gard

☎ +33 (0) 4 66 84 95 11
📠 +33 (0) 4 66 84 27 68

✉ contact@maison-diocesaine-nimes.cef.fr

🖥 www.maison-diocesaine-nimes.cef.fr

💶 price to be negotiated.

☞ Take the train to Gare de Nîmes. The château is less than 1 kilometre from the station.

✝ **Sunday Mass**
1000 & 1900.
Cathédrale Notre-Dame-et-Saint-Castor de Nîmes, Rue St-Castor, Nîmes.

♿ Discuss your needs in advance of arriving, ideally when booking.

♨ Open to men, women & groups

PLACES OF INTEREST ❧ **Nîmes** is situated halfway between **Avignon** and **Montpellier**. Spanish and Roman influences are evident in the classical buildings, elaborate fountains, tapas bars and 1st-century BC colosseum, **Les Arènes**, which is in the centre of the town. It is perfectly preserved and its design is similar to that of the Colosseum in Rome.

❧ The artists' town of **Arles**, south of Nîmes, also has a Roman amphitheatre, though not on the same scale. Bullfights are held here but thankfully they are mostly bloodless, with the bull, the matador and the spectators all surviving. Dutch Impressionist artist **Vincent Van Gogh** (1853–1890) lived here in the 'yellow house' on the Place Lamatine (depicted in one of his paintings). In 1888 Van Gogh's friend, the painter **Paul Gauguin** (1848–1903), spent 9 weeks painting in Arles while living at the yellow house. During this time the two artists were involved in a heated argument which led to Van Gogh cutting off part of his ear.

❧ Further north is the village of **St-Rémy**, where Van Gogh also lived for a time and was inspired to paint over 150 works. Visit the tourist office for the map of the self-guided Van Gogh walking tour. Arles is 30 kilometres east of Nîmes.

❧ It's not all that easy to believe, but Nîmes was the birthplace of **denim**. In the early 20th century this fabric was called *serge de Nîmes*, and only later labelled 'denim'. The Italian town of **Genoa** came up with 'jeans', which were made in bell-bottom style for sailors in the Italian navy from the Nîmes cloth; the bottoms could be easily rolled up and the pants (baggy in those days) could be jettisoned quite quickly if a sailor unexpectedly found himself in the ocean.

❧ The **Musee des Beaux-Arts** in Nîmes displays works from the 15th century by French and European artists, including **Peter Rubens** (1577–1640) and **James Pradier** (1792–1852).

❧ Also in the region is the **Pont du Gard**, a three-tiered Roman aqueduct built to provide Nîmes with fresh water. The area around the aqueduct is now a national park, popular for walking and picnicking; it has been listed as a World Heritage site.

Open Houses
Languedoc-Roussillon Nîmes

❦ The mountain walking and hiking area of the **Cévennes** is to the north and the beaches to the south are just 90 minutes away by car. The locals know that during autumn the wild chestnut trees in the mountains are laden with nuts free for the taking. Many a family has a fun day out following the walking trails, buckets and containers in hand to gather chestnuts to roast over an open fire.

❦ Beat the breathalyser and take a barge along **Languedoc's** 240 kilometres of canals and waterways to the local vineyards. Situated on the 17th-century Canal du Midi, the town of **Béziers** is in the centre of Languedoc's wine-growing region. The canal flows into the Mediterranean via the **Étang de Thau**, (*Thau Basin*) south of **Montpellier**.

FOOD AND DRINK ❦ Sample your way around the lively Arles street market, the largest and one of the best in Provence. The **Marché Provençal** is held on Saturday mornings along the Boulevard des Lices until 1200. The market is a one-stop shop for souvenirs and a taste of all things Provençale. A smaller farmers' market is held on Wednesday mornings in the Boulevard Émile Combes.

❦ The **Van Gogh Café** (formerly the Café Terrace) in the colourful, umbrella-filled Place du Forum in Arles is often crowded with devotees of the great Dutch artist who captured the building in his celebrated painting titled *The Café Terrace on the Place du Forum*. If no tables are available there are multiple choices for relaxed outdoor dining in the umbrella filled Place du Forum in front of the café.

❦ The wine growers around **Montpellier** have grouped together to form a combined point of sale and tasting area at the **Caveau** (*cellar*) **de St-Geniès des Mourgues** in the town of the same name. Wednesday is a good day to visit as the local market should be underway. St-Geniès des Mourgues is 38 kilometres south of Nîmes and 15 kilometres north-east of Montpellier.

OPEN HOUSE

16

Château du Parc Ducup

The **Château du Parc Ducup** is situated 3 kilometres west of the centre of **Perpignan** in a scenic, leafy location 10 kilometres from the beaches of the **Mediterranean** and 20 kilometres from the Spanish border. Constructed in local pink and white granite, the stately, rather grand-looking structure was once the privately owned Château Ducup de St-Paul and stands in 5 hectares of park and gardens which are overlooked by many of the guestrooms.

¶ Today the Château du Parc Ducup is owned by the local Catholic Diocese which runs the complex with the assistance of Carmelite nuns. The centre has 90 guestrooms and caters primarily for groups and families. Single, double and family-size guestrooms are available; all are modestly furnished. Some guestrooms have en suite bathrooms. General facilities include a television room, lift and plenty of car parking.

¶ The château's dining room serves a mix of French and Spanish cuisine, but for a change you could try the popular, reasonably priced local restaurant **La Yucca** which is situated near the château in a building which once belonged to it. Concerts, weddings, celebrations and cultural events are often held in the spacious grounds of the Parc Ducup estate. The complex can cater for large school groups and conferences and some rooms are suitable for the disabled.

✉ Allée des Chênes
F-66000 Perpignan
Pyrénées-Orientales.

✆ +33 (0) 4 68 68 32 40
✆ +33 (0) 4 68 85 44 85

✐ parcducup@wanadoo.fr

✐ www.parcducup.com

🛏 from €35.00 pp,
including breakfast.

☞ Take the train to Gare de Perpignan, the town's main train station, then a taxi to the château.

✝ **Sunday Mass**
0800, 1000 & 1830.
Cathédrale St-Jean-Baptiste de Perpignan, place de Gambetta, Perpignan.

♿ Discuss your needs in advance of arriving, ideally when booking.

☯ Open to men, women & groups

Open Houses
Languedoc-Roussillon Perpignan

PLACES OF INTEREST❦ **Perpignan** has much to offer the visitor—including sunshine and the proximity to safe beaches fronting colourful artists' villages and glamorous resorts. Even without a car it is not difficult to get to the beach by public transport; buses depart Perpignan on a regular basis for the sandy shores of **Canet Plage**, 12 kilometres away.

❧ The town is dominated by the **Palais des Rois de Majorque** (*Palace of the Kings of Majorca*), built in the 13th century when Perpignan was the capital of Majorca. The palace is the oldest royal residence in France.

❧ Some 30 kilometres south of Perpignan is the oceanfront town of **Collioure**, a favourite haunt of artists and craftspeople, many of whom sell from their studios and conduct courses for visitors. **Pablo Picasso** (1881–1973) and **Henri Matisse** (1869–1954) both painted here and reproductions of their works can be seen on the **Fauvism Footpath**, so named after the art movement Matisse promoted. To make sure you don't miss seeing any of the paintings, collect a map from the tourist office in the Place du 18 Juin.

❧ The art and techniques of patchwork quilting are taught at the **Centre European du Patchwork** (*European Centre of Patchwork*) in Sallèles-d'Aude, 70 kilometres north of Perpignan.

❧ For five centuries a sealed stone tomb in the garden of the **Abbaye Ste-Marie d'Arles-sur-Tech** (*Abbey of St Marie of Arles-sur-Tech*), in the Pyrénées-Orientales, containing the relics of **St-Abdon** and **St-Sennen**, the Patron Saints of the village, has constantly—and mysteriously—flowed with fresh, pure water, the source of which is still not known. The water is sometimes distributed to Mass-goers but has no miraculous properties.

❧ The **Chemin de la Liberté** (*The Way of Freedom*) is an old escape route from the French Pyrenées into northern Spain, once used by Allied servicemen during World War II. The now signposted route is open to the public and has become a well-used but difficult walking trail. Other such trails are expected to open in the near future.

❡ **L'Abbaye de St-Martin du Canigou** (*Abbey of St Martin*) clings to a rocky precipice high in the Pyrénées and can only be reached on foot. From the village of **Casteil**, 50 kilometres west of Perpignan, it is a 40-minute climb up a rocky mountainside to reach this 11th-century, former Benedictine abbey, now occupied by a Christian religious group, the Communauté Catholique des Béatitudes (*Catholic Community of the Beatitudes*). The community conduct guided tours of the abbey for a small fee.

❡ Twelve kilometres from St-Martin du Canigou, the **Petit Train Jaune** (*Little Yellow Train*) departs from one of the most beautiful villages in France, the walled, medieval **Villefranche-de-Conflent**. The train stops at Mont-Louis, 30 kilometres west and then travels to **Bolquere**, the country's highest train station; from there it's on to **Esquavar**, **Err** and back to **Villefranche**. A thrilling, panoramic journey if vertigo isn't a problem.

FOOD AND DRINK ❧ The university town of Perpignan is close to the beaches and nightlife of the Mediterranean coast, and to the Spanish border. Spanish-style *gazpacho* and *paella* are served in the town's restaurants, along with French *cassoulet* and *soufflé*. On summer Thursday evenings buskers and magicians roam the streets.

❡ **Seafood** and **tapas** feature on most restaurant menus in Perpignan. You can have your fill of tapas here quite cheaply and maybe share *paella* at one of the lively restaurants in the **Place de la Loge**, the pedestrian-only section of the old town.

❡ Dine indoors amongst the memorabilia or eat outside on the narrow laneway at the convivial bistro, **Casa Sansa**. While seafood features strongly on the menu, there is plenty to keep meat (and garlic) lovers satisfied.

✉ 2, Rue Fabriques Nadal.

☎ +33 (0) 4 68 34 21 84   €€€-€€€€

❡ The **cherry** season starts mid-May and walking paths trail through the cherry orchards surrounding the village of **Céret**, south of Perpignan. If it's **wine** you fancy, then head to the hills of the **Corbières** region where the vineyards outnumber the ruined châteaux and abbeys.

17

OPEN HOUSE

Chartreuse de Valbonne

The Chartreuse de Valbonne is a former monastery established in 1204 by the Bishop of Uzes, Guilhem de Vénéjan for the Carthusian order. The property was occupied by the Carthusians up until early in the 20th century when it was purchased by a Protestant Christian group, l'Association de Secoure, who established a hospital on the premises. The association closed the hospital in the 1990s and the building was completely renovated and re-opened as a tourist hotel. The association retains ownership of the property and the old cloisters, corridors and ecclesiastical adornments remain. The complex is situated in a wooded valley, 55 kilometres north of **Avignon**. Its reputation for hospitality has made it a popular destination, with many repeat guests.

❡ The guestrooms, which comprise 13 renovated single and twin monks' cells, are comfortably furnished and have en suite facilities. The Bishop's Apartment is available for families or small groups and consists of three bedrooms and a small kitchen. All meals can be taken in the on-site restaurant where local specialities are served with the monastery's own Côtes du Rhône wine, made from grapes grown in vineyards cultivated by monks since the 13th century. Facilities include a television lounge and a kitchen for the use of guests. There is ample on-site parking. Guided tours of the monastery take place each day between March and December and conclude in the old cellars, with a tasting of monastery wine. It was Carthusian monks who created the alcoholic, green **Elixir Vegetal de la Grande-Chartreuse** (*Chartreuse herbal liqueur*), the ingredients of which are only known to Carthusian monks to this day.

✉ F-30130 St-Paulet de Caisson Gard.

📞 +33 (0) 4 66 90 41 03
📠 +33 (0) 4 66 82 76 10

✉ hotellerie@
chartreusedevalbonne.
com

🌐 www.
chartreusedevalbonne.
com

🛏 from €32.00 pp (single room).

☞ Avignon, 45 kilometres south of St-Paulet, is the closest train station to the monastery. A bus departs from the Avignon Centre train station (not from the new TGV station on the outskirts of the town) to the commune of St. Alexandre which is 5 kilometres from the monastery. Please check bus connection times before departure and arrange a pick-up from St Alexandre.

✝ **Sunday Mass 1030.**
Chapelle de la Chartreuse de Valbonne.

⚭ Open to both men & women

PLACES OF INTEREST ❧ From **St-Paulet de Caisson** beautiful **Avignon** can be visited in a day. However, bear in mind that as the town is a designated UNESCO World Heritage site there is much to see. Known as the 'city of Popes', Avignon is a web of cobblestone streets, medieval towers and churches and an old town surrounded by impenetrable stone bulwarks, built to protect the ostentatious residence of long-departed pontiffs, known as the 'anti-popes'.

❦ Between 1305 and 1403 the town was the seat of the Papacy. **Pope Clement V** (1264–1314) was the first of the 'anti-popes' and it was he who moved the seat of the papacy away from Rome in 1305. A supporter of **Philippe IV** (Philip the Fair, 1268–1314), the French king, the two men plotted to quash the wealthy and powerful Catholic military order of the Knights of Templar (over a monetary dispute) and establish Avignon as the seat of the papacy. On dissolving the order the king seized its Treasury and the last remaining members of the order were burnt at the stake.

❦ Seven Popes from **Pope Clement V** (ruled 1305–1314) to **Pope Gregory XI** (1370–1378) resided at the enormous **Palais des Papes** (*Palace of the Popes*). Even after Pope Gregory XI moved the seat of the papacy back to Rome, his replacement, **Clement VII** (1378–1394) continued to live in the sumptuous palace, as did his successor, **Benedict XIII** (Pedro de Luna, 1328–1422/23), who lived here until 1403.

❦ The **Palais des Papes** is now the centre of the town's cultural life and a ready-made venue for concerts, art exhibitions and festivals.

❦ From the town of **Pont St-Esprit**, 4 kilometres east of St-Paulet de Caisson, it is possible to travel by boat to **Avignon**. The ruins of the 12th century **Pont d'Avignon** (*Bridge of Avignon*) once formed part of the medieval pilgrimage route to Santiago de Compostela in Spain. The bridge is the focus of the famous song 'Sur le Pont d'Avignon' ('*On he Bridge of Avignon*'). According to the legend a young shepherd, Bénézet (now **St-Bénézet**) miraculously heaved a large boulder into the Rhône, having followed the instructions of a voice from Heaven, and thereby laying the foundation stone of the bridge that was subsequently built. To-day only half the bridge remains standing.

Open Houses
Languedoc-Roussillon St-Paulet de Caisson

The remains of a settlement known as **Camp-de-César** (*Caesar's camp*) in the town of **Laudun l'Ardoise**, between St-Paulet de Caisson and Avignon, refers to the significant Roman ruins situated above the town. The camp is thought to have been in use for almost 1,000 years from the 5th century BC. The **Via Domitia**, the old Roman road which once linked Italy to Spain, is now a scenic motoring route passing through Saint-Rémy-de-Provence, Nîmes, Béziers, Narbonne and Perpignan.

The wetlands of the **Crau** area near the town **St-Martin-de-Crau** 45 kilometres south-east of Nîmes, is a protected area of France and a haven for ornithologists and naturalists. Learn more at the **L'écomusée de St-Martin-de-Crau**, the local natural history museum.

FOOD AND DRINK There are a number of cafés, a baker's shop (*boulangerie*) and a delicatessen in the central area of **St-Paulet-de-Caisson**. The town is only small but the area is notable for its vineyards. Wine produced by over 100 local vignerons can be tasted and purchased at the local **Cave des Vignerons** (*wine cellars*) in St-Paulet.

The **Chartreuse de Valbonne** can arrange guided tours of its vineyards followed by a little sampling of the vintage *crus* in the old monastery cellar. You could continue on and follow the walking trails through the hills surrounding the château and stop by some of the other vineyards in the district to compare tasting notes.

The restaurant in the **Chartreuse de Valbonne** complex is run by professional caterers and is also open to those not staying in the complex. Reservations are necessary and fixed-price menus are available.

☎ +33 (0) 4 66 90 41 24   €€

Pont St-Esprit and **Uzès** have a market each Saturday morning. The **Uzès market** in the **Place aux Herbes** has a well-deserved reputation as one of the best Provençal markets.

Pays-de-la-Loire

O LESS THAN AN HOUR FROM PARIS by the TGV fast train, Pays-de-la-Loire is a region of grand abbeys, regal châteaux and exquisite gardens. It's also the home of the international motor racing track and car museum in Le Mans and the Cadre Noir military riding school, the home of French horsemanship.

Throughout Pays-de-la-Loire, country clubs with impeccably groomed fairways provide sanctuaries for golf lovers. Along the coast, cycling trails and walking paths offer plenty of chances for both exercise and exploration.

If you're seriously into castles you'll think you're in Heaven in the Loire Valley. Fairytale châteaux line both sides of the River Loire, and a themed motoring trail makes finding some of the largest ones easy. Postcard-pretty castles can be reached by barge from Paris. Some barges carry bicycles on board so guests can make further forays onto dry land.

The medieval cathedrals and abbeys of the Loire also invite closer inspection and many offer a place of rest and shelter. The soothing sounds of Gregorian chants, revived in the subdued spiritual ambience of a Loire abbey, are likely to stir even the most wayward of religious hearts.

18

Centre de l'Etoile

Located in the heart of **Le Mans**, just 55 minutes by TGV fast train from Paris, the **Centre de l'Etoile** was, up until the early 20th century, the Monastère de la Visitation Sainte-Marie (*Monastery of the Visitation*), occupied by a contemplative order of Catholic nuns. These days it is owned by the Catholic Diocese of Le Mans and run as a place of accommodation by the local branch of the Sisters of Providence, who are assisted by members of the local parish.

❡ The centre is open to solo travellers but is well suited to group accommodation as it is set up for meetings and conferences, and has the catering facilities to cope. The centre can handle meals for 150 day guests. The sisters offer accommodation in a choice of guestrooms, each sleeping between one and up to six people. All guestrooms have en suites and some are suitable for the disabled. The centre has a self-service cafeteria which caters for all meals and in-between snacks, and there are outdoor areas where, weather permitting, meals can be enjoyed. The residence is close to the centre of town and is set in 2 acres of attractive, spacious grounds overlooked by some of the guestrooms. There is plenty of on-site parking and a bus stop is nearby. Facilities include communal sitting rooms with television, a table tennis and billiard room, and a small chapel. A sister is usually at reception but after midnight an entrance code arrangement is in place.

✉ 26, Rue Albert Maignan F-72000 Le Mans Sarthe.

☎ +33 (0) 2 43 54 50 00
📠 +33 (0) 2 43 76 46 31

✉ etoile@centre-etoile.com

🖥 www.centre-etoile.com

🛏 from €25.00 pp, including breakfast. A €10.00 membership fee is extra.

☞ Take the train to Le Mans. From the Le Mans train station take bus number 5 and get off at the 'Etoile' stop. Le Mans is approximately 200 kilometres south-west of Paris.

✝ **Sunday Mass** 0830 & 1030. Cathédrale St-Julien, Rue de la Reine Bérengère, Le Mans.

♿ Discuss your needs in advance of arriving, ideally when booking.

⚥ Open to men, women & groups

PLACES OF INTEREST ❧ **Le Mans** is probably best known for its **endurance car race** and the 24-hour circuit is only 4 kilometres from the Centre de l'Etoile. The race is held in June when the town is invaded by car-racing enthusiasts. Tours of the track and driver-training courses are conducted here. A car museum is located at the entrance to the circuit.

❦ **Le Vieux Mans**, the old town of Le Mans, is one of the best-preserved medieval town centres in France. Ancient towers and large sections of the Roman walls remain intact. **The Cathedral of St Julien**, famed for its stained-glass windows, dates back to the 12th century.

❦ Should burial places be your passion, two of the world's most famous people are buried in the Loire's château country. Painter and sculptor **Leonardo da Vinci**'s (1452–1519) remains are interred in the **St-Hubert Chapel** in the grounds of **Château Amboise**, 125 kilometres south-east of Le Mans. English king **Richard the Lionheart** (reigned 1189–1199) rests in peace at the now secular, 12th-century **Fontevraud Abbey**, near Chinon, between Le Mans and Poitiers.

❦ Amongst the harbours and fishing villages along the Pays coastline stretch long white sandy beaches, including **La Baule**, said to be one of the best beaches in France. The **Île d'Yeu** (*Island of Yeu*), one of the 15 ruggedly beautiful **Îles du Ponant**, is a 10 × 4 kilometre dot in the ocean, 18 kilometres off the Pays coast. Its capital, the fishing town of **Port-Joinville**, can be accessed by ferry from **Fromantine** on the mainland. It seems that the most popular tourist activity is to hire a bike in Port-Joinville and head off on one of the numerous cycling paths, stopping to swim or nibble on some fresh seafood in a harbourfront café at **Port-de-la-Meule**, 4 kilometres away and on the opposite side of the island. The neighbouring island of **Noirmoutier** has a history of salt mining, an industry that was first established by Benedictine monks around the 5th century.

Open Houses
Pays-de-la-Loire Le Mans

The **House of St-Thérèse** in Rue de St Blaise, **Alençon**, 55 kilometres north of Le Mans, is the birthplace of **St-Thérèse of Lisieux** (1873–1897), commonly known as 'The Little Flower'. It is now a museum and a place of pilgrimage. Lisieux, where St-Thérèse lived as a Carmelite nun and died at the age of 24, is 100 kilometres north of Alençon. In 1977 Pope John Paul ii honoured St-Thérèse by declaring her a Doctor of the Church, following in the footsteps of St Teresa of Ávila and St Catherine of Siena. In 2008 relics of St-Thérèse were carried into space on the NASA space-shuttle *Discovery*.

The prehistoric caves, **le Grotte et Canyon de Saulges** in Thorigné en Charnie at **Saulges**, 55 kilometres west of Le Mans, are said to have been inhabited up to 25,000 years ago. On tours of the caves, the guides relate entertaining tales of witches and warlocks, myths and legends. Not for claustrophobics or the vertically challenged.

FOOD AND DRINK Hungry tourists are well catered for in **Le Mans** with numerous bistros, restaurants and cafés in the old town, many serving the local speciality *rillettes du Mans*, a type of pork paté. Book early in race season.

Get into the spirit of Le Mans at the city's iconic **Legends Café**, a cross between a museum of motor sports and a very busy brasserie.

✉ 9, Rue du Port.

☎ +33 (0) 2 43 77 15 09   €€€

Behind the peek-through lace curtains in the window of classic French bistro, **La Ciboulette** is a warm, cosy little nook serving above-average French regional cuisine.

✉ 14, Rue de la Vieille Porte.

☎ +33 (0) 2 43 24 65 67   €€–€€€

The area around the village of **Ste-Maure de Touraine**, 140 kilometres south of Le Mans produces a unique, creamy goats cheese of the same name. Each separate cheese is log-shaped and held together with a rye straw inserted end to end through the middle. The cheese is usually on sale at the daily produce market on the **Place du Marché** in Le Mans, or at the Friday market in Ste-Maure.

Provence / Alps / Côtes d'Azur

 ENOWNED FOR ITS SUNFLOWERS as much as its glorious sunshine, Provence soothes the spirits of travellers and pilgrims alike with an abundance of sensory riches. A luminous sapphire blue sky, vast expanses of fragrant lavender, the muted shades of olive groves and row upon row of cheery, golden sunflowers make for glorious backdrops to convents and monasteries whose stunning locations and 5-star views surely make them the envy of major hotel chains.

In short, the region has everything a visitor dreams about—a warm, dry climate, sunny beaches, snow-covered mountains and fascinating medieval villages where the daily life continues, as it has done for centuries, at an unhurried pace.

Long after the Romans settled in Provence, Mary Magdalene introduced Christianity to the region. Several Popes lived here for a time and post-Impressionist painters couldn't resist the place on account of the special effects of its mellow, translucent light.

In a tranquil valley near the hilltop village of Gordes, every summer a medieval Cistercian monastery is drenched in the fragrance of lavender. A Cistercian-owned ferry sails to an abbey on an idyllic island in the Mediterranean where monks still live, work and pray in relative solitude. Visitors are welcome and during the warmer months, the quiet is likely to be disturbed only by the humming of cicadas or a weary traveller in search of rest and renewal.

If you crave a bit more 'buzz', go window-shopping in the exquisite shops and boutiques on the boulevards of the French Riviera.

Open Houses
Provence / Alps / Côtes d'Azur Cannes

19

Centre International Marie Eugénie Milleret

The Centre International Eugénie Milleret is owned and run by the sisters of the Religious of the Assumption and named after the founder of the order, the Blessed Marie Eugénie Milleret (1817–1898). The order was established in Paris in 1939 and is now represented in 35 countries.

❧ The rather impressive building housing the CIMEM appears to have been, in its heyday, a typical south-of-France-style mansion, and even with today's slightly 'well used' appearance retains its attractiveness. The centre is situated in 2 hectares of garden in a quiet, suburban area of Cannes, 2 kilometres from the main beach and waterfront promenade. Slender palm trees and sun-loving scarlet bougainvillea create a tropical scene.

❧ The guestrooms are airy and comfortable and accommodate from between 2 and six guests; most have en suite bathrooms. The gardens and some of the front facing guestrooms have sea views. There is an attractive outdoor terrace which doubles as an eating area in the summer, as well as an indoor dining room where French home-style cooking is the norm. Facilities include a television room, a large parking area and a lift. On-site conference facilities are available for groups. Visa and Mastercard are accepted. A surprisingly large chapel, where guests can join the sisters in liturgical activities, is within the building.

✉ 37, Avenue du Commandant Bret F-06400 Cannes Alpes-Maritimes.

☎ +33 (0) 4 97 06 66 70
📠 +33 (0) 4 97 06 66 76

✉ contact@cimem.com

🌐 www.cimem.com

🛏 from €50.00 pp, including breakfast.

☞ The nearest train station is Gare de Cannes which is approximately 2 kilometres from the convent. However, you might prefer to take a taxi to the convent as it is situated on a steep hill.

✝ **Sunday Mass 1800.** Chapel of the Centre International Marie Eugénie Milleret.

⚤ Open to both men & women

PLACES OF INTEREST ❧ Glamorous **Cannes** is internationally known for its **film festival** which is generally held in May each year. It is just as well known for its extravagant hotels, casinos, exclusive boutiques and the well-heeled glitterati it attracts. Observe all the above on a stroll along the broad, elegant, palm-lined, waterfront **Boulevard de la Croisette** which leads from one end of the beach to the other.

❧ For some extraordinary window-shopping, wander along **Rue d'Antibes**, the major—and expensive—shopping street of Cannes. The more affordable **Galeries Lafayette** has a small branch at 6 Rue du Maréchal-Foch which runs off the Rue d'Antibes.

❧ **Grasse**, the **perfume** centre of Provence, is only 18 kilometres north of Cannes. Grasse is surrounded by perfumeries but the three major perfume factories open to the public— **Fragonard**, **Galimard** and **Molinard**— are all within walking distance of each other in the centre of town. Create your own signature perfume with the help of a master perfumier. The town is bathed in the fragrance of roses each May when the country's most beautiful smelling rose is chosen during the **Fête de la Rose** (*Rose Festival*).

❧ The **Planaria Ferry** (Line), owned by the monks of the Abbaye Notre-Dame de Lérins, departs daily from Cannes Quay for the **Îles de Lérins**, (*the Lerin Islands*) where the 18th-century monastery, its 10th-century predecessor, and the monks' vineyards and olive groves can be explored. The rail journey from **Cannes** to **Nice** takes 45 minutes (fast train), with swanky **Monaco** a further 15 minutes away. Choose a waterside seat so as not to miss the lavish oceanfront mansions and exclusive private beaches.

❧ **L'Abbaye de Valbonne**, in the village of **Valbonne**, 15 kilometres north of Cannes, was founded in 1199 by the monks of the Order of Chalais. It is a testament to 12th-century builders and architects that the monks' quarters and a section of the cloisters still stand. The building also houses a museum of local history.

Open Houses
Provence / Alps / Côtes d'Azur Cannes

❧ The works of French painter **Fernand Léger** (1881–1955) are on display in the village of **Biot** (pronounced *Bee-ot*) in the museum which bears his name. This ancient hilltop village, 15 kilometres east of Cannes, is known for its glassblowers and potters. **La Verrerie de Biot** (*Biot Glass*) located on the edge of the village has a huge collection of glass and ceramics on sale and offers a handy post home service.

❧ Escape the sun and the heat on the **Sentier de la Brague**, an 18-kilometre (round trip) walking trail between the ancient villages of **Biot** and **Valbonne**. The trail follows the River Brague through a national park where thick clusters of oak and pine trees provide welcome shade.

❧ If you have any French francs hidden away in a drawer somewhere you could spend them in the village of **Collobrières**, east of **Toulon** where some of the local stores take the old currency as well as the Euro.

FOOD AND DRINK ❧ The cafés and restaurants along the **Cannes Promenade** have great ocean views— but at a price. And why pay to sit on the private beaches when the sandy beaches on the **St Tropez** side of the port have free access? The **Plage du Midi** in front of the Boulevard du Midi has much the same outlook, cheaper food and drink, a less touristy atmosphere and the beaches are more family-orientated.

❧ If you have a sweet tooth then head for the **Café Lenôtre** where you can pick up a French feast for a picnic on the beach, or dine in and sample the almost 'too hard to choose' pastries and desserts. If it's summer, delicious lavender ice-cream might be on the menu. And you could always enrol in the café's **pastry school** and learn the trade secrets.

✉ 9, Rue d'Antibes.
☏ +33 (0) 4 97 06 67 67 €€€

❧ The **Rue Félix Faure**, behind the port, is lined with a string of casual street cafés and restaurants, many owned by local fishermen and most serving the local catch of the day.

OPEN HOUSE

20

Maison du Séminaire

This is surely one of the city's best kept accommodation secrets, given that many visitors to **Nice** would be happy paying large sums of money for a hotel room with **views** akin to those from the guestrooms of the Maison du Séminaire. The guesthouse is situated on a slight rise near the ocean ferry terminal in an exclusive, quite fashionable area of Nice and was once the local diocesan seminary for trainee priests, who could only have been inspired by the views from the front-facing windows. The modestly furnished abodes of the former occupants have made way for small but modern, renovated guestrooms, most with views extending across the Mediterranean and over the **Baie des Anges** (*Bay of Angels*) from one end of the beach to the other. Expensive yachts, fishing boats and the ferries to Corsica regularly sail past.

❧ Run along hotel lines by an association known as Friends of the Seminary, the guestrooms all have en suites, televisions and telephones. The first-floor **restaurant** opens out on to a large outdoor terrace where meals and wine are served and from where guests can watch the rich and famous at play on the water.

❧ There is a large car parking area, lifts and wheelchair access. A bus stop is less than 500 metres away. Cross the road to swim in the **Mediterranean** with the locals (be prepared for a rocky clamber down to the water) or turn right out of the Maison to discover the well-priced, breezy waterside restaurants and outdoor cafés by the quay.

✉ 29, Boulevard Franck Pilatte
F-06300 Nice Alpes-Maritimes

☎ +33 (0) 4 93 89 39 57
✆ +33 (0) 4 93 26 79 99

✉ mds@maison-du-seminaire.com

✉ www.maisonduseminaire.fr

🛏 from €40.00 pp.
Breakfast €8.00 pp.

☞ Take the train to the main Nice train station, Nice-Centre Ville. Take a taxi to the guesthouse which is 5 kilometres from the station.

✝ **Sunday Mass 1000.**
Église Notre-Dame du Port, Place Ile de Beauté, Nice.

⚭ Open to men, women & groups

Open Houses
Provence / Alps / Côtes d'Azur Nice

PLACES OF INTEREST ✔ The panoramic views from the hilltop village of **Eze**, 10 kilometres east of Nice, are worth the climb along the narrow rocky pathways which lead past old stone houses, artists' studios, cafés and in summer masses of multi-coloured bougainvillea. Most roads lead to a ruined 15th-century castle in the grounds of the **Jardin Exotique** (*exotic garden*) where thousands of cacti and tropical plants flourish under the often scorching Mediterranean sun.

❧ A day or so following the various **lavender** trails is bound to be rewarding. Flowering season is from late June to early September and local tourist offices can supply maps for walking the trails or motoring. Meandering through sprawling purple fields, you will be led from picturesque Provencale villages to distilleries and perfume museums. Along the way you can indulge in some lavender tasting: lavender tea, honey, lemonade, cake, sweets, ice-cream—a seemingly endless list.

❧ The **Musée Escoffier de l'Art Culinaire** (*Escoffier Museum of Culinary Art*) in the village of Villeneuve Loubet is dedicated to the life of chef extraordinaire Auguste Escoffier (1846–1935) and is in a former home of the master chef. In 1893 Escoffier created the renowned dessert 'Peach Melba' in the kitchens of the Savoy Hotel in London in honour of the great Australian opera singer and international soprano Dame Nellie Melba (1861–1931). The village is 20 kilometres west of Nice.

❧ The **Monastère Notre-Dame de Cimiez** (*Monastery of Cimiez*) in suburban Nice is not only a fully working monastery but features a museum which chronicles the Franciscan way of life from medieval times to the present. The formally designed monastery garden is open to the public and commands panoramic views over the city and to the sea.

✝ Sunday Mass 0930 & 1130

❧ French painter and one-time resident of Nice, **Henri Matisse** (1869–1954) is buried alongside his former wife, **Amélie Noellie Parayre** (1872–1958) in the well-kept graveyard of the Monastery of Cimiez. **The Matisse Museum** where many of the artists' works are on display is nearby at 164, Avenue des Arènes de Cimiez. Matisse and his wife separated in 1939.

❧ The **Musée Renoir** (*Renoir Museum*) in Cagnes-sur-Mer, 12 kilometres south-west of Nice, is the final residence of French Impressionist painter Auguste Renoir (1841–1919) who lived here from 1907 until he died. Situated in a park of olive and orange trees are the artist's two studios containing a number of his paintings, sketches, sculptures and personal possessions. Renoir's grandson Jacques Renoir (b. 1942), a photographer of note, lives in Cagnes-sur-Mer.

❧ The graves of Princess Grace and Prince Rainier of Monaco lie side by side in the **Monaco Cathedral**, in the Place St-Nicholas near the Grimaldi Palace. On the day they were married in 1956 the royal couple paid a visit to the **Église Ste-Dévote** (*Church of St Devota*), near the harbour to honour the Patron Saint of Monaco, Ste-Devote (282–304) who is buried in the church.

☩ Sunday Mass Cathédrale de Monaco 1030
   Église Ste-Dévote 1030 & 1800

❧ And if you fancy a movie (in English) *en plein air*, the outdoor screenings during summer at the **Cinéma d'Été** in Monaco must surely make for the most picturesque cinema in the world. The bus from Nice to Monaco stops a few blocks from the Maison du Séminaire.

FOOD AND DRINK ❧ Take in the sights and the fresh sea air on a pre-dinner stroll along the **Promenade des Anglais**, or hire a beach chair and relax on the famous pebbly beach. You can eat while enjoying the view at one of the stylish seafront cafés—but do check the prices before sitting down.

❧ **Salade Niçoise**, the local salad speciality made with tuna, potato, green beans, eggs, tomatoes and olives, features on most menus in this part of the world and never tastes better than when eaten in the city of its origin.

❧ Close to the **Maison du Seminaire**, the waterfront restaurants strung around the port are competitively priced with waiters vying for the attention of any hungry-looking pedestrians.

❧ Almost opposite La Maison du Seminaire is the up-market restaurant **La Réserve** where the cost of dining on the exclusive terrace can be around €400 for a seven-course meal. However, the restaurant on the terrace of **La Maison du Seminaire** (not open every night) has the same view and a *tout compris* menu around €40pp. Wine is also available.

✉ Restaurant La Réserve, Boulevard Franck Pilatte

☏ +33 (0) 4 97 08 29 98 60   €€€€€

✉ Restaurant La Maison du Seminaire, Boulevard Franck Pilatte

☏ +33 (0) 4 93 89 39 57   €€

21

Maison d'Accueil Lacordaire

Run by the Dominican Sisters of the Rosary, the Maison d'Accueil Lacordaire is tucked away in quiet suburbia approximately 20 minutes' walk from the centre of **Vence**. The Chapelle Matisse (*Matisse Chapel* or Chapelle du Rosaire), which was designed and decorated by **Henri Matisse** (1869–1954) between 1947 and 1951, is in the front garden of the convent. This was Matisse's final work, the artist having taken the project on at the age of 77 at the behest of his one-time nurse, model and good friend Sister Jacques-Marie (1921–2005), a Dominican nun who lived at Lacordaire. **Guided tours** of the chapel can be arranged with the sisters and members of the public can attend Mass here. After Mass on Sunday the chapel is closed but it is open most afternoons. It's best to check before setting out.

❦ Overlooking the gorgeous town of Vence and the Mediterranean, accommodation here consists of two separate villas containing 24 single and double guestrooms. All have en suites. The sisters have a minimum night stay which at the moment is 3 nights (may change). A feature of the convent is the colourful **Mediterranean-style garden** with vine-covered archways, flower-laden stone urns and a tiny fish pond. The establishment has a dining room and all meals are available if required. There is a terrace for eating outdoors. Facilities include a television room, lift and conference amenities. The Dominican sisters have a similar establishment in the village of St-Paul de Vence 2 kilometres away.

✉ 466, Avenue Henri Matisse
F-06141 Vence Alpes-Maritimes

☎ +33 (0) 4 93 58 03 26
☏ +33 (0) 4 93 58 21 10

✉ dominicaines@wanadoo.fr

✉ www.pagesperso-orange.fr/maison.lacordaire

💳 from €50.00 pp, including all meals.

☞ Take the train to Cagnes sur Mer, 10 kilometres south of Vence, then bus number 400 or 410. A taxi is the other alternative. Vence is situated in the hills behind the Riviera, about 20 kilometres north-west of Nice and 30 kilometres north-east of Cannes.

✝ **Sunday Mass** 1000.
Chapelle du Rosaire de Vence, 466, Avenue Henri Matisse.

⚤ Open to both men & women

PLACES OF INTEREST ❧ Caressed by gentle ocean breezes in summer, **Vence** is quite an artists' paradise with studios, galleries and museums spread throughout the old town. The smaller, walled medieval village of **St-Paul de Vence** is far more touristy. Painter Henri Matisse famously said of Vence, 'This morning while walking near my house, seeing all these girls, women and men riding their bikes to market, I thought I was in Tahiti.'

❧ An easy way to explore the town without missing anything is to pick up a map from the local tourist office and take a self-guided walking tour around the historic **Vieille Ville**, the old town of Vence.

❧ The works of local artists are on sale at **La Galerie de l'Éveche**, 1, Place Cahours. Local artisans specialising in modern art display their wares in the **Gallerie Beauborg** in the **Château Notre-Dame des Fleurs** (on the road between Vence and Tourettes-sur-Loup) which also has a sculpture garden.

❧ Or perhaps take some lessons at the art school in **Henri Matisse's** former home, the **Villa La Reve**, which is quite close to the Lacordaire convent. Back in Nice, a collection of works by the master are on display at the Matisse Museum.

❧ It is just a short bus ride to the astonishingly attractive village of **St-Paul de Vence** which is overrun with tourists all summer long. Despite the crowds and the prices it is still a charming little town to explore. However, there are hundreds of steps leading up and down steep inclines which the less mobile would be well to consider before embarking on a sightseeing expedition.

Open Houses
Provence / Alps / Côtes d'Azur Vence

❧ **Henri Matisse's** last work was the design and building of the chapel at the **Lacordiare Convent**. The history behind the chapel begins in 1942 when the 73-year-old artist became ill and needed full-time care after a major operation. He advertised in the local newspaper for a 'pretty' night nurse. A local girl, 21-year-old **Monique Bourgeois**, was given the job. Over time Monique and Henri became the best of friends, and she even modelled for some of his paintings (*Monique in Gray Robe*, *Green Dress and Oranges*, *The Idol* and *Tabac Royale*). In return he taught her to paint. Henri was devastated when, two years later, Monique informed him that she was going to become a nun. He did his best to dissuade her, but after completing her novitiate in Monteils, Monique was finally professed and given the name **Sister Jacques-Marie**. Her first posting was to the Dominican convent in Vence. Not long afterwards Henri moved to live in Vence, quite near the convent.

❧ The good friends kept in touch and after Sister Jacques sought the artist's advice about a sketch she had been working on, Henri decided to adapt the design into one for a stained-glass window which would serve as the inspiration for a new chapel for the convent. Amid much controversy within the cloisters, on account of Matisse's modern approach and the fact that he was a non-practising Catholic, the chapel took 4 years to complete. Today it stands in the convent's front garden. Some believe it to be Matisse's greatest work.

❧ When Matisse died in 1954 he was buried at the cemetery of the **Monastère Notre-Dame de Cimiez** in suburban Nice. Fearing a media circus, Sister Jacques' superiors would not allow her to attend the funeral. She lived the last years of her life in a convent in **Bidart** in Aquitane; when she died at the age of 84 her funeral service was conducted in the Matisse Chapel and she was laid to rest nearby.

❦ Her friendship with Matisse created such interest that in 1993 Sister Jacques wrote a book, *Henri Matisse, La Chapelle de Vence*. In 2003, Barbara Freed, Professor of French Studies at Carnegie Mellon University in Pittsburgh, was sufficiently intrigued to film a documentary about the friendship, *A Model For Matisse: The Story of the Vence Chape*l. In the film, the down-to-earth Sister Jacques says she thought of Matisse as her grandfather: 'No one could say there was anything improper between us because there never was.' Nevertheless the documentary makes fascinating viewing.

FOOD AND DRINK ❦ In the **Vieille Ville**, the lovely old town of Vence, you'll be pleasantly surprised by the interesting mix of shops and restaurants. Some are seriously expensive, but souvenir hunters as much as foodies are well catered for.

❦ Near the Vence–St-Paul bus stop on the edge of the village of St-Paul, the **Café de la Place** overlooks the local 'petanque' pitch which provides engaging entertainment for the sometimes excitable patrons. It seems that every Provencale village has its own petanque pitch and the game is taken quite seriously. Judging by the crowds trying to find a table, this is the 'in' place to sit and enjoy a drink while watching the troops of tourists make their way into the town.

❦ Join the locals at the fountain in the **Place Peyra** in Vence and fill your water bottles with the local mineral water which is free of charge. The pre-bottled variety is branded *La Foux* and has to be paid for.

Spiritual Retreats
Paris

22

Maison St-Pierre-Julian Eymard

The Maison St-Pierre is run by the Blessed Sacrament Fathers, an order of Catholic priests founded in Paris by St-Pierre Julian Eymard in the mid-1800s. The centre is wonderfully well located near the **Arc de Triomphe** and around the corner from the **Rue de Fauborg St Honore**, one of the city's most prestigious shopping streets and the avenue along which Marie Antoinette was led from imprisonment in the Conciergerie to her death by guillotine at the Place de La Bastille on 16 October 1793.

The Maison St-Pierre provides simple, clean accommodation in both single and double guestrooms, each of which has a wash basin and telephone. Bathrooms are on a shared basis. Breakfast is taken with the community; lunch and dinner are available if required, and are inexpensive at around €12 each. Guests are asked to help with small chores such as cleaning up after meals. There is a rather old-fashioned lift and a sitting room downstairs for the use of guests. The fathers request that visitors arrive between 0900 and 1200 or between 1400 and 1730 Monday to Saturday as the reception area is not open at other times. The centre is closed for arrivals on Sundays (except for nuns and priests).

Guests are invited to take part in **religious services** with the priests, including the adoration of the Blessed Sacrament. The monastery has a strict no smoking policy. Visa and MasterCard are accepted. There is an underground (pay) car park 50 metres away.

Tourists and visitors to Paris who are sympathetic to the resident fathers' way of life are able to stay here.

✉ 23, Avenue de Friedland F-75008 Paris

☎ +33(0) 1 40 76 30 30
☎ +33(0) 1 40 76 30 00

✉ maison-eymard@wanadoo.fr
www.maison-eymard.fr

🛏 from €28.00 pp, including breakfast.

☞ Take the Metro to the Charles de Gaulle–Étoile Metro Station (Line 6) and exit the station onto the Avenue de Friedland for a 300-metre walk to the convent. The Arc de Triomphe and the Champs Élysées are an easy walk from the Maison St-Pierre and bus stops are strung along the avenue.

✝ **Sunday Mass** 1100 & 1830 Chapelle du Corpus Christi, Maison St-Pierre-Julian Eymard.

⚭ Open to both men & women

PLACES OF INTEREST ❧ If a trip to Grasse and the perfume factories is out of the question the next best thing is to visit a branch of one of the **perfumeries** in Paris. The headquarters of **Fragonard** is in Grasse and their four Paris outlets are located in the centre of the city. The Fragonard museum of perfume and a boutique shop are at 9, Rue Scribe near the Opera Metro Station.

❧ While you are in a shopping mode and in the vicinity of the Opera Metro Station you could browse in the largest department store in France, **Galeries Lafayette** on Boulevard Haussmann. If nothing there tempts, pop into the enormous **Printemps** department store next door. The illustrious **Paris Opera House** is opposite these stores. The department store **Le Bon Marché** is in the Rue de Sévres, near the Sévres–Babylone Metro Station on the opposite side of the Seine. Sale time for shops and department stores is in January and July. And all manner of unusual shops can be found in the tiny back-street arcades— like the antique walking stick shop in the Passage Jouffroy; the snuff-box shop in the Arcades du Palais-Royal; Deyrolle, the taxidermy shop on the Rue du Bac; and the unpretentious **Librairie Ulysses** on the Île Saint-Louis, a treasure trove of travel books.

❧ **L'Arc de Triomphe**, a memorial to Napoleon's victories, stands conspicuously at the top of the most famous boulevard in Paris, the **Avenue des Champs-Élysées**. Over 250 steps lead to the roof of the monument which commands an enthralling view of the broad, tree-lined avenue below.

❧ **The Avenue de Foch**, which runs off the Arc de Triomphe, is considered one of the best residential addresses in Paris and the home of the seriously rich— think Grimaldi, Rubenstein and Onassis. Many of the city's exclusive designer label stores are located on the **Avenue George v**, which runs off the Champs-Elysées near l'Arc de Triomphe.

❧ The **Église de la Madeleine** (*Church of St Mary Magdalene*) in Paris is named after reformed 'sinner' Mary Magdalene. Paris society weddings take place in this almost temple-like church and it is also the scene of many of the city's impressive state funerals. In May 1992 the funeral service for German actress **Marlene Dietrich** (1901–1992) was held here. African-American singer **Josephine Baker** (1906–1975), French composer **Gabriel Urbain Fauré** (1845–1924) and Polish-born composer Frédéric Chopin (1820–1869) were laid to rest following Requiem Mass at the Madeleine.

✝ Sunday Mass 0930, 1100

(Solemn Mass with the Madeline Choir) & 1900

Spiritual Retreats
Paris

❦ **The Paris Opera House** is near the Madeleine church; the public areas are open for visitors each day. However, for a glimpse of ballerina Anna Pavlova's dancing shoes take a guided tour of the building. The Opera House shop sells souvenirs, memorabilia and unique flower-scented honey produced by bees from the city's most scenic apiary – on the roof of the building! The owner, Jean Paucton, who works at the Opera House moved to an apartment so had to find somewhere else to keep his bees.

FOOD AND DRINK ❦ You can support the Benedictine fathers who are attached to Church of the Madeleine at their congenial public restaurant underneath the church building (on the right-hand side). **The Foyer de la Madeleine** is one of the cheapest, largest and friendliest eating places in Paris and well supported by local shopkeepers. It won't win a Michelin star but it is worth a visit for the experience alone. And where else in Paris can you get 3 courses and wine for around €10.00? Open for lunch only between Monday and Friday (1145–1400).

✉ 14, Rue de Surène

☎ +33 (0) 1 44 51 69 00   €€

❦ The more upmarket restaurant, **Maxims** attracts a well-dressed, well-heeled crowd; the adjoining gift shop sells gourmet food and elegant knick-knacks.

✉ 3, Rue Royale

☎ +33 (0) 1 42 65 27 94   €€€€€

❦ Not as expensive but still 'French', the restaurant chain **Chez Clément** has a branch in the Avenue des Champs-Elysées where traditional French cuisine is served in a typically French environment at untraditionally reasonable prices.

✉ 23, Avenue des Champs-Elysées

☎ +33 (0) 1 40 73 87 00   €€–€€€

❦ Learn to cook with French flair on a half-day cookery course at the **Ritz-Escoffier** cooking school in the **Hôtel Ritz** on the salubrious Place Vendôme. **Le Cordon Bleu** at 8, Rue Léon Delhomme near the Vaugirard Metro Station also offers day cooking classes, market tours and gourmet workshops.

❦ The renowned Parisian food and wine stores **Fauchon** and **Hédiard** are located on the Place de la Madeleine near the Madeleine Metro Station. Opera House honey is sold at both stores.

23

Maison d'Accueil des Soeurs du Très St-Saveur

The convent is situated near the historic village of **Oberbronn** in what was once the town castle. Originally established in the 12th century, it was rebuilt in the early 1800s. The Soeurs du Trés St-Saveur (*Sisters of the Most Holy Saviour*) have occupied the building since 1857. The order was established in 1849 by a pious French woman, Elisabeth Eppinger (1814–1867), who became head of the order under the name of Mother Alphonse-Marie. The order now has hundreds of members in convents across Europe.

❡ The house in Oberbronn is in a convenient location for visitors who wish to use the thermal baths at **Niederbronn-les-Bains** just 3 kilometres away. The thermal springs take care of the physical ailments while the Sisters of St-Sauveur tend to the spiritual needs of those making a retreat or participating in the liturgical activities of the convent.

❡ The guest quarters consist of single and double rooms, all with telephone and most en suite facilities. Some guestrooms share a bathroom. Large groups are catered for and meeting and function rooms are available. All meals are provided. Lifts are on each floor; there is a large dining area and a separate television room. The house has access for the disabled and parking facilities. The surrounding area is ideal for exploring as the convent is situated in a forested area laced with walking and hiking trails.

✉ 2, Rue Principale
F-67110 Oberbronn
Bas-Rhin

☎ +33 (0) 3 88 80 84 59
☎ +33 (0) 3 88 80 84 70

✉ accueil@soeurs-stsauveur.fr

🖰 www.soeurs-stsauveur.fr

💶 price to be negotiated.

☞ From Strasbourg take the Regional Express train to Niederbronn-les-Bains which is 3 kilometres from Oberbronn. Take a taxi to Oberbronn from here. Oberbronn is 50 kilometres north of Strasbourg.

✝ **Sunday Mass**
1030.
Église Saint-Etienne, Oberbronn.

♿ Discuss your needs in advance of arriving, ideally when booking.

👥 Open to men, women & groups

Spiritual Retreats
Alsace Oberbronn

PLACES OF INTEREST ❧ **Oberbronn** is surrounded by 480 kilometres of walking and cycling routes, many of which trail through the forested areas surrounding the village. If motoring seems like a better option, discover such typically Alsatian villages as **Zinswiller**, **Rothbach**, **Mulhausen**, **Uhrwiller** and **Uttenhoffen** on a scenic drive from Oberbronn. This is a return journey of around 30 kilometres. Uttenhoffen, 8 kilometres south of Oberbronn, is said to have the smallest parish church in Alsace.

❧ To the north of Oberbronn are the ruins of dozens of castles with many on the castle motoring route which crosses into Germany. Also in the north are reminders of **World War II** where the old fortresses along the **Maginot Line** can be inspected. The Marginot Line was established in 1930 as a line of impenetrable steel bunkers to form part of the defences to protect north-east France from German invasion. Hundreds of fortifications were built up and down the Line, many masking complete underground wartime cities. **The Citadel of Bitche** can be toured on foot; **Fort Simserhof**, in Siersthal and **Fort Hackenberg**, near Veckring, the largest fort on the Line (big enough to house 1,000 people), can be visited by a train which travels underground.

❧ **Le Jardin Alpestre de la Grotte St-Vit** (*Alpine Garden and Grotto of St-Vit*) is an ancient hermitage in the **Saverne Forest**, about 1 hour on foot along a path located near the ruined **Château du Griffon** (*Greiffenstein*). Masses of flowers and greenery tumble down a rocky knob to a limestone cave, the Grotte de St-Vit, now converted into a tiny chapel where locals come for prayer and seeking silence. The Cave of St-Vit was once a place of pilgrimage; a visit here was believed to be of help in curing the nervous disorder St Vitus' Dance. **St-Vit** (Vitus) is the Patron Saint of Epileptics. Mass is celebrated in the cave five times each year, including on 15 June, St Vitus' Feast Day.

❡ **The International Centre for Glass Art** in **Meisenthal**, on the Alsace and Lorraine border 30 kilometres east of Oberbronn, is renowned for the colourful Christmas baubles created by the glassblowers. Prior to the 19th century, red apples were hung on European Christmas trees. According to Brother René Stockman, Superior General of the international Catholic religious order the Brothers of Charity, 'As a consequence of a bad apple crop at the beginning of the 19th century, there were no more red apples by Christmas time, which gave a glassblower from Meisenthal the idea to blow baubles made of glass and paint them red. That was how the first baubles were created. In the years after that, the red apples were replaced ever more frequently by red glass baubles.'

❡ In times past, fresh apples featured in the **Lenten fast of the Cistercians**; six apples were allocated daily to each monk to prevent constipation during this 40-day period of abstinence.

FOOD AND DRINK ❧ **Chestnut season** commences in October and lasts for 3 months. During this time hot chestnuts are almost always on sale at any Alsatian Christmas market. The locally made chestnut brandy, the **Elixir d'Oberbronn**, is served in Oberbronn's restaurants. Many of the town's eateries can be found quite close to each other in the Rue Principale, with hungry tourists easily able to peruse the menu of each before deciding which to patronise.

❡ Exotic tastes are sometimes catered for at the **Restaurant au Boeuf Noir** in Oberbronn where kangaroo and crocodile steak are known to have been served. Traditional French fare such as duck, rabbit, veal and fish feature on the fixed-price menus which range from around €25. The restaurant is located in a traditional Alsatian house.

✉ 28, Rue Principale.

☎ +33 (0) 3 88 09 61 39   €€€

❡ You will never go hungry or thirsty in Alsace. Apart from the wine route, other food and drink-related driving trails include the Hop Route, the Sauerkraut Route, the Fish Stew Route, and the Cheese, Trout and Carp Routes.

Spiritual Retreats
Alsace Rosheim

Hôtellerie La Paix St-Benoît

The Hôtellerie La Paix St-Benoît is run by a congregation of Benedictine nuns who live in an adjacent monastery. The convent has been owned by the order since 1862 and the sisters have traditionally made their living by making Communion hosts. The sisters meet in the chapel of the monastery seven times each day for liturgical celebrations. Once a month the nuns conduct a 'night of prayer' for religious vocations; members of the public are invited to attend. The evening commences at 2100 in the monastery church and ends at 0800 the next day.

⸿ The sisters encourage visitors who are interested in spending time in reflection and prayer to stay overnight at the convent's hôtellerie. Accommodation consists of single, twin and triple guestrooms, all of which have en suite facilities. In an outer building which is also used to house visitors, larger, family-style rooms which sleep up to six people are available. All meals are served and facilities include a lounge room, library, car park and a peaceful garden. In 2009 the sisters embarked on extensive renovations to upgrade the accommodation and add wheelchair accessible guestrooms.

✉ Monastère des
Bénédictines
3, Rue St-Benoît
F-67560 Rosheim
Bas-Rhin.

☎ +33 (0) 3 88 50 28 95
📠 +33 (0) 3 88 48 94 50

✉ lapaixstbenoit@
orange.fr

🖳 www.benedictines-
rosheim.com

💶 price to be negotiated.

☞ Take the train to
Rosheim, then a taxi
to the hôtellerie which
is a little more than 2
kilometres from the
station.

✝ **Sunday Mass**
0930. *(sung)*.
Monastère des
Bénédictines,
1, Rue St-Benoît.

♿ Discuss your needs in
advance of arriving,
ideally when booking.

⚤ Open to both men &
women

PLACES OF INTEREST ❦ The ancient Alsatian village of **Rosheim** is nestled at the foot of the **Vosges Mountains** among the vineyards strung along the Alsatian wine trail, an easy day trip from Strasbourg. Thick, 14th-century arched stone gateways lead to the medieval streets in the old town.

❧ The striking medieval architectural treasures include the turrets, towers and intricate stonework of the Romanesque **Église St-Pierre et St-Paul** (*Church of St Peter and St Paul*) which shares the local limelight with the **Heidehüss** (*Romanesque House*) in the Rue du Gal de Gaulle, reputed to be the oldest (12th century) building in Alsace.

❧ A local **wine trail** leads out of **Rosheim** on the Rue de Rosenwiller; during the warmer months those on foot can meet the growers and taste some of the local wine, though possibly not during September/October when winemakers are busy with the new harvest. However, festivals and parades are held all over Alsace to celebrate the new vintage, with plenty of opportunities for comparing grape varieties. Occasionally during summer, night-time walks through the vineyards are arranged. The tourist office in the town can supply maps.

❧ If travelling south on the wine route you will pass the **Domaine Weinbach**, near Kayserberg, producers of the *Clos des Capucins* appellation which features a monk on the label. Until the French Revolution the complex was a monastery owned by Capuchin monks who grew grapes on the surrounding slopes. Today the vineyard is run by three generations of women from the Faller family which has the reputation of producing some of Alsace's finest wine.

❧ If you are not a wine drinker, Alsace is also well known for producing the refreshing, fruit-flavoured water **eau-de-vie** (*water of life*).

❧ South of Rosheim, the **Unterlinden Museum** in **Colmar**, with its collection of sculptures and paintings from the late Middle Ages, many of religious scenes, is housed appropriately within the Gothic cloisters of a 13th-century Dominican monastery. The most valuable piece in the museum's collection is the **Issenheim Altarpiece**, depicting Christ's Crucifixion and painted for the monks of Colmar's St Anthony's Monastery in 1515 by German Renaissance artist **Matthias Grünewald** (c. 1475–1528). The monastery is no longer in existence.

Spiritual Retreats
Alsace Rosheim

❧ The remains of the former **Natzweiler Concentration Camp** in **Struthof**, 28 kilometres south-west of Rosheim, stand as a sombre memorial to the tens of thousands of people who lost their lives here, in the only such camp established on French territory.

❧ Further south, in **Muttersholtz**, you could call into the weavers' cottage, Tissage Gander at 10A, Rue de Verdun where hand-crafted tablecloths with matching napkins, pillowcases and all sorts of embroidery are on sale. Now, weathervanes are not the usual take-home souvenir, but Bernard Stinner's are quirky enough to be irresistible and make an eye-catching addition to any drab old roof. The workshop is at 6 Ehnwihr near Muttersholtz.

❧ Markets are held in **Rosheim** on Friday mornings and in **Obernai** on Thursday mornings.

FOOD AND DRINK ❧ Often cited as one of Rosheim's best restaurants, the **Hostellerie du Rosenmeer** features a choice of all-inclusive *gastronomique* menus ranging in price from €50 to over €100. A less expensive a la carte menu is available in the more casual winestub.
✉ 45, Avenue de la Gare.
☎ +33 (0) 3 88 50 43 29   €€€–€€€€€

❧ Take your willpower to the wonderland at **Fortwenger**, the 18th-century gingerbread factory and shop in the village of Gertwiller, 15 kilometres south of Rosheim. The gingerbread made here and sold in the Hansel and Gretel-style shop is baked in all shapes, sizes and designs—and tastes as good as it looks. The shop is packed to the rafters with all manner of enticing sweet treats.
✉ 144, Route Strasbourg.
☎ +33 (0) 3 88 08 96 06

❧ Some 50 kilometres further south is the town of **Colmar** where visitors can walk the old cobblestoned pedestrian zone in the area known as Little Venice. True to its namesake, the canals are lined with shops, bistros and cafés where the local gastronomic speciality ropfkueche (*almond cake*) is a tasty temptation. Restaurants with wall-to-wall charm and quaint cafés serving traditional cuisine can be found in the delightful Place de l'Ancienne Douane.

25

Abbaye St-Joseph de Clairval à Flavigny

The movie *Chocolat* starring Juliette Binoche and Johnny Depp was filmed on location in the medieval village of **Flavigny-sur-Ozerain**, 60 kilometres north of Dijon (2000). However, if there is a hint of sweet fragrance in the Flavigny air it is most unlikely to be chocolate, but rather anís (*aniseed*)—and it is sure to be coming from the confectionery factory adjoining the old Benedictine Abbaye St-Pierre which up until the French Revolution was the home of Ursuline nuns. Anis de Flavigny had been made here since the 8th century and the sweets are sold in unique, painted, oval-shaped tins. Each tiny, round sweet has a tangy anís seed surprise in the centre.

¶ For the last 30 years, the Benedictines of St-Joseph have resided in their handsome abbey which was once a château constructed in the 18th century. Throughout the year they conduct a series of guided, 5-day, men-only retreats which are based on the spiritual exercises of St Ignatius Loyola, the founder of the Jesuit religious order. Individuals (men only) can stay at the abbey when undertaking a retreat. Guestrooms are modestly furnished and bathroom facilities are shared. Meals are provided. A guesthouse is operated by the monks and is located outside the monastery estate. Men and women who wish to participate in liturgical services at the abbey, or make a private retreat, may stay here.

¶ The monks publish a monthly newsletter for those who are unable to attend a retreat personally. The newsletter is available online in a choice of seven languages. Please email the abbey to subscribe (free).

✉ F-21150 Flavigny-sur-Ozerain Côte-d'Or.

☏ +33 (0) 3 80 96 22 31
📠 +33 (0) 3 80 96 25 29

✉ abbaye@clairval.com
🌐 www.clairval.com

💶 price to be negotiated.

☞ Take the train to Les Laumes–Alésia train station which is 9 kilometres from Flavigny, or to the Montbard train station, 25 kilometres from Flavigny. A taxi from either station will take you into the town. To call a taxi from Les Laumes–Alésia, telephone (0)3 80 96 12 69 or (0)3 80 96 02 81.

✝ **Sunday Mass**
1000 & 1700.
Abbaye St-Joseph de Clairval à Flavigny.

♂ Only men may stay in the abbey.

🏠 A separate guesthouse is provided for men & women.

Spiritual Retreats

Burgundy Flavigny-sur-Ozerain

PLACES OF INTEREST ✦ While staying
in the tiny town of **Flavigny** (population
around 400), you could take a tour of
the aniseed **confectionery factory**,
adjacent to the ruins of the former
Benedictine Abbaye de St-Pierre, where
tons of pastilles of various flavours
are produced each year. The factory
is closed during August and over
Christmas; otherwise it's open each
weekday morning from 0900 to 1045.
The monks are no longer involved in
confectionery production. The factory
was first established by the Benedictine
monks but was taken over by the locals
after the monastery was dissolved
during the French Revolution. The
monks returned in 1976 and established
the Benedictine Monastère St-Joseph
de Clairval which was later granted the
higher status of 'Abbey'.

❦ From the aniseed factory and under
the old monastery church, the 8th-
century 'crypt of St Reine' can be
accessed. **Ste-Reine** (*St Regina*) was
beheaded for her Christian beliefs in
the nearby village of Alise Ste-Reine in
the year 253. Today the villagers of Alise
Ste-Reine commemorate the event each
September with a traditional festival
and parade.

❦ Flavigny's Gothic, 13th-century **Église
St-Genest** (*Church of St Genest*) has
been renovated and rebuilt over the
years—recently because of lightning
strikes. The interior with its 12th-
century stone statue of the Madonna
and Child and exquisite carved wooden
stalls, complete with 'misericords' or
'mercy seats' (to relieve the suffering of
tired or unwell clergy), is most certainly
worth investigating. Concerts are held
in the medieval church during the
summer.

❦ During May and June each year the
town of **Semur en Auxois**, 16 kilometres
west of Flavigny, celebrates its Gallic
ancestry with a medieval festival.
The village is one of the prettiest
in Burgundy and its residents have
a reputation for being among the
friendliest people in France. The village
is illuminated on summer evenings with
a spectacular lighting display.

L'Abbaye de Fontenay, near the town of Montbard, is a UNESCO World Heritage Site and one of the oldest and most beautiful Cistercian abbeys in Europe. Founded by St Bernard in 1118 and now privately owned and restored, most of the abbey remains remarkably intact. The abbey is 25 kilometres north of Flavigny-sur-Ozerain. Scenes from the movie *Cyrano de Bergerac* starring French actor Gérard Depardieu (b. 1948) were filmed at Fontenay Abbey.

During the year, **weaving classes** are conducted in **Flavigny** by textile artisan and atelier Daniel Algranate from his studio at the Maison des Matières in the Rue Lacordaire. Art enthusiasts might like to inspect the works of local painters in the gallery of **La Licorne Bleue** (*The Blue Unicorn*) on Rue de la Poterne, where art lessons are sometimes conducted. There are a number of craft and clothing shops in the village; hand knitted sweaters are a speciality of Antoinette Rigitano of Antoilaine in Rue de la Abbaye. However, frustrated shopaholics could visit Troyes, the factory outlet shopping capital of France, 120 kilometres north of Flavigny, about an hour's drive on the N71.

FOOD AND DRINK If it's July or August and you find yourself in Flavigny, you are in luck. The local farmers here have come together and opened a café, **La Grange des Four Hours Soupatoire** (*The Barn Soup Kitchen*). Not only do they provide the farm-fresh food daily but, along with family members, they prepare and serve it as well.

✉ Place de l'Église.   *Closed Mondays*
☎ +33 (0) 3 80 96 20 62   €€

The hotel **Le Relais de Flavigny** is in the centre of town near the ruins of the Benedictine Abbey of St Pierre. The hotel's restaurant offers a good value, fixed-price menu.

✉ Place des Anciennes Halles.
☎ +33 (0) 3 80 96 27 77   €€€

The restaurant **Le Cheval Blanc** in the town of Alise Ste-Reine just a few kilometres north of Flavigny is one of the most popular and authentic French country restaurants in the area.

✉ Rue du Miroir.
☎ +33 (0) 3 80 96 01 55   €€€–€€€€

Nicknamed the *King of Cheese* (a title shared with Rocquefort), **Époisses** cheese was first made by Cistercian monks in their monastery at Époisses, 40 kilometres west of Flavigny. The disk-shaped cheese has a firm, orange-coloured rind and a creamy, pungent interior; it is said to have been one of Napoleon's favourites.

26

Communaté de Taizé

The **Taizé Community**, a Christian religious order of male monastics, welcomes tens of thousands of young adults from across the world every year. The community is multi-denominational and every day young people, individuals, families and children meet together in Taizé and join with the brothers in praying for world peace. Singing plays a major role in the spiritual activities here and guests are welcome to bring musical instruments.

❧ Taizé is a tiny hamlet surrounded by lush Burgundian countryside with small villages within walking distance. Accommodation and living conditions at Taizé are simple: shared dormitories, tents, cabins, shared bathrooms and simple meals taken outdoors for most of the year. A small shop on site sells provisions. Visitors are required to bring a sleeping bag. Cheap, picnic-style meals are available.

❧ The community's roots can be traced back to 1940 when **Brother Roger Schutz** (1915–2005), then 25 years old, settled alone in Taizé. He intended to create a community that would be a 'parable of communion'. Today there are more than 100 brothers—Catholics and from various Protestant backgrounds—from 25 countries. They earn their living through publishing, pottery and painting.

❧ Brother Roger Schutz was a personal friend of the late **Pope John Paul II**. He was the first to receive Communion (from his wheelchair) at the Pope's funeral Mass in April 2005. Brother Roger died tragically on 16 August 2005, 4 months after the Pope, after being attacked by a deranged woman during the evening prayer service in the Taizé Community church. He was 90 years old. **Brother Alois** (b. 1954), born in Germany of Czech parents, has succeeded him as prior.

✉ F-71250 Taizé Saône et Loire.

✆ +33 (0) 3 85 50 30 02
✆ +33 (0) 3 85 50 30 16

✉ meetings@taize.fr

✉ www.taize.fr

suggested donation of up to €25.00 pp.

☞ The monastery of the Taizé Community is situated between Chalon sur Saône and Mâcon (closer to Mâcon). Take the train to Mâcon-TGV, Mâcon-Ville or to Chalon sur Saône and then a bus to the monastery. Please check train/bus connections to Taizé before departure.

✝ **Sunday Mass**
1000.
Communaté de Taizé.

Open to men, women & groups

PLACES OF INTEREST ❧ **Taizé** is 11 kilometres north of the remains of the medieval **Abbey of Cluny**, once the religious heart of Europe, the abbot being the most powerful religious ruler after the Pope. The abbey was founded c. 910 by **William the Pious**, Duke of Aquitane (875–918), for the Benedictine Cluniac Order. Situated near the town of **Mâcon**, the abbey was an influential centre of Christianity; hundreds of abbeys founded in Europe were all under its control.

From the 12th century a gradual deterioration of the abbey began, brought about by the wars of religion and, not least, the lavish lifestyle chosen by the monks. This once mighty abbey was finally destroyed in 1798 after being suppressed at the beginning of the French Revolution; only fragments of the original imposing edifice remain. However, visitors to the **Musée Ochier**, the Musée d'Art et d'Archéologie (*Museum of Art and Archaeology*) can view a 3D film which captures some of the abbey's former greatness. The museum is located in the former palatial residence of **Abbot Jean de Bourbon** (ruled 1456–1480) and exhibits many of the abbey's salvaged artworks. A scale model reconstruction of the original abbey is on display. Capture an overall picture of the town from the top of La Tour de Fromages (the *Cheese Tower*).

The picturesque **Romanesque art trail** begins in Cluny and leads to 11th- and 12th-century chapels, churches, abbeys and châteaux. The trail mirrors the **Mâconnais wine trail** which means you can squeeze in a little wine tasting along the way.

Napoleon I founded the **Cluny National Stud Farm** in 1806 specifically to breed the thousands of war horses needed by his fighting forces. Today the stud breeds thoroughbred stallions for horse racing and is situated within the old Benedictine Abbey estate on the outskirts of the town. Tours of the facility are conducted between July and March.

The **Monks' Chapel** in **Berzé la Ville**, 19 kilometres south of Taizé was the former private chapel of the abbots of Cluny who had a summer residence in the village. The vaulted interior is embellished with 12th-century frescoes and Cluniac art, which was once painted over by a former owner. The artwork was accidentally discovered in the late 1800s and has since been restored. The village is 19 kilometres south of Taizé.

Spiritual Retreats
Burgundy Taizé

¶ The scenic **Lamartine motoring trail**
commences in Tournus, 25 kilometres
north-east of Taizé, and weaves through
the favourite countryside of French
poet and politician **Alphonse de
Lamartine** (1790–1869). The trail passes
by the moated Château de Cormatin
(on the outskirts of Taizé) where the
poet often holidayed—well worth a
visit for its sumptuous interiors and
magnificent gardens.

¶ French portrait painter **Jean-Baptiste
Greuze** (1725–1805) is one of Tournus'
most famous; a permanent exhibition
of his paintings is displayed in the
Musée Greuze.

FOOD AND DRINK ✦ There are few cafés
and places to eat in Taizé. However, the
Café Les Dolmens is not far from the
monastery and caters for foodies on a
tight budget.
✉ 8, Rue de Poitiers.
☎ +33 (0) 5 49 66 28 42   €€

¶ The poultry-breeding town of **Bourg-
en-Bresse** is said by serious chefs and
dedicated gourmets to raise the best-
tasting chickens in France. To taste the
superior flavour look for the restaurants
with a statue of a giant chicken outside
the premises. Bourg-en-Bresse is 75
kilometres south-east of Taizé, near the
town of Mâcon.

¶ Find that special bottle of wine at
the **Au Plaisir Dit Vin** in the centre
of **Cluny** where hundreds of different
labels from the surrounding area are
on sale.
✉ 19, Rue Mercière.
☎ +33 (0) 3 85 59 16 29
¶ Nearby is an exquisite pâtisserie and
chocolaterie, **Au Péché Mignon**, which
also has a branch in Mâcon.
✉ 25, Rue Lamartine, Cluny.
☎ +33 (0) 3 85 59 11 21
✉ 10, Rue de la Barre, Mâcon.
☎ +33 (0) 3 85 29 05 66
¶ Saturday is market day in Cluny. A
market is held in Bourg-en-Bresse each
Wednesday and in Chalon-sur-Saône
each Wednesday and Sunday morning.
In Mâcon, a market is held from Tuesday
to Friday in the Place aux Herbes and on
Saturday mornings on Quais Lamartine.

Spiritual Retreats

Pays-de-la-Loire Solesmes

(27)

Abbaye St-Pierre de Solesmes

The tiny village of **Solesmes** is endowed with two great abbeys. **The Abbaye St-Pierre** (*Abbey of St Peter*) is run by a community of Benedictine monks; and the **Abbaye Ste-Cécile** (*Abbey of St Cecilia*), by nuns of the same order. The monks and nuns of Solesmes are credited with reviving the ancient liturgical music of the **Gregorian chant**. Their interpretations of the chant can be heard in either abbey at various times throughout the day. The Abbaye Ste-Cécile is named after **St Cecilia**, the Patron Saint of Music.

❧ The monks of the Abbey of St Peter welcome male guests only, singly or in groups, to take part in spiritual retreats, celebrations of the liturgy and days of silence and meditation within the monastery cloisters. Single guestrooms and shared bathrooms are provided and all meals are taken with the monks. Contact the guestmaster for further information.

❧ The monastery has two separate buildings off the estate which are used to accommodate groups, both male and female, and especially groups of young people. Accommodation is hostel-style with communal bathrooms, a kitchen and rooms for meetings or just relaxing. Mixed groups can stay in the guesthouses but accommodation is only offered to those visiting the abbey for spiritual purposes. Restaurants and cafés can be found in the village.

❧ The monks run a well-stocked gift shop which is attached to the Abbey of St Peter where books and religious articles and copies of the monks' CDs are on sale. Nearby is a small museum with a scale model of the massive abbey complex.

✉ 1, Place Dom Guéranger
F-72300 Solesmes
Sarthe.

📞 +33 (0) 2 43 95 03 08
📠 +33 (0) 2 43 95 03 28

📧 hospes@solesmes.com

🌐 www.solesmes.com

🛏 from €30.00 pp (single), including all meals.

☞ Take the TGV (fast train) from Paris Montparnasse station direct to Sablè-sur-Sarthe which is 3 kilometres from Solesmes.

☦ **Sunday Mass** 1000.
Abbaye St-Pierre.
Daily Chant Schedule 0730, 1000, 1300, 1345, 1700 & 2030.
On Thursday the usual 1700 service commences at 1600 in summer and 1730 in winter.

☦ **Sunday Mass** 0945.
Abbaye St-Cécile.
Schedule of Offices 0630, 0730, 0945 (*Mass*), 1230, 1430, 1630, 2000 & 2045.

⚥ Only men may stay in the Abbaye St-Pierre.

⚥ Men, women & groups may stay in a separate house owned by the monks.

Spiritual Retreats
Pays-de-la-Loire Solesmes

PLACES OF INTEREST ❧ Pretty **Solesmes** straddles the River Sarthe. Its clean, neat streets are lined with tidy houses obviously inhabited by some very keen gardeners. The town is particularly attractive in summer when hanging baskets spill over with brightly coloured petunias and geraniums; the ancient buildings of **St Peter's Abbey** add a medieval flavour. This grand edifice stands majestically on the riverbank as it has done for almost 200 years. Close by, a narrow, walled laneway leads to the equally lovely **Abbey of St Cecilia**. Until recently the sisters ran a guesthouse in the town, which owing to council regulations has been closed, hopefully temporarily. However, the sisters do take guests (women only) for spiritual retreats and accommodation is provided in the abbey.

❧ The monks, many of whom look surprisingly young, begin their day with Matins at 0530. The last service of the day is Compline at 2030. At the women's abbey the sisters meet eight times each day and sit in a separate section of the church to the congregation.

❧ A street café opposite St Peter's attracts a lunchtime crowd, and in the late afternoon well-dressed locals emerge into the sunshine for a genteel stroll, a refreshing café au lait or an afternoon *pastis*.

❧ **Sablé-sur-Sarthe** (pronounced *Sab-blee*) is a cruise boat and river-touring centre, 2 kilometres from Solesmes; it can be reached on foot by following the river. **Cruises** of up to 2 weeks in length can be arranged here. Boats sail north towards **Laval** and **Le Mans** or south to **Angers** on the edge of the Loire Valley. The abbeys can be appreciated from a different angle on the river and if time is not an issue you could enjoy a lunchtime cruise—or hire a canoe. A spectacular photo of the Abbey of St Peter can be taken from the bridge crossing the River Sarthe, behind the abbey.

❡ **Sablé-sur-Sarthe** stages a summer music festival, the **Festival de Sablé**, for 4 days each August. This festival of ancient music is a major event on the Loire cultural calendar and both abbeys feature prominently in the performances. The **Basilique Notre-Dame du Chêne**, a few kilometres away in **Vion**, and Sablé's parish church, the **Église Notre-Dame**, are both concert venues.

❡ The moated, Renaissance **Château du Plessis-Bourré** in the hamlet of **Écuillé**, 35 kilometres south of **Sablé-sur-Sarthe**, was the location for the French films *Jeanne d'Arc* and *Louis XI*. The château is now in private hands but the owners welcome visitors for guided tours.

❡ If heading for the **Pays** (*Loire Atlantique*) **coast** and **St-Nazaire** you could visit the **Chantiers de l'Atlantique**, one of the world's largest shipyards, where the **Cunard** ocean liner *Queen Mary II* was constructed. On the outskirts of the town and near the airport is a giant **Airbus** factory where the A380 (in 2010 the world's largest passenger aircraft) is assembled. Guided tours of the shipyard and the factory can be arranged.

FOOD AND DRINK ✎ A few casual eateries and cafés are located near the Abbey of St Peter. The **Restaurant des Saveurs** in the Grand Hôtel de Solesmes (opposite the abbey) features an a la carte menu of French classics and a 'degustation', tasting menu.

✉ 16, Place Dom Guéranger.

✆ +33 (0) 2 43 95 45 10   €€€€

❡ Do try the locally produced delicacy **'le Sablé'**, a crispy almond biscuit which can be purchased from the local pâtisserie, **Le Sablesienne de Biscuiterie** in Sable-sur-Sarthe; but be warned—they are habit forming.

✉ La Denisière.

✆ +33 (0) 2 43 95 04 53

❡ If travelling on to **La Flèche**, a 30-minute drive south of Solesmes there is a rather charming restaurant called **Le Moulin des Quatre Saisons**; it's on the banks of the River Loire and traditional French favourites (lots of sauces and leaning towards seafood) are featured on the menu.

✉ 2, Rue du Général Gallieni.

✆ +33 (0) 2 43 45 12 12   €€€–€€€€

❡ All sorts of sweet treats are on display at **Le Pâtisserie Guillemard** in La Flèche and there's a cosy tea room for eat-in patrons.

✉ 24, Grande-Rue.

✆ +33 (0) 2 43 94 02 11   €€

Spiritual Retreats
Pays-de-la-Loire Vion

28

Maison Notre-Dame du Chêne

The spiritual complex of the **Maison Notre-Dame du Chêne** in the commune of **Vion**, 4 kilometres south of the **Abbaye St-Pierre**, is run by the local Catholic diocese as a pilgrimage centre and provides alternative accommodation for those visiting **Solesmes**. A guesthouse is available for the use of pilgrims, and bed and breakfast can be arranged for those who wish to spend some days in silence and reflection and take part in liturgical services here or at the abbeys in Solesmes. Day pilgrimages are also conducted here. A separate self-contained house can be rented by groups and families for meetings and celebrations. All guestrooms have en suite bathrooms.

⁋ **The Basilica of Notre-Dame du Chêne** in Vion is visited each year by some thousands of pilgrims and religious who come to make a pilgrimage or a retreat or to pray, as has been the custom for hundreds of years. According to legend, over 6 centuries ago a local priest, Father James Buret, placed a statue of Mary and the child Jesus in the branches of an oak tree which once stood on the site of the present-day 16th-century basilica. From that time on, locals began to visit and offer prayer before the statue. Miracles are said to have occurred and word quickly spread. Fittingly, the theme running through the interior of the church is one of carved oak leaves and acorns. Near the basilica stands a stone copy of the Holy Sepulchre in Jerusalem.

✉ 2, Rue des Bleuets
F-72300 Vion Sarthe

☎ +33 (0) 2 43 95 48 01
☎ +33 (0) 2 43 92 31 72

✎ ndchene@wanadoo.fr

🖰 www.notredameduchene.com

🛏 from €35.00 pp (single), including breakfast.

☞ Take the TGV (fast train) from Paris Montparnasse station direct to Sablè-sur-Sarthe which is 7 kilometres from Vion.

✝ **Sunday Mass**
1000.
Basilique Notre-Dame du Chêne.

♿ Discuss your needs in advance of arriving, ideally when booking.

👪 Open to men, women, families & groups

PLACES OF INTEREST ❧ Reputedly one of the most naturally picturesque golf courses in the region, the **Sablé-Solesmes Golf Club** on the Route de Pince is scenically located on the banks of the River Sarthé; it is open to visitors all year.

❧ Golf with a twist can be played at the **Belmondières Farm Course** in the tiny hamlet of **Brûlon**, near Le Mans. Called Swin Golf, it's a cross between croquet and golf and is played with a single club with a three-sided head. The object of the game is the same—get the ball in the hole with the least number of hits.

❧ The medieval village of **Asnières-sur-Vègre** is 7 kilometres north of Solesmes and is said to be one of the most beautiful in Sarthe. Its history can be traced back to the 7th century. Ancient buildings include medieval bridges, 16th century houses and the parish church, the **Église St-Hilaire** (*Church of St Hilary*), with its interior replete with Roman art.

❧ The village of **Malicorne**, 18 kilometres east of Solesmes, is renowned for its decorative earthenware. The local pottery museum, **L'Espace Faïence**, sells **Malicorne** earthenware and the village's many pottery workshops offer a variety of finished pieces.

❧ Lovers of all things equestrian will be right at home at the **French Cadre Noir**, the National Riding School. Situated in **Saumer**, this mammoth complex houses hundreds of horses. If visiting the school you could watch a performance of the students of the Cadre Noir. And if you need a new pair of hand-crafted riding boots, the workshop of master bootmaker **J. Albert Bottier** is nearby in Place Sénatorerie.

❧ In the **Maine-et-Loire**, the **Château d'Angers**, a fortress-like castle supported by 17 massive towers, stands solidly in place beside the River Maine in the centre of Angers. A collection of irreplaceable medieval tapestries titled **Tapisseries de l'Apocalypse** (*Tapestries of the Apocalypse*) is on display in the tapestry museum within the château. The linked tapestries depict a series of biblical scenes which lead the viewer to an illustration of the end of the world; they were commissioned by **Louis I**, Duke of Anjou (1339–1384) and designed by Flemish painter **Hennequin de Bruges** (aka Jean Bondol, c. 1350).

Spiritual Retreats
Pays-de-la-Loire Vion

❡ Medieval tapestries are also on display at the stately **Château de Serrant** in **St-Georges sur Loire**, a privately owned, elaborately furnished medieval castle (restored in the 17th century) open to the public. Evening torchlight tours commencing at 2200 reveal a grand, fully restored interior, including a private chapel, a 12,000-book library and some colourful history.

❡ Who is responsible for the hundreds of enigmatic sculptures in the caves of **Dénezé sous Doué**? The answer remains a mystery. Said to have religious significance, the sculptures are mainly of male and female figures; the heads have been carbon dated to the 16th and 17th centuries. The town is 35 kilometres south of Angers.

FOOD AND DRINK ✆ The **Golf Club of Sablé-sur-Sarthe** on the outskirts of Solesmes has two dining areas. One serves sandwiches, snacks and casual meals on the terrace overlooking the club grounds; the other is the 'epicurian' restaurant **Martin Pêcheur** with fixed-price degustation menus. *A la carte* is also available.

✉ Route de Pincé.

✆ +33 (0) 2 43 95 97 55   €€-€€€€

❡ The **Restaurant Campanile** in the hotel of the same name is in **Vion**, 6 kilometres south of Solesmes. The hotel has a casual dining room where buffet meals are served and at reasonable prices.

✉ L'Arme au Coeur.

✆ +33 (0) 2 43 92 44 92   €€-€€€

❡ One of the most unique restaurants in the Loire area is located in the Troglodyte village of **Rochemenier**, near **Louresse**, south of **Angers**, where there is a complete underground village first excavated in the 13th century. Visitors can take a tour of the subterranean rooms complete with farmyards, animals, and an underground chapel. The **Restaurant Les Caves de la Genevraie**, an atmospheric underground restaurant, is located nearby.

✉ 11, Rue du Musée.

✆ +33 (0) 2 41 59 34 22   €€€

29

Abbaye Notre-Dame de Senanque

The Cistercian Fathers of the Immaculate Conception first came to **Sénanque** in 1150. They occupied this thriving abbey until the tumultuous late 1700s when not only religious intolerance but the French Revolution intervened, forcing the monks to abandon the abbey for three centuries. Despite the order returning briefly during the mid-19th century the monks were forced out once more when an 'anti religion' law was passed by the French Government. In 1926 the order returned to the abbey and the monks have remained there since.

❧ The abbey is situated in an isolated Provençal valley 4 kilometres from the ancient perched village of **Gordes** in the Luberon National Park. During May, June and up to mid-July visitors will know they are close to **Sénanque** by the delicate bouquet of lavender on the breeze. This is when the monks' purple carpets are in glorious full bloom, lavender growing being a flourishing industry which supports the abbey financially.

❧ Throughout the year the monks welcome visitors to share their lives of prayer, silence and meditation. The guestrooms reflect the Cistercian lifestyle and are quite spartan; bathrooms are shared. The maximum stay is 8 days and all meals are taken with the monks and in silence. Guests are also invited to take part in liturgical services with the community. Visitors are requested not to use their cars while staying at the monastery; instead, they are encouraged to explore the surrounding area on foot.

❧ The monks have strict arrival times and it's best to check when these are.

✉ Hôtellerie du Monastère
F-84220 Gordes
Vaucluse.

📞 +33 (0) 4 90 72 17 92
📠 +33 (0) 4 90 72 17 95

✉ frere.hotelier@senanque.fr

🌐 www.senanque.fr

🚫 Closed on Mondays and through January and February.

💶 from €30.00 pp, including all meals.

☞ Gordes does not have a train station. The abbey is best accessed by car.

✝ **Sunday Mass**
1000.
Abbaye de Notre-Dame de Sénanque.

Open to both men & women

Spiritual Retreats
Provence / Alps / Côtes d'Azur Gordes

PLACES OF INTEREST ❧ Pay a visit to the **monastery shop** where a range of lavender products (water, perfumes, antiseptics, soaps, balms and oil) are sold alongside religious literature and CDs of spiritual music.

❧ **Walking and hiking tracks** skirt by the abbey and the trails are popular with horseriders as well. There are riding schools in the area offering excursions and trail rides through the valley.

❧ The monks conduct **guided tours** of the monastery (in French, but guidebooks in other languages are available); as these are very popular it is necessary to reserve a place by emailing *visites@senanque.fr*

❧ The cobblestone village of **Gordes** is one of a number of Luberon 'perched' villages and one of the most beautiful villages in France. However, probably much better known is the village of **Ménerbes**, 10 kilometres south, where author and Francophile **Peter Mayle** wrote his jaunty memoir, *A Year in Provence*. These days Ménerbes is full of tourists seemingly arriving by the busload. Much less fashionable but equally attractive, the village of **Goult** is quieter and less touristy.

❧ Peter Mayle's later book, *A Good Year*, was filmed in 2006 at the **Château La Canorgue** near Bonnieux. The movie starred Australian actor Russell Crowe (b. 1964) and was directed by Sir Ridley Scott (b. 1937), an English film producer who has a house in the Luberon village of **Oppède le Vieux**.

❧ The tiny 15th-century hilltop village of **Oppède le Vieux**, 10 kilometres south of Gordes, is a charming little hamlet to explore. Oppède's Lilliputian village square and lovingly restored stone houses attract artists, writers and creative types who would find it hard not to be inspired by the setting and its environs.

❧ The perched village of **Lacoste** is known for the ruined château once belonging to the **Marquis de Sade** (1740–1814), the infamous writer of pornographic literature. French fashion designer **Pierre Cardin** now owns the property.

❧ If you collect antiques, **l'Isle sur la Sorgue**, sometimes referred to as 'Little Venice', 17 kilometres west of Gordes, has a plethora of antique and second-hand shops lining the canals. This lovely town hosts annual antique fairs each Easter and in mid-August.

❦ The **Moulins de Bouillons** (*Olive Oil Mill*) in **St-Pantaléon** near Gordes is one of the oldest mills (1762) in the country. Nearby is the **Museum of Stained Glass** which details the history of this art form in the area. The French Heritage-listed **Village of Bories** (on the outskirts of Gordes) is a reconstructed rural settlement of stone, beehive-shaped huts known as *bories*, which were used as houses and workshops in the 14th and 15th centuries.

❦ The **Musée de la Lavande** (*Museum of Lavender*) in **Cabriéres**, near Coustellat, 8 kilometres south of Gordes is open all year except for January. The flowers are harvested in July and August and lavender products can be purchased from the ever-scented museum shop.

FOOD AND DRINK ❦ The Michelin-starred **Restaurant Les Bories**, near the Abbey of Senanque, is one of the area's finest eateries; it offers a number of fixed-price degustation menus—dress up; this is fine dining at its best.

✉ 51, Route de l'Abbaye de Senanque.

☎ +33(0) 4 90 72 00 51   €€€€€

❦ Take home the flavours of Provence with olive oil from a local mill or some nougat from **Montelimar**, the nougat capital of France. The confiserie **Diane de Poytiers Nougaterie** in Montelimar is worth a stop for this rich, chewy, local speciality—and for a little bit of juicy, 16th century gosssip. The original Diane (1499-1566) was the mistress of King Henri II of France (1519–1559). Henri married Catherine de' Medici (1519-1589), daughter of a noble Florentine when they were both 14 years old. When Diane was 35 she infamously fell in love with the 16 year old Henri. The liason produced a daughter, Diane, Duchess d'Angoulême (1538-1619). Henri and Catherine had ten children of their own.

✉ 99, Avenue Jean Jaurès.

☎ +33(0) 4 75 01 67 02

❦ **Markets** are held in Gordes on Tuesday mornings, in Bonnieux on Fridays and in Oppède-le-Vieux on Saturdays. Coustellet has a farmers' market each Sunday; market days are Thursdays and Sundays at l'Isle sur la Sorgue. You could pick up some olives, ham and cheese, some fresh baguettes and picnic in true Provençal style.

Spiritual Retreats
Provence / Alps / Côtes d'Azur Île de St-Honorat

(30)

Abbaye Notre-Dame de Lérins

As with the Abbey of Senanque the Lérins abbey is occupied by the monks of the Congrégation Cistercienne de l'Immaculée Conception (*Cistercian Congregation of the Immaculate Conception*) and was founded in the early 5th century by St-Honoratus, a former Archbishop of Arles. It is believed that St Patrick came here to study before he departed on his journey to Ireland. Large sections of an earlier, 11th-century monastery still stand at the water's edge.

❡ For centuries Cistercian monks have been welcoming visitors to the island for prayer and reflection; they conduct retreats throughout the year. Retreatants and general visitors can participate in the liturgical ceremonies if desired. Maximum stay is 5 days but single-day retreats are also offered. Accommodation is in single and twin rooms; some are fitted with en suite bathrooms. All meals are available and are taken with the monks, in silence. The abbey is open to visitors for 11 months of the year but closed in November.

❡ The community of 30 monks run a thriving commercial enterprise through their work in the vineyards, gardens and apiary on the island. Guests can offer assistance if they wish. The monks also run a well-stocked gift and produce shop selling souvenirs, food items and their award-winning organic wines. Their tasty and quite unique Lerina Liqueur comes in a variety of flavours and is made from a concoction of dozens of aromatic herbs and plants grown on the island. Tastings can be arranged at the monks' restaurant, La Tonnelle.

SPIRITUAL RETREAT

✉ Île de St-Honorat
F-06406 Cannes
Alpes-Maritimes.

☎ +33 (0) 4 92 99 54 20
📠 +33 (0) 4 92 99 54 21

✆ hotellerie@
abbayedelerins.com

🖥 www.abbayedelerins.
com

💶 price to be negotiated.

☞ Take the Planaria Ferry
from Cannes Quay.
Owned by the monks,
this line is the only
way of getting to the
island. Ferry tickets
are available from the
ticket office on the
quay. The journey
takes approximately
15 minutes.

✝ **Sunday Mass**
0950.
Abbaye Notre-Dame
de Lérins.

⚭ Open to both men &
women

PLACES OF INTEREST ❧ **St-Honorat** and **Ste-Marguerite** are part of a group of four islands (two smaller islands are uninhabited) known as the **Îles de Lérins** (*Lerins Islands*) which lie a few kilometres off the coast of Cannes.

❧ The **Île de St-Honorat** is such a tourist attraction that to control the number of visitors (including nudists who, in the past, came for the secluded beaches) the monks purchased a ferry boat, the *Horizon IV*, and established their own ferry service, thereby excluding access to the island to all others. The Cannes ferry boat operators took umbrage at this and the monks soon found themselves in court. The monks won the case, however—and the appeal that followed. A separate ferry must now be taken from Cannes to visit the neighbouring island of **Ste-Marguerite**.

❧ **Île de St-Honorat** can be well explored on a day-long excursion. The ferry lands at a jetty near the **La Tonnelle** café/restaurant where visitors can stop for a cold drink or continue on down the gravel laneways past olive groves and vineyards to the main abbey entrance. Sections of the abbey are closed to day visitors and the guesthouse is also off limits. However, there is still much to see. Stone cloisters lead to the simple, remarkably beautiful abbey church and on to the monastery shop which, with its array of all manner of food, literature, religious objects, wine and liqueur, gently loosens the purse-strings. A path leads to the 11th-century remains of the original abbey where in summer groups of enthusiastic, multi-lingual young people conduct guided tours for visitors who will be rewarded with spectacular views of the Riviera coastline.

Spiritual Retreats

Provence / Alps / Côtes d'Azur Île de St-Honorat

❡ The **Île de Ste-Marguerite** was named after St Honoratus' mythical sister, supposedly a Cistercian nun, who is said to have established a convent on the island. The island is larger than the Île de St-Honorat and more touristy. The walking tracks on Ste-Marguerite weave through hectares of pine and oak forests which offer blessed relief from the blazing summer sun. If swimming in any of the coves here, speeding jet skis can sometimes be a nuisance.

❡ The major attraction on the island is the **Fort of Ste-Marguerite**, once a 17th-century prison, where the 'Man in the Iron Mask' of movie fame spent years in an isolated cell. The fort and the cell are open to visitors and a section now forms part of the **Musée de la Mer** (*Museum of the Sea*) which displays objects retrieved from local shipwrecks.

❡ The waters around the islands bob with marine activity. The area between the two islands, the **'plateau du milieu'** (*plateau in the middle*), is a safe, protected anchorage for pleasure boats. Explore more of the Riviera by taking a sightseeing tour to places further along the coast. Some tour companies use a bus in one direction and cruise boat in the other.

FOOD AND DRINK ❧ The **Restaurant La Tonnelle**, near the wharf on the Île de St-Honorat, is the island's only restaurant. It serves anything from a snack to a full meal and on a scorching day much-needed cold drinks and ice-creams. Dine indoors or more casually outside on the terrace. The wine and liqueurs produced by the monks are served here and fixed-price menus are offered. All in all a pleasant place to sip something cold and while away some time until the next ferry arrives.

✉ Île de St-Honorat.

☎ +33 (0) 4 92 99 18 07   €€€

❡ One of the most idyllically situated restaurants on the Riviera has to be the **Restaurant La Guérite** on the water's edge (next to the Fort Royal) on Île Ste-Marguerite. Flop into a chair under a shady umbrella, drink in the view and enjoy the house speciality—bouillabaisse. Simple, tasty baguettes (*sandwiches*) are available from the snack bar.

✉ Île Ste-Marguerite.

☎ +33 (0) 4 93 43 49 30   €€€–€€€€

❡ Back in **Cannes** there are numerous cafés and restaurants, either in the back streets or along the waterfront, close to the ferry station. Behind the quay fresh seafood, fruit and vegetables are sold at the undercover **Marché Forville** (*Forville Market*) every Tuesday to Sunday between 0700 and 1300.

Spiritual Retreats
Provence / Alps / Côtes d'Azur St-Etienne le Laus

31

Hôtellerie Notre-Dame du Laus

The isolated village of **St-Étienne le Laus**, high in the French Alps and some 18 kilometres south-east of the town of **Gap**, is a hallowed site where Our Lady is said to have appeared to a 17-year-old shepherdess, Benoîte (*Bernadette*) Rencurel (1647–1718), in the year 1664. The hamlet is now a place of pilgrimage with pilgrims converging on the site of the appearances as well as to see Benoîte's tomb which is behind the main altar in the church that Mary asked the young girl to establish. Daytime and torchlight pilgrimages are held in and around the church.

❧ **The Hôtellerie de Notre-Dame** is run by Oblate priests of the Missionaries of Laus who have been active here since 1819. It has small, modestly furnished guestrooms, most with en suite bathrooms and many with views over the valley. All meals are available, including take-away picnic lunches for those who want to explore the countryside. Facilities include a lift, television room, panoramic beer garden, café and a large restaurant. There is a well-stocked souvenir shop and plenty of parking.

❧ The Hôtellerie is situated among the mountain ranges of the Hautes-Alpes and is a popular base for bushwalkers and hikers. Located as it is in an isolated area, St-Étienne le Laus is a true sanctuary which has been forever free from war, plagues and conflict. Legend has it that centuries ago when it took weeks to reach the monastery on foot, the Pope at the time, recognising the difficulties people had in getting here, issued a decree that all who reached the monastery would gain Eternal Life—so a visit here could well be worth the effort!

✉ F-05130 St-Étienne
Le Laus
Hautes-Alpes

☎ +33 (0) 4 92 50 30 73
📠 +33 (0) 4 92 50 90 77

✉ accueil@notre-dame-du-laus.com

🖱 www.notre-dame-du-laus.com

🛏 from €25.00 pp, including breakfast.

☞ Take the train to Gap. The monastery runs a shuttle bus (pre-arranged) between Gap train station and the hôtellerie.

✞ **Sunday Mass
0700 & 1030.**
Basilique Notre-Dame du Laus.

♿ Discuss your needs in advance of arriving, ideally when booking.

👪 Open to men, women, families & groups

Spiritual Retreats
Provence / Alps / Côtes d'Azur St-Etienne le Laus

PLACES OF INTEREST ❧ The monastery is in a high mountainous position and the stunning views it commands can really only be fully appreciated from the difficult, uphill 'Calvary' climb to the 14th Station (of the Cross), which is also an ideal picnic spot. An enormous statue of a winged angel welcomes those who make it to the top.

❧ Lake Serre Ponçon, 20 kilometres east of Gap, provides summer opportunities for swimming, fishing and windsurfing. The Museoscope du Lac (*Lake Museum*) in the commune of Rousset has interesting background material on the lake's construction (it's Europe's largest) and the now submerged villages at the bottom. The only visible remains of the former townships is the tiny island Chapelle St-Michel (*Chapel of St Michael*), seemingly afloat on the lake but perched on the crest of a submerged hill. Cruise boats depart from the villages of Savines de Lac, Chorges, Rousset and La Bréole; most sail past the chapel.

❧ In summer the Plateau de Bayard, 7 kilometres north of Gap, is a popular hiking area. In winter, this becomes a snow lover's paradise with over 50 kilometres of cross-country ski trails and snowshoe walking tracks.

❧ The French National Alpine Botanical Academy forms part of the grounds of the 17th-century Château de Charance, once the summer residence of former bishops of Gap. Over 1,400 varieties of apple and pear trees and thousands of rose bushes, including many ancient species, flourish on over 200 hectares of land.

❧ The Heritage-listed Cathédrale Notre-Dame du Réal, a 12th-century Gothic masterpiece in the medieval village of Embrun, 35 kilometres east of St-Etienne, is still in prized condition and often the venue for summer concerts.

❧ The village of St-Véran, 80 kilometres north-east of St-Étienne-le-Laus, is the highest village in Europe, at 2,040 metres. At the Musée Le Soum, situated in St-Véran in a perfectly preserved village fuste (*old house*), visitors will discover the customs and traditions of the former occupants.

❧ **The Route Napoléon**, used by the Emperor and his soldiers on their way to Paris in 1815, passes through **Gap** and leads either north to **Grenoble** or south to **Sisteron**, **Grasse** and **Cannes**.

❧ The 12th-century **Abbaye de Boscodon** in **Crots**, 30 kilometres east of St Étienne, once belonged to the now defunct Order of Chalais (1100–1300). This enormous abbey is now occupied by a small community of Dominican sisters who have embarked on an ambitious project of restoration—an ongoing venture since 1972. Tourists come to visit or join the sisters on 'spiritual days'. To arrange such a day or a tour of the abbey please call the sisters.

☎ +33 (0) 4 92 43 14 45

❧ The **Italian border** and the mountainous **Piedmont** region are approximately 100 kilometres east of St-Étienne le Laus. The French town of **Briançon** is 20 kilometres from the border town of **Cesana** in Italy, which hosts the annual **Bobsleigh World Cup** each February.

FOOD AND DRINK ❧ The restaurant of the **Hotel St-Étienne du Laus** is open for breakfast, lunch and dinner. The main meal of the day is served at lunchtime, when the French guests like to partake of a little wine. The kitchen staff prepare wonderful, hearty picnics for those who want to spend the day hiking—fresh baguettes, pâté, slices of chicken, lentils, salad, homemade fruit cake and fresh fruit.

❧ The monastery also has an outdoor café and bar where a large terrace overlooks the valley below, providing sweeping views. Snacks are available here along with cold drinks, beer (including a very drinkable non-alcoholic variety) and wine from the monks' vineyards below the mountain.

❧ **Markets** are held in Gap on Wednesday mornings in the Place de la Republique. There is a Saturday morning market in the Place Jean Marcellin where cafés and bistros are also located.

❧ If you are looking for somewhere a bit different you could try dining at **La Rôtisserie des Cordiers**; the décor evokes the submarine *Nautilus* and the inspiration comes from Jules Verne's book *Twenty Thousand Leagues under the Sea*. It's not expensive, serves grills, pizza and pasta, and the kids will love it.

✉ Rue des Cordiers.

☎ +33 (0) 4 92 56 13 52   **€€–€€€**

PILGRIMAGES

PILGRIMAGE ROUTES ❧ There are numerous established pilgrimage routes commencing from various towns and cities in France which trail through the country and into Spain to join the **Camino de Santiago** (*Way of St James*) which leads to the **Shrine of the Apostle St James in Santiago de Compostela** in Galicia in north-west Spain. It is believed that the relics of St James, one of Christ's Apostles, lie here. All the pilgrimage routes are way-marked with a scallop shell, the emblem of St James and a symbol of the Santiago Pilgrimage. Each of the pilgrimage routes has some hundreds of variations and a detailed guide map is recommended.

ROUTE MAPS and information can be found on the following websites:
❧ American pilgrims
www.americanpilgrims.com
❧ UK pilgrims
www.csj.org.uk
❧ Australian and New Zealand pilgrims
www.caminodownunder.com

Via Turonensis

❧ The pilgrimage route to **Santiago de Compostela** which begins in Paris is called the **Via Turonensis** (approximately 1630 km); it tracks south through either **Orleans** or **Chartres** to the city of **Tours** and in particular to the **Basilique de St-Martin-de-Tours** (*Basilica of St Martin de Tours*), where lies the tomb of the town's 4th-century bishop. The route continues on through **Poitiers** to the **Église St-Hilaire-le-Grand** (*Church of St Hilary the Great*) which is situated in the town and named after **St Hilary**, the first Bishop of Poitiers (4th century). The church has been designated a World Heritage site. The **Église Ste-Radegonde** (*Church of St Radegunda*) also in Poitiers, is dedicated to the Patron Saint of the town, **Ste-Radegonde** (d. 587) who founded a monastery here in the 6th century. The saint's tomb is inside the church. Sightseeing in Poitiers is made easy with themed routes to various tourist sights and attractions marked on the streets with red, blue or yellow lines. A map is available from the tourist office at 45, Place Charles de Gaulle.

✝ Sunday Mass

1030. Église St-Hilaire-le-Grand, Poitiers.

0930 & 1100. Église Ste-Radegonde, Poitiers.

❧ The trail continues on to **Aulnay** in the Charente-Maritime and to **Saintes** in Poitou-Charentes. The city of **Bordeaux** in Aquitaine is a major stop on the route for a feast of World Heritage-listed monuments, including the **Cathédrale St-André de Bordeaux** (*Cathedral of St Andrew*) and two basilicas dedicated to **St-Seurnin** and **St-Michel**. Some 15 kilometres south-east of the city and also on the French heritage list, is the 11th-century **l'Abbaye de-la Sauve-Majeure** (*Great Saviour Abbey*), once occupied by some hundreds of Benedictine monks. The area is also noted for the quality of its red wine and the Bordeaux appellation has been awarded AOC status, the highest classification in France. The route tracks down through the Aquitaine region to the hamlet of **Vieux-Richet** and a tiny 11th-church and graveyard, the **Église St-Jean-Baptiste** (*Church of St John the Baptist*). From the thermal spa centre of **St-Paul-lès-Dax** it is on to the lovely walled town of **St-Jean-Pied-de-Porte** on the River Nive at the base of the Pyrénées, before the hard trek over the mountains and into Spain.

✝ Sunday Mass

1100. Cathédrale St-André de Bordeaux.

0930 & 1100. Basilique St-Seurnin, Bordeaux.

1100. Basilique St-Michel, Bordeaux.

Via Podiensis

❡ **Le-Puy** has for centuries been one of the starting points for the pilgrimage to **Santiago de Compostela** and today many pilgrims begin their journey here following the **Via Podiensis** (1460 km). Pilgrimage season in Le-Puy-en-Velay extends from 25 March to 15 October and during this time thousands of pilgrims descend on the town. The Le-Puy pilgrimage traditionally commences after a 0700 Mass celebrated every day in the **Cathédrale Notre-Dame du Puy** (*Cathedral of Our Lady of Puy*) and where a much-visited statue of the Black Madonna takes pride of place in the cathedral's Chapel of the Blessed Sacrament. On the Feast of the Annunciation, 25 March, a pilgrimage led by clergy holding aloft the statue of the Black Madonna departs from the cathedral in a holy procession through the medieval streets of the town.

❡ While in the town it is almost compulsory to visit the 10th-century **Chapelle St-Michel d'Aiguilhe** (*Chapel of St Michael on the Peak*), built in honour of **St James** and hovering at the top of a volcanic rock on the outskirts of the town. Masses (irregular times) are celebrated at the foot of the rock and in the high-rise chapel. However, it is a climb of almost 270 steps to the top.

✝ Sunday Mass 0700 & 1100.

Cathédrale Notre-Dame du Puy.

❡ The local Catholic diocese in Le-Puy has a Department of Pilgrimages situated at 4, Rue St-Georges where walks to religious sites and personal pilgrimages can be arranged.

❡ Le-Puy's famous green lentils make tasty, easy-to-carry and filling pilgrim food and the hearty Auvergne classic, peasant-style *La Potée Auvergnate* or Auvergne stew (made with potatoes, various cuts of pork, whatever sausage is on hand and a chopped head of cabbage fried in bacon) will keep the hunger pangs at bay. Each village has its own particular way of making this dish.

From Le Puy the route weaves through the dramatic volcanic landscapes of Auvergne south through **Saugues, St-Chély-d'Aubrac, St-Côme-D'Olt** and **Conques** in the Midi-Pyrénées. Conques is one of the most beautiful villages in France and in the centre of the village stands a medieval Benedictine abbey, the **Abbaye Ste-Foy** (*Abbey of St Foy*). During the summer months the abbey church is the venue of the *Festival de Musique de Conques* (Conques Music Festival). Pilgrim accommodation is available in the town.

✝ Sunday Mass 1100. Abbaye Ste-Foy, Conques.

From **Conques,** pilgrims can choose the route via **Cahors** (where a produce market is held in the square outside the local cathedral every Wednesday and Saturday morning) and **Lauzerte** (where traditional goose *foie gras* and a sweet meringue cake, *Le Macaron de Lauzerte*, are local specialities). The other choice is to walk via **Villeneuve d'Aveyron** where the 14th-century **Église du St-Sepulcre** (*Church of St Sepulche*) is of interest for the ancient frescoes of pilgrims walking the Santiago trail. Both routes eventually lead to **Moissac** and the 11th-century Romanesque cloisters in the Augustinian **Abbaye St-Pierre** (*Abbey of St Peter*). The area is known for growing sweet, golden Chasselas grapes and a grape festival is held each September. The well-marked trail continues on through **Lectoure** and **Eauze** to the last stop on the French side, **St-Jean-Pied-du-Port**, which is approached through the Heritage-listed **Porte St-Jacques** (*Gate of St James*). The town's medieval **Église de Notre-Dame-du-Bout-du-Pont** (*Church of Our Lady at the End of The Bridge*) is much visited by pilgrims. Then it's up and over the Pyrénées and into Spain.

✝ Sunday Mass 1030. Abbaye St-Pierre, Moissac.

Via Lemovicensis

❧ The town of **Vézeley** in Burgundy, and in particular the **Basilique Ste-Marie-Madeleine** (*Basilica of St Mary Magdalene*), is a starting point on the **Via Lemovicensis** (1630 km) route to **Santiago de Compostela**. Some believe that the genuine relics of Mary Magdalene are those kept in the cathedral here in Vézeley, although this is disputed by the Dominicans who care for the Mary Magdalene shrine at **La Baume** in Provence.

❧ The Vézeley shrine is tended by the Brothers and Sisters of the Monastic Fraternities of Jerusalem who take an active role in conducting guided tours of the religious sites in the town and mingling with visitors and tourists.

✝ Sunday Mass 1100.

Basilica of St Mary Magdalene, Vézeley.

❧ Pilgrims will find plenty of reasonably priced cafés and restaurants in Vézelay. However, for an indulgent culinary pilgrimage before hitting the footpaths of the Via Lemovicensis, one of France's best restaurants just happens to be in Vézelay—French chef extraordinaire **Marc Meneau**'s 3-Michelin star **L'Esperance**.

☎ +33 (0) 3 86 33 39 10

❧ From Vézelay pilgrims can choose to go via **La Charité-sur-Loire**, a former religious centre founded by the Benedictine Abbot of Cluny in the 11th century, and on to **Bourges** and **Chateauroux**, skirting the Centre region, and then from **Limoges** to **Périgueux**. Or they can proceed from Vézelay via **Nevers**, where **St-Thérèse of Lisieux** (1873–1897) lived as a Carmelite nun, and then from **Neuvy-Saint-Sepulches** on to **Limoges** and **Périgueux**. The route then trails through **Bergerac** in the Dordogne, **La Reole** and **Bazas** in Aquitaine where pilgrims can visit the magnificent former cathedral, the **Cathédrale St-Jean-Baptiste** (*Cathedral of John the Baptist*). On the day after Ash Wednesday, pilgrims in Bazas compete for space with the local cattle as the town celebrates the annual *Fete des Boeufs Gras* (Festival of the Bazas Cattle), a colourful procession of '*Bazadaise*' in line with an age-old royal tradition of each butcher donating one beast to the church every year. Needless to say, tender steak cooked in any style features on most of the restaurant menus in the town. The route continues on to **St-Sever** in Aquitaine and through to the Spanish border.

Via Tolosana

❧ The Via Tolosana (1540 km) pilgrimage route to the **Santiago de Compostela** is commonly referred to as the *Arles Route* and is less popular than the routes heading down from the north, possibly because the trail is more difficult to negotiate and more hilly in parts. The well-marked trail leads from **Arles** to the town of **Montpellier** where pilgrims can visit the national monument, the **Cathédrale St-Pierre** (*Cathedral of St Peter*) with its turrets and gargoyles and 14th-century heritage before trekking on to one of France's most beautiful villages, **St-Guilhem-le-Désert**, the site of a 9th-century abbey founded by **St-Guilhem** (*St William of Gellone*, 755–c. 814). The beautiful **Abbey of Gellone** houses a reliquary of what is believed to be a piece of the true Cross. The reliquary is always at the head of a religious procession held in the town on the Feast of St-Guilhem on 3 May. From time to time cross-shaped biscuits are sold here as a symbol of good luck for pilgrims to carry with them on the journey (only to be eaten in an emergency). From St-Guilhem-le-Désert where the eerie crystallised shapes in the **Grotte de Clamouse** (*Clamouse Caves*) divert many a steadfast pilgrim, the route leads on to **Lodève** and its 6th-century **Cathédrale St-Fulcran de Lodève** (*Cathedral of St Fulcran*).

❧ The first stop on the Midi-Pyrénées section of the Arles route is **La Salvetat-sur-Agout** and its 11th-century **Église St-Étienne** (*Church of St Etienne*), followed by the town of **Castres** on the River Agout. If it's Saturday you could stop by the market on the Place Jean-Jaures in Castres to pick up something tasty and sustaining. A visit to the parterre gardens behind the former **Episcopal Palace** (now the Goya Museum) is recommended. The gardens were designed by **André Le Nôtre** (1613–1700), former gardener of **King Louis XIV** of France (1638–1715).

✟ Sunday Mass

1100. Église St-Étienne, La-Salvetat-sur-Agout.

❧ Then to **Toulouse**, also in the Midi-Pyrénées, and the eccesliastical treasures and collections of **La Basilique St-Sernin** (*Basilica of St Sernin*), in particular the relics of St-Sernin (d c. 257), the town's first (3rd century) bishop.

✟ Sunday Mass

1000 & 1200. Cathédrale St-Pierre, Montpellier.

1100. l'Abbaye-de-Gellone, St-Sernin, Toulouse.

0900, 1030 & 1830. La Basilique St-Sernin, Toulouse.

Via Tolosana

❧ Pilgrims continue on to **Auch** and the striking interior of the **Cathédrale Ste-Marie** (*Cathedral of St Mary*), and then head to **Morlaàs** in Aquitaine and the treasured medieval artworks of the newly restored Romanesque **Église Ste-Foy** (*Church of St Foy*). Morlaàs is famous for both its local veal and for the hearty pilgrims' dish *aligot*, a delicious, filling, creamy mash of potato and garlic. Then it's on to **Pau**, the birthplace of **King Henry IV** (1553–1610), where you could pick up a bag of the local speciality, *coucougnettes*, an ambrosial mixture of chocolate, raspberries, almonds, and ginger doused in Armagnac. The last stop on the French side, **Oloron-Ste-Marie** is in the Pyrénées-Atlantiques and pilgrims generally pay a visit to the city's medieval cathedral. The Belgian chocolate company **Lindt** has a factory shop in the town and the mouth-watering aroma of chocolate often hangs in the air. Pilgrim-style food in the form of *garbure* (a thick, nourishing and sustaining peasant-style soup, crammed with vegetables and flavoured with whatever meat happens to be on hand) is a speciality of the area. The trail crosses the Spanish border through the **Col du Somport** mountain pass.

✝ Sunday Mass

1030. Cathédrale Ste-Marie, Auch.

1030. Cathédrale Ste-Marie, Oloron-Ste-Marie.

Paris-Centre
Ile-de-France

❡ Each Pentecost weekend (Pentecost Sunday is 50 days after Easter Sunday) a 3-day **Pèlerinage de Chretienté** (*Pilgrimage of Christians*) departs from **Paris** for **Chartres**, 120 kilometres south-west in a revival of a tradition dating back to the Middle Ages. The walk commences with a pilgrims' blessing in the **Cathédrale Notre-Dame de Paris** (*Cathedral of Notre Dame*) in Paris at 0630 on the Saturday and concludes at a Pontifical High Mass celebrated in **Chartres Cathedral** on the following Monday. Pilgrims stop for Mass and other religious activities along the way. This is a tough pilgrimage. Accommodation is available in tents and the only food provided is bread and soup. Water is also available. Back-up and support vehicles proceed to and fro along the route but only those in good health should attempt this walk.

✟ Sunday Mass

0900, 1100 & 1800. Chartres Cathedral.

❡ Those who have a devotion to **Our Lady of the Miraculous Medal** could visit the National Shrine in the **Chapelle Notre-Dame de la Médaille Miraculeuse** (*Chapel of the Miraculous Medal*) at 140, Rue du Bac in Paris. It is said that here in 1830 a young nun, **Catherine Labouré** (1806–1886), a member of the order of the Daughters of Charity, experienced visions of Our Lady. The Lady asked Catherine to strike a medal in her honour with the promise of 'great blessings' to all who wore it. The medal is known as the Miraculous Medal. Sister Catherine was canonised by **Pope Pius XII** on 27 July 1947 and her incorrupt body lies in a glass coffin in the church.

✟ Sunday Mass

0730, 1000 & 1115. Chapelle Notre-Dame de la Médaille Miraculeuse, Paris.

Pilgrimages

Paris-Centre
Ile-de-France

❦ Standing majestically on the Île de la Cité, the **Cathédrale Notre-Dame-de-Paris**, (*Cathedral of Our Lady*) is believed to be one of the largest Gothic cathedrals in the world. It's a place of pilgrimage not only for those interested in the ecclesiastical but for historians, art lovers and tourists alike. On 14 August each year, the eve of the Feast of the Assumption, pilgrims can join in a procession led from the cathedral by clergy carrying a statue of Our Lady of Notre-Dame to a barge in the River Seine. The boat proceeds along the water accompanied by a small flotilla and sails around the Île de St-Louis and the Île de la Cité before returning to moorings near the cathedral. A similar procession is held the following day, the Feast of the Assumption, but this procession takes place on land through the streets of the two small islands.

✝ Sunday Mass 0830, 1030, 1130, 1245 & 1830. Cathédrale Notre-Dame-de-Paris.

❦ The **Chapelle St-Vincent-de-Paul** (*Chapel of St Vincent de Paul*) at 95, Rue de Sevres is situated within the headquarters of the Vincentian order which was founded by **St-Vincent-de-Paul** (1576–1660). Open every day, pilgrims are drawn to the chapel to pray before the incorrupt heart of St Vincent which is kept above the church altar.

✝ Sunday Mass 1030. Chapelle St-Vincent-de-Paul.

❦ The stunningly beautiful and now deconsecrated Gothic church, the **Sainte-Chapelle** (*Holy Chapel*) on the Boulevard du Palais on the Île de la Cité was built by **King Louis IX of France** (1214–1270) to hold precious religious objects said to have been from the Crucifixion of Christ. The relics are no longer here but were stored in a reliquary in the Upper Chapel, a monument in itself to 13th-century stained-glass artisans. The relics are now kept in the Treasury of the Cathedral of Notre-Dame.

❡ The Basilique du Sacre-Coeur de Montmartre (*Basilica of the Sacred Heart*), which overlooks the city from its hillside perch in **Montmartre**, has for over 100 years been a mecca for pilgrims and tourists. The Benedictine Sisters of Montmartre (the order is also located in London at the Tyburn Convent near Marble Arch) run a large guesthouse catering for those who wish to come here to pray (guided prayer sessions are conducted by priests and nuns in French and English), make a private or guided retreat, or participate in the Perpetual Adoration of the Blessed Sacrament. From time to time the sisters conduct retreats for other nuns and members of religious orders. The Carmelites also have a convent near the basilica. Every evening the sisters of Sacré-Coeur conduct 'a night of adoration' commencing at 2030. After Mass at 2000 a roster of prayer before the Blessed Sacrament operates through the night. Reservations are necessary and can be made by telephone.

☎ +33 (0) 1 53 41 89 09

✝ Sunday Mass 1100, 1800 & 2200.

Basilique du Sacre-Coeur de Montmartre.

❡ The Dutch Christian fellowship association the *Capella Sancti Servatii Nunhem* (**Church of St Servais** in Nunhem, the Netherlands) arranges pilgrimages throughout Europe, particularly for young people. Each year the association is represented in the **Paris-to-Chartres** pilgrimage, the **Tóchar Phádraig** in Ireland, and in the **Leffe to Foy-Notre-Dame** pilgrimage in Belgium.

✍ *www.nunhem.nl/cssn*

Alsace

❧ **Le Mont Ste-Odile** (*Mount St Odile*), high above the village of **Ottrott** south of **Strasbourg**, has long been a place of pilgrimage in honour of **Odile**, an 8th-century saint who was cured of blindness here. Today, both pilgrims and tourists come to the mountain to sightsee, rest and pray and follow the pilgrims' paths to sites connected with the saint. Pilgrims can also join in the celebration of the **Perpetual Adoration** which takes place in the church 24 hours each day. Nuns, priests and lay helpers are available to assist.

❧ The pilgrimage centre has a number of restaurants and eating places serving meals, snacks and the local Ottrotter red wine. **Ottrott**, the village at the foot of the mountain, is in the centre of a wine-growing area with cafés and restaurants offering traditional home cooking and local vintages to match.

✟ Sunday Mass 1000, 1130 & 1800.

Église du Mont Ste-Odile, Ottrott.

❧ Not far from Mont Ste-Odile and in a peaceful rural setting, the restored **Couvent du Bischenberg** (*Convent of Bischenberg*) nuzzles into the Bischenberg Hill, high above the village of Bischoffsheim. Leading up a gentle rise from the convent's **Chapelle Notre-Dame des Sept Douleurs** (*Chapel of Our Lady of Seven Sorrows*) is an 18th-century, 14 station Chemin de Croix (*Way of the Cross*). Each 'station' is sheltered in its own tiny chapel. Each year, on Our Lady's Feast Day, 15 August, the Redemptorist fathers (the order has occupied the convent since 1820) lead the **Pèlerinage Notre-Dame du Bischenberg** (*pilgrimage of Our Lady of Bischenberg*) from the village and along the Way of the Cross to a closing ceremony in the chapel.

Auvergne

❧ Many people make a private pilgrimage to the sites frequented by **Ste-Jeanne d'Arc** (*St Joan of Arc*, 1412–1431) who was born in the village of **Domremy la Pucelle** near Nancy, in the Alsace/Lorraine region, 300 kilometres east of Paris. The house she lived in can be visited; it is now a National Monument. Nearby, the sisters of the French Missionary order known as Les Travailleuses Missionaries (*The Working Missionaries*) run an excellent restaurant, **l'Accueil du Pélerin** (*The Welcome Pilgrim*). As in their French restaurant, **L'Eau Vive** (*Water of Life*) in central Rome, during the meal diners are asked to join with the sisters in singing the hymn '*Ave Maria*'. The sisters pass around hymn sheets on which are printed the words so everyone can participate.

✉ L'Accueil du Pélerin, Domremy la Pucelle.

☎ +33 (0) 3 29 94 14 38
📠 +33 (0) 3 29 94 02 51

✉ L'Eau Vive, Via Monterone, 85, Rome, Italy.

☎ +39 (0) 6 6880 1095
📠 +39 (0) 6 6880 2572

🖱 www.restaurant-eauvive.it

❧ **The St Gilles Way**, a north–south, 200-kilometre-long medieval pilgrimage trail (separate to the Santiago de Compostela route) leads from **Le-Puy-en-Velay** to **St-Gilles-du-Gard** in Languedoc, situated between the towns of Arles and Nîmes. On average the walk takes 2 weeks and trails through villages and hamlets in the volcanic areas of Auvergne and past old Roman settlements in Languedoc to the town of Alès (not to be confused with Arles in nearby Provence) and on to St-Gilles-du-Gard. The town's **Abbey of St Gilles** was once part of an ancient Benedictine monastery and is now a UNESCO World Heritage site as well as a stop on the **Santiago de Compostela** pilgrimage trail. Relics of the Greek-born **St-Gilles-Aegidius** (c. 710–724), the first abbot of the monastery and a Patron Saint of the Disabled, are kept here.

✝ **Sunday Mass 1100**. Abbaye St-Gilles-du-Gard.

Bourgogne
Burgundy

❧ The monastic town of **Paray le Monial** has been a place of pilgrimage since the 17th century when Jesus is said to have appeared to a young nun, **Marguerite Marie Alacoque** (1647–1690), and revealed His Sacred Heart. The apparition appeared in what is now **la Chapelle des Apparitions** (*the Chapel of the Apparitions*) where Margaret Mary, now Ste-Marguerite Marie (*St Margaret Mary*), is buried. Sisters of the Visitation Order live in a monastery next door and celebrate liturgical services in the chapel daily; pilgrims and tourists are welcome to join in. Every day religious celebrations take place in the town and many are conducted in the 12th-century **Basilique du Sacré-Coeur** (*Basilica of the Sacred Heart*). Pilgrims can relax in the Parc des Chapelains (the *Chaplain's Park*) behind the basilica where during summer a sound and light display traces the background story of the Apparitions.

✝ Sunday Mass

0945. La Chapelle des Apparitions, Paray-le-Monial.

1100. Basilique du Sacré-Couer, Paray-le-Monial.

Bretagne
Brittany

❧ Since the 13th century it has been a Catholic tradition in Brittany to make the **Tro Breizh** (*Tour of Brittany*) pilgrimage to honour the seven saints who introduced Christianity to this region. The circular route is almost 600 kilometres long and it is permissible to complete the pilgrimage in various sections, over the course of a lifetime. The towns, and the saints who are buried there, are: **Dol** (**St-Samson**, c. 490–565, who founded the Monastery of Dol in the 6th century); **St-Malo** (**St-Malo**, c. 520–c. 620, a Welsh missionary who worked in Brittany); **St-Brieuc** (**St-Brieuc**, c. 420–510, who founded a monastery near St-Brieuc); **Tréguier** (**St-Tudwal**, d. 564, a former Bishop of Treher or Tréguier); **St-Pol-de-Léon** (**St-Pol** or Paul Aurelian, d. 572, a preacher of Christianity); **Quimper** (**St-Corentin**, d. 490, a former Bishop of Quimper); and **Vannes** (**St-Patern**, c. 440, the first Bishop of Vannes).

❧ The little town of **Ste-Anne-d'Auray** is often referred to as the religious capital of Brittany. The Bretons' devotion to **Ste-Anne**, Jesus's maternal grandmother and Brittany's Patron Saint, stems from the early 17th century when the saint is said to have appeared to a local peasant with the request that a church be established in her name.

Languedoc

❧ The **Basilique de Ste-Anne d'Auray** (*Basilica of St Anne of Auray*) was established soon after this vision and, some centuries later in 1996, was visited by **Pope Jean-Paul II** (1920–2005). The little village bursts at the seams on Ste-Anne's feast day, 26 July, when pilgrims flood the basilica to receive a traditional pardon for past sins. A pilgrims' Mass is celebrated in the church on most days at 1500.

✞ Sunday Mass 1500.

Basilique de Ste-Anne d'Auray.

❧ During the pilgrimage season, between March and October, traditional '**pardon**' ceremonies are conducted in parish churches all over Brittany.

❧ There are some excellent restaurants in the town of **Auray** situated a few kilometres from **Ste-Anne-d'Auray**. Seafood and pancakes feature on many of the menus along with *Gâteau Breton* (Breton Cake), a light, buttery favourite which makes a perfect dessert or a satisfying snack with a traditional *café au lait*. During the summer the local artists sell their works along the medieval St-Gouston harbourfront in Auray, where there is also a number of eating places.

❧ Thousands of people visit the town of **Rennes-le-Château** each year in search of buried treasure following the escapades of the village's renegade priest, **Father François Bérenger Saunière** (1852–1917), who appeared to have accumulated great personal wealth during his lifetime. When rumours spread that the priest had hidden his supposed treasure, masses of people descended on the area after his death. Some believe that the character in Dan Brown's novel *The Da Vinci Code*, Jacques Saunière, the curator of the Louvre Museum and head of the mysterious organisation the Priory of Sion (*Prieuré de Sion*), is linked to Father Bérenger.

Midi-Pyrénées

❡ **Lourdes** is probably the most famous of all the French pilgrimage sites and the shrine has been a place of faith, hope and peace since 1858 when the Blessed Virgin is believed to have appeared to a local girl, **Bernadette Soubirous** (1844–1879). From this time a spring of pure water began to flow from a rocky cave now known as the **Massabielle Grotto**. The water is said to have miraculous properties and visitors can access the spring 24 hours each day.

❡ The incorrupt body of **St Bernadette**, Patron Saint of the Sick, lies in the chapel of the **Convent of St-Gildard** in **Nevers** in Burgundy where she lived as a member of the order of the Sisters of Charity and was given the name Sister Marie-Bernard. The sisters at the convent in Nevers take overnight guests for retreats and prayer (*see* page 133).

❡ Some millions of pilgrims visit **Lourdes** each year to pray and meditate, out of curiosity or to seek relief from their suffering. There are numerous hotels and eating places in the town and souvenir shops line the streets. Some are rather tawdry and are stocked to the rafters with all manner of unlikely products invoking the name Bernadette—soap, coffee mugs, tea towels, corkscrews and even hats and wallets. The most popular confectionery on sale in Lourdes are the sweets produced at the **Pastillerie Malespine** factory, which uses the water from the Massabielle Grotto in all their products.

❡ **Pope Benedict XVI** visited Lourdes in 2008.

✟ Sunday Mass 0830. Massabielle Grotto, Lourdes.

❧ The remarkably attractive cliff-hanging village of **Rocamadour** has been a place of pilgrimage from around the time of **Zaccheus**, who lived in the 1st century and who was the spouse of **St Veronica**, the woman who wiped the face of Jesus on his way to Calvary. Zaccheus is said to have lived here in a rocky cave as a hermit and had in his possession a statue of a Black Madonna. When Zaccheus died pilgrims began to visit to pray for the intercession of the Black Madonna and the statue was moved to the **Chapelle de Notre-Dame** (*Chapel of Our Lady*) next to the town's **Basilique St-Saveur** (*Basilica of St Saviour*). In the 12th century an incorrupt body was discovered here which is believed to be that of **St Amadour** who, again in legend, has been linked with Zaccheus. However, despite some curious myths the fact remains that the **Chapelle Miraculeuse** (*Chapel of Miracles*) which houses the tomb of St Amadour and the statue of the Black Madonna are still the major focus of today's pilgrims.

❧ The little town is divided into upper and lower with the religious epicentre and its chapels, shrines, a Way of the Cross and the Black Madonna in the higher town. A 200-step staircase leads to the upper town; in the past, penitents and pilgrims would climb the steps on their knees. For those who can't manage this feat, a lift is in operation.

❧ **Rocamadour** is a stop on the **Santiago de Compostela** pilgrimage route from Vezelay; the local disc-shaped Rocamadour goat's cheese comes in a handy size to throw in a backpack for later.

✝ Sunday Mass 1100 & 1700. Sanctuaire du Rocamadour.

Nord-Pas-de-Calais

❧ **Boulogne-sur-Mer** is the largest fishing port in France. The legend attached to the **Shrine of Boulogne-sur-Mer** dates back to the 7th century when a lone boat carrying a statue of the Virgin Mary was found floating in the sea nearby. The statue was hence known as the **Notre-Dame de Boulogne-sur-Mer** (*Our Lady of The Sea*), and placed in the village church. When miracles were said to have occurred here the site became a place of pilgrimage, and subsequently a new church was erected. The present-day cathedral was established in the 19th century with a special 'Lady Chapel' built to house the precious statue and where pilgrims, particularly sailors and fishermen, come to pray. For the past 150 years it has been a town tradition to celebrate the Virgin of Boulogne-sur-Mer in a procession through the streets.

❧ **Boulogne-sur-Mer** was once taken over by Napoleon as he prepared for his invasion of England. The Emperor and his men must have eaten well; local fishing fleets have unloaded their bountiful catches here for centuries.

✝ Sunday Mass 1100 & 1830.

Cathédrale Notre-Dame de Boulogne-sur-Mer.

Normandy

❧ The island Abbey of **Mont St-Michel** (*St Michael's Mount*) was founded by **St-Aubert** (d. 669), Bishop of Avranches, in the 8th century after he is said to have experienced a vision of St Michael the Archangel. Soon after his experience, St-Aubert established a religious settlement on the island to honour St Michael. Catholic Benedictine monks came to live on Mont St-Michel and it soon became an important place of pilgrimage and a stop on the way to the Shrine of St James de Compostela in Spain. The route to **Santiago de Compostela** from Mont St-Michel, known as the **Plantagenet Way**, trails south through Angers and by the Chateau d'Angers where hang the 100-metre-long and almost 6-metre-high, 14th-century **Les Tapisseries de l'Apocalypse** (*Apocalypse Tapestries*) which depict events leading to the end of the world; the Plantagenet Way then joins the route of the **via Turonensis** from Paris in St-Jean d'Angely. A 20th-century copy of the Apocalypse Tapestries by French artist **Jean Lurçat** (1892–1966) is on display at the Jean Lurçat Museum on the Boulevard Arago in Angers and titled *Le Chant du Monde* (Song of the World).

The Benedictines left **Mont St-Michel** prior to the French Revolution when the abbey was turned into a jail. However, in 2000, after extensive restorations, the religious men and women of the **Les Fraternités Monastiques de Jerusalem** (*Monastic Communities of Jerusalem*) settled here. They conduct religious services on a daily basis and official pilgrimages from time to time. Nonetheless, thousands of people visit the island each week to make a private pilgrimage or to participate in an overnight retreat.

✟ Sunday Mass 1100. *Église Abbatiale*
(Fraternités Monastiques de Jérusalem).

There are restaurants and cafés on the island, many in the **Old Town** and some with marvellous views.

St Thérèse, the Little Flower (1873–1897), was born in **Alençon** in Normandy and many make a private pilgrimage to the sites associated with the saint. Through the local **Lisieux** tourist office pilgrims and tourists can organise a 2-day self-guided tour or pilgrimage commencing in Alençon and ending in the **Carmel Chapel** in Lisieux where the saint's incorrupt body lies in a glass reliquary. Thérèse joined the Carmelite Order when she was 15 years old and died just 9 years later. Thérèse's parents, Louis Martin and Marie Zélie Guerin, are buried in the crypt of the **Basilique St Thérèse** in Lisieux; in 2008 they were beatified (the first steps towards sainthood) by **Pope Benedict XVI**.

✟ Sunday Mass

0800, 0900 & 1130. La Chapelle du Carmel de Lisieux.

1030. Basilique St Thérèse, Lisieux.

If motoring, be aware that driving in **Alençon** can be difficult as it is a maze of one-way streets. However, the town is old and quite beautiful and it's well worth parking the car and taking a self-guided walking tour—details from the tourist office in **La Maison d'Ozé**, a particularly elegant medieval structure which was once home to a local family.

Picardie
Picardy

❧ The Heritage-listed 13th-century **Cathédrale Notre-Dame d'Amiens** (*Amiens Cathedral*) is a magnet for pilgrims and tourists alike who are inspired by its size, soaring ceilings, sculptures and exquisitely decorated choir stalls. On the floor is a medieval labyrinth where some visitors make their own private pilgrimage. A plaque inside the cathedral stands as a memorial to the Australian soldiers who lost their lives defending Amiens during World War I. In 1920 the Bishop of Amiens, **Pierre-Florent-André du Bois de la Villerabel** (1864–1938), dedicated the plaque with the words: "We bow to you, Messieurs les Australiens, for the magnificent deeds that you did in those days, now happily at an end, for your country and for France, and for the victory of hope and sanity. The soil of France is transfigured to a new divinity by your sacrifices. In the whole of history we cannot find an army more marvellous in its bravery, and in the war there was none that contributed more nobly to the final triumph." *www.diggerhistory.info*

Provence

❧ **The Sanctuaire Notre-Dame de Valcluse** (*Sanctuary of Our Lady of Valcluse*), in **Auribeau-sur-Siagne** near **Grasse**, is visited by pilgrims who come to pray before a 13th-century shrine honouring the Virgin Mary. The sanctuary is cared for by the Community of the Beatitudes, a religious order of priests, nuns and lay people which is now active in five continents. Members of the Community of the Beatitudes are attached to the Catholic Church and take the traditional religious vows.

✝ Sunday Mass 1700.

Sanctuaire Notre-Dame de Valcluse

❧ **Auribeau-sur-Siagne** is a tiny, enchanting, perched village with narrow, crooked medieval lanes and in summer masses and masses of colourful blooms. Lovely views and some good eating places add to the attraction.

❧ Every year for three days following 24 May an unusual pilgrimage and celebration is held in the **Église Stes-Maries-de-la-Mer** (*Church of the St Marys by the Sea*) in the town of the same name in Bouches-du-Rhône department in the Carmargue region. Thousands of Gypsies from all over Europe descend on the town to honour the Patron Saint of Gypsies, **St Sarah the Black**, whose statue stands in the Church of **St Mary's by the Sea**. It is known as the *Pelerinage de Gitans* (Gypsies' Pilgrimage). The legend of St Sarah relates to the supposed arrival in this area by boat of three 'Marys': the repentant sinner, **Mary Magdalene**; **Mary Jacob** (St Mary the Gypsy), a relative of the Blessed Virgin Mary; and possibly **Mary Salome**, the mother of the Apostle James. Legend and myth dictate that Sarah may have been the maidservant of one of the women. The church is said to have been erected over the graves of two of the women. During the pilgrimage the statues of Sarah and the three Marys are taken in procession down to the sea and then returned to the church in the same way. There is much celebration in the town at this time, and pilgrims have a wide choice of restaurants and cafés to choose from, although as the town is on the coast, most specialise in seafood. Just-caught seafood platters are on almost every menu along with fresh, fragrant local *Paella*.

❧ The coastal town of **St-Baume** is steeped in the history of **Mary Magdalene**, who as mentioned previously may have landed near here by boat. It is said that she walked to the top of a mountain near St-Baume and found a large cave where she lived for 30 years. From St-Baume two separate pilgrimage trails lead to this cave. Both have a steep ascent and, on average are a 30-minute walk in each direction. The paths are scattered with ancient stone shrines and lead through a thick forest of beech, elm and ash trees to the hillside cave and grotto which has now been converted into a chapel where religious services are frequently conducted. Relics believed to be those of Mary Magdalene are kept in the grotto which is open from 0730 every day.

Provence

❧ **Mary Magdalene** is the (unofficial) Patron Saint of Provence and on 22 July each year, her Feast Day, (and on Christmas Eve) pilgrims make a trek to the cave by torchlight to celebrate a midnight Mass. Pilgrims also visit the 13th-century Gothic **Basilique Ste-Marie-Madeleine** (*Basilica of St Mary Magdalene*) in the little town of **St Maximin-la-Ste-Baume** situated at the foot of the mountain where more relics are kept. **St Maximin** (c. 346) is said to have been a companion of Mary and with her help spread the Gospel throughout Provence. The convent of Ste-Baume, and a hotel for pilgrims and tourists which is run by the Dominican Order, is situated at the beginning of the paths leading to the grotto (*see* page 140). La Baume is approximately 50 kilometres north-east of **Marseilles** and 40 kilometres east of **Aix-en-Provence**.

✝ Sunday Mass

   1100. Grotte de la Ste-Baume.

   1030. Basilique Ste-Marie-Madeleine,

❧ The **Hôtellerie du Couvent Royal** in St-Maximin-la-Ste-Baume was for centuries the home of Dominican monks. The food served in the hotel's **Chapter Room Restaurant**, once an ancient refectory, may have improved considerably since, but the medieval stone walls still lend a monastery atmosphere to every meal.

❧ On a clear day, the hilltop pilgrimage site of **Mont Ste-Victoire** can be seen across the plains from **La Baume**. Centuries ago pilgrims would climb to the top of the mountain where a monastery was established, to pray before the shrine dedicated to **Ste-Victoire** and to spend the night. A bonfire, visible to those below, would be lit as a sign of having arrived safely. In recent times the ancient buildings on the site have been restored to provide a place to pray and a refuge for hikers. A large cross, **La Croix de Provence**, visible from afar, has been reconstructed near the site of the original monastery. Rebuilding has been undertaken by the association of the *Confrères de Ste-Victoire* (Friends of St Victoire), an energetic and admirable group of local people who give freely of their expertise. Mass is sometimes celebrated in the chapel at the summit.

❧ The mountain paths can be quite dangerous and are closed at certain times. Pilgrims and hikers should seek information and advice from the tourist office in Aix-en-Provence before setting out. However, Mont Ste-Victoire remains a popular destination for hikers, many of whom begin their ascent from the hamlet of **Vauvenargues** at the foot of the mountain and in particular from the **Château de Vauvenargues**, which was once the home of painter **Pablo Picasso** (1881–1973), who is buried in the grounds.

Rhone-Alps

❡ **Le Sanctuaire Notre-Dame-de-La-Salette** (*The Sanctuary of Our Lady of Salette*) is located on the slopes of **Mont Planeau**, approximately 10 kilometres from the town of **Corps**, south of Grenoble, and has been established on the site of where it is believed the Blessed Virgin appeared to two children in 1846. The children reportedly said that a 'Beautiful Lady' passed on messages for the people of the world imploring them to change their ways. In the following years miracles are said to have occurred here and a dry spring ran once more with water, said to have miraculous properties. The appearances were finally ratified by the authorities and some 6 years later work commenced on a church, a monastery and a building to accommodate pilgrims.

❡ Two Catholic religious orders were established: the **Missionaries of Our Lady of La Salette** and the **Sisters of Our Lady of La Salette**. Over 150 years later, with the support of lay helpers, the priests and nuns conduct spiritual programs and arrange pilgrimages, prayer and liturgical services in honour of Our Lady of Salette. A 14-station Way of The Cross leads pilgrims higher up the mountain following the path said to have been taken by Our Lady.

❡ The children who experienced the vision described a silver cross that Our Lady was wearing as having a hammer and open pincers on either side of the cross bar. The hammer is said to represent human failings and the open pincers, prayer and penance. Replicas of the cross (necklace) are on sale in many shops in the area.

✝ Sunday Mass 1015, 1145, 1600, 1830.

Basilique du Sanctuaire Notre-Dame-de-La-Salette.

Additional Accommodation

Paris

🔸 PARIS

🄢 Groupe Scolaire Saint-Nicolas

✉ 19, Rue Victor Hugo
F-92130 Issy-les-Moulineaux
Paris.

📞 +33 (0) 1 41 46 15 23
📠 +33 (0) 1 40 93 50 90

✆ accueil@st-nicolas.org
✆ www.st-nicolas.org

☞ Métro: Mairie d'Issy or
Corentin Celton

🛏 Only school groups may stay
here

🄣 Hébergement Kellerman

✉ 17, Boulevard Kellermann
F-75013 Paris

📞 +33 (0) 1 43 58 96 00
📞 +33 (0) 1 43 58 95 14

✆ reservation@cisp.fr
✆ www.cisp.fr

☞ Métro: Porte d'Italie

🛏 Only groups of young people
may stay here

🄣 Hébergement Maurice Ravel

✉ 6, Avenue Maurice Ravel
F-75012 Paris

📞 +33 (0) 1 43 58 96 00
📠 +33 (0) 1 43 58 95 14

✆ reservation@cisp.fr
✆ www.cisp.fr

☞ Métro: Bel-Air–Porte de
Vincennes–Porte Dorée

🛏 Only groups of young people
may stay here

🄣 Hôtel Dieu Hospitel

✉ 1, Place du Parvis Notre-Dame
F-75004 Paris

📞 +33 (0) 1 44 32 01 00
📠 +33 (0) 1 44 32 01 16

✆ hospitelhoteldieu@wanadoo.fr
✆ www.hotel-hospitel.com

☞ Metro: Saint-Michel or Cité

🛏 Open to both men & women

🄢 L'Accueil St-Paul

✉ 22 Rue de l'Abbé Derry
F-92130 Issy-les-Moulineaux
Paris

📞 +33 (0) 1 45 29 16 06
📠 +33 (0) 1 55 95 88 66

☞ Métro: Mairie d'Issy

🛏 Open to men, women & groups

🄢 L'Enclos Rey

✉ 57, Rue Violet
F-75015 Paris

📞 +33 (0) 1 44 37 34 00
📠 +33 (0) 1 44 37 34 31

✆ accueil@psa.asso.fr
✆ www.assomption-psa.org

☞ Métro: Commerce or
Avenue Émile Zola

🛏 Open to men, women & groups

🄢 Maison d'Accueil Ephrem

✉ Basilique du Sacre-Coeur de
Montmartre
33, Rue du Chevalier-de-la-Barre
F-75018 Paris

📞 +33 (0) 1 53 41 89 09
📠 +33 (0) 1 53 41 89 19

✆ pax@sacre-coeur-montmartre.com
✆ www.sacre-coeur-montmartre.com

☞ Metro: Anvers, Abbesses,
Château Rouge

♿ Discuss access when you book

🛏 Open to both men & women

🄣 MIJE Hostels

✉ 6, Rue de Fourcy
F-75004 Paris

✉ 11, Rue du Fauconnier
F-75004 Paris

✉ 12, Rue des Barres
F-75004 Paris

📞 +33 (0) 1 42 74 23 45
📠 +33 (0) 1 40 27 81 64

✆ info@mije.com
✆ www.mije.com

☞ Metro for all: Saint-Paul, Pont
Marie

🛏 Only young people may stay
here

Centre/ Île-De- France

🌸 BROU SUR CHANTEREINE

Ⓢ Prieuré St-Joseph

✉ 1, Avenue Victor Thiébaut
F-77177 Brou sur Chantereine
Seine-et-Marne

📞 +33 (0) 1 60 20 11 20
📠 +33 (0) 1 60 20 43 52

📧 pr.stjoseph.brou@club-internet.fr
🖥 www.benedictinesjc.org

♿ Discuss access when you book

🕮 Open to both men & women

🌸 EPERNON

Ⓢ Prieuré St-Thomas

✉ 29, Rue du Prieuré
F-28230 Epernon Eure-et-Loir

📞 +33 (0) 2 37 83 60 01
📠 +33 (0) 2 37 83 44 00

📧 prieure-epernon@wanadoo.fr
🖥 www.soeursduchrist.fr

🕮 Open to both men & women

🌸 JOUARRE

Ⓢ Abbaye Notre-Dame de Jouarre

✉ 6 Rue Montmorin
F-77640 Jouarre Seine-et-Marne

📞 +33 (0) 1 60 22 84 18
📠 +33 (0) 1 60 22 31 25

📧 hotes@abbayejouarre.org
🖥 www.abbayejouarre.org

🕮 Open to both men & women

🌸 MOLINEUF

Ⓢ Carmel de Blois

✉ La Chambaudière
F-41190 Molineuf Loir-et-Cher

📞 +33 (0) 2 54 70 04 29
📠 +33 (0) 2 54 70 05 76

📧 carmeldeblois@yahoo.fr
🖥 www.carmel.asso.fr/Molineuf-Blois

🕮 Open to both men & women

🌸 MONTMORENCY

Ⓢ Congrégation des Pallotins

✉ 34, Chemin des Bois Briffaults
F-95160 Montmorency Val-d'Oise

📞 +33 (0) 1 39 89 32 96
📠 +33 (0) 1 34 12 02 08

📧 info@centrumdialogu.org
🖥 www.centrumdialogu.org

🕮 Open to men, women & groups

🌸 ST-CHÉRON

Ⓢ Centre Morogues Saulty

✉ 4, Rue Paul Payenneville
F-91530 St-Chéron Essonne

📞 +33 (0) 1 64 56 63 12
📠 +33 (0) 1 64 56 63 44

🖥 www.centre-morogues-saulty.abcsalles.com

🕮 Only groups may stay here

🌸 VERSAILLES

Ⓢ Notre-Dame du Cénacle

✉ 68, Avenue de Paris
F-78000 Versailles Yvelines

📞 +33 (0) 1 39 50 21 56

📧 cenacle.versailles@wanadoo.fr
🖥 www.ndcenacle.org/soeurs/pages/versailles

🕮 Open to both men & women

Additional Accommodation

Alsace

🐾 ERGERSHEIM

Ⓢ **Abbaye Notre-Dame d'Altbronn**

✉ 16, Rue Principale
F-67120 Ergersheim Bas Rhin

📞 +33 (0) 3 88 47 95 40
📠 +33 (0) 3 88 47 95 47

📧 abaltbronn@wanadoo.fr

🛏 Open to both men & women

🐾 LUCELLE

Ⓣ **Maison Saint-Bernard**

✉ F-68480 Lucelle Haut-Rhin

📞 +33 (0) 3 89 08 13 13
📠 +33 (0) 3 89 08 10 83

📧 cerl3@wanadoo.fr
🌐 www.cerl-lucelle.fr

🛏 Open to both men & women

🐾 MARIENTHAL

Ⓢ **Hôtellerie Notre-Dame de Marienthal**

✉ 1, Place de la Basilique
F-67500 Marienthal Bas-Rhin

📞 +33 (0) 3 88 93 90 91
📠 +33 (0) 3 88 93 97 01

📧 accueil@basiliquemarienthal.fr
🌐 www.basiliquemarienthal.fr

♿ Discuss access when you book

🛏 Open to both men & women

🐾 OTTMARSHEIM

Ⓢ **Prieuré St-Bernard**

✉ 3, Rue du Couvent
F-68490 Ottmarsheim
Haut-Rhin

📞 +33 (0) 3 89 26 00 27
📠 +33 (0) 3 89 26 19 71

📧 sjm.saintbernard@freesurf.fr
🌐 www.serviteurs.org

♿ Discuss access when you book

🛏 Open to both men & women

🐾 STRASBOURG

Ⓣ **Foyer Notre-Dame**

✉ 3, Rue de Echasses
F-67061 Strasbourg Bas-Rhin

📞 +33 (0) 3 88 32 47 36
📠 +33 (0) 3 88 22 68 47

📧 foyernotredame.fjt@orange.fr

♿ Discuss access when you book

🛏 Open to both men & women

🔳 Open university holidays only

🐾 THAL-MARMOUTIER

Ⓢ **Congrégation des Petites Sœurs Franciscaines**

✉ 1, Rue du Couvent
F-67440 Thal-Marmoutier
Bas-Rhin

📞 +33 (0) 3 88 03 1203
📠 +33 (0) 3 88 03 1200

📧 accueil-st-françois@orange.fr
🌐 sjm.couventdethalmarmoutier.com

🛏 Open to both men & women

Aquitaine

🐾 BAYONNE

Ⓢ **Maison Diocésaine**

✉ 10, Avenue Jean Darrigrand
F-64115 Bayonne Pyrénées
Atlantic

📞 +33 (0) 5 59 58 47 47
📠 +33 (0) 5 59 52 33 98

📧 maisondio@numericable.fr

🛏 Open to both men & women

🐾 DAX

Ⓢ **L'Arrayde**

✉ 26, Rue d'Aspremont
F-40100 Dax Landes

📞 +33 (0) 5 58 58 30 30
📠 +33 (0) 5 58 58 30 31

📧 reservations@arrayade.cef.fr
🌐 www.arrayade.cef.fr

🛏 Open to both men & women

🐾 PERIGUEUX

Ⓣ **Centre Madeleine Delbrêl**

✉ 38, Avenue Georges
Pompidou
F-24000 Perigueux Dordogne

📞 +33 (0) 5 53 35 70 70
📠 +33 (0) 5 53 46 72 94

📧 CAMD24@wanadoo.fr
🌐 www.prh-perigueux.com

♿ Discuss access when you book

🛏 Open to both men & women

Auvergne

🔥 BROMONT-LAMOTHE

Ⓢ Maison Saint-François

✉ Anschald
F-63230 Bromont-Lamothe
Puy-de-Dôme

📞 +33 (0) 4 73 88 99 40
📠 +33 (0) 4 73 88 30 66

🖰 accueilsaintfrancois.anschald@
wanadoo.fr
🖰 www.catholique-clermont.cef.fr

🎎 Only groups of young people
may stay here

🔥 CHANTELLE

Ⓢ Abbaye Bénédictine
St-Vincent

✉ 14, Rue Anne de Beaujeu
F-03140 Chantelle Allier

📞 +33 (0) 4 70 56 62 55
📠 +33 (0) 4 70 56 15 30

🖰 snfb.chantelle@wanadoo.fr
🖰 www.benedictines-chantelle.com

🎎 Open to both men & women

🔥 CONDAT

Ⓣ Maison St-Nazaire

✉ F-15190 Condat Cantal

📞 +33 (0) 4 71 78 53 42

🖰 deceukeleire.mireille@neuf.fr
🖰 www.cantalhebergement.com

🎎 Open to both men & women

🔥 LA CHAISE-DIEU

Ⓢ Communauté Saint-Jean

✉ 2, Place de l'Écho
F-43160 La Chaise-Dieu
Haute-Loire

📞 +33 (0) 4 71 00 05 55
📠 +33 (0) 4 71 00 05 12

🖰 lachaisedieu@stjean.com
🖰 www.abbaye-chaise-dieu.com

🎎 Open to both men & women

🔥 LANGEAC

Ⓢ Monastère Ste-
Catherine de Sienne

✉ 2, Rue du Pont
F-43344 Langeac Haute-Loire

📞 +33 (0) 4 71 77 01 50
📠 +33 (0) 4 71 77 27 61

🖰 dominicaines.langeac@orange.fr
🖰 www.langeac.op.org

🎎 Open to both men & women

🔥 LE-PUY-EN-VELAY

Ⓢ Grand Séminaire
Saint-Georges

✉ 4, Rue Saint-Georges
F-43000 Le-Puy-en-Velay
Haute-Loire

📞 +33 (0) 4 71 09 93 10
📠 +33 (0) 4 71 09 93 17

🖰 accueilstgeorges43@wanadoo.fr
🖰 www.catholique-lepuy.cef.fr

🎎 Open to both men & women

🔥 MARCENAT

Ⓢ Russian Orthodox
Monastère de la Mère
de Dieu du Signe

✉ La Traverse
F-15190 Marcenat Cantal

📞 +33 (0) 4 71 78 84 68
📠 +33 (0) 4 71 78 80 01

🖰 www.ndjasg.club.fr/MDduSigne/

🎎 Open to both men & women

🔥 TAUVES

Ⓣ Maison d'Accueil
St-Joseph

✉ Place du Foirail
F-63690 Tauves
Puy-de-Dôme

📞 +33 (0) 4 73 21 12 49
📠 +33 (0) 4 73 21 11 19

🖰 stjoseph.tauves@orange.fr
🖰 www.village-vacances-auvergne.
com

🎎 Open to both men & women

**Additional
Accommodation**

Brittany
Bretagne

🏠 BREST

🆂🆃 Centre Keraudren

✉ Rue Ernestine de Trémaudan
F-29200 Brest Finistère

📞 +33 (0) 2 98 34 66 34

📧 centre.de.keraudren@wanadoo.fr
🌐 www.centrekeraudren.com

♿ Discuss access when you book

🛏 Open to both men & women

🏠 DINARD

🆂🆃 La Maison Saint-François

✉ 1, Avenue des Acacias
La Vicomté
F-35802 Dinard Ille-et-Vilaine

📞 +33 (0) 2 99 88 25 10
📠 +33 (0) 2 99 88 24 15

📧 st.francois@wanadoo.fr
🌐 www.tressaint.com/cte/dinard/
presntdin.htm

♿ Discuss access when you book

🛏 Open to both men & women

🏠 SAINT-GILDAS-DE-RHUYS

🆂 Abbaye de Rhuys

✉ Place Monseigneur Ropert
F-56370 Saint-Gildas-de-Rhuys Morbihan

📞 +33 (0) 2 97 45 23 10
📠 +33 (0) 2 97 45 35 81

📧 abbaye.de.rhuys@wanadoo.fr
🌐 www.abbaye-de-rhuys.fr/
contact-abbaye-rhuys

♿ Discuss access when you book

🛏 Open to both men & women

🏠 SAINT-JACUT-DE-LA-MER

🆂🆃 L'Abbaye St-Jacut-de-la-Mer

✉ F-22750 Saint-Jacut-de-la-Mer
Côtes d'Armor

📞 +33 (0) 2 96 27 71 19
📠 +33 (0) 2 96 27 79 45

🌐 www.abbaye-st-jacut.com

♿ Discuss access when you book

🛏 Open to both men & women

🏠 SAINT-PIERRE-QUIBERON

🆂🆃 Association Saint Joseph de l'Océan

✉ 16, Avenue de Groix
F-56510 Saint-Pierre-Quiberon Morbihan

📞 +33 (0) 2 97 30 91 29
📠 +33 (0) 2 97 30 80 18

📧 info@relaisdelocean.com
🌐 www.relaisdelocean.com

♿ Discuss access when you book

🛏 Open to both men & women

Burgundy
Bourgogne

🏠 JOIGNY

Ⓢ Centre Sophie Barat

✉ 11, Rue Davier
F-89300 Joigny Yonne

📞 +33 (0) 3 86 92 16 40
📠 +33 (0) 3 86 92 16 49

✉ centre-sophie-barat@wanadoo.fr
🌐 www.centre.barat.free.fr

🛏 Open to both men & women

🏠 NEVERS

Ⓢ Espace Bernadette

✉ Convent of the Sisters of
Charity
34, Rue Saint Gildard
F-58000 Nevers Nièvre

📞 +33 (0) 3 86 71 99 50
📠 +33 (0) 3 86 71 99 51

✉ contact@espace-bernadette.com
🌐 www.sainte-bernadette-nevers.
com/anglais/sanctu_infos

♿ Discuss access when you book

🛏 Open to both men & women

Ⓢ Le Monastère de la Visitation

✉ 49, Route des Saulaies
F-58000 Nevers Nièvre

📞 +33 (0) 3 86 57 37 40
📠 +33 (0) 3 86 57 25 98

✉ visitation.nevers@orange.fr
🌐 www.catho58.cef.fr/diocese/
dreligieux

♿ Discuss access when you book

🛏 Open to both men & women

🏠 PARAY LE MONIAL

Ⓢ Foyer Nazareth

✉ 10, Ave de Charolles
F-71600 Paray le Monial
Saône-et-Loire

📞 +33 (0) 3 85 81 11 88
📠 +33 (0) 3 85 81 56 19

✉ yvette.lecourieux@wanadoo.fr
🌐 www.paroisse-paray.fr/
communautes/srs-foyer-nazareth

🛏 Open to both men & women

🏠 VÉZELAY

Ⓢ Centre Ste-Madeleine

✉ Rue St-Pierre
F-89450 Vézelay Yonne

📞 +33 (0) 3 86 33 22 14

✉ centre.saintemadeleine@
orange.fr
🌐 www.vezelay.cef.fr/fr/ressourcer/
ste_madeleine.php

🛏 Open to both men & women

Champagne
Ardennes

🏠 MESNIL-SAINT-LOUP

Ⓢ Monastère Notre-Dame de la Sainte-Espérance

✉ F-10190 Mesnil-Saint-Loup
Aube

📞 +33 (0) 3 25 40 40 82
📠 +33 (0) 3 25 40 56 35

✉ contact@monastere-mesnil.fr
🌐 www.monastere-mesnil.fr

🛏 Open to both men & women

**Additional
Accommodation**

Corsica

France Compté

Languedoc-Roussillon

🕯 CATERI

Ⓢ Prieuré de St-Esprit

✉ Marcassu
F-20225 Cateri Haute-Corse

📞 +33 (0) 4 95 61 70 21
📠 +33 (0) 4 95 61 71 15

✉ marcassu@wanadoo.fr
✉ www.notredamedesperance.com

👥 Open to both men & women

🕯 L'ILE ROUSSE

Ⓢ Convent of Corbara

✉ Congrégation St-Jean
F-20220 l'Ile Rousse Haute-Corse

📞 +33 (0) 4 95 60 06 73
📠 +33 (0) 4 95 60 09 08

✉ hotellerie.corbara@stjean.com
✉ www.stjean-corbara.com

👥 Open to both men & women

🕯 CONSOLATION-MAISONNETTES

Ⓢ Centre d'Accueil

✉ Fondation de Val
F-25390 Consolation-Maisonnettes Doubs

📞 +33 (0) 3 81 43 67 67
📠 +33 (0) 3 81 43 67 68

✉ fondation.consolation@wanadoo.fr
✉ www.val-consolation.com

👥 Open to both men & women

🕯 LONS LE SAUNIER

Ⓣ Maison d'Accueil de Montciel

✉ 23 Avenue de Montciel
F-39016 Lons le Saunier Jura

📞 +33 (0) 3 84 47 87 60
📠 +33 (0) 3 84 47 87 55

✉ montciel@eglisejura.com
✉ www.montciel.eglisejura.com

♿ Discuss access when you book

👥 Open to both men & women

🕯 CARCASSONNE

Ⓣ Centre Diocésain Notre-Dame de l'Abbaye

✉ 103, Rue Trivalle
F-11000 Carcassonne Aude

📞 +33 (0) 4 68 25 16 65
📠 +33 (0) 4 68 11 47 01

✉ contact@abbaye-carcassonne.com
✉ www.abbaye-carcassonne.com

♿ Discuss access when you book

👥 Open to both men & women

🕯 CASTEIL

L'abbaye de Saint-Martin du Canigou

✉ F-66820 Casteil Pyrénées-Orientales

📞 +33 (0) 4 68 05 50 03
📠 +33 (0) 4 68 05 54 73

✉ visitezabbayestmartin@wanadoo.fr
✉ www.stmartinducanigou.org

🔳 Day visitors only. Bookings necessary.

🕯 MONTPELLIER

Ⓣ Accueil en Famille Organization

✉ 63, Impasse du Brestalou
F-34070 Montpellier Herault

📞 +33 (0) 4 67 56 73 87

✉ accueilenfamille@free.fr
✉ www.accueilenfamille.org

👥 Only groups of young people may stay here

Limousin

🌺 BRIVE-LA-GAILLARDE

⑤ Maison Saint-Antoine

✉ Grottes de Saint Antoine
41, Avenue Edmond Michelet
F-19100 Brive-la-Gaillarde
Corrèze

📞 +33 (0) 5 55 24 10 60
📠 +33 (0) 5 55 17 18 50

✍ hotellerie@fratgsa.org
✍ www.fratgsa.org

♿ Discuss access when you book

🍴 Open to both men & women

Lorraine

🌺 GORZE

⑤ Bethanie Christian Community

✉ Prieuré Notre-Dame et St-Thiébault
F-57680 Gorze
Moselle

📞 +33 (0) 3 87 52 02 28
📠 +33 (0) 3 87 69 91 79

✍ centre.bethanie@wanadoo.fr
✍ www.centre-bethanie.org

🍴 Open to both men & women

🌺 MOULINS-LÈS-METZ

⑤ Ermitage Saint-Jean

✉ 7, Rue des Moulins
F-57160 Moulins-Lès-Metz
Moselle

📞 +33 (0) 3 87 60 02 78
📠 +33 (0) 3 87 60 06 63

✍ www.ermitagesaintjean.fr

🍴 Open to both men & women

Midi-Pyrénées

🌺 BELLEGARDE STE-MARIE

⑤ Abbaye Ste-Marie du Désert

✉ F-31530 Bellegarde Ste Marie
Haute Garonne

📞 +33 (0) 5 62 13 45 45

✍ abstemariedesert@wanadoo.fr
✍ www.abbayedudesert.com

🍴 Open to both men & women

🌺 BOULAUR

⑤ Cistercian Abbey of St. Mary Boulaur

✉ Sister Hôtelière
F-32450 Boulaur Gers

📞 +33 (0) 5 62 65 49 39
📠 +33 (0) 5 62 65 49 37

✍ hotellerie@boulaur.org
✍ www.boulaur.org/fp/Hotellerie.htm

🍴 Open to members of religious orders, men, women & families

🌺 CONQUES

⑤ Abbaye Sainte-Foy

✉ F-12320 Conques Aveyron

📞 +33 (0) 5 65 69 85 12
📠 +33 (0) 5 65 69 89 48

✍ accueil-conques@mondaye.com
www.mondaye.com

🍴 Open to both men & women

⑦ Maison de la Abbaye Sainte-Foy

✉ F-12320 Conques Aveyron

📞 +33 (0) 5 65 69 86 18
📠 +33 (0) 5 65 69 86 18

✍ demandebrochure@capfrance.com
✍ www.capfrance.com

🍴 Open to both men & women

**Additional
Accommodation**

Midi-Pyrénées

🏠 LOURDES

🏠 La Maison Bellevue

✉ Route de Bartrès
F-65100 Lourdes Hautes-Pyrénées

📞 +33 (0) 5 62 94 91 82
📠 +33 (0) 5 62 42 08 75

✉ pmk-lourdes@club-internet.fr
✉ www.mission-catholique-polonaise.net/

🛏 Open to both men & women

🏠 Monastère des Dominicaines

✉ Avenue Jean Prat
F-65100 Lourdes Hautes-Pyrénées

📞 +33 (0) 5 62 46 33 30
📠 +33 (0) 5 62 94 89 76

✉ moplourdes@free.fr
✉ www.moplourdes.com

♿ Discuss access when you book

🛏 Open to both men & women

🏠 Soeurs Dominicaines de la Présentation

✉ 2, Avenue Saint-Joseph
F-65100 Lourdes Hautes-Pyrénées

📞 +33 (0) 5 62 94 07 51
📠 +33 (0) 5 62 94 57 14

✉ foyerfamilial.dominicaines@wanadoo.fr.
✉ www.dominicaines-lourdes.com

🛏 Open to both men & women

🏠 Village des Jeunes

✉ Rue Monseigneur Rodhain
F-65100 Lourdes Hautes-Pyrénées

📞 +33 (0) 5 62 42 79 95
📠 +33 (0) 5 62 42 79 98

✉ village.jeunes@lourdes-france.com
✉ www.lourdes-france.org

🛏 Only groups of young people may stay here

🏠 ROCAMADOUR

🏠 La Maison à Marie

✉ Le Château
F-46500 Rocamadour Lot

📞 +33 (0) 5 65 33 23 23
📠 +33 (0) 5 65 33 243 24

✉ relais.des.remparts@wanadoo.fr

🛏 Open to both men & women

Nord-pas-de-Calais

STELLA-PLAGE

ⓢ Stella Maris

✉ 376, Chemin du Baillarquet
F-62780 Stella-Plage Pas de Calais

📞 +33 (0) 3 21 94 73 65
📠 +33 (0) 3 21 94 63 55

✍ contact@stellamaris-vacances.com
✍ www.stellamaris-vacances.com

♿ Discuss access when you book

✠ Open to men, women & groups

WISQUES

ⓢ Abbaye St-Paul

✉ 50, Rue de l'Ecole
F-62219 Wisques Pas de Calais

📞 +33 (0) 3 21 12 28 50
📠 +33 (0) 3 21 12 28 72

✍ www.abbaye-stpaul-wisques.com

✠ Open to both men & women

Normandy
Normandie

BAYEUX

ⓢ Monastère des Bénédictines

✉ 48, Rue Saint Loup
F-14400 Bayeux Calvados

📞 +33 (0) 2 31 92 85 74
📠 +33 (0) 2 31 92 82 52

✍ hotellerie@lajoiesaintbenoit.com
✍ www.lajoiesaintbenoit.com

✠ Open to both men & women

GOUVILLE-SUR-MER

ⓣ Château des Forges

✉ 121, Rue du Littoral
F-50560 Gouville-Sur-Mer Manche

📞 +33 (0) 2 33 47 85 68
📠 +33 (0) 2 33 45 16 17

✍ asso.escal@wanadoo.fr
✍ www.manche-decouverte.com

✠ Open to men, women & groups

JUAYE-MONDAYE

ⓢ Abbaye St-Martin Mondaye

✉ F-14250 Juaye-Mondaye Calvados

📞 +33 (0) 2 31 92 58 11

✍ hotelier@mondaye.com
✍ www.mondaye.com

✠ Open to both men & women

Additional Accommodation

Normandy
Normandie

🕭 LA CHAPELLE-MONTLIGEON

ⓈⓉ Sanctuary of Our Lady of Montligeon

✉ F-61400 La Chapelle-Montligeon Orne

📞 +33 (0) 2 33 85 17 02
📠 +33 (0) 2 33 85 17 15

📧 infos@sanctuaire-montligeon.com

🖰 www.sanctuaire-montligeon.com

♿ Discuss access when you book

⚤ Open to both men & women

🕭 LE MONT SAINT-MICHEL

Ⓢ Fraternité Monastique de Jérusalem

✉ F-50170 Le Mont-Saint-Michel Manche

📞 +33 (0) 2 33 58 31 71

📧 hotellerie@abbaye-montsaintmichel.com

🖰 www.abbayedumontsaintmichel.cef.fr

⚤ Open to both men & women

ⓈⓉ Maison du Pèlerin
(House of the Pilgrim)

✉ F-50170 Le Mont-Saint-Michel Manche

📞 +33 (0) 2 33 60 14 05

📧 sanctuaire.saint.michel@wanadoo.fr

🖰 www.abbayedumontsaintmichel.cef.fr

⚤ Open to men, women & groups

🕭 LISIEUX

ⓈⓉ Ermitage Sainte Thérèse

✉ 23, Rue du Carmel
F-14100 Lisieux Calvados

📞 +33 (0) 2 31 48 55 10
📠 +33 (0) 2 31 48 55 27

📧 ermitage-ste-therese@therese-de-lisieux.com
🖰 www.therese-de-lisieux.cef.fr

⚤ Open to both men & women

ⓈⓉ Foyer Louis et Zélie Martin

✉ 15, Avenue Sainte-Thérèse
F-14100 Lisieux Calvados

📞 +33 (0) 2 31 62 09 33
📠 +33 (0) 2 31 62 88 65

📧 foyer-martin@therese-de-lisieux.com
🖰 www.therese-de-lisieux.cef.fr

⚤ Open to men, women & groups

🕭 SAINT-JEAN-LE-THOMAS

ⓈⓉ Centre d'Accueil L'Etoile de la Mer

✉ Allée du Presbytère
F-50530 Saint-Jean-le-Thomas Manche

📞 +33 (0) 2 33 48 84 24
📠 +33 (0) 2 33 48 99 80

📧 galaxie@etoiledelamer.org
🖰 www.etoiledelamer.org

♿ Discuss access when you book

⚤ Open to men, women & groups

🕭 SÉES

ⓈⓉ Centre d'Accueil La Source

✉ 25, Rue de Loutreuil
F-61500 Sées Orne

📞 +33 (0) 2 33 27 96 90
📠 +33 (0) 2 33 28 86 18

📧 la.source.accueil@wanadoo.fr
🖰 www.diocesedeseez.cef.fr

♿ Discuss access when you book

⚤ Only groups may stay here

🕭 SOLIGNY LA TRAPPE

Ⓢ Abbey of La Trappe

✉ F-61380 Soligny La Trappe Orne

📞 +33 (0) 2 33 84 17 00

📧 hotelier@latrappe.fr
www.latrappe.fr

♿ Discuss access when you book

⚤ Open to both men & women

Pays-de-la-Loire

✿ ANGERS

ⓢ Bon-Pasteur Accueil

✉ Rue Marie-Euphrasie Pelletier)
F-49045 Angers Maine-et-Loire

📞 +33 (0) 2 41 72 12 80
📠 +33 (0) 2 41 72 18 99

✉ info@bpaccueil.org
🖱 www.buonpastoreint.org

♿ Discuss access when you book

👪 Open to men, women & groups

✿ PONTMAIN

ⓢ Relais Le Bocage

✉ 2, Rue de Mausson
F-53220 Pontmain Mayenne

📞 +33 (0) 2 43 30 26 00
📠 +33 (0) 2 43 30 26 01

✉ relais.bocage@wanadoo.fr
🖱 www.relais-le-bocage.com

♿ Discuss access when you book

👪 Open to men, women & groups

✿ SAINT-JEAN D'ASSÉ

ⓢ Monastere de Notre-Dame de la Merci-Dieu

✉ F-72380 Saint-Jean-d'Asse Sarthe

📞 +33 (0) 2 43 25 25 49
📠 +33 (0) 2 43 25 20 36

✉ monastere@merci-dieu.com
🖱 www.merci-dieu.com

👤 Only priests, nuns & religious office holders may stay here

✿ ST-LAURENT SUR SÉVRE

ⓣ Maison d'Accueil Montfortaine

✉ 2, Rue Jean-Paul II
F-85290 St-Laurent sur Sévre Vendée

📞 +33 (0) 2 51 64 37 05
📠 +33 (0) 2 51 64 87 34

✉ maiacc.montfort@orange.fr
🖱 www.vendeesevretourisme.fr

👪 Open to men, women & groups

📅 Open in July and August only

Picardy
Picardie

✿ AMIENS

ⓢ Centre St-François de Salles

✉ 384, Rue St-Fuscien
F-80000 Amiens Somme

📞 +33 (0) 3 22 33 27 10
📠 +33 (0) 3 22 95 14 03

✉ centre-st-francois@diocese-amiens.com
🖱 www.catholique-amiens.cef.fr

👪 Open to men, women & groups

**Additional
Accommodation**

Provence/
Alps/
Côtes d'Azur

🎎 AIX-EN-PROVENCE

🅢 La Baume

✉ 1770, Chemin de la Blaque
F-13090 Aix-en-Provence
Bouches du Rhone

☎ +33 (0) 4 42 16 10 30
📠 +33 (0) 4 42 26 88 67

🖅 www.labaumeaix.com

🛏 Open to men, women & groups

🎎 ARLES

🅢 Prieuré Notre-Dame-des-Champs

✉ Domaine de Bouchard
F-13200 Arles Bouches-du-Rhône

☎ +33 (0) 4 90 97 00 55
📠 +33 (0) 4 90 97 00 74

🖅 hotelleriebouchaud@orange.fr

🛏 Open to both men & women

🎎 GOULT

🆃 Hôtellerie Notre-Dame de Lumières

✉ F-84220 Goult Vaucluse

☎ +33 (0) 4 90 72 22 18
📠 +33 (0) 4 90 72 38 55

🖅 hotellerie@notredamedelumieres.com
🖅 www.notredamedelumieres.com

♿ Discuss access when you book

🛏 Open to men, women & groups

🎎 GRASSE

🅢🆃 La Maison Ste-Antoine

✉ 6, Boulevard Gambetta
F-06130 Grasse Alpes-Maritimes

☎ +33 (0) 4 93 36 21 72
📠 +33 (0) 4 93 36 10 60

🖅 foyer.stantoine@wanadoo.fr
🖅 www.foyer-stantoine.com

👤 Open to women only

🎎 LA CRAU

🅢🆃 Château de la Castille

✉ Route de la Farlède
F-83260 Solliès-Ville La Crau Var

☎ +33 (0) 4 94 00 80 40
📠 +33 (0) 4 94 00 80 42

🖅 fondation@domaine-castille.fr
🖅 www.domaine-castille.fr

🛏 Open to men, women & groups

🎎 LA TRINITÉ

🅢🆃 Sanctuaire Notre-Dame de Laghet

✉ F-06340 La Trinité Alpes-Maritimes

☎ +33 (0) 4 92 41 50 50
📠 +33 (0) 4 92 41 50 59

🖅 sanctuairelaghet@orange.fr
🖅 www.sanctuaire-laghet.cef.fr

♿ Discuss access when you book

🛏 Open to men, women & groups

🎎 MENTON

🅢🆃 Maison d'Accueil Le Home

✉ 6, Rue du Louvre
F-6500 Menton Alpes-Maritimes

☎ +33 (0) 4 93 35 75 51
📠 +33 (0) 4 92 10 38 34

🖅 www.homelouvre.fr.st

🛏 Open to men, women & groups

🎎 SAINTE-BAUME

🅢🆃 Hôtellerie de la Ste-Baume

✉ F-83640 Plan d'Aups Sainte-Baume Var

☎ +33 (0) 4 42 04 54 84
📠 +33 (0) 4 42 62 55 56

🖅 hsbaume@gmail.com
🖅 www.hotellerie-saintebaume.com

🛏 Open to both men & women

🎎 ST-PAUL DE VENCE

🅢🆃 Dominicaines de la Sainte-Famille Passe-Prest

✉ F-06570 St-Paul de Vence Alpes-Maritimes

☎ +33 (0) 4 93 32 53 93
📠 +33 (0) 4 93 32 83 09

🖅 couventpasseprest@wanadoo.fr

🛏 Open to both men & women

🎎 TARASCON

🅢 Abbaye St-Michel de Frigolet Hotellerie St-Michelle

✉ Route de l'Abbaye de Frigolet
F-13151 Tarascon Bouches de Rhone

☎ +33 (0) 4 90 90 52 50

🖅 hotellerie@frigolet.com
🖅 www.frigolet.com

🛏 Open to both men & women

🎎 VILLEDIEU

🆃 La Magnanarié

✉ F-84110 Villedieu Vaucluse

☎ +33 (0) 4 90 28 92 58
📠 +33 (0) 4 90 28 92 58

🖅 infos@magnanarie.com
🖅 www.magnanarie.com

🛏 Open to men, women & groups

Rhone-Alps

🕯 AIX-LES-BAINS

ⓢ Hotel Notre Dame des Eaux

✉ 6, Boulevarde des Côtes
F-73015 Aix-les-Bains Savoie

📞 +33 (0) 4 79 61 13 87
📠 +33 (0) 4 79 34 06 96

✎ contact@notredamedeseaux.fr
✎ www.notredamedeseaux.fr

🕮 Open to men, women & groups

🕯 BELLEY

ⓣ Maison St-Anthelme

✉ 37, Rue Ste-Marie Belley
F-01300 Belley Ain

📞 +33 (0) 4 79 81 02 29
📠 +33 (0) 4 79 81 02 78

✎ stanthelme@orange.fr
✎ www.maisonsaintanthelme.com

🕮 Open to men, women & groups

🕯 COLOMBIER-LE-CARDINAL

ⓣ Le Château des Célestins

✉ F-07430 Colombier-le-Cardinal Ardèche

📞 +33 (0) 4 75 34 83 31
📠 +33 (0) 4 75 34 15 65

✎ chateaudescelestins@orange.fr
✎ www.chateaudescelestins.com

🕮 Open to men, women & groups

🕯 EVIAN

ⓢ Prieuré Saint-François de Sales

✉ 12, Route du Monastère
F-74500 Evian Haute Savoie

📞 +33 (0) 4 50 75 24 20

✎ evian.monatiscali@wanadoo.fr

🕮 Open to men only

🕯 LA SALETTE

ⓢ Sanctuaire de Notre Dame de La Salette

✉ F-38970 La Salette Isère

📞 +33 (0) 4 76 30 32 90
📠 +33 (0) 4 76 30 03 65

✎ infos@lasalette.cef.fr
✎ www.lasalette.cef.fr

🕮 Open to both men & women

🕯 ST BERNARD DU TOUVET

ⓢ Monastère Notre-Dame des Petites Roches

✉ F-38660 St-Bernard du Touvert, Isère

📞 +33 (0) 4 76 08 31 13
📠 +33 (0) 4 76 08 32 17

✎ hotellerie.petitesroches@gmail.com
✎ www.bernardine.org/touvete.html

🕮 Open to both men & women

🕯 ST-LAURENT-LES-BAINS

ⓢ Abbaye Notre Dame des Neiges

✉ Maison de Zachée
F-07590 St-Laurent-les-Bains Ardèche

📞 +33 (0) 4 66 46 59 00
(only between 1000–1200 on Mon, Thurs and Fri)
📠 +33 (0) 4 66 46 59 10

✎ maisondezachee@notredamedesneiges.com
✎ www.notredamedesneiges.com

🕮 Open to both men & women

U

ALL OUTWARD FORMS OF RELIGION ARE
almost useless, and are the causes of endless
strife. Believe me there is a great power silently
working for all things for good—behave
yourself and never mind the rest.

BEATRIX POTTER
BRITISH CHILDREN'S AUTHOR (1866–1943)

UK

HERE'S SOMETHING IN GREAT BRITAIN to keep the fussiest traveller content, be it a ruined castle, a showpiece village, serene countryside, the trappings of royalty or the prevailing sense of a robust history. You can wander around a country garden, or barter for a bargain in a bustling street market. If the weather turns inclement, head to a gallery or museum—or use a rainy spell as the perfect excuse to spend up big in the trendy department stores.

Romantic Gretna Green is just across the border in Scotland, and Edinburgh and its famous castle at the top of the Royal Mile, is further north. St Andrews, where monks attached to the village cathedral are reputed to have invented the game of golf, is the legendary home of the sport. Or draw on the rich cultural heritage of Wales with its medieval castles and rugged countryside. Try speaking 'Wenglish', a dialect mix of Welsh and English.

Come rain or shine, though, the centre of much British social life is the pubs. These mostly cosy establishments are the perfect places to meet the locals over a pint and a plate of bangers and mash.

Sadly, things have been somewhat less friendly over the years when it comes to religion, especially after Henry VIII abandoned the Catholic Church and set up his own flourishing Church of England.

Notwithstanding these religious troubles, in days of yore English parish priests continued to provide hospitality—the original 'bed and breakfast'?—for many a weary traveller, a custom which survives into the 21st century among both Catholic and Protestant orders.

London

SOME SAY A LIFETIME IN LONDON is not long enough to see the place properly. The simplest way to take in this huge, always-on-the-move city—one of the world's greatest—is to get out the A–Z and head off on foot. Wander the streets at your leisure or, if you need some quiet 'down time', this vibrant, cosmopolitan metropolis has a surprising number of green spaces. Hyde Park is perfect for a leisurely stroll—unless it's Sunday morning when Speakers' Corner comes to life. Or sit by the Thames and watch the world float by.

As the cultural capital of England, London is home to first-class theatre, ballet and opera, and an extraordinary number of theatres and concert halls are within easy distance of the tube. Summer kicks off with fairs and festivals and the entire population seems to head outdoors. If any sunshine doesn't last, stay in and watch the best of the British—or the football—on the telly, or retreat to the 'local' for a pint.

Indulge in a formal high tea, something of a tradition ever since the 18th-century Duchess of Bedford complained of that late afternoon 'sinking feeling' and invented a cure. You can splurge on posh sandwiches and cakes at the Ritz, Claridges or Fortnum & Mason. Otherwise, jostle with all and sundry among the street stalls in Brick Lane Market where you can feast on cockles and mussels, whelks and winkles, and the ubiquitous jellied eel.

These days, in a melting-pot of religious diversity, just about every mainstream and obscure religious denomination can be found in this vast city. Christian monasteries, convents and religious hostels are scattered throughout, a number close to tourist attractions. Many welcome overnight guests—of all faiths and none.

01

Franciscan Sisters of Malta

The Catholic religious order of the Franciscan Sisters of The Sacred Heart of Jesus (more commonly known as The Sisters of Malta) was co-founded in Gozo, Malta in 1880 by Mother Margherita De Brincat, the first Mother General, and local priest Father Joseph Diacono. The order is now international; members follow the teachings of St Francis of Assisi.

❧ In 1960 the order established a branch in **Pimlico** where the traditional role of the sisters is to offer accommodation to Maltese families who are seeking medical treatment in London. However, the sisters also welcome tourists on a 'room available' basis, a service provided throughout the year. The convent is in a typical five-storey, 18th-century Victorian house, in a handy corner position in the heart of London. Single and twin guestrooms are available and all share a bathroom on the same floor. There is a small lounge room for the use of guests and meals are available.

❧ Shops, cafés, pubs and restaurants are in easy distance of the convent. The local Tachbrook Street market is nearby and is open Monday to Saturday from 0800 until 1800.

❧ The guesthouse is close to the major Victoria Bus, Underground and National Rail transport hub, and is in walking distance of **Buckingham Palace**, **Westminster Cathedral** and the **Houses of Parliament**.

✉ 9 St George's Drive
Pimlico
London SW1V 4DJ
(On the corner of St George's Drive and Hugh Street)

🏨 from £30.00 pp, including breakfast.

☎ +44 (0) 20 7834 4020
📠 +44 (0) 20 7976 6862

✉ fransisuk@btopenworld.com

🖥 www.fcjmalta.org

☞ Take the train or bus to Victoria Station from where it is a short distance to the convent.

✝ **Sunday Mass**
0700
Chapel of the Franciscan Sisters
9 St George's Drive
Pimlico

⚭ Open to both men & women

Open Houses
London

PLACES OF INTEREST ⟨ The **Chelsea Flower Show**, one of Britain's best-loved events, is held for a week at the end of each spring in the gardens of the Royal Hospital in Chelsea. Visitors can wander through the display gardens, seek the advice of horticultural experts and inspect hundreds of exhibits.

⟨ Nearby is **Cheyne Walk**, one of the area's most fashionable and exclusive streets. English guitarist **Keith Richards** (b. 1943) and singer **Sir Mick Jagger** (b. 1943), both of Rolling Stones fame, were near neighbours here for a while. Soccer star **George Best** (1946–2005), suffragette **Emmeline (Emily) Pankhurst** (1858–1928) and actor **Lord Olivier** (1907–1989) also lived in the street. Blue plaques mark the houses once lived in by the rich and famous.

⟨ The houses in Cheyne Walk are modest, however, compared to English royal residences, especially the grandeur of **Buckingham Palace**. Nearby **Clarence House** in The Mall was once home to **Queen Elizabeth the Queen Mother**. Today it's the London residence of the **Prince of Wales**, the **Duchess of Cornwall**, and **Princes William** and **Harry**. Many of the rooms open to the public remain unchanged since the Queen Mother's death in 2002. Both palaces have sections open to the public during summer.

⟨ **Lambeth Palace**, the official London home of the **Archbishop of Canterbury, Dr Rowan Williams** (b. 1950), and his family, stands on the banks of the Thames across from the Houses of Parliament near Westminster Bridge. Group visits can be arranged by contacting the Lambeth Palace Events Administrator who can organize guided tours of the crypt, chapel and library. At designated times throughout the year the gardens are open to the general public.

⟨ These days the de-consecrated parish church of **St Mary** at **Lambeth** has a new role as London's **Garden Museum**. Royal gardeners in the 17th century and importers of exotic flora, John (1608–1662) and John the Elder (1570–1638) of the Tradescant family, are buried in the churchyard where they once toiled.

❦ On the riverside near Lambeth Palace, you can get a bird's eye view of the city from the **London Eye**, otherwise known as the Millennium Wheel. This 440-foot-high landmark on Westminster Bridge Road circles on a 30-minute, slow-moving panoramic 'flight'. On a clear day passengers can see **Windsor Castle** almost 30 miles away. Next to the London Eye a permanent exhibition of surrealist **Salvador Dali**'s (1904–1989) sculptures are on display in the **County Hall Gallery**. One of the artist's 'melted clocks' statues is displayed outside the hall and draws much attention. More melted clocks, Dali's lobster telephone and his iconic Mae West Lips Sofa are inside.

❦ The **Tate to Tate Boat** (catamaran) operates every 40 minutes during gallery opening times between the **Tate Britain** (from a state-of-the-art new pier) and the **Tate Modern** galleries, with a stop at the London Eye.

❦ The Pimlico Road **Farmer's Market** (near Ebury Street) is held every Saturday morning and is gaining a reputation as one of London's best. The nearest tube is Sloane Square.

FOOD AND DRINK ❦ Fancy a pint? The old English pub **The Black Friar** was built on the site of an old monastery beside Blackfriars Station. A jolly—and obviously well-fed—monk welcomes guests from above the front door and the monastic theme continues inside where, if it were not for the bartenders pulling pints, you might think you were in a very busy and very thirsty monastery. *Please note Blackfriars Station will be closed for renovation until the end of 2011.*

✉ 174 Queen Victoria Street, Blackfriars

✆ +44 (0) 20 7236 5474 £££

❦ No wonder Princess Diana and Fergie enjoyed an occasional night out at the **Admiral Codrington** ('the Cod') where Australian singer Kylie Minogue celebrated receiving an OBE award. The comfortable, welcoming pub in Kensington boasts a thoroughly up-market English bar, good food and a pleasant outdoor garden area.

✉ 17 Mossop Street, Kensington

✆ +44 (0) 20 7581 0005 £££–££££

❦ After a day out at the Chelsea Flower Show you could dine in fine style at the nearby **Restaurant Gordon Ramsay**. This Michelin 3-star restaurant is owned by television's celebrated chef and serves the finest of French cuisine.

✉ Royal Hospital Road, Chelsea

✆ +44 (0) 20 7352 4441 £££££

02

More House

Located in **South Kensington**, More House, a Catholic Chaplaincy Centre for the Universities of London, is named after the English saint **Thomas More** (1478–1535). The More House guesthouse is run by the Canonesses of St Augustine, an order of Augustinian nuns who have branches in France and Belgium and, since 1886, a convent at Hayward's Heath in West Sussex.

❡ For most of the academic year More House operates as a student hostel. However, single and twin rooms are let to tourists during university holidays (July and August). The guestrooms are basic, but adequately furnished. None have en suite facilities and shared bathrooms are located on each floor. The rooms facing Cromwell Road can sometimes be noisy but quieter rooms towards the rear of the building are available. Continental or full English breakfast is the only meal served but pubs, cafés and restaurants are only a short stroll away. Facilities include a lift, telephone, Internet access, a television lounge, a games room and a laundry with coin-operated washers and dryers. Daily Mass is celebrated in the chapel. One of the advantages of staying at More House is its premier position, just yards from the main Underground line (Gloucester Road Station on the Piccadilly Line) to Heathrow Airport, with easy access to all directions.

✉ 53 Cromwell Road
South Kensington
London sw7 2eh

🏨 from £38.00 pp, including breakfast.

🗓 Open in July and August, during university holidays.

☎ +44 (0) 20 7584 2040
+44 (0) 20 7581 5748

✉ office@morehouse.co.uk
🖱 www.morehouse.co.uk

🚇 Take the tube to Gloucester Road Station. Exit onto Cromwell Road and turn right. More House is only yards away on the right-hand side.

✝ **Sunday Mass**
0700, 0800, 0900, 1100 (sung Latin), 1230, 1630 & 1900.
Brompton Oratory
Brompton Road
South Kensington

⛪ Open to men, women & groups

PLACES OF INTEREST ❧ More House is situated opposite both the **Victoria and Albert Museum** and the **Natural History Museum**, and close to the Gloucester Road Underground train station. **The Science Museum** and its ever-popular IMAX 3D Cinema is just around the corner in Exhibition Road.

❧ Further along Cromwell Road stands **Brompton Oratory**, one of London's major Catholic landmarks. The Oratory choir performs during the dramatic sung Latin Mass at 1100 each Sunday. Notwithstanding the solemn religious ceremony, the Mass is also an absorbing piece of theatre. **Jennifer Paterson** (1928–1999) of *The Two Fat Ladies* (television cookery program produced by the BBC) fame was a regular worshipper at Brompton Oratory and her funeral Mass was celebrated here. Paterson lived in a flat behind Westminster Cathedral. Her co-star, **Clarissa Dickson-Wright** (b. 1947), remarked on her friend's death: 'Jennifer is no doubt sitting on a cloud, with her bike parked beside her, smoking a fag and discussing menus with St Peter, singing hymns with St Lucy and writing recipes with St Honore before going off to lunch with Noel Coward.' [*www.bbc.co.uk/food*]

❧ Walk further along Brompton Road and you will find yourself at London's iconic, up-market department store. **Harrods'** sales are renowned events, taking place each January and June/ July. A celebrity is always on hand to declare the sale 'open'. In 2009 English-born actor Mischa Barton opened the summer sale, following in the footsteps of Welsh soprano Katherine Jenkins and actor Kim Cattrell (*Sex in the City*). Exclusive shops and restaurants have proliferated in this area.

❧ Take a leisurely ramble around the 270-acre **Kensington Gardens**, once the private playground of the royal tenants of Kensington Palace. The royal residence is situated at the western end of the park; the **Diana, Princess of Wales memorial** and children's playground can be found just off Rotten Row, the track used by horseriders in the park. A handy café has opened next to the playground. Exhibitions are often staged inside the palace with one of the most popular being a display of Princess Diana's gowns.

❧ **Spencer House** at 27 St James Place is the ancestral home of Princess Diana. The 18th-century house overlooks Green Park and its extensive gardens are open to the public on set days.

Open Houses
London

¶ Expansive **Hyde Park** is nearby. Note that those comfortable-looking, lolling-about-in canvas chairs scattered around are only for those willing to pay.

¶ Fans of British television will be tempted by the chance to have a look behind the scenes of many BBC-produced shows in a backstage tour at the BBC **Television Centre** in Shepherd's Bush. Tours run for around 2 hours and must be pre-booked.

◿ www.bbc.co.uk/tours

☏ +44 (0) 28 9053 5904
☏ 0370 901 1227 (local call)

¶ Take a guided tour of the **Royal Albert Hall** in Kensington Gore any day between Friday and Tuesday. Sometimes concert rehearsals coincide with a tour—a real treat.

¶ A branch of **Christies Fine Art Auctioneers** is at 85 Old Brompton Road. The company offers a free, no-obligation valuation service to curious sellers and it is just the place to start a unique art collection or pick up a well priced piece of jewellery. Auctions are held two or three times each week.

FOOD AND DRINK ¶ The Anglican Church of **St Martin-in-the-Fields** in Trafalgar Square is an unlikely venue for a good restaurant. However, tucked away beneath the church, under sweeping arches and thick stone pillars the **Café in the Crypt** serves modern British cuisine every day of the week. Tables are arranged over the graves of such notables as **Thomas Chippendale** (1718–1779), whose furniture workshop was located nearby, and actress **Nell Gwynne** (1650–1687), the mistress of **King Charles II** (1630–1685). The café is open every day for eat-in or take-away meals, tea and coffee, and even a full English breakfast. It's also an intriguing venue for a romantic dinner by candlelight. Wine is served.

✉ Duncannon Street, Trafalgar Square

☏ +44 (0) 20 7766 1158   ££–£££

¶ Enjoy a taste of Paris at *L'heure du thé* in the gracious **Ladurée Tea Room** at **Harrods** department store. The menu lists a curiously named *Religieuse pistache*. Apparently this sinful delicacy is so called because it resembles a nun's (*religieuse*) habit. A tenuous connection perhaps—but they do taste rather divine!

✉ Ground Flr, 87–135 Brompton Road, Knightsbridge

☏ +44 (0) 20 7893 8293   ££££

03

Newman House

Named in honour of the Catholic Cardinal and Englishman **John Henry Newman** (1801–1890), and situated in an area of university colleges, Newman House is run by the Central Catholic Chaplaincy to the London Universities and operates as a hall of residence for students of the nearby **University of London**. The centre is open to tourists during university holiday periods. The single and twin guestrooms are small but adequately furnished, with a wash basin and refrigerator included. There are no en suite facilities but bathrooms are located on all floors. The house is centrally heated throughout with television rooms, telephones, kitchens, library, chapel and a small bar.

◖ Breakfast is on a self-serve basis and no other meals are available. There is a coin-operated laundry with iron provided. BYO towel.

◖ In 2008, to fulfil a Vatican request, Cardinal Newman's remains were excavated from the Oratorian graveyard in Rednal near Birmingham and reburied in the Chapel of St Charles Borromeo at the Birmingham Oratory of St Philip Neri in Edgbaston. This was in the wake of the Cardinal becoming a candidate for sainthood, but the exhumation caused much controversy. Cardinal Newman's last wishes were that he be buried near his dear friend and companion of 30 years, fellow Oratorian Father Ambrose St John (1815–1875). Both Cardinal Newman and Father St John converted from Anglican clergy to Catholic priests in 1845. In 2009, Pope Benedict XVI approved the beatification of Cardinal Newman, the stage before canonisation.

✉ 111 Gower Street
Bloomsbury
London WC1E 6AR

🛏 from £22.00 pp,
including breakfast.

🗓 Open during university holidays.

📞 +44 (0) 20 7383 6370

✉ enquiries@
universitycatholic.com

✎ www.londoncatholic.
com/newman

☞ Gower Street is just a short walk from Warren Street or Goodge Street tube stations.

✝ Sunday Mass
1030, 1930 and during university vacation at **1030.**
Newman House Chapel
Gower Street
Bloomsbury.

⚇ Open to men, women & groups

Open Houses
London

PLACES OF INTEREST ❧ Newman House is within walking distance of the **British Museum**, the **West End** theatres and **Oxford Street**'s major department stores. The complex is part of the historic **Bloomsbury** area, playground of London's artistic and literary jet set, an exclusive club known as the Bloomsbury Group, whose members included writers **Virginia Woolf** (1882–1941, author of *Mrs Dalloway*, later to inspire the film *The Hours* starring Nicole Kidman), **Vita Sackville-West** (1892–1962, *All Passion Spent*), **E. M. Forster** (1879–1970, *A Room with a View*) and **John Maynard Keynes** (1883–1946, *The General Theory of Employment, Interest and Money*). Woolf resided at 29 Fitzroy Square, Bloomsbury between 1907 and 1911; blue metal plaques mark the homes formerly occupied by other Bloomsbury members. Later, Sackville-West and her husband Sir **Harold Nicolson** (1886–1968) moved to **Sissinghurst Castle** in Kent. After Vita's death her son **Nigel Nicolson** (1917–2004) wrote a fascinating account of his parents' 'open' marriage titled *Portrait of a Marriage* (University Of Chicago Press)

❧ The nightingales may have long gone from the city's first 'garden square' but **Bloomsbury Square** is still a peaceful, semi-private oasis where music groups often perform on summer weekends. Across the street, the leafier **Russell Square** has a pleasant park café, a splashy fountain and—if you're in luck—a Punch and Judy show on the weekends. Close by is the **British Museum** and, with a collection of more than 1 million artefacts covering a period of 2 million years, there is no excuse for boredom.

❧ Two of the loveliest streets in Bloomsbury are **Woburn Walk** and **Sicilian Avenue**. Both are closed to traffic and a delight to explore. One, where the Irish poet **W. B. Yeats** (1865–1939) once lived, reflects the refinement of the Victorian era. The other, thought to be paved with Sicilian limestone, is more laid-back 'Italian flair meets English charm'.

¶ Take in the sights, sounds and atmosphere of **Covent Garden Market**, one of London's favourites. In the 13th century, the area was named *Convent Garden* as it was originally an expansive walled estate used by Benedictine monks as a market garden to grow fruit and vegetables to raise revenue. The monastery has disappeared and today the market showcases the best of British art, crafts and fashion; there are speciality shops, restaurants, cafés and bars, with atmosphere provided by wandering minstrels and street musicians. The original fruit, flower and vegetable market has moved to a 60-acre site in the **Nine Elms** district near Wandsworth in south-west London.

¶ Homesick Aussies can drop by the **Australia Shop** at 27 Maiden Lane in the Covent Garden Complex to stock up on Vegemite, eucalyptus drops and Bundy rum.

¶ Some 'high' culture can be had at the **Royal Opera House**, home of The Royal Opera and The Royal Ballet, opposite the market, where you can take a fascinating backstage tour.

FOOD AND DRINK ✆ Cheap and cheerful, the **Spaghetti House** and **Wagamama Noodle Bars** both serve comforting, filling food, equally satisfying for the taste buds and wallets alike.

✉ Spaghetti House 20 Sicilian Avenue, Bloomsbury
☎ +44 (0) 20 7405 5215 ££
✉ Wagamama 4 Streatham Street, Bloomsbury
☎ +44 (0) 20 7323 9223 ££

¶ Treat the kids to dinner at the **Rainforest Café** in London's West End where they'll get a close-up view of some of Africa's exotic animals. Book in advance. Children are always welcome.

✉ Shaftesbury Avenue, Piccadilly Circus
☎ +44 (0) 20 7434 3111 £££-£££££

¶ **The Refectory Restaurant** in **St Paul's Cathedral** is open every day for lunch, as well as morning and afternoon tea. The café is situated in the Cathedral Crypt where distinguished naval and military heroes **Admiral Lord Nelson** (1758–1805) and the **Duke of Wellington** (1769–1852) rest in peace alongside other English luminaries.

✉ St Paul's Church Yard, City of London
☎ +44 (0) 20 7248 2469 ££-£££
✝ Sunday Services 0800, 1015, 1130, 1515 & 1800

¶ The salubrious restaurant at **Claridge's** in Brook Street, still the refuge of princes and prime ministers, has now been taken over by celebrity chef Gordon Ramsay. If you love mushy comfort food, give it a miss.

✉ Upper Brook Street, Westminster
☎ +44 (0) 20 7499 0099 ££££

Open Houses
London

04

The Highbury Centre

The Highbury Centre is a homely Christian guesthouse run by the Centre for Global Christian Leadership in the former premises of the Foreign Missions Club. Located in Highbury in North London, it has been offering hospitality since 1893. The club has comfortably furnished single, double and family guestrooms available to overseas visitors of all religious denominations, with a maximum stay of 3 months for students. The club is family friendly and children are made welcome. Family rooms are furnished with bunk beds for the kids, and standard single and double guestrooms are available with en suite facilities or on a share bathroom basis. All guestrooms are centrally heated. Hairdryers are provided, and tea and coffee making facilities are available in each room. Be aware that there are a number of interior stairs, no lift and no wheelchair access.

◖ Well-furnished common rooms overlook well-tended gardens and a small children's playground. Guests can relax in a television room or in the spacious lounge room. There is a large dining room where breakfast is served, a laundry for the use of the guests, a children's play room and parking is free. Credit cards are accepted (except for AMEX). Football fans will note that the centre is ½ mile from the home of the Arsenal Club's **Emirates Stadium**.

✉ 20–26 Aberdeen Park
Highbury
London N5 2BJ

🏨 from £37.00 pp,
including breakfast

📞 +44 (0) 20 7226 2663
📠 +44 (0) 20 7704 1853

✍ enquiries@
thehighburycentre.org

✍ www.thehighburycentre.
org

☞ The Highbury Centre
is ½ mile north-east of
Highbury and Islington
tube and National
Rail stations. There
is no taxi rank at the
station.

✝ Sunday Services
0900, 1100 & 1800.
Christ Church
(Anglican)
155 Highbury Grove
Highbury.

👥 Open to men, women
& groups

PLACES OF INTEREST ❧ **Highbury** was once home to **George Orwell** (1903–1950). The English novelist and renowned author of *Animal Farm* lived at 27b Canonbury Square, possibly a little less fashionable in those days than in more recent times when nearby 1 Richmond Crescent was the home of former British Prime Minister **Tony Blair** (b. 1953) and wife **Cherie** (b. 1954). The Blairs later upgraded to a prime location in Downing Street.

❧ Once famous for its antique shops, the **Camden Passage Mall** has now been taken over by a developer, although some dealers continue to trade in the surrounding laneways. In another blow, the **Camden Lock Market** on Chalk Farm Road was recently devastated by fire. The good news is that the market has re-opened, with hundreds of stalls selling fashion, jewellery, artworks— you name it. The nearest stations are Camden or Chalk Farm, or get there by waterbus along the Regent's Canal.

❧ Local artists work from studios inside the **Candid Arts Trust** building in Torrens Street near the Angel tube station. The artists exhibit their creations at the **Angel Art Market** on Torrens Street each weekend between 1100 and 1800. **The Nag's Head** (covered) flea market in Seven Sisters Road, Holloway is open every day. Get off at the Holloway Road tube station.

❧ Scenes from English film director **Sir Richard Eyre**'s (b. 1943) movie *Notes on a Scandal* starring leading ladies **Cate Blanchett** (b. 1969) and the highly respected York-born actor **Dame Judy Dench** (b. 1934) were filmed at the Islington Arts and Media School in Turle Road.

❧ You might like to check out the program at the **Pleasance Theatre** in Carpenters Mews, a tiny independent venue, staging theatre, comedy, music and dance. **The Little Angel Theatre** in Dagmar Passage, located in an old temperance hall, is now a dedicated puppet theatre (classes are also conducted) where adults have as much fun during the performances as the children. **The Almeida Theatre,** on Almeida Street, is one of London's most respected, frequently attracting star names to appear in the intimate auditorium that started life as a working men's institute.

Open Houses
London

❡ **Sadlers Wells Theatre** in Rosebery Avenue, Islington is the UK's home of dance. The theatre opened in 1683. When mineral springs were discovered on the property, the water was promoted as 'health giving'. People came from far and wide to 'take the waters' and watch the shows. The well can be seen inside the theatre today.

❡ Football fans can take the requisite tour of the museum at the **Emirates Stadium** where the history of the **Arsenal Football Club** is on display. Walk from Highbury and Islington station.

❡ The **Gillespie Park Nature Reserve** in Highbury is a pleasant area to commune with nature. The park is the headquarters of the Islington Ecology Centre which offers information on the latest 'green' innovations.

❡ The unusual **London Canal Museum** in New Wharf Road depicts the history of London's waterways. Included in the price of admission is a guided boat tour along the 19th-century Islington tunnel, part of the Regent's Canal. Bookings are necessary.

FOOD AND DRINK ❧ Refuel on generous servings of traditional, home-cooked British food at **The S & M Café** (Sausages & Mash Café) in Islington. Open every day and with an extensive menu, the sausages and mash with home-made gravy and mushy peas is a best-seller, closely followed by Toad in the Hole and Stilton pie.

✉ 6 Essex Road, Islington

☎ +44 (0) 20 7359 5361   ££

❡ The lively Italian restaurant **San Daniele del Friuli** is more or less an institution in the Highbury area. Friendly wait staff, tasty Italian pasta and pizza, and an informal atmosphere attract a keen local following.

✉ 72 Highbury Park, Highbury

☎ +44 (0) 20 7226 1609   £££

❡ The **Hen and Chickens** in Islington is more than just a good English pub. The theatre upstairs is the venue for small concerts, plays and stand-up comedy. With only 50 or so seats, the atmosphere is cosy and intimate.

✉ 109 St Paul's Road, Islington

☎ +44 (0) 20 7704 2001 (Box Office)   ££

❡ The Islington area is scattered with an eclectic range of restaurants, with Indian, Japanese, Vietnamese, Italian and Thai cuisines all represented, along with plenty of choices for a good English fry up.

05

Methodist International Centre Hotel and Hostel

The Methodist International Centre Hotel is run according to the guidelines of the Methodist Church and consists of a commercial hotel, with a hostel for students attached. The hotel has 35 air-conditioned guestrooms, all of which are located on the top floor of the building and have en suite bathrooms, plasma televisions, room safes and Internet access. A full English breakfast is provided and the hotel is open year round. It is rated as 4-star accommodation by England's Automobile Association (AA) guide.

❡ The MIC hostel is in the same building and is open to tourists during university holiday periods. The hostel has a range of single and twin guestrooms furnished student style, with bed, wardrobe, bookcase and desk. The single rooms are available in three sizes from small to extra large. The majority of the hostel rooms share a bathroom with a neighbouring room. Twin rooms are fitted with a wash basin. There are fully equipped kitchens for guests to prepare and cook their own meals. Facilities include a television room and a fitness centre with modern exercise equipment. The hotel's **Atrium** restaurant and bar is open to the centre's guests and their friends.

❡ The MIC is handy to both **University College London** and the **British Library**.

✉ 81–103 Euston Street
Regent's Park
London NW1 2EZ

Hotel
🏨 from £60.00 pp,
including breakfast.

☎ +44 (0) 20 7380 0001
📠 +44 (0) 20 7387 5300

✉ acc@micentre.com

🖥 www.micentre.com

Open to men, women
& groups

Hostel
🏨 price to be negotiated.

☎ +44 (0) 20 7691 1439
📠 +44 (0) 20 7387 5300

🖥 www.micentre.com/
student

Open during university
holidays.

Open to men, women
& groups

☞ The Methodist
International Centre
Hotel and Hostel is just
450 yards from Euston
Station. Euston Square
tube station is also
nearby.

✝ **Sunday Services**
1400.
First London African
Methodist Episcopal
Church
Camden Square
Camden.

Open Houses
London

PLACES OF INTEREST ❧ The department stores of Oxford Street are just 1 mile south west of the hotel. The gigantic **Selfridges** store is here, along with **Mothercare, Marks & Spencer, Debenhams, John Lewis** and every young woman's idea of shopping nirvana, **Top Shop**. Winter sales commence just after Christmas and summer sales commence on 30 June. Most stores are open on Sundays.

❧ **Regents Park and Zoo** is less than ½ mile from the MIC Hotel. The park was one of the former London hunting grounds of Henry VIII (1491–1547) and there are miles of paths and walkways to explore. You can get there by boat which departs from **Little Venice** near the Warwick Avenue Underground Station. Enjoy the balmy English evenings at a concert at the **Regent's Park Open Air Theatre** which opens in summer for a 15-week season. Arrive in time for a drink and snack before the show or pre-order a picnic.

❧ Mix with the famous at **Madame Tussaud's** wax museum in Marylebone Road, and have your photograph taken with a celebrity. Royalty, Hollywood and sports stars are all well represented, as are luminaries of the Catholic Church. If you can't get to Rome during your travels you can have your photo taken with Pope Benedict right here—no-one need ever know!

❧ The first ever edition of *The London Times* (18 March 1788) is on display at the **British Library** in Euston Road, St Pancras. The library is also the home of the original Magna Carta (1215) and the world's oldest Christian Bible, the Greek handwritten 1600-year-old *Codex Sinaiticus* (the Sinai Book), which was purchased from former leader of the Soviet Union, **Joseph Stalin** (1878–1953) in 1933. In 2009 fragments thought to be from the original *Codex Sinaiticus* were found in the library of the isolated **St Catherine's Monastery** in Sinai, Egypt.

❧ The house that is now the **Sherlock Holmes Museum** in Baker Street, Marylebone is said to be the home referred to by writer **Arthur Conan Doyle** (1859–1930) as that of the fictional private eye Sherlock Holmes and his companion Doctor Watson.

¶ Step back in time at **Ye Olde Cheshire Cheese** in Fleet Street, one of Charles Dickens' favourite pubs, or visit **Ye Olde Curiosity Shop** in Portsmouth Street, which is claimed to be the oldest shop in London (1567).

¶ The **Churchill Museum** and the **Cabinet War Rooms** in St James are part of the Imperial War Museum which houses a permanent exhibition dedicated to **Sir Winston Churchill** (1874–1965). The exhibition includes the underground 'flat' he shared with his wife **Clementine** (1885–1977) during World War II.

¶ **Wigmore Hall** in Marylebone is one of London's premier recital halls for chamber music; classical concerts are presented on most days. The hall's restaurant is open for lunch and dinner and attracts non-concertgoers as well.

¶ During the year the **Church of St Martin-in-the-Fields** on Trafalgar Square conducts a program of free lunchtime concerts of classical music. Concerts start at 1300, though they may not be performed every day.

✝ Sunday Services 0800, 1000, 1700 & 1830

FOOD AND DRINK ✦ Like most of the pubs along Fleet Street, the **Old Bell Tavern** (300 years old) caters for editors and scribes—and if any praying needs to be done, it has the advantage of a back exit leading to **St Bride's Church**.

✉ 145 Fleet Street, City of London

☎ +44 (0) 20 7583 0216   ££

¶ If you are looking for somewhere unique to eat try **Inamo**, in Soho where the tables are interactive computer screens where guests press and click to set the 'mood' of the surroundings, place an order, check out the local area and call a cab to go home.

✉ 134–136 Wardour Street, Soho

☎ +44 (0) 20 7851 7051   ££££

¶ Meanwhile, over near the **British Library** the Irish former landlady of **Mabel's Tavern** continues to haunt the place (after hours only). Traditional pub food is served.

✉ Mabledon Place, Camden

☎ +44 (0) 20 7387 7739   ££

¶ **Belgo Noord**, a lively Belgian restaurant in Camden, serves the house speciality, *moules et frites*, with a vast range of Belgian beer, including Trappist-brewed varieties. 'Monks' (most definitely not members of any religious order) wait on the tables here.

✉ 72 Chalk Farm Road, Camden

☎ +44 (0) 20 7267 0718   £££

06

Kings College Hall

Founded in the traditions of the Church of England, the following two establishments are both part of the **Kings College University Campus** and offer accommodation to tourists during university holidays.

❧ **Kings College Hall** provides ideal accommodation for people travelling on a budget. The complex is pleasantly situated in acres of leafy gardens, 1 mile from the Oval Cricket Ground, 3 miles from the centre of London, and handy to the shops and pubs of **Camberwell** and **East Dulwich**. Accommodation is provided in single guestrooms (no twin) all of which are furnished 'student' style. Each room is fitted with a wash basin and guests share a bathroom on the same floor. In-room refrigerators can be hired if needed. Towels and linen are supplied and the rooms are serviced daily. A full English breakfast is the only meal available and is served in the college cafeteria; however areas are provided for guests to make tea or coffee and light snacks.

❧ Facilities include television lounges, coin-operated laundry, library, conservatory, music room, table tennis area and squash courts. A handy swipe card entry system is in operation. The minimum age for unaccompanied guests is 18; however, there are no facilities for young children. The complex has limited on-site parking, no curfew and credit cards are accepted.

✉ Champion Hill
Denmark Hill
London SE5 8AN

🛏 from £27.00 pp (single),
including breakfast.

📅 Open during university
holidays.

📞 +44 (0) 20 7733 2166
📞 +44 (0) 20 7848 1700
📠 +44 (0) 20 7737 0235
📠 +44 (0) 20 7848 1717

✉ stopover@kcl.ac.uk

✉ www.kcl.ac.uk/kcvb

☞ The nearest National
Rail (overground) train
station is Denmark
Hill, 250 yards north
of Kings College Hall.
Champion Hill runs
off Denmark Hill Road.
There is a bus stop
near the college.

✝ **Sunday Services
1000.**
St George's Anglican
Church, Coleman Road,
Camberwell.

⛪ Open to men, women
& groups

PLACES OF INTEREST ❧ The **Eurostar** (the under-the-Channel train to Europe) now leaves from the cavernous rebuilt **St Pancras Station** in Pancras Road which took over international services from Waterloo Station in 2007. For some continental retail therapy take the Eurostar to **Paris** and you could be browsing in **Galleries La Fayette** in just over 2 hours.

❧ The saint and hermit **St Giles** (of Assisi), the Patron Saint of the Crippled, figures prominently in modern **Camberwell**. According to Catholic Culture: 'churches named for St Giles were built so that cripples could reach them easily… That in his name charity was granted the most miserable is shown from the custom that on their passage to Tyburn for execution, convicts were allowed to stop at St Giles' Hospital where they were presented with a bowl of ale called St Giles' Bowl, thereof to drink at their pleasure, as their last refreshment in this life.' The St Giles Hospital chapel has survived to become the Camberwell parish church.

✝ Sunday Service 1000

❧ The centuries old trees, lush vegetation and eclectic monuments in the once neglected **Nunhead Cemetery** in **Southwark** have created one of the most attractive (though sometimes eerie) burial grounds in London. This atmospheric venue is the backdrop for concerts and musical performances during the summer months. Guided tours leave from the Lindon Grove entrance at 1415 on the last Sunday of the month.

❧ Under the **Brunel Museum** in Railway Avenue, Rotherhithe is part of an original walkway under the Thames which now forms a section of the London tube network. Once an underwater fairground the tunnel is today a tourist attraction offering floodlit tunnel tours.

❧ **The Pilgrim Fathers** departed on their journey to America from **The Mayflower** pub in Rotherhithe Street in 1620. In line with its historic American connections the pub is the only public house in England licensed to sell both British and US postage stamps.

❧ **The Old Nun's Head** public house at 15 Nunhead Green stands on the site of a former 'nunnery' which was dissolved by Henry VIII (ruled 1509 to 1547). Henry ordered that the abbess be decapitated and her head paraded around on a stake for all to see, hence the pub's name.

Open Houses
London

❧ The residents of Kennington claim comedy actor and boy made good, **Charlie** (Sir Charles) **Chaplin** (1889–1977) as one of their own. Chaplin was born in East Street and attended school in Kennington Road. A plaque identifies the house where he once lived at 287 Kennington Road.

❧ Movie buffs can take potluck at the **British Film Institute** next to the Royal Festival Hall, Southbank which conducts daily screenings of films on a wide range of topics. A film journalism course by correspondence is also available.

❧ The **Peckham Farmers' Market** in Peckham High Street is open every Sunday between 0930 and 1330.

FOOD AND DRINK ❧ **Tony Blair** treated **Bill Clinton** to lunch at the elite, riverside **Le Pont de la Tour** restaurant over a decade ago. According to Wikipedia: 'In May 1997, the motorcade of United States President Bill Clinton was divided by the "unexpected" opening of the Tower Bridge. President Clinton arrived just as the bridge was rising. The bridge opening split the motorcade in two, much to the consternation of security staff. A spokesman for Tower Bridge is quoted as saying, "We tried to contact the American Embassy, but they wouldn't answer the phone."'

✉ Butlers Wharf, 36d Shad Thames, London Bridge
☎ +44 (0) 20 7403 8403   **£££££**

❧ The food served in the refectory of **Southwark Cathedral** is not standard fare by any means and dining facilities are run by one of London's leading caterers.

✉ South Bank, London Bridge
☎ +44 (0) 20 7407 5740   **£££**
✟ Sunday Services 0900, 1100 & 1830

❧ **Manze's Noted Eel and Pie House** has a branch in Peckham and another in Tower Bridge Road, just south of Tower Bridge. Pie and mash, sausages with baked beans, and eel stewed or jellied are the menu staples and your eels and beans can be home delivered to anywhere in the UK.

✉ 105 High Street, Peckham
☎ +44 (0) 20 7277 6181   **££**

07

Kings College Hampstead Residence

The Hampstead Campus is situated on the outskirts of **Hampstead Village**, one of London's oldest and quietest tree-lined neighbourhoods, and within close proximity of the open expanses of the famous heath. Kidderpore Avenue, the location of various college and university buildings, is a quiet, leafy street. The guest accommodation is much like that in **King's College Hall** except that twin and single rooms are available. Small groups of up to 20 people are catered for. Children staying with an adult are welcome. The minimum age for unaccompanied guests is 18.

¶ All guestrooms have a washbasin and shared bathrooms are located on all floors. Towels and linen are supplied. Rooms are serviced daily Monday to Friday. Facilities include a coin-operated laundry and a television room, but there is no communal kitchen. Continental breakfast is provided, and a wide choice of shops, cafés and pubs can be found in Hampstead Village. There is no access for the disabled and no parking facilities in the grounds, although parking is available on the surrounding streets.

¶ The **Oval Cricket Ground** is two stops from Finchley Road station, the closest to the Hampstead residence. The complex is a few blocks from the Sandy Road entrance to **Hampstead Heath** and approximately 1 mile from Hampstead High Street.

✉ Kidderpore Avenue
Hampstead
London NW3 7ST

from £29.00 pp, including breakfast.

Open during university holidays.

☎ +44 (0) 20 7435 3564
☎ +44 (0) 20 7848 1700
+44 (0) 20 7431 4402
+44 (0) 20 7848 1717

stopover@kcl.ac.uk

www.kcl.ac.uk/kcvb

☞ The nearest Underground is Finchley Road, 1 mile away.

✝ **Sunday Services 1100 & 1900.**
St Luke's Anglican Church, Kidderpore Avenue, Hampstead.

Open to men, women & groups

Open Houses
London

PLACES OF INTEREST ❦ **Hampstead Heath** is a 400-acre expanse of lush parkland with ponds, walking tracks and sporting fields with extensive views of the city of London. In the 10th century, much of this land was owned by the Benedictine monks of the **Abbey of St Peter** in Westminster. Today the largest properties here are owned by the Saudi Royal Family which, it is said, has extensive holdings in The Bishop's Avenue, alongside numerous celebrities and self-made millionaires.

❦ Cricket fans won't want to miss the **Lords Cricket Ground** (MCC) tour which includes the Long Room and the players' dressing rooms, the indoor cricket school and the MCC Museum. Lords is just 2 miles from the campus.

❦ Once the home of Austrian psychologist **Sigmund Freud** (1856–1939) and his family, the **Sigmund Freud Museum** is located in Maresfield Gardens, Hampstead. It contains a large collection of books, antiques and furniture as well as that famous couch.

❦ Another well-known local was 20th-century Hungarian architect **Ernö Goldfinger** (1902–1987) who lived in what is now **Goldfinger House** at 2 Willow Road. Hampstead was considered the 'arty' area of London at the time. Goldfinger designed the house in 1939 and lived here with his family. Once considered a house of horrors, architecturally speaking, the building is now owned by the National Trust. The 'Goldfinger' of **James Bond** fame is said to be named after the architect who was deemed a considerable villain at the time, on account of his unpopular, albeit innovative, designs.

❦ **Hampstead** has lost none of its 'artiness' over the years and the impressive **Kenwood House** on the edge of the Heath is a treasury of precious artworks. Courtesy of the philanthropic Guinness family who donated the property to the State, these include masterpieces by Dutch painters **Rembrandt van Rijn** (1606–1669) and **Jan Vermeer** (1632–1675) as well as English landscape painters **William Turner** (1775–1851) and **Thomas Gainsborough** (1727–1788) and portrait painter **Joshua Reynolds** (1723–1792).

❧ The poet **John Keats** (1795–1821) also lived for a time in Hampstead and his house in Keats Grove is now preserved as a museum. Poetry readings, book launches and other literary events are often conducted here. The house is close to the heath where no doubt the poet found inspiration.

❧ The **Hampstead Theatre** in Eton Avenue was established 70 years ago but the new theatre has only been open for a short time. Already, however, it is recognised as a leading promoter of the works of talented young playwrights—which have included a controversial play about former Russian President **Mikhail Gorbachev** (b. 1931) called *The President's Holiday*.

❧ The **Swiss Cottage Farmers' Market** in Eton Road, is held opposite the Hampstead Theatre each Wednesday from 1000. Stock up on buffalo cheese, organic fruit and maybe some traditional English pork pies.

FOOD AND DRINK ❧ Enjoy a summer evening picnic and concert in the grounds of **Kenwood House** in Hampstead. No need to book—and it's free. Nearby are the cordial and inviting **Spaniard's Inn** and the **Holly Bush**, both pubs with a history of attracting poets, artists and academics as well as a few highwaymen of note.

✉ Holly Bush 22 Holly Mount, Hampstead

☎ +44 (0) 20 7435 2892 **££–£££**

✉ Spaniards Inn Spaniard's Road, Hampstead Heath

☎ +44 (0) 20 8731 8406 **££–£££**

❧ The **Everyman Cinema** in Holly Bush Vale, opposite the Hampstead tube station, is not your usual picture theatre. Patrons can get comfy in posh armchairs or leather sofas with a bottle of wine within easy reach. No choc tops here, but they sometimes have gummy bears, chocolate-coated raspberries and salt-and-pepper cashews—all delivered to your seat.

✉ 5 Holly Bush Vale, Hampstead

☎ 0870 066 4777

❧ The ultra-modern **Gaucho's Restaurant** is one of a chain of restaurants in London. Argentinian beef, thick chorizo sausages and tasty empanadas are on the menu along with a choice of South American wine, margaritas or Mojitos. Tango music is on the side.

✉ 64 Heath Street, Hampstead

☎ +44 (0) 20 7431 8222 **£££**

Herefordshire

LTHOUGH IT SHARES A BORDER WITH WALES,
Herefordshire is still only 155 miles from London. The
county's capital, Hereford, has been a cattle market
centre for centuries, the particular breed being named
after the town. Today Hereford, along with other
market towns in the county, still swarms with activity.
Vintage bookstores, antique shops, abbeys, cider mills, literary
festivals and themed walking trails all help shape the county's
appeal. Sections of the 150-mile circular Herefordshire Walking
Trail link tiny hamlets, quiet villages and busy towns. The
considerably shorter 21-mile-long Cider Cycling Route, which starts
in Ledbury, passes nine cider mills. It is considered something of a
feat not to stop and taste the local brew!

A church has stood on the site of Hereford Cathedral since
676. Now it houses two of the county's most significant medieval
spoils—a 13th-century map of the world and a tiered, chained library
containing books and manuscripts over 500 years old.

Some of finest gardens in all England can be found in
Herefordshire. The formal gardens and traditional blooms of
Abbey Dore Court are situated near the ruins of Dore Abbey which
was once a Cistercian monastery. Part of the medieval abbey
has been restored and is now a fully operational parish church—
Herefordshire's last convicted witch, Jane Wenham (convicted in
1912 but eventually pardoned), would be aghast!

Open Houses
Herefordshire Hereford

08

Hedley Lodge
at Belmont Abbey

Hedley Lodge is situated in the magnificent formal gardens of **Belmont Abbey**, less than 3 miles from the centre of Hereford, which the estate overlooks. Run by monks, who follow the Rule of Saint Benedict, the lodge caters for tourists and business people, as well as for those taking part in spiritual programs at the abbey. The lodge is a perfect base from which to explore Herefordshire and parts of Wales. Each of the modern single, twin and double (king size beds) guestrooms is comfortably furnished and has an en suite bathroom. Facilities include hairdryer, telephone, television and tea and coffee-making facilities, and daily newspapers are delivered to the room. Cots can be arranged and one family room is available; guests have access to an iron, and a laundry service is provided. The lodge has ample car parking. Breakfast is served and all meals are taken in the lodge's **Cantilupe Restaurant** which overlooks sheltered, leafy gardens. The fully licensed restaurant offers an extensive international menu and takes its name from **St Thomas de Cantilupe**, a former Bishop of Hereford (1275–1282), who is buried in Hereford Cathedral.

¶ The monks conduct programs of guided retreats and guests can join them in liturgical services in the abbey church, which is a jewel in itself. The stained glass windows, carved angels, monks' stalls and soaring roof were designed by English architect **Edward Welby Pugin** (1834–1875) who inherited his father **A. W. Pugin**'s (1812–1852) talent along with his business. Augustus Welby Pugin was a leading 19th-century English architect who specialised in religious and grand public buildings.

Hedley Lodge
✉ Abergavenny Road, Hereford HR2 9RZ

🛏 from £38.00 pp, including breakfast.

📞 +44 (0) 1432 374 747
📠 +44 (0) 1432 277 318

✉ hedley@belmontabbey.org.uk

🖥 www.hedleylodge.com

Accommodation at Hedley Lodge is also available to those making a retreat at Belmont Abbey. Contact details for retreat bookings are:

Belmont Abbey
✉ Abergavenny Road, Hereford HR2 9RZ

📞 +44 (0) 7799 811 646
📠 +44 (0) 1432 277 597

✉ retreats@belmontabbey.org.uk

🖥 www.belmontabbey.org.uk

☞ The nearest train station is Hereford which is 3 miles from the abbey. A taxi is available at the station.

✝ **Sunday Mass**
0830, 0930 & 1100. Belmont Abbey Church Abergavenny Road Hereford.

⚭ Open to men, women & groups

Open Houses
Herefordshire Hereford

PLACES OF INTEREST ✻ Take a guided tour of **Belmont Abbey**. On some occasions this may include a short talk by a Benedictine monk on monastic life and the history of the Benedictine Order. ❡ The **Burghill Valley Golf Club** is on the northern outskirts of Hereford; rumour has it that the local Anglican bishop enjoys a round here when time permits. This may account for a signpost near the 6th tee promoting attendance at the local churches. According to the magazine *Christian Today*, the church turned down suggestions of a sign reading 'The fairway to Heaven' or 'For when your life is in the rough' and came up instead with 'A branch in every village'. ❡ Hereford has two famous attractions, both on display in **Hereford Cathedral**: the **Mappa Mundi** (c. 1290), a unique ancient map of the world; and a 1400-volume of literary treasures in the world's largest chained library. As a deterrent to medieval light fingers, each volume was attached to a lectern with enough chain to allow the reader to take the book to a nearby table. The oldest book, the *Hereford Gospels*, was written in the 8th century.

❡ For over 300 years an annual, week-long festival of classical music has been held alternately in the grand cathedrals of **Hereford**, **Worcester** and **Gloucester**. Hereford's turn came in August 2009 and will be followed by Gloucester and Worcester. The cathedral choirs take a starring role, assisted by international musicians and soloists. ❡ Somewhat smaller, but with a history dating back to 1140, the **Church of St Mary and St David** with its tiny burial ground stands alone in a remarkably picturesque location in rural **Kilpeck**. The church is decorated with elaborate, stone carvings of all manner of religious imagery although one or two are most decidedly on the ungodly side.

✝ Sunday Service 1000, *every third Sunday*

❡ Discover everything you've ever wanted to know about snail breeding at **L'Escargot Anglais**, the National English Snail Farming Centre at Credenhill, near Hereford or perhaps take a peek into the lives of the seriously well-to-do, at **Croft Castle** in Yarpole, the ancestral home of the aristocratic Croft family.

❧ Not your usual pottery shop, **Bronte Porcelain** in **Malvern**, across the border in Worcestershire, is one of the principal ceramic manufacturers in England. Take home a delicate work of art or a 'one-off' collectible.

❧ **Malvern** is known for the purity of its water, which retails throughout England but can be sampled free of charge at many of the area's public wells. One particular source, known as the **Holy Well**, is said to have curative properties. Plans are afoot to bottle the water from the Holy Well; this was once an activity of the Benedictine monks of the 11th-century **Great Malvern Priory**, which was taken over by Henry VIII in 1539. The old priory has been restored and is now a working parish church.

☦ Sunday Services 0800 & 1030

FOOD AND DRINK ☙ Taste-test delicious cheeses at the **Monkland Cheese Dairy** near Leominster where the rich, cheddar-like Little Hereford Cheese is produced. Or quench your thirst at the **Westons Cider Mill**, in Much Marcle, 14 miles east of Hereford, where you can evaluate the subtle difference between apple cider and apple juice.

✉ **Monkland Cheese Dairy** The Pleck, Monkland

☎ +44 (0)1568 720 307

✉ **Westons Cider Mill**
The Bounds, Much Marcle, Ledbury

☎ +44 (0)20 8731 8406

❧ **The Bell Inn** in Yarpole is a highly rated local pub/restaurant. The food is Herefordshire fresh—think Hereford beef and wine from the vineyards of nearby **Croft Castle**. Guests have the choice of sitting under an umbrella in the garden, under rugged, old oak beams in the main dining room, or—temperature permitting—by a crackling log fire.

✉ Green Lane, Yarpole, nr Leominster

☎ +44 (0)1568 780 359   £££

❧ Enjoy a water view along with good food at the **Saracen's Head Inn** in Symonds Yat East, in the Wye Valley south of Hereford. Here guests can dine on the outside terrace and watch the cruise boats and kayakers glide along the River Wye. If you get the urge to join them you could always take the self-operated, hand-pulled (by you!) rope ferry across the river to Symonds Yat West.

✉ Symonds Yat East

☎ +44 (0)1600 890 435   £££

Kent

ENT IS POSSIBLY MOST FAMOUS for the White Cliffs of Dover—from where, on a clear day, you can see across the English Channel to France. Dover came to television sets in the early 1990s when the popular television series *The Darling Buds of May* was filmed there. The town also has strong associations with World War II.

Kent is known as 'the garden of England', and perhaps deservedly so. One of the most celebrated gardens is the Sissinghurst estate near Maidstone. Sissinghurst is the creation of writer Vita Sackville-West (1892–1962) and her husband, diplomat and author Harold Nicolson (1886–1968).

East of Sissinghurst lies Canterbury Cathedral, the epicentre of Anglicanism and the headquarters of the Archbishop of Canterbury, the head of the Church of England. It has been a place of pilgrimage for over 800 years, since the 1170 murder of Archbishop Thomas Becket (c. 1118–1170), now St Thomas Becket, by soldiers of King Henry II.

The ancient pilgrims' path known as the Pilgrims' Way commences at Winchester in Hampshire and trickles down through Kent to the Trinity Chapel in Canterbury Cathedral and the memorial to Becket. The pilgrims in Geoffrey Chaucer's *Canterbury Tales* made this arduous journey in the 14th century. Today's pilgrims don't have to sleep rough; they can stay overnight in the relative luxury of the cathedral's accommodation centre.

OPEN HOUSE

09

Aylesford Priory

Aylesford Priory, better known as The Friars, is nestled among the evergreen meadows of rural Kent, a smooth, picturesque, hour-long rail journey from London. The Friars dates back to the 13th century when local Englishman and gentleman farmer **Richard de Grey** (1199–1271) donated land for the monastery to the Order of Carmelites. The order occupied the monastery until the Dissolution in 1538 when it was lost to the Carmelites for almost 400 years. Not until 1949 was the order able to buy back the property. The Friars is tucked away in acres of spectacular, park-like grounds. Accommodation is in single, double and family rooms; the guestrooms are simple and basically furnished, though comfortable and adequate. The age of the building doesn't allow for more than a few en suites; in most cases bathrooms are on a share basis. Children are welcome at The Friars as are travellers looking for quiet, safe accommodation while they explore the surrounding area. There is a large dining hall which caters for all meals, a separate restaurant and numerous pubs and restaurants in the surrounding area (a car is needed). A car park is on site.

❦ The friars organise pilgrimages and guided retreats throughout the year and some guests come to make their own private retreat. A simple, handsome chapel contains a reliquary of **St Simon Stock**, who founded many Carmelite communities and who instituted the Marian devotion of the Brown Scapular. One of the oldest and most picturesque villages in the county, Aylesford was once a stop on the ancient Pilgrims' Way between Winchester and Canterbury Cathedral. Canterbury is 21 miles from Aylesford.

✉ The Friars
Aylesford ME20 7BX

🏠 from £26.00 pp,
including breakfast.

📞 +44 (0) 1622 717 272
📠 +44 (0) 1622 715 575

✍ guesthouse@thefriars.org.uk

✍ www.thefriars.org.uk

☞ The nearest train station is Maidstone East, 2½ miles south-east of Aylesford. A taxi is available from the station to the priory, or take bus number 155 or 156 (135 on Sunday) from the bus stop outside the station to The Friars.

✝ **Sunday Services**
0800 & 1015.
The Friars, Aylesford.

⚭ Open to men & women

Open Houses

Kent Aylesford

PLACES OF INTEREST ❧ **The Aylesford School of Ceramics** is based at The Friars, and curios and collectibles can be purchased here. Day-long pottery courses are also conducted.

❧ **Maidstone**, on the southern outskirts of Aylesford, is the home of the unusual **Museum of Carriages**. Located in 14th-century stables, it houses a collection of royal state carriages and horse-drawn sledges, antique sedan chairs and various miniature carriages used by Queen Victoria.

❧ **Leeds Castle**, 5 miles east of Maidstone, is claimed to have been **Henry VIII**'s favourite royal residence. Home to a handful of medieval English queens, the castle is spread over two islands in the centre of a small lake. Within the meticulously restored estate is an aviary of native and exotic birds, a nature trail and a quirky museum displaying medieval dog collars.

❧ **Brogdale** near **Faversham** is the home of the **National Fruit Collection**, where visitors can wander in the apple, cherry and pear orchards. Some of the varieties propagated here date back to the 16th century. Faversham is 19 miles east of Aylesford. **The Bedgebury National Pinetum** is near the village of Goudhurst. Over 10,000 evergreen pine trees thrive here; cycling routes, horse trails and walking paths of varying difficulty enable access to the forest.

❧ Explore Kent by boat. The cruiser *Kentish Lady* plies the **River Medway** on hour-long trips between the **Archbishop's Palace** on the riverbank in Maidstone and Allington Lock, almost 2 miles north. At Allington Lock, you can tour the outdoor **Museum of Kent Life** to glean insights into the Kentish lifestyle of the 1800s. The Kentish Lady is suitable for the elderly and the disabled. The Archbishop's Palace was once a residence of the Archbishop of Canterbury and provided accommodation to clergy travelling between London and Canterbury. The palace and gardens are open to the public on set days in summer.

The village of **Groombridge**, where the 17th-century moated **Manor House** in **Groombridge Place** is one of the area's major tourist attractions, is 24 kilometres south of Aylesford. It is easy to while away a day here wandering around the spectacular formal gardens (the Drunken Garden is clever and amusing). An 'enchanted forest' and 'giant's swings' keep the kids occupied. **The Crown Inn** across from Groombridge Place was established in 1585, making it one of the oldest pubs in this part of England. The cast and crew made the Crown their local when English film director **Joe Wright**'s (b. 1972) 2005 version of novelist **Jane Austen**'s (1775–1817) *Pride and Prejudice*, starring English actors **Keira Knightley** (b. 1985), **Brenda Blethyn** OBE (b. 1946) and **Dame Judi Dench** (b. 1934), was being filmed here.

The scenic, 28-mile Tunbridge Wells 'circular walk' trails through Kent's **High Weald** Area of Outstanding Natural Beauty. Worn-out ramblers can always cheat a little and take the **Spa Valley Railway** steam train from Groombridge back into Tunbridge Wells, a 7 mile sector.

FOOD AND DRINK **The Aylesford Priory** has a large self-service restaurant/tea room located in a restored, thatched, 17th-century barn on the monastery estate. Lunch as well as morning and afternoon teas are served. Attached to the restaurant is the monks' well-stocked gift and bookshop. West Barn, near the Priory car park.

✆ +44 (0) 1622 717 272   ££

Indulge in some fine English cider at the **Biddenden Vineyard** where Monk's Delight (an alcoholic concoction of apple cider, honey, herbs and spices) is reputed to be the nectar of the gods. The vineyard's non-alcoholic home-pressed apple juice is available for those doing the driving.

✉ Gribble Bridge Lane, Biddenden
   (16 miles south-east of Aylesford)
✆ +44 (0) 1580 291 726

You could meander down to **The Hengist** in Aylesford's main street, an intimate, upscale restaurant serving modern French cuisine in a choice of elegant dining rooms; a tasting menu is available for those who want to sample the regional produce.

✉ 7/9 High Street, Aylesford
✆ +44 (0) 1622 719 273   ££££

Open Houses
Kent Canterbury

10

Canterbury Cathedral Lodge

Canterbury Cathedral Lodge is run by the Anglican Church of England and offers high quality accommodation to tourists, families, pilgrims or business people. It is hard not to be inspired by the location—in the centre of **Canterbury**, within the ancient city walls and in the grounds of this remarkable cathedral and UNESCO World Heritage Site. The guestrooms are modern and comfortable and well furnished up to 3-star hotel standard. Rooms are available in single, twin or double configuration and all have en suite facilities. Many of the guestrooms overlook the private cathedral gardens. A number of rooms are suitable for the disabled and all are equipped with television, telephone and fast Internet connection. Bathroom toiletries are provided. Continental breakfast is served daily.

⸭ A fully-furnished and separate apartment is available for small groups. The apartment contains six en suite guestrooms and a fully equipped kitchen. The apartment is offered on a self-catering basis and is not suitable for the disabled as it has no lift access.

⸭ The cathedral shop sells gifts, clothing and souvenirs.

✉ Canterbury Cathedral
The Precincts
Canterbury CT1 2EH

🛏 from £35.00 pp, including breakfast.

☎ +44 (0) 1227 865 350
📠 +44 (0) 1227 865 388

✉ stay@canterbury-cathedral.org

🖥 www.
canterburycathedrallodge
.org

☞ Take the train to Canterbury West or Canterbury East Station and follow the signs to the cathedral. It is approximately a 10-minute walk from either station.

♿ Discuss your needs in advance of arriving, ideally when booking.

✝ **Sunday Services**
0800, 0930 & 1100.
Canterbury Cathedral
The Precincts
Canterbury.

👥 Open to men, women & groups

PLACES OF INTEREST ❦ Kent is home to many gracious, well-connected residences. **Chartwell**, home of the late **Sir Winston Churchill** (1874–1965), is near Sevenoaks, north of Tunbridge Wells. The 13th-century **Hever Castle**, the (possible) birthplace and childhood home of **Anne Boleyn** (c. 1507–1536, one of the six wives of **Henry VIII**) is located near Edenbridge; her ghost is said to roam the castle. The **Sissinghurst** estate and the famous rose gardens of author **Vita Sackville-West** (1892–1962) are near Cranbrook, 27 miles south-west of Canterbury.

❧ Literary links continue at the stately **Great Maytham Hall** in Rolvenden where **Frances Hodgson Burnett** (1849–1974) wrote the children's classic *The Secret Garden*. Author **Rudyard Kipling** (1865–1936, *The Jungle Book*) lived in Etchingham, a few miles from Sissinghurst Castle. The interior of his Jacobean home is unchanged from the time he lived there; his Rolls Royce is still parked in the garage.

❧ Take a memorable journey into Merry England at **The Canterbury Tales** exhibition at St Margaret's Church in Canterbury. In a condensed re-creation of **Geoffrey Chaucer's** (c. 1343–1400) 14th-century stories guests join Chaucer's pilgrims in a 'walk' from the Tabard Inn in London to the shrine of St Thomas Becket at Canterbury Cathedral. Lots of (tall) tales are told along the way and some rollicking good fun is guaranteed.

❧ According to news reports in 2008, the Anglican Bishop of **Ebbsfleet**, on the east coast of Kent, the Right Reverend **Andrew Burnham** (b. 1948), objected to the vote by the Anglican General Synod to allow women bishops and is believed to have had discussions with the Vatican to open the way for him and his followers to defect. The See of Ebbsfleet was especially created in 1994 to fulfil a role in assisting those parishes that refuse to accept women who are ordained as priests.

Open Houses
Kent Canterbury

❡ **Dover** on the Kent coast is just across the Channel from **Calais** in France which can be reached by fast catamaran or ferry. The ferry crossing takes 75 minutes; the faster catamarans take 45 minutes. Many people visit Calais for the shopping—taxes are lower there than in the UK. However, closer to home the massive **Bluewater** shopping complex near Dartford boasts over 330 shops.

❡ The **Battle of Britain** between the Royal Air Force (RAF) and the German Air Force (*Luftwaffe*) began in the skies over the port of Dover in 1940. In recognition of this, the **Shoreham Aircraft Museum** in Sevenoaks exhibits a collection of memorabilia retrieved from the aftermath of the historic battle.

❡ The 17th century market town of **Royal Tunbridge Wells** grew around the site of the Chalybeate Mineral Spring situated in an area known as **The Pantiles**, where in days long gone people would come to drink the health-giving water. Modern day visitors can draw a glass of the iron rich liquid courtesy of a suitably attired 'dipper'.

FOOD AND DRINK ❧ The **Star and Eagle Pub** in the centre of the village of **Goudhurst** has been dispensing hospitality and refreshment for centuries. Its low ceilings, old stonework and half-timbered walls lend a truly old-world atmosphere. The building is thought to have once been a monastery.
✉ High Street, Goudhurst
✆ +44 (0) 1580 211 512   £££

❡ If it's July you could catch the week-long **Oyster Festival** held at **Whitstable** down on the Kentish east coast (8 miles north of Canterbury) and enter the oyster-eating competition. In the 12th century the bountiful Whitstable area was designated an official supplier of oysters to the kitchens of Canterbury Cathedral to help feed the hungry pilgrims who converged on the cathedral after the murder of Thomas Becket.

❡ The **Kent Tea and Trading Company Factory Shop** near **Ashford** is open weekdays between 0900 and 1400. The shop sells a range of quality coffee, loose-leafed tea and tea bags from all over the world. Refresh with an exotic blend from Colombia or maybe a gentle tisane from Nepal.
✉ Pivington Mill, Egerton Road, Pluckley, nr Ashford
✆ +44 (0) 1233 840 265

Lancashire, Manchester & Merseyside

THE NORTH-WEST IS A LIVELY MIX of industry, bustling market towns and seaside holiday resorts. Throngs of Lancastrians head for Blackpool each summer to enjoy the balmy weather, the warm water and the entertainment. Others prefer slightly more out-of-the-way places—like the once-tiny fishing village of Lytham St Anne's, home of the renowned golf club, the Royal Lytham & St Anne's.

For many, Liverpool is identified with its famous football club. But this cosmopolitan city also boasts racecourses, a famous river, Georgian architecture and, of course, the Beatles.

If you're an avid watcher of the long-running television soapie Coronation Street, head for Manchester. The series has been produced at the Granada Studios since 1960.

As well as offering accommodation, some religious communities in Lancashire are extending their tradition of hospitality by opening their premises to the public for meals. These days you don't have to be a pilgrim to eat in the refectories of The Priory in Lancaster (next to Lancaster Castle) and the Liverpool Anglican Cathedral in Cathedral Close.

11

Park House Guesthouse

Park House is a well-known landmark for locals in Merseyside. In the past it has been a private hospital and a convalescent home. However, the Augustinian sisters who own and run the complex have converted the building into a comfortable and popular guesthouse which is set in 2 acres of established gardens featuring a small private lake.

❡ The single and twin guestrooms are well furnished in a homely, old-fashioned style and all have en suites. Facilities include television, tea and coffee making equipment, and a trouser press. Hairdryers are available on request. Bed and breakfast or full board can be arranged. Car parking is available and a bus stop is nearby. The sisters accept credit cards.

❡ Sister Carmel of Park House writes, 'All guests are welcome. When they go they are very happy with the accommodation and the service they receive. Park House Guesthouse is their first choice once they have experienced the hospitality. They compare us to a 5-star hotel!'

❡ A theatre and a library are next to Park House; shops, restaurants and a cinema are close by.

✉ Haigh Road
Waterloo
Liverpool L22 3XS

🛏 from £32.00 pp,
including breakfast.

✆ +44 (0) 1519 284 343
📠 +44 (0) 1519 490 947

✉ bookings@parkhse.
wanadoo.co.uk
✉ www.parkhse.com

☞ Take the train to
Liverpool's Waterloo
Station which is
500 yards from the
convent.

✝ **Sunday Services**
0830 & 0930.
Church of St Thomas
of Canterbury,
22 Great Georges Road,
Prescot.

👥 Open to men &
women

OPEN HOUSE

PLACES OF INTEREST ❧ Once, the most famous Liverpudlian entertainers were **Frankie Vaughan** (1928–1999, 'Tower of Strength') and **Jean Alexander** (b. 1926, *Coronation Street*) but without a doubt the **Beatles** wrested the title from them. **Rita Tushingham** (b. 1942, *The Girl With Green Eyes*), **Cilla Black** OBE (b. 1943, 'Anyone Who Had a Heart') and **Kim Cattrell** (b. 1956, *Sex in the City*) were also born here, as was actor **Tony Booth** (b. 1931), father of **Cherie Booth** QC (b. 1954), the wife of ex British PM **Tony Blair** (b. 1953). **Sir Paul McCartney** MBE (b. 1942) lived at 20 Forthlin Road, Allerton, and the Beatles wrote music and practised here. Guided tours of 20 Forthlin Road can be combined with a visit to 'Mendips' in Woolton, the childhood home of **John Lennon** MBE (1940–1980). **Ringo Starr**'s MBE (born Richard Starkey in 1940) early childhood home at 9 Madryn Street has been demolished but his home at 10 Admiral Grove where he celebrated his 21st birthday is, at the time of writing, still there. The Beatles got their first break at the **Cavern Club** at 10 Mathew Street.

❦ Liverpool's other obsession is football and soccer fans can tour the stadium and museum of the **Liverpool Football Club.** Down at the **Everton Football Club** in Goodison Park, stadium tours include a visit to the players' lounge, the TV interview room and a run-down the tunnel.

❦ The annual **River Festival** carnival is held in June with tall ships and hundreds of boats participating. Dockside onlookers are kept occupied with music and entertainment. Take a trip across the Mersey in the aptly named **Yellow Duckmarine**.

❦ Those with an eye for sculpture could follow sections of the 33-mile-long **Irwell Valley Sculpture Trail** which runs from Salford Quays (near Manchester, 30 miles east of Liverpool) and through the Irwell Valley to Bury, Ramsbottom and on to Bacup. Dotted along the trail are dozens of contemporary sculptures and works of art. In summer, ferries run between Liverpool and Salford Quays.

Open Houses
Lancashire, Manche∫ter & Merseyside Liverpool

❡ The **East Lancashire Steam Railway** makes a 13-mile round trip from Rawtenstall (on the Irwell Sculpture Trail) to Heywood for those who prefer to do their sightseeing sitting down. Refurbished Pullman-style coaches are used, and special lunch and dinner trips are often arranged.

❡ The imposing **Lancaster Castle** has a history of beheadings and hangings, but is most infamous for the imprisonment of children. The dungeons, the Grand Jury Room, the hanging corner and ancient instruments of torture are all on display.

❡ Less grisly outings are to the **Planet Earth Centre** in Todmorden or the **Fusiliers Museum** in Bury. For something more mundane, head to the **British Lawnmower Museum** in Southport.

❡ The **Tate Liverpool**, the home of the National Collection of Modern Art, complements its London counterparts with innovative displays of sculpture, art and photography.

FOOD AND DRINK ❦ After touring Liverpool's massive **Anglican Cathedral** visitors are more than likely to feel the need for some light refreshment. The cathedral's **Mezzanine Café Bar** and the Refectory Restaurant are open every day for meals and snacks.

✉ St James Mount, Liverpool
☎ +44 (0) 1517 096 271   ££

❡ **The London Carriage Works Restaurant** in Liverpool enjoys a reputation as one of the city's premier eating houses. Taste the best of seasonal local produce here including vegetables from a nearby farm, fish fresh out of Liverpool Bay and prime Lancashire beef.

✉ Hope Street Hotel, Liverpool
☎ +44 (0) 1517 052 222   ££££

❡ If you happen to be near Lancaster Castle, you will notice the Priory Church next door. Meals and light snacks are available in the **Priory Refectory**. Run by a band of friendly local volunteers to aid the priory maintenance program, it is open from Easter to the end of October. The Refectory is closed for meals on Sundays but you could always go to a church service instead.

✉ Castle Hill, Lancaster
☎ +44 (0) 152 465 338   ££
✝ Sunday Services 0800, 1000 & 1830

Yorkshire

ILM AND TELEVISION BUFFS will be familiar with Yorkshire's landscape. Such much-loved productions as *All Creatures Great and Small*, *The Full Monty*, *Brideshead Revisited* and *Calendar Girls* have all been shot there.

Author Charlotte Brontë (1816–1855) of *Jane Eyre* fame is one of Yorkshire's most well-known literary figures. The Brontë family lived in the tiny stone village of Haworth north of Halifax. Other villages of much character, charm and quirkiness include the somewhat eccentrically named Hutton le Hole, Osmotherley, Appletreewick, Giggleswick and Wigglesworth.

Religious orders, attracted by the scenic splendour and rural isolation of the Yorkshire moorlands, hills and dales, once flocked to the area to establish abbeys and monasteries. Some have survived and today welcome visitors and sightseers and travellers seeking rest and refuge.

The World Heritage-listed Fountains Abbey near Harrogate (founded by the Cistercians 800 years ago) also offers 'work'. The 800-acre abbey estate and its historic buildings have proven to be something of a conservation nightmare and volunteers are always needed to help direct the more than 300,000 people who each year come to visit this impressive reminder of Yorkshire's Christian ancestry.

Open Houses
Yorkshire York

12

The Bar Convent

Established within an elegant Georgian building just beyond the centre of York in 1686, the historic **Bar Convent** is one of the oldest (working) convents in England. The Catholic sisters of the Institute of the Blessed Virgin Mary, who run the convent, take a hands-on role in looking after their guests. They offer a bed and breakfast service to tourists, with accommodation in single and double rooms. Most guestrooms share a bathroom but a couple of rooms, including a family room, have en suites. All guestrooms have tea and coffee making facilities, a hand basin and a hairdryer, and each floor has a fully equipped kitchen and television room. A recreation room with a snooker table is available for the use of the guests. Continental breakfast is provided but a full English breakfast can be ordered for a small charge. Over the years the convent has been the recipient of awards for hospitality and tourism.

¶ General facilities include a lift to all floors and guestrooms with wheelchair access. A 'park and pay' car park is situated opposite the convent. **The Bar Convent Garden Café** is open to the public for snacks and meals up until late afternoon but is closed for dinner. The convent museum outlines the early history of Christianity in the north of England and the background of the religious order which occupies the convent today is depicted in a video featuring the voice of York-born actor Dame Judi Dench (b. 1934).

✉ 17 Blossom Street
York YO24 1AQ

🛏 from £33.00 pp, including continental breakfast.

📞 +44 (0) 1904 643 238
📠 +44 (0) 1904 631 792

✉ info@bar-convent.org.uk

✉ www.bar-convent.org.uk

☞ Take the train to York station. The convent is a short walk following the outside city walls to Micklegate Bar.

✝ **Sunday Services**
0830 & 1100.
St Wilfrid's Church, Duncombe Place, York.

♿ Discuss your needs in advance of arriving, ideally when booking.

⚤ Open to men, women & groups

PLACES OF INTEREST ❧ York's majestic Gothic cathedral dominates the walled city. **York Minster** was first established on the site of a Roman fort and was then followed by a Norman church, the remains of which can be seen on an underground tour of the cathedral which is almost 1,000 years old.

☦ Sunday Services *(may change)*

0800, 1000, 1130 & 1600.

❡ The cathedral is presided over by the Anglican Archbishop of York, the Ugandan-born **John Sentamu** (b. 1949), who can be seen (and heard) in a fascinating video, streaking across the sky in tandem with a Red Devil from the Parachute Regiment Freefall team of the British Army. The archbishop made the jump to raise money for the families of British soldiers killed in Afghanistan. View the jump at *www.archbishopofyork. org/1844.* The Archbishop of York holds the second-highest office of the Church of England.

❡ Meet a Viking at the **Jorvik Viking Centre** which occupies the site of a 10th-century Viking settlement discovered in 1979. Jorvik is run in conjunction with DIG, a local organisation established to protect York's considerable archaeological heritage. Interested visitors can participate in an excavation at the DIG **centre** at St Saviour's Church in St Saviourgate.

❡ The York city walls are over 2 miles in length; a leisurely circuit of them can be completed in around 2 hours. Once inside the walls you can take the informative 'snickleways' walking tour. **Snickleways** are old, narrow alleys often used by those in the know as shortcuts. The tour is a great way to see something of medieval York. Popular evening 'ghost walks' also lead through many of the snickleways.

❡ The Yorkshire moors blossom with purple heather during August and September. A section of the 250-mile **Pennine Way** National Trail, Britain's long-distance footpath, weaves through the Yorkshire Dales. In the same area, the 220-mile Coast to Coast Walk trails from St Bees on the Irish Sea to Robin Hood's Bay on the opposite side of Yorkshire.

❡ If you don't mind getting lost, spend some time at the **York Maize** near Grimston Bar. Cropped out of 1.5 million maize plants, in a design that changes annually, the maze covers an area equivalent to approximately 15 football grounds. The maze is thought to be the largest in the world.

Open Houses
Yorkshire York

¶ Home to the aristocratic Howard family since the 16th century, the grand and imposing **Castle Howard** was the spectacular and unforgettable location of the television series *Brideshead Revisited*, based on the novel of the same name by English author **Evelyn Waugh** (1903–1966). The series was produced by Granada Television in the early 1980s. In 2008, Miramax and the BBC jointly produced the movie version, which was filmed on location at Castle Howard. The castle is open to the public and tours of the sprawling estate are conducted daily. Castle Howard is the present day home of Eton educated the **Hon. Simon Howard** and his family and is situated 15 miles north-east of York.

¶ **York Castle Museum** is housed in the former county prison, a sprawling Georgian edifice. The atmospheric cells may still be explored—including the condemned cell that housed highwayman **Dick Turpin** (1705–1739) prior to his execution on York's Knavesmire, on the site of the city's present-day racecourse. The museum's founder, local surgeon **Dr John L Kirk** (1869–1940) assembled a huge collection of domestic objects and curiosities from five centuries. The highlight is an evocative Victorian street recreated with original shopfronts, cobbles and gaslight. Youngsters will enjoy meeting (or evading) the policeman who's often on the beat.

¶ The **National Coal Museum** at the Caphouse Colliery in Overton, between Wakefield and Huddersfield (south of York) pays tribute to Yorkshire's coal miners. Visitors don a helmet and belt and are taken on a tour of the pits 140 feet below.

¶ The **Captain Cook Memorial Museum** in the seafaring town of Whitby occupies the house where James Cook (1728–1779) served as an apprentice to Captain John Walker.

¶ The town of **Ripon** is known for its outdoor market held each Thursday where, in a centuries-old tradition, the 'bellman' signals that the market has opened (at 1100).

¶ The Royal Horticultural Society's **Harlow Carr** botanical gardens are found on the western edge of **Harrogate**, a spa town threaded with parkland. Handsome stone buildings in the town house upmarket antique, art, clothes and gourmet food stores.

FOOD AND DRINK ❦ Dine under the soaring steeples of **York Minster**, in the 15th-century **St William's College**. There's both indoor and outdoor seating; guests can feast on roast beef and hearty serves of authentic Yorkshire pudding.

✉ College Street, York

☎ +44 (0) 1904 634 830   ££

❦ Eat at the award-winning **Blue Bicycle** in York and enjoy the views over the placid River Foss. The restaurant was once a thriving bordello which was open for business whenever the owner's blue bicycle was parked outside.

✉ 34 Fossgate, York

☎ +44 (0) 1904 673 990   £££–££££

❦ **Betty's Tea Rooms** in York are considerably stylish with elaborate tiers of Viennese-style cakes and dainty sandwiches, all served in an atmosphere of Victorian refinement.

✉ 6 St Helen's Square, York

☎ +44 (0) 1904 659 142   £££

✉ 46 Stonegate, York

☎ +44 (0) 1904 622 865   £££

❦ It may be the size of a postage stamp, but locals 'in the know' head to the award-winning **Café Number 8**. A menu based on fresh local produce is cooked with a light touch. In summer, the small garden overlooking the city walls is a leafy haven.

✉ 8 Gillygate, York

☎ +44 (0) 1904 653 074   £££

❦ Ever-popular **Weeton's Cafe** in **Harrogate**, 20 miles west of York is a 'pasture to plate' type of establishment as it is owned and run by local farmers who have a readymade outlet for their free-range beef and lamb and home grown vegetables. All meals are available and a first-rate deli is stocked wall to wall with a huge variety of produce made or grown in Yorkshire.

✉ 23–24 West Park, Harrogate

☎ +44 (0) 1423 507 100   £££

❦ In 2008, **Starkey's**, the local butcher shop at **Sherburn-in-Elmet**, 16 miles south of York, won a prestigious award for 'the Best Sausage in Yorkshire for a Sarnie'. Starkey's sausages are served on the sarnies (*aka* sandwiches) at the local **Squire's Biker's Café** in **Newthorpe**, where you can also order a comforting hot chip butty with either a pint of tea or a pint of hot chocolate and cream.

✉ Newthorpe Lane, Newthorpe, South Milford

☎ +44 (0) 1977 684 618   £

Spiritual Retreats
London

13

Tyburn Convent

The Catholic order of the Sisters of the Adorers of the Sacred Heart of Jesus of Montmartre, was founded in Paris in 1898 by Frenchwoman Marie Adele Garnier (Mother Mary of St Peter). The congregation moved to London in the early 1900s when numerous religious orders in France were dissolved after the introduction of the laws against religion by the country's left-wing government of the time.

❧ The Tyburn nuns invite women only to make a private, undirected retreat at the historic **Tyburn Convent** and to join them in liturgical services including daily Mass, the Liturgy of the Hours and Eucharistic Adoration. The sisters meet for prayer eight times each day between 0530 and 2015. At certain times during the year retreats are offered to males.

❧ The sisters have set aside six simple, single rooms for guests within the convent grounds but outside the nuns' enclosure. Meals are taken in a small guests' dining room. The last meal of the day is served at 1830; facilities are available to make tea, coffee and light snacks.

❧ It was Mother Mary of St Peter who introduced the practice of 24-hour devotion of the Blessed Sacrament, a tradition which continues today. At various times throughout the year members of the public are invited to join in the all-night adoration. On most days the church of the Tyburn Convent is open to the public between 0615 and 2000. When in the church the sisters are separated from the public by a wall of tall, white grilles symbolising they belong to an enclosed religious order.

✉ 8 Hyde Park Place
Westminster
London W2 2LJ

🛏 from £30.00 pp,
including all meals.

☏ +44 (0) 20 7706 4507

✉ admin@tyburnconvent.
org.uk

✉ www.tyburnconvent.
org.uk

☞ The nearest tube
station is Marble
Arch from where the
convent is a short
walk down Edgware
Road, in the opposite
direction to Oxford
Street. Bus numbers 12
and 88 stop near the
convent.

✝ **Sunday Services
0730.**
Church of Tyburn
Convent, Marble Arch.

👤 Women only

⚘ Occasional retreats
are offered to men;
contact the convent
for details

PLACES OF INTEREST ❧ The convent is situated 100 yards from **Marble Arch** and the site of the **Tyburn Gallows**, where scores of Catholics were martyred over a 100-year period up to 1783, after which **Newgate Prison** (located near the Central Criminal Court or 'Old Bailey') became the place of public executions. Executions often attracted crowds of up to 50,000 onlookers. If you look closely at Edgware Road (near the Bayswater Road intersection) you can just make out a small cross memorial to the Tyburn Martyrs.

❧ **The National Shrine of the Martyrs of England and Wales** is at Tyburn. Visitors to the convent can tour the crypt and the Shrine of the Martyrs where the relics of many of those murdered on the gallows are kept. A sister leads guided tours at 1030, 1530 and 1730 each day.

❧ The **Tyburn Sisters** live under a strict rule of silence, with speaking permitted only during a 1-hour recreation period each afternoon. Some years ago, when raising funds for renovations to the convent roof, the enterprising nuns ran a snooker tournament and invited members of the public to sponsor them according to how many balls they could land in the pot. The idea created much attention and the necessary repairs were eventually carried out.

❧ In 2001 the sisters inaugurated the highly regarded, invitation-only **Tyburn Lecture**, whereby a prominent person is invited to speak on the subject of their choice. Previous speakers include **Cherie Booth** QC (b. 1954), and the **Rt. Hon. Chris Patten** (b. 1944), former governor of Hong Kong. The Deputy Chairman of international news service Reuters, Irishman **Niall Fitzgerald** KBE, (b. 1945), delivered the 2009 lecture. The speakers at **Speakers' Corner** (opposite the convent) may not be so polished, but the right of free speech is alive and well come Sunday mornings when anyone can voice an opinion—and even be listened to.

❧ The smallest house in London is only 3ft 6ins wide! At **10 Hyde Park Gate**, it forms part of the Tyburn Convent. It is thought that the area covered by the house was once a passageway leading to the former St George's cemetery on St George's Field—apparently a handy place for a little bodysnatching. The city's largest house, the residence of **Her Majesty Queen Elizabeth II**, is across the park opposite the convent, on land once owned by the monks of **Westminster Abbey**. The enormous estate, now known as **Hyde Park**, was procured by **Henry VIII** (1491–1547) in 1536 for use as another of his private hunting grounds.

Spiritual Retreats
London

⸙ At 1200 on **Horseman's Sunday**
(3rd Sunday in September) the Vicar
of St John's Church in Hyde Park
Crescent mounts a trusty steed to lead a
procession of scores of horses and riders
to a religious service and a traditional
blessing of the horses.

✝ Sunday Service 1000

⸙ Horse riding in the centre of London
is a popular sport. You can hire a well-
schooled steed at **Hyde Park Stables**
at 63 Bathurst Mews and take a trail
ride along the 5 miles of bridle paths in
peaceful Hyde Park. Children, beginners
and the experienced rider are catered for.

FOOD AND DRINK ⸙ The **Tyburn
Convent** is near **Park Lane**, home to
some of London's finest hotels and
expensive eateries in the posh **Mayfair**
area—no greasy spoons around here.
However, you could head in the opposite
direction, down Bayswater Road to the
local 'chippie' **Mr Fish** for a plate of
the house favourite—fried fish of your
choice with chunky chips, squashy peas
and a glass of French wine. To dine on
seafood in more elegant surroundings,
try Ian Fleming's favourite restaurant,
Scott's Oyster Bar in Mayfair, where
dry martinis are served a-la-James
Bond—'shaken, not stirred'.

✉ Mr Fish 9 Porchester Road, Bayswater
📞 +44 (0) 20 7229 4161   ££
✉ Scott's Oyster Bar 20 Mount Street, Mayfair
📞 +44 (0) 20 7495 7309   ££££–£££££

⸙ The royal grocer, **Fortnum & Mason**,
is just around the corner. Pick up a
hamper, some ritzy champagne and
picnic like a king.

✉ 181 Piccadilly, Westminster
📞 +44 (0) 20 7734 8040

⸙ Escape the hustle and bustle and
wander through St James's Park
feeding—or avoiding—the hungry
squirrels along the way, to the
impressively located **Inn the Park**. To be
waited on, take a table on the verandah
and watch the swans and ducks drift by,
or sit inside where there is a self-service
cafeteria.

✉ St James Park, Westminster
📞 +44 (0) 20 7451 9999   £££–££££

14

St Edward's House

St Edward's House is brilliantly situated in the shadow of Westminster Abbey, near the Houses of Parliament and Big Ben. St Edward's is the home of the Anglican monastic community of the Society of St John the Evangelist, the oldest community in the Anglican Church, which was founded in 1866 by priest **Richard Meux Benson** (1824–1915), the Vicar of Cowley, in Oxford.

❡ The priests of St Edwards conduct days of retreat or 'just quiet' days at the monastery to visitors of every religious shade and opinion, though the priests themselves fit the traditionalist Anglican mould. Fifteen centrally heated guestrooms within the monastery itself are available for overnight visitors. Each guestroom has a wash basin; bathrooms are shared. Meals are available on request and guests are invited to share in the spiritual activities of the community. The chimes of Big Ben can often be heard in the distance and the monastery's roof garden has views of the Houses of Parliament. Near the monastery on Abington Street a small, but often crowded park known as College Green is commonly used by television studios and political correspondents to interview MPs.

❡ **The Chapel of St Peter and John** is open daily and guests and passers-by can join the priests in their daily prayers, which commence with Matins at 0700 (0730 on Sunday) and finish with Compline at 2130.

✉ 22 Great College Street
Westminster
London SW1P 3QA

💷 price to be negotiated.

📞 +44 (0) 20 7222 9234

✉ guestmaster@ssje.org.uk

✉ www.ssje.org.uk

☞ The nearest tube station is Westminster Station, less than 500 yards from St Edwards.

✝ **Sunday Services**
0730 & 0800.
Chapel of St Peter and John, St Edward's House, 22 Great College Street, Westminster.

👥 Open to men & women

Spiritual Retreats
London

PLACES OF INTEREST ❦ **Westminster**
is graced with well-known tourist
attractions, namely **Westminster
Abbey** (Anglican), **Westminster
Cathedral** (Catholic) and the **Houses
of Parliament**. From the monastery
you can walk along the river towards
Vauxhall Bridge and to the **Tate Britain**
gallery on Millbank which exhibits
British art from 1500 to the present
day. Something unique is always on
display. British artist **Martin Creed**'s
(b. 1968) exhibition has been one of the
Tate's most controversial. *Work No. 850*
involved a team of athletes running
separately, at 30-second intervals and
at full speed, around the Tate's Duveen
Galleries in a celebration of physical and
mental vigour.

✝ **Westminster Abbey** Sunday Services
0800, 1000, 1115, 1500, 1745 & 1830

✝ **Westminster Cathedral** Sunday Mass
0800, 0900, 1030, 1200, 1730 & 1900

❧ Art and religion combine at the
Church of St John in Smith Square near
Great College Street. Open to the public,
this lovely 18th-century church is now
used as a concert venue, especially
for productions of classical music.
The design of the church resembles
an upturned footstool, possibly an
architectural aberration after **Queen
Anne** (1665–1714), in a moment of
displeasure, informed architect **Thomas
Archer** (1668–1743) that she wanted the
church to look 'like that' as she booted a
footstool across the room.

❧ In 2005 hundreds of nuns,
monks, priests and other religious
protested (peacefully) against Tony
Blair's government on the streets of
Westminster, in a bid for increased aid to
poverty-stricken Third World countries.
The protest was followed by a service in
St Margaret's Church. The Anglican
Church of St Margaret in Parliament
Square, between Westminster Abbey
and the Houses of Parliament, is known
as the 'parish church of the House of
Commons'. Since the 17th century a
pew has always been reserved for the
sole use of the Speaker of the House
of Commons. **Sir Winston Churchill**
married here in 1908.

✝ Sunday Services 0800, 1000, 1115, 1500 & 1830

❧ **Australia House** in The Strand, London is the workplace of the Australian Ambassador to the UK. Australians can apply here for tickets to events such as the **Trooping of the Colour**, **Royal Garden Parties** and the **Royal Ascot Race Meeting**. Apply before you leave home at *www.australia.org.uk*. The Ambassador may not be aware that in the basement of Australia House is a little known 'holy well', these days only accessible via a trapdoor. Holy wells have their origins in Celtic times when the waters were said to have had healing properties.

❧ If you are male and in need of pampering, head for **Trumpers**, the gentlemen's barber in Curzon Street in the gentrified Mayfair area. Meanwhile, ladies could browse in the nearby jewellery shops of **Old Bond Street** or at **Floris** in Jermyn Street, the historical home of fine English fragrances. Recover in the old-world charm of **The Audley**, a traditional English pub in Mount Street.

FOOD AND DRINK ❧ You may be glared at by some pre-eminent ecclesiastics as you take your refreshment in **The Cardinal**, an old English pub near Westminster Cathedral. Named after **Henry Edward Manning** (1808–1892), the Catholic Archbishop of Westminster Cathedral from 1865 until his death,

it serves reasonably priced food in a sometimes hushed atmosphere but with a little bit of history thrown in.

✉ 23 Francis Street, Westminster
📞 0871 984 3496   ££

❧ **The Footstool Restaurant** in the crypt of St John's Church in Westminster is open for weekday lunches and for dinner on concert evenings.

✉ Smith Square, Westminster
📞 +44 (0) 20 7222 2779   ££

❧ The menu at **Tate Britain's Rex Whistler Restaurant** usually offers some intriguing choices, such as English asparagus with soft-boiled duck egg, elderflower sorbet, fresh Cornish crab and a by-the-glass international wine list. Morning and afternoon tea are also served.

✉ Millbank, Westminster
📞 +44 (0) 20 7887 8825   £££–££££

❧ The elegant, fine dining restaurant the **Cinnamon Club** is situated among book-lined walls in the refined environment of **Old Westminster Library**. The Bombay tasting plate offers an exotic introduction to one of the city's best Indian eateries.

✉ 30 Great Smith Street, Westminster
📞 +44 (0) 20 7222 2555   ££££

Devon

NE OF THE LARGEST ENGLISH COUNTIES, Devon lies
on the south-west peninsula of the country, some
190 miles from London. Traditional fishing villages
are strung along its rugged coastline and its seaside
towns—with safe, sheltered, sandy beaches, many
of which are lined with multi-coloured beach huts—
make great family holiday destinations. Torquay is as popular as ever
and still known to many as the 'English Riviera'. Lively as the town
is, however, it is easy to escape the crowds—and enjoy the sweeping
ocean views—by taking to one of the coastal footpaths.

Scattered across Devon's moors are numerous small villages. Many
boast pretty, charming cottages with oak beams and thatched roofs,
and most have a couple of friendly walkers' pubs with names like
The Ring of Bells and The Plume of Feathers which welcome tired
ramblers with a restorative tipple.

Monastery ruins, old stone churches and historical abbeys
throughout the county all offer glimpses into Devon's past. Various
orders and religious groups offer accommodation for overnight
guests looking for a haven of tranquility.

15

Southgate Guesthouse, Buckfast Abbey

St Mary's Abbey, or **Buckfast Abbey**, is situated in the heart of the tiny village of Buckfastleigh. The original monastic complex was established in the 11th century but the stately abbey you see today was built in the 19th century. It was established by French Benedictine monks who came to England having been ordered out of their monastery in France during religious upheavals.

❧ The guesthouse and residential centre of the abbey offers accommodation for men and women seeking spiritual enlightenment or those who wish to make a self-guided retreat. Accommodation is in a well-heated 19th-century manor house which has its own chapel, library, common room, kitchenette and telephone. There is a walled garden where guests can relax.

❧ The monks own a number of properties around the abbey estate where visitors to the area can also be accommodated. These are ideal for families and groups (minimum number 4 people) as the houses have full kitchens as well as washing and drying facilities.

❧ The abbey is in extensive grounds with a restaurant and a monastic shop selling items made by the monks, including Buckfast Bee Honey (some tons of honey are produced each year) and Tonic Wine which the monks brew according to an original 130-year-old recipe passed down from monks living in France. Cosmetics and perfumes are also sold. The shop is within a moated stone cottage accessed via a narrow bridge. Separate well-stocked stores sell a range of gifts and religious literature.

❧ As a mark of respect, professed Benedictine monks are addressed by the title '*Dom*'—not 'Father'—a term which stems from the Latin word *Dominus*, meaning 'Lord' or 'master'.

✉ St Mary's Abbey
Buckfastleigh TQ11 0EE

💷 price to be negotiated.

Retreats
☎ +44 (0) 1364 645 558

Group Accommodation
☎ +44 (0) 1364 645 532
✆ +44 (0) 1364 645 615

✉ guests@buckfast.org.uk

✉ www.buckfast.org.uk

☞ Buckfastleigh is located off the A38 between Exeter and Plymouth. The nearest train stations are Newton Abbot, 11 miles north-east, and Totnes, 8 miles south-east. Take a bus or taxi to the abbey from either station. In summer you could take the scenic route via the South Devon Steam Railway which runs from Totnes (the SDR station is a 20-minute walk from the town centre) to Buckfastleigh where a vintage bus waits to take visitors to the abbey (on set days only).

♿ Discuss your needs in advance of arriving, ideally when booking.

✝ **Sunday Mass**
0900, 1030 & 1730. St Mary's Abbey Church, Buckfastleigh.

⚭ Open to men, women & groups

Spiritual Retreats
Devon Buckfastleigh

PLACES OF INTEREST ❧ The **Buckfast Butterfly and Dartmoor Otter sanctuaries** are both located next to the South Devon Steam Railway station in Buckfastleigh. For a unique outing, add the hedgehog hospital at **Prickly Ball Farm**, Newton Abbot to your itinerary. Watch out for the prickles and be careful where you sit.

❧ The **Berry Pomeroy Castle** near Totnes is said to be one of the most haunted castles in England. It was once the subject of Living TV's *Britain's Most Haunted*.

❧ The goings-on in the seaside town of **Torquay**, 14 miles east of Buckfastleigh, provided a fertile source of ideas, plots and intrigue for crime writer **Dame Agatha Christie** (1890–1976); the Agatha Christie Mile, a walking trail around the town, leads to some of the places mentioned in her novels and includes clues to a mystery for wannabe crime busters to solve. If you fancy yourself as a 21st-century sleuth, travel to **Tatton Park**, a 19th-century stately home and historic estate near Knutsford in Cheshire and take *The CSI Experience*, a course in solving crimes, particularly grisly murders.

❧ A **Poetry Trail** in **Stover Country Park**, 10 miles north-east of Buckfastleigh, is dedicated to former Poet Laureate the late **Ted Hughes** (1930–1998); many of his poems are displayed on wooden 'poetry posts' along the route which on average takes about 2 hours to walk.

❧ If you're drawn to the unusual, there is a paperweight museum at **Yelverton** and a museum which features barometers at **Merton**. Otherwise the **West Putford** Gnome Reserve provides a diversion; it's compulsory that all visitors don a gnome hat (kindly provided) before gaining entry.   ∘

❧ The talent of Devon's craftsmen and women is on display in the gallery and showrooms of the **Devon Guild of Craftsmen** in Bovey Tracey which exhibits the work of over 200 artists. Elsewhere in this town, the **House of Marbles** is the home of games, novelties, toys and puzzles. Take home a genuine Jack-in-the-Box, a bag of mixed, brightly-coloured eyeballs or a handy musical key ring. Or just relax in the **Old Pottery Cafe Restaurant** and let the kids play marbles on the longest marble run in the UK.

❧ **Honiton**, 39 miles north-east of Buckfastleigh, was once a centre for lace-making. The **Allhallows Lace Museum** interprets the history of Honiton lace combined with lace-making demonstrations during summer. **The Lace Shop** in Honiton specialises in antique lace and lace-making tools. Tuesday and Saturday are market days in the town.

❧ The ancient craft of the cobbler is alive and well in the workshop of **Brodequin Shoemakers**, in the port town of **Teignmouth**, where casual boots, sandals and walking shoes are carefully hand-made to measure.

❧ It hasn't always been easy living in the remote, barren wilderness of **Dartmoor** and the **Museum of Dartmoor Life** in Okehampton, 45 miles north-west of Buckfastleigh, tells of the struggles of the people who lived on the moors in the days before cars, electricity and modern conveniences. Open during summer.

FOOD AND DRINK ❧ **The Grange Restaurant** in Buckfast Abbey offers a high-quality, well-run cafeteria service with healthy offerings among the usual café food. The restaurant has a sunny outdoor sitting area overlooking the abbey estate.

✉ St Mary's Abbey, Buckfastleigh

☎ +44 (0) 1364 645 504   ££

❧ From Buckfastleigh it is 3 miles to the **Riverford Organic Farm** where self-guided tours of the organic dairy, grassy pastures and vegetable gardens are followed by a healthy, tasty lunch of freshly gathered produce in Riverford's **Field Kitchen** restaurant.

✉ Wash Barn, Buckfastleigh

☎ +44 (0) 1803 762 074   ££

❧ A traditional Devonshire tea with fresh, warm scones, lashings of double Devon cream (less fat than the clotted type so don't feel guilty) and home-made strawberry jam can be taken in the thatched-roofed **Primrose Cottage** in the gorgeous village of Lustleigh, 15 miles north of Buckfastleigh.

✉ Lustleigh

☎ +44 (0) 1647 277 365   ££

❧ **The Dartbridge Inn** in Buckfastleigh is open for meals and drinks 7 days a week. Pull up a chair by the log fire or sit outdoors, weather permitting.

✉ Totnes Road, Buckfastleigh

☎ +44 (0) 1364 642 214   £££

Gloucestershire

HE PHOTOGENIC COTSWOLDS district lies largely in Gloucestershire between Worcester in the north and Bath in Somerset to the south. The gentle hills and sprawling valleys of the county can be explored on foot via the 100-mile-long Cotswolds Way scenic path.

Throughout Gloucestershire are magnificent gardens, castles and stately homes, and some very grand cathedrals and churches. Henry VIII (1491–1547) and Anne Boleyn (c. 1507–1536) once resided at Thornbury Castle and Henry's last wife, Catherine Parr (1512–1548), lived at Sudely Castle at Winchcombe. The county's centuries of royal associations continue, and these days Gloucestershire is home to Charles, the Prince of Wales, and Camilla, the Duchess of Cornwall, who married in 2005.

The Regency spa town of Cheltenham is one of the gateways to the area and many a punter has been drawn to Cheltenham's racecourse for the National Hunt and Gold Cup festivals.

Scenes from the *Harry Potter* movies were filmed in the 1,300-year-old cloisters of Gloucester Cathedral, which up until the Dissolution in the 16th century was known as Gloucester Abbey, part of a Catholic Benedictine monastery. Even today the cathedral is still blessed with a timeless medieval beauty. Gloucestershire's cornucopia of abbeys and churches points to a robust Christian past, while present-day members of various religious orders continue the tradition of contributing to the spiritual and economic vigour of their local communities.

16

Glenfall House

Glenfall House in the Cheltenham suburb of Charlton Kings is a Church of England conference and retreat centre. It was established by the Diocese of Gloucester when the estate was passed on as a gift by the Anglican Sisters of the Society of St Peter, who moved to a convent in Edgeware, London.

❧ Situated on a rise, the house overlooks the Malvern Hills and retains a gracious atmosphere with large, private gardens and refined Regency design and furnishings. Visitors of all Christian denominations are welcome to participate in Glenfall's programmed residential retreats. The diocese also conducts non-residential 'days of reflection' throughout the year. There are 27 comfortably furnished single and twin guestrooms, of which 20 have en suites. The grounds and garden pavilion are secluded sanctuaries for meditating or just enjoying the silence. Glenfall has rooms and conference facilities available to groups. All meals are provided, picnic lunches can be arranged, there is plenty of on-site parking and the centre of Cheltenham is only a few minutes' drive away. From time to time residential 'walking retreats' are conducted in the surrounding area.

✉ Mill Lane
Charlton Kings
Cheltenham GL54 4EP

price to be negotiated.

☎ +44 (0) 1242 583 654
+44 (0) 1242 251 314

✉ enquiries@glenfallhouse.org

🖰 www.glenfallhouse.org

☞ The nearest railway station is Cheltenham Spa, 3 miles from Charlton Kings. Take a taxi from here.

✝ **Sunday Mass**
1000 & 1800.
Anglican Church of the Holy Apostles,
London Road,
Charlton Kings.

Open to men, women & groups

Spiritual Retreats
Gloucestershire Cheltenham

PLACES OF INTEREST ❧ Enjoy Regency **Cheltenham** by taking an escorted walking tour of the town centre, run by the local tourist office on the Promenade. Or pick up a map and take a stroll around some of Gloucestershire's historical villages. Ramble along the 9-mile **Daffodil Way** in the leafy Leadon Valley during March and April when the wild daffodils run amok. The village of **Dymock**, 25 miles west of Cheltenham, is one of the starting points on the circular walk. The route can also be joined at Oxenhall or Kempley.

❧ Whatever the season, spectacular blooms are always on display at the **National Arboretum** on the outskirts of **Tetbury**. However, there's no formal design to the 25,000 acres of the ancient **Royal Forest of Dean**, in the west of Gloucestershire on the border of Wales and Herefordshire, where walking trails cut through woods, meadows and banks of wildflowers—and past the **Three Choirs Vineyard** near Newent. Set among manicured rows of grape vines, the vineyard's terrace restaurant provides an idyllic setting for a relaxed meal and a refreshing glass of good English wine.

❧ **Highgrove Estate**, Prince Charles' country home, is on the edge of Tetbury, 22 miles south of Cheltenham. Royal watchers might be tempted to wander past, but don't bank on taking a tour of the Highgrove gardens anytime soon— the waiting list stretches for almost 2 years. The Prince's 37-acre estate is landscaped with hundreds of trees and miles of hedgerows and topiary. The farm operates a vegetable box scheme whereby Highgrove's organic produce is picked, packed and delivered to local families who wish to participate in the scheme.

❧ If you are well brushed up on your English history you will know that in 1327 **King Edward II** (1284– 1327) was supposedly murdered in Gloucestershire's **Berkeley Castle** by his wife and her lover, with a red-hot poker lodged in a rather unorthodox place. **Catherine Parr**, the sixth wife of Henry VIII, lived at **Sudeley Castle** between 1543 and 1548; she is buried in the churchyard in the castle grounds.

Cheltenham's **National Hunt Festival** (hurdles) is held at Cheltenham Racecourse over a 4-day period each March. The feature race of the festival is the Cheltenham Gold Cup, run over 3 miles and 15 energy-sapping jumps.

The **Badminton Horse Trials** are held in May at the Duke of Beaufort's **Badminton House** estate, 5 miles south of Cheltenham. Riders from all over the world compete in this Olympic-class event. Show-jumping, dressage, cross-county, and speed and endurance events form part of the program. And yes, it is believed the game of badminton (shuttlecock) was first played on English soil, here in 1873.

The **International Centre for Birds of Prey** in **Newent**, 17 miles west of Cheltenham, conducts courses in the art of falconry and bird handling using owls, hawks and falcons. Open daily.

Markets are held in **Tetbury** in a purpose-built 17th-century market hall each Wednesday. **Gloucester's Country Market** is held every Thursday morning at Northgate Hall, St John's Lane and a **Farmer's Market** is held on Friday. The produce on sale may include the locally made cheese with the distinguished name of *Stinking Bishop*. The cheese was originally made by Cistercian monks and possibly named after a tiff with their local superior. Don't take it home on the bus!

FOOD AND DRINK The coffee shop in **Gloucester Cathedral** serves drinks, snacks and light meals such as soups and sandwiches. It is open every day. Around the corner from the coffee shop you will find the fragrant, traditionally designed monastic herb garden.

✉ 13 Pitt Street, Gloucester
☎ +44 (0)1452 527 701   ££
✝ Sunday Services 0800, 1215, & 1500

French restaurant **Le Champignon Sauvage** in Cheltenham has been serving fine food for over 20 years and is still winning awards and accolades for distinguished food and service. Not cheap but you do get what you pay for.

✉ 24 Suffolk Road, Cheltenham
☎ +44 (0)1242 573 449   ££££

We're not sure if Prince Charles ever pops in for a cup of properly drawn Earl Grey, but **Café 53**, in Tetbury, near his Highgrove residence is a cheery, busy place and open every day for drinks and meals. The café is near the Prince's Highgrove shop at 10 Long Street, which sells produce from his estate.

✉ Long Street, Tetbury
☎ +44 (0)1666 502 020   ££–£££

Local ales and Cotswold lager are served at **The Snooty Fox** in Tetbury, along with high-class pub food.

✉ Market Place, Tetbury
☎ +44 (0)1666 502 436   ££££

Spiritual Retreats
Lancashire, Merseyside and Cumbria Carnforth

17

Monastery of Our Lady of Hyning

The **Carnforth** area is noted for its natural scenic beauty and the **Monastery of Our Lady of Hyning** is situated in an attractive rural landscape on the edge of the Lakes District on the Lancashire-Cumbria border. The monastery is run by Catholic sisters of the Bernadine Cistercians of Esquermes, a branch of the Cistercian order founded by St Robert of Molesme (c. 1029–1111) in Cîteaux in Burgundy, France in 1098. The Bernadine Cistercians took their name from St Bernard of Clairvaux (1091–1153), who was instrumental in establishing monasteries for both men and women.

❡ The sisters in Carnforth conduct a program of guided or individual retreats and days of silence throughout the year (closed January/July/August). The guesthouse is open to people of all Christian faiths and denominations who wish to make a retreat or spend some quiet days in a monastic environment. The sisters meet in the chapel for prayer six times each day and guests are welcome to participate.

❡ Guest accommodation comprises of a number of single, twin and double guestrooms in the main monastery building while cottages on the estate provide additional guestrooms. A lift is available in the main monastery building and some rooms have wheelchair access. Bathrooms are shared as there are no en suites. Guests are requested to bring a towel and soap. Tea and coffee making facilities are provided. All meals are served and guests are asked to help with light cleaning duties. The guesthouse has a residents' lounge, library and gift shop.

✉ Warton
Carnforth LA5 9SE

🛏 from £67.00 pp per weekend, including all meals.

📞 +44 (0) 1524 732 684
not after 8:00pm *or on Sundays*
📠 +44 (0) 1524 720 287

✉ hyningbookings@yahoo.co.uk

✉ www.bernardine.org/hyninge

☞ The nearest train station is Carnforth, 3 miles south of the monastery. Take a taxi from here or travel on the Carnforth Connect Bus (line 1) which stops at the monastery.

♿ Discuss your needs in advance of arriving, ideally when booking.

✝ **Sunday Mass 0900.**
Church of St Mary, 2 Yealand Road, Yealand Conyers nr Carnforth.

⚭ Open to men & women

PLACES OF INTEREST ❧ Films produced over 50 years apart have brought fame to **Carnforth Train Station**. Scenes from the movie version of **Noel Coward**'s (1899–1973) *Brief Encounter* were shot on location here in 1945. The Hogwarts' Express of *Harry Potter* fame is stored at the West Coast Railway Depot in Carnforth and is occasionally put on public view. Unfortunately, because of a dispute between local tourism authorities and the film series' producers, the train cannot be used as an everyday tourist attraction, and so it remains locked away.

❧ The Jacobean **Gawthorpe Hall** in Padiham, 49 miles south of Carnforth, exhibits a world-renowned collection of lace and embroidery kept by the last family member to live there, the **Hon Rachel Kay-Shuttleworth** (1886–1967). The Kay-Shuttleworths (Rachel's grandparents, James and Janet) were friends of the Brontës. **Charlotte Brontë** (1816–1865) was a regular visitor to Gawthorpe Hall which is now the final stop on the 43-mile Brontë Way. This waymarked walking trail links places associated with the Brontë family, particularly Charlotte. The walk commences at the Elizabethan manor house **Oakwell Hall** in **Kirklees**, after which the family home 'Fieldhead' in Charlotte Brontë's novel *Shirley* is named.

❧ On Easter Monday, the ancient and tricky custom of egg rolling takes place in **Preston**, south of Carnforth. Easter eggs are rolled down a grassy slope with the winner being the roller of the first egg to reach the bottom still intact. And there is no rule stating that they can't be eaten!

❧ **Ulverston**, a scenic 30-mile drive from Carnforth through Cumbria, is a town of old-world charm and cobbled streets. Its street market is regarded as the oldest in the South Lakeland with a Market Charter dating back to 1280. The Town Crier opens the market which trades on Thursdays and Saturdays from 0800 to 1630. **The Kendal Street Market** (indoors) is open each Wednesday and Saturday from 0800 to 1630; the local chocolate speciality, Kendal Mint Cake, is sure to be on sale.

❧ **The Cumbria Crystal Factory** at The Lakes Glass Centre in Ulverston is open every weekday. Visitors to the factory can take a tour of the premises and browse the factory shop which retails crystal with minute imperfections. Or visit the **Laurel and Hardy Museum**. Comedian Stan Laurel (1890–1965) was born in Ulverston.

Spiritual Retreats
Lancashire, Merseyside and Cumbria Carnforth

The **Lancaster Canal Walk** from **Kendal** to **Tewitfield** follows the canal tow path for 14 pretty miles through peaceful Lancashire countryside. The shorter **Kendal** to **Sedgewick** route is 4 miles long. Discover more of the canal in a self-drive narrowboat.

The **Leeds–Lancaster–Morecambe** scenic railway through the Dales countryside departs up to five times each day. Passengers can get off and explore towns and villages en route before re-joining the train. The tiny, stone village of **Giggleswick** is the first stop on the route; **Carnforth** and **Lancaster** are also on this line. The **Brief Encounter Tearoom** on Carnforth Station is open every day between April and October and a gift shop sells an assortment of collectibles.

FOOD AND DRINK The **Hazelmere Café** in **Grange-over-Sands** is a winner of the English Tea Guild's Award for Excellence. As expected, the café serves a vast range of unusual teas from different continents. Tea is poured from 'proper' teapots and served in fine bone china tea cups. Take home some home-made damson conserve.

✉ Yewbarrow Terrace, Grange-over-Sands

☎ +44 (0) 1539 532 972   £££

The **Wolfhouse Gallery and Restaurant** in **Silverdale**, north of Carnforth, is a family-run gallery and restaurant presenting an assortment of contemporary ceramics, glassware, paintings and jewellery. The gallery's smart Wolfhouse Restaurant is open for all meals.

✉ Lindeth Road, Silverdale, nr Carnforth

☎ +44 (0) 1524 701 405   ££££

A good, cheap, no-frills meal can be had at **The Heron Café** in the coastal town of **Arnside**. The traditional menu often includes the old English standbys of crumbed plaice, haddock and roast lamb. Special prices for seniors. The Heron is open for lunch and dinner. Not licensed.

✉ The Promenade, Arnside

☎ +44 (0) 1524 762 482   ££

Spiritual Retreats

Lancashire, Merseyside and Cumbria Prescot

18

Loyola Hall
Jesuit Spirituality Centre

The small village of **Rainhill** on the outskirts of Liverpool is the location of **Loyola Hall**. Once the Manor of Rainhall, since 1923 the hall has been a house of prayer run by Jesuit priests who are assisted by religious sisters and laity. Situated in large beautiful grounds, the team welcomes Christians from all denominations, along with those who have no religious affiliation, to take part in a program of individual, guided or themed retreats. A three-dimensional approach is taken to all retreats and spiritual exercises with healing of the body, mind and spirit being the aim. As well as a chapel and prayer rooms, the complex includes a small gym with a sauna, an 'art room', and plenty of reading material is on hand. Other facilities include conference and meeting rooms and guest lounge rooms. All 45 guestrooms have en suite facilities. Twin and double rooms are available. Occasionally, retreats are offered in languages other than English.

❧ Loyola Hall is surrounded by tranquil gardens and well-trodden walking paths weave from the property through the surrounding countryside. Parking is provided for overnight guests.

✉ Warrington Road,
Rainhill,
Prescot L35 6NZ

🚆 from £35.00 pp,
including all meals.

📞 +44 (0) 1514 264 137
📠 +44 (0) 1514 310 115

✉ mail@loyolahall.co.uk

✉ www.loyolahall.co.uk

☞ The nearest railway station is Rainhill which is 1 mile north of the centre. Prescot is 9 miles east of the centre of Liverpool.

✝ Sunday Mass
0830 & 1000.
St Bartholemew's Catholic Church, Chapel Road, Rainhill.

👥 Open to men, women & groups

Spiritual Retreats
Lancashire, Merseyside and Cumbria Prescot

PLACES OF INTEREST ✆ In 2008 the
Rev John Davies, the Rector of the
Good Shepherd Anglican Church
in **West Derby**, a few miles north of
Rainhill, embarked on an unusual
method of attracting parishioners'
attention. He undertook a 2-month,
108-mile walk along the busy M62 from
Hull in Yorkshire, through Leeds and
Manchester to Liverpool. During the
walk he kept a detailed diary of the
places he visited and the people he met
along the way. His book *Walking the
M62* makes fascinating reading and can
be purchased at *www.lulu.com*.

⚜ Sunday Services 1030 *(1st & 3rd Sundays)*,
1830 *(2nd, 4th & 5th Sundays)*

❡ **Prescot** is a medieval market town on
the outskirts of Liverpool. Within the
Prescot Museum there is an exhibition
of clock and watchmaking, a craft for
which the town was once famous. Items
from the town's former pottery and
ceramic workshops are also on display.
The museum's exhibits highlight the
heritage of the local area. A little further
north at **Leyland** and south of **Preston**,
the **British Commercial Vehicle
Museum** displays the Popemobile made
especially for **Pope John Paul II** when
he visited the UK in 1982.

❡ A 5-mile motoring trail through the
Knowsley Safari Park in Prescot leads
past camels, buffalo, white rhino and
tigers. The park is on land owned by the
18th Earl of Derby, a notable wildlife
conservationist; **Knowsley House**
is the seat of his family, the Stanleys.
The Earl also runs a successful horse
stud in Newmarket. **The Epsom Derby**
horse race was named after his ancestor
Edward Smith-Stanley, the 12th Earl of
Derby (1752–1834), in 1779. The race was
previously called the Epsom Oaks.

❡ If snow sports appeal, you don't
need to wait for winter to go skiing
in Lancashire. **The Chill Factor^e**, a
state-of-the-art all-season snow sports
centre in Manchester, has slopes, ski
lifts, snowboarding facilities and a
challenging, high-speed luge track for
the extremist. Open every day.

❡ The racecourse, stables and equine
museum of **Aintree**, 8 miles north
of Prescot, is the site of the **Grand
National Steeplechase**, held each
April. When visiting the course and
museum, be sure to saddle up on the
Grand National steeplechase simulator,
an experience you won't easily forget.
Ladies Day at the Grand National race
meeting in Aintree is usually on a Friday,
an occasion when the fashion off the
field attracts more attention than the
fillies galloping around it.

❡ **The National Wildflower Centre** in Roby Road, **Liverpool** is open from March until the end of August and visitors are more than likely to be greeted with a blaze of colour.

❡ Golf enthusiasts can be well challenged in Lancashire. **Tiger Woods** (b. 1975) of the USA won the 2006 British Open at the **Royal Liverpool Golf Club**, and in 2008 Lancashire's **Royal Birkdale** was the venue of the British Open won by Irishman **Padraig Harrington** (b. 1971).

❡ Shop for clothing bargains at **McArthur Glen Designer Outlet** at Cheshire Oaks.

FOOD AND DRINK ❡ **The Three Fishes** pub in **Mitton** was established some 400 years ago and is linked to the nearby **Whalley Abbey** (*see Additional Accommodation*, page 240). The coat of arms of the last abbot of Whalley, Abbott Parslew, can be seen above the pub's front entrance. Fresh local farm produce, Morecambe Bay shrimps and Lancashire cheeses feature on the restaurant menu.

✉ Mitton Road, Mitton, nr Whalley

✆ +44 (0) 1254 826 888   £££

❡ Devotees of the up-market, contemporary British cuisine served at the 'special occasion' **Longridge Restaurant** near **Preston** can always book in for a day-long cookery class which is based on the Longridge menu.

✉ 106 Higher Road, Longridge, nr Preston.

✆ +44 (0) 1772 784 969   £££££

❡ Remember sarsaparilla? Treat yourself to a pint of blood cleansing sarsaparilla cordial at **Fitzpatrick's Temperance Bar** in **Rawtenstall**, 28 miles north-east of Prescott, the country's last original temperance bar. Ice-cream floats, herbal tonics, cream soda and ginger beer are also available.

✉ 5 Bank Street, Rossendale, nr Rawtenstall

✆ +44 (0) 1706 231 836

❡ For a quick bite try the **Deanes House** pub near the historical St Mary's Church and the Clock Museum in Prescot. A casual outdoor eating space opens in summer.

✉ Church Street, Prescot

✆ +44 (0) 151 289 1881   ££

Sussex

HINK OF SUSSEX AND THINK OF CRICKET played on village greens, pukka polo tournaments and the mellow, rolling landscapes of the Sussex Downs. For sun-worshippers the county means Brighton with its famous gaudy pier and pebbly beach—an easy day trip from London.

The Sussex landscape has had its share of literary luminaries too. A. A. Milne (1882–1956) created the inspirational Pooh Bear classics in the village of Hartfield. Virginia Woolf (1882–1941) and her husband Leonard (1880–1969) lived and worked at Monk's House in Rodmell, not far from the River Ouse, the site of Woolf's tragic drowning. Her ashes are buried in the garden at Monk's House.

In 1066 history was written at Battle Abbey, a few miles north of the seaside town of Hastings, when the Battle of Hastings was fought and lost to the Normans led by William the Conquerer.

Christianity in Sussex harks back to Saxon times when St Wilfred of York, a Benedictine monk, established the county's first monastery at Selsey in 681 AD. Benedictines went on to establish Battle Abbey. Much of the county is steeped in customs and traditions from centuries past; in the town of Lewes it was once (but is now controversial) the custom to publicly burn an effigy of Pope Paul V each 5 November. This goes back to the same date in 1605 when Guy Fawkes (1570–1606), encouraged by some high-ranking officials of the Catholic Church, tried to set fire to the British Houses of Parliament. Thankfully, today's Catholic hierarchy are a more peace-loving lot!

SPIRITUAL RETREAT

19

Worth Abbey

Worth Abbey, the sister of **Downside Abbey** in Bath, is run by monks of the Benedictine Order. They offer an 'open cloister' arrangement for those who want to take time out from their daily life and routine to spend some time in the peace and calm of a monastic environment. Christians of all denominations are invited to attend the retreats and join in the religious services organised by the monks. Special programs are also conducted for those who have no experience of attending a formal retreat or participating in guided prayer.

‹ Accommodation is offered in the abbey guesthouse, St Bruno's, which has large family rooms and twin bedrooms, some of which are en suite. Single bedrooms are available in a separate house on the estate. The guests' lounge has 'help yourself' tea and coffee facilities, comfy armchairs and a large fireplace. All meals are available but continental breakfast is on a self-serve basis. Guests are requested to bring their own towels and to lend a hand with minor chores.

‹ Those who are unable to stay overnight can participate in single days of retreat and prayer. The abbey's 100-year-old garden is part of a worldwide network of 'quiet gardens' where the surroundings encourage prayer and meditation. The monks of Worth Abbey also run a 'Soul Gym', an ethics workshop for businessmen and women. The Abbot of Worth, **Dom Christopher Jamison**, recently criticised the Disney Corporation for its 'commercial exploitation of spirituality.' Crawley is 20 miles north of the seaside town of Brighton and 20 miles south of the centre of London.

✉ The Bookings
Secretary
The Open Cloister
Worth Abbey
Paddockhurst Road
Turners Hill
Crawley RH10 4SB

▣ price to be negotiated.

☏ +44 (0) 1342 710 318
☏ +44 (0) 1342 710 311

✎ TOC@worthabbey.net

✎ www.worthabbey.net

☞ The nearest rail station is Three Bridges, which is the station after Gatwick Airport coming from the direction of London. Take a taxi from Three Bridges to the abbey, 4 miles away. You may need to telephone for a taxi.

♱ **Sunday Mass** 0930.
Worth Abbey, Crawley.

⚭ Open to men, women & groups

🛏 Accommodation for up to 250 people is offered to groups during the English school holidays. Conference facilities are available. Please contact:

✉ The Bursar,
Worth Abbey

☏ +44 (0) 1342 710 225
☏ +44 (0) 1342 710 291

✎ amurray@worth.org.uk

Spiritual Retreats
Sussex Crawley

PLACES OF INTEREST ❧ A pleasant way of rediscovering some of Sussex's major historical events is to take the **1066 Country Walk** from **Pevensey Castle** to **Battle Abbey** and back down to the town of **Rye**, re-tracing the footsteps of **William the Conqueror** (c. 1028–c. 1087). Pevensey is on the coast between Hastings and Eastbourne; the 31-mile walk can be taken in shorter sections.

❧ The historic **Battle Abbey** remained Benedictine-owned up until the Dissolution of the monasteries. It is now the site of an independent co-educational school while the old abbey gatehouse is the Museum of Monastic Life. The Benedictines re-established themselves in Sussex with the founding of **Worth Abbey** in 1933. In 2005 Worth Abbey featured in the hugely successful BBC television series *The Monastery* which traced the lives of five men training for the priesthood.

❧ **Winchelsea** on the Sussex coast is the smallest town in England, with less than 400 houses. English novelist **Ford Madox Ford** (1873–1939), for many years in a liaison with Australian war artist **Stella Bowen** (1893–1947), lived in Winchelsea between 1901 and 1907. During his time here Ford wrote *A History of the Cinque Ports*, of which Winchelsea is one.

❧ The 11th-century ruins of **Lewes Castle**, 27 miles south of Crawley provide a spectacular backdrop for theatrical and musical performances during the summer months. Much of the history of the area is revealed at the **Lewes Folk Museum**, once the home of **Anne of Cleves**, the fourth wife of **Henry VIII** who in 1540, after a marriage of just six months, left Anne the house as part of the divorce settlement.

❧ The moated 800-year-old Augustinian **Michelham Priory** in **Upper Dicker** (near **Hailsham**, and 18 miles north-east of Brighton) was formerly an Augustinian monastery. Fully restored and open to visitors, it included a guesthouse, which—unfortunately for this publication—closed a few centuries ago.

❧ Followers of Pooh, Piglet and Eeyore can pick up a map from the **Shop at Pooh Corner** in the village of **Hartfield** and take the 'enchanted places' walk, stopping at many of the places mentioned in the tales written by children's author A. A. Milne (1882–1956). Hartfield is 18 miles east of Crawley.

❦ Father David Buckley of **Our Lady Immaculate and St Philip Neri Catholic Church** in **Uckfield**, East Sussex has taken a 21st-century approach to religion. He commissioned **Marcus Cornish** (an up-and-coming young English sculptor) to design a statue of a 'modern' looking Christ, for the church. Dubbed 'Jesus in Jeans' the figure is dressed in a pair of daggy jeans and a stylish shirt, complete with well-groomed hair and beard.

❦ **East Grinstead** is just 8 miles east of Crawley and from here the number 473 bus (which does not operate every day) can be taken to **Kingscote**, at the start of the **Blue Bell Steam** (scenic) **Railway** to Sheffield Park, 9 miles south. The steam railway is on the most popular tourist attractions in Sussex and afternoon tea and full meals are available on some services. The railway is manned by volunteers and operates on weekends and during school holidays.

❦ You could take home a 'trug' from **The Truggery** in **Herstmonceux** near Hailsham. A 'trug' is a traditional, hand-crafted willow or chestnut basket. The craftspeople at The Truggery make them according to the traditional method.

FOOD AND DRINK ❦ Succulent, meaty **Rye Bay** scallops can be polished off at the local **Rye Fish Café**, which serves seafood fresh from the fishing trawlers. Diners have a great view of the chefs preparing the orders. A smattering of meat dishes are also on the menu.

✉ 17 Tower Street, Rye.

☎ +44 (0)1797 222 226   £££

❦ **The Parson's Pig** in **Crawley** serves all meals every day with the speciality being the Sunday roast. The big plasma screen ensures it is well supported by locals who are into their football.

✉ Balcombe Road, Crawley.

☎ +44 (0)1293 883 104   ££

❦ The Crown at Turner's Hill is not far from Worth Abbey and along with traditional ales serves 'proper' English pub food including pork pie, sausages and mash, and ploughman's lunch. The locally produced, award-winning Duddleswell cheese and wines from the local Carr Taylor vineyard might feature on the menu.

✉ Turner's Hill, East Crawley.

☎ +44 (0)1342 715 218   ££

❦ There are plenty of homely, cosy tea rooms in the **Rye** area and all serve delicious English cream tea.

Pilgrimages
England

London

❧ Just over 100 years old, **Westminster Cathedral** is the 19th-century seat of the current Catholic Archbishop of London, **Cormac Cardinal Murphy-O'Connor** (b. 1932). Since 1066 the Anglican **Westminster Abbey** has been the majestic setting of coronations, a place of prayer for kings and prime ministers, and the burial place of monarchs and statesmen. However, **Canterbury Cathedral** in Kent is the 'mother' church of the Church of England and the seat of the Archbishop of Canterbury, the Primate of All England the Most Reverend and Right Honourable **Rowan Douglas Williams** (b. 1950)—Archbishop number 104.

❧ For almost 20 years the parish of the central London Church of **St Martin-in-the-Fields** has organised a pilgrims' walk from this popular church in Trafalgar Square, south to **Canterbury Cathedral**, following the footsteps of those pilgrims mentioned in Geoffrey Chaucer's *Canterbury Tales*. The walk is traditionally held on the last weekend of May and covers the 72-mile-long old **Pilgrims' Way. Aylesford Priory** (*See page 173*) is one of the overnight stops on the 3-night walk.

❧ The annual Tyburn Way Pilgrimage from the **Church of St Sepulchre** in Holborn to the **Tyburn Priory** in Edgware Road, Marble Arch honours the memory of over 100 Catholics who were martyred on the Tyburn Gallows between 1535 and 1681. The Church of St Sepulchre stands near the site of the **Newgate Prison** where (St) **Oliver Plunkett**, a former Archbishop of Armagh and Primate of All Ireland (1669–1681), and numerous other Catholics were imprisoned. The 3-mile route is the same path along which these early martyrs were taken to the site of their execution. A tiny cross-shaped plaque can be seen in the middle of busy Edgware Road where the 'Tyburn Tree' gallows once stood (between 1196 and 1783.)

❧ The sisters of the **Tyburn Convent**, near Marble Arch, conduct a program of continuous adoration of the Blessed Sacrament. On one evening of each month members of the public are invited to join the sisters in maintaining the all-night vigil. The sisters are members of the Adorers of the Sacred Heart of Jesus of Montmartre and take turns in keeping watch day and night. The church is open to the public between 0615 and 2000 every day.

☦ Sunday Mass 0730.

Tyburn Convent Church, 8 Hyde Park Place.

❧ In medieval times pilgrims who were unable to visit the Holy Land would follow the custom of 'walking the labyrinth', which was recognised as a type of pilgrimage in itself. The labyrinth in **St Paul's Cathedral** in London can be followed in person (headphones supplied) or online at *www.labyrinth.org.uk*. Visitors to the site can also light a candle and post a prayer.

❧ The architect of the great cathedral, **Sir Christopher Wren** (1632–1723), had two of his previous designs rejected before the third was finally approved by **King Charles II** in 1675.

☦ Sunday Services 0800, 1015, 1130, 1515 & 1800.

St Paul's Cathedral.

❧ The **Rosminian Church of St Etheldreda** in Ely Place in Holburn was once part of the Palace of the Bishops of Ely. Dedicated to **St Etheldreda** (c. 636–679), who was the inspiration for the great **Ely Cathedral** in Cambridgeshire), St Etheldreda's is the oldest Catholic church in England with a history dating back to 1250. It is thought that a nearby pub, the **Mitre Tavern**, was built by one of the Ely bishops. The bishops were renowned for growing the most delicious strawberries in the country and a strawberry fair is held here every June.

☦ Sunday Mass 0900 & 1100 (*Sung Latin*).

Church of St Ethedreda.

❧ The London-based **St Francis of Assisi Catholic Ramblers' Club** was established 75 years ago. The mainstay of the club is the Sunday ramble which takes place rain, hail or shine in or around the city of London. Each walk is led by an experienced guide and pilgrimage walks in other counties in the UK as well as in parts of Europe are arranged from time to time.

❧ *www.stfrancisramblers.org.uk*

Pilgrimages
England

Cambridgeshire

❦ **Ely Cathedral** has been a place of pilgrimage since medieval times when people came to visit the **Shrine of St Etheldreda**, who established a monastery here in the 7th century. She became the first Abbess of the **Monastery of Ely** in 673. The monastery was subsequently destroyed by Danish invaders in 870. A church was established on the site in the 12th century but a shrine dedicated to St Etheldreda was destroyed in 1541 on the orders of **Henry VIII**. The place where the shrine stood is now the site of the present-day Ely Cathedral where pilgrims still come today to pray to St Etheldreda.

✟ Sunday Services 0815, 1030 & 1600.
   Ely Cathedral.

❦ Drinks and sandwiches are available from the cathedral's **Refectory Café** and more substantial offerings are served at **The Almonry Restaurant and Tea Rooms** on Ely's High Street.

❦ The tiny **Anglican Church of St John** at **Little Gidding**, 37 miles north of Cambridge, has a history dating back to the early 1200s when the Bishop of Lincoln, **John de Stanford** (1313–1335), was appointed the first rector. This gorgeous church nestles in the heart of rural Huntingdonshire and its intriguing interior is a time capsule of the past 800 years. Poet **T. S. Eliot** (1888–1965) wrote about Little Gidding in his poem 'Four Quartets'.

So, while the light fails
On a winter's afternoon, in a
*   secluded chapel*
History is now and England.

✟ Sunday Services 1500 & 1800.
   Church of St John, Little Gidding.

Channel Islands: Jersey

❧ The Patron Saint of **Jersey**, **St Helier** (*St-Hélier*, d. 555), established a monastery on the island in the 6th century. His Feast Day, 16 July, is a day of celebration and pilgrimage to the hermitage where he once lived. The hermitage stands high on a rocky outcrop next to the site of the original monastery and can only be reached on foot at low tide.

❧ Ferries depart the mainland at **Poole** and **Portsmouth** for **St Helier** which is 2 hours away by fast boat. A day trip to France can be arranged from St Helier; travelling time by ferry to **St Malo** in Brittany is approximately 1 hour.

❧ **St Helier**'s prime export is its locally produced pear cider which can be purchased on the island and sampled at the **La Mare Winery** in the Parish of St Mary. There is a strong French influence on St Helier, reflected in the local cuisine. Many of the restaurants serve seafood and have fine views, some overlooking wide, white sandy beaches or picturesque harbours bobbing with leisure craft and fishing boats. Nature has been kind to the island which can be easily explored; specially marked 'lanes' are set aside for walkers, cyclists and horse riders—just go easy on the cider!

Cornwall

❧ Once the site of a Benedictine monastery, **St Michael's Mount** became a mecca for pilgrims during the 5th century after an apparition said to be **St Michael the Archangel** was reportedly seen by a local fisherman. Miracles were said to have occurred and from then on pilgrims arrived in their droves. St Michael's Mount can be reached on foot at low tide via a man-made causeway or by boat from the coastal town of **Marazion**. The castle on the island has been occupied by the descendants of the same family, the **St Aubyns**, for more than 300 years. They have a 999-year lease on the island estate.

❧ Visitors to **St Michael's Mount** are well catered for with a garden café and an island restaurant offering various dining options. The National Trust is the custodian of the island and runs a well-stocked gift and souvenir shop.

Durham

❧ **Durham Cathedral** is the final resting place of **St Cuthbert** (635–687) and **St Bede** (672–735). St Cuthbert was the Prior of the **Lindisfarne** monastery on Holy Island and the Bishop of Lindisfarne; St Bede was a member of the Benedictine monastery of **Monkwearmouth** in Sunderland.

❧ Visitors to **Durham Cathedral** can make a private pilgrimage by following instructions in a booklet written by the current dean of the cathedral, the Very Rev **Michael Sadgrove** (b. 1950). From time to time the Benedictine monks who reside here conduct live-in retreats which commence with the dean leading a pilgrimage around the cathedral. Pilgrimages further afield can be arranged. Accommodation is provided in the nearby **St Chad's College** (*see* page 238).

✝ Sunday Services 0800, 1000, 1115 & 1530.
   Durham Cathedral.

Essex

❧ Those looking for spiritual solace could make a private pilgrimage to the 7th-century **Chapel of St Peter-on-the-Wall** at **Bradwell-on-Sea** (strictly speaking *Bradwell-on-the-River Blackwater*). The annual Bradwell pilgrimage is held on the first Saturday of July each year and 'quiet days' of contemplation are conducted here during the year. The Chaplain of the Church of St Peter-on-the-Wall, along with the Othona Eucumenical Christian Community, organise the pilgrimage. The community offers hostel-style accommodation with shared bathrooms and simple meals to pilgrims and visitors. Reflecting its multi-denominational focus, the pilgrimage has been led at various times by hierarchy of the Catholic and Anglican churches and leaders of other Christian religious denominations.

❧ There is a very pleasant old English pub in the village, **The Green Man**, where meals and drinks are available. A rustic beer-garden overlooks the River Blackwater.

Hampshire

◖ The 155-mile long **Hampshire to France Pilgrimage Trail** commences at the **Shrine of St Swithun** (also spelt *Swithin*) in **Winchester Cathedral** and weaves down to **Portsmouth** on the southern English coast, 28 miles away. From Portsmouth pilgrims can take the ferry to **Cherbourg** in France and travel south on a well-marked trail to the island **Abbey of Mont St-Michel**. Some pilgrims then join the trail to the **Shrine of St James** in **Santiago de Compostela** in Galicia, Spain.

◖ A separate **Pilgrims' Way** route leads from **Winchester Cathedral** to the **Shrine of Thomas Becket** in **Canterbury Cathedral** in Kent, a distance of 120 miles. The pathways of the National Trail form part of the route.

◖ The section known as **St Swithun's Way**, named after **St Swithun** (800–862), a former Bishop of Winchester, heads out from Winchester Cathedral to **Farnham** where it links with the **North Downs Way** (National Trail) and stretches further to Canterbury. St Swithun, the Patron Saint of Rain, expressed a desire to be buried outdoors 'where the rain would fall on him and the feet of ordinary men could pass over him'. His wishes were granted, but in 870, when local monks attempted to move his body to a spectacular shrine inside Winchester Cathedral, they were prevented from doing so by a deluge of torrential rain which lasted for 40 days and 40 nights. This led to the legend that if it rains on St Swithun's Day on 15 July, 40 days and nights of rain will follow. However, the monks finally got their way, although the shrine was later destroyed and relics of St Swithun somehow ended up in various churches across the land.

♰ Sunday Service 0800. Winchester Cathedral.

◖ The award-winning **Refectory Restaurant**, part of Winchester Cathedral, is open daily for lunch or Hampshire cream teas.

Pilgrimages
England

Hertfordshire

❡ The cathedral in the town of
St Alban's, around 50 minutes' drive
up the M25 from London, was founded
on the site where **St Alban** (d. 304) was
beheaded for refusing to relinquish his
Christian beliefs. St Alban was born in
the town, at the time called Verulamium,
and was Britain's first Christian martyr.
Every year, around the time of St Alban's
Feast Day on 17 June, a pilgrimage
commences at the **Roman Verulamium**
(museum), the site of St Alban's trial,
and follows a path to the Shrine of
St Alban in the local cathedral. At
other times during the year thousands
of people make their own personal
pilgrimage to the shrine. Legend
says a red rose bush appeared before
St Alban as he was led to his execution;
hence, it is traditional for pilgrims to
carry or wear a red rose during the
pilgrimage walk. St Alban's relics were
removed from the shrine during the
Dissolution of the Monasteries and were
subsequently lost.

✟ Sunday Services 0800, 0930 & 1830.
   St Alban's Cathedral.

❡ Lighthearted activities on the day
of the annual pilgrimage may include
chariot racing and 'lion' taming.
The Cathedral Café is open for tea
and meals.

Kent

❧ **The Friars** at **Aylesford** is a stop on the **Pilgrims' Way** to Canterbury and beyond and has been so since medieval times. The Carmelite friars who live and work in this beautiful priory conduct special days of pilgrimage throughout the summer months and all are welcome to join in. Throughout the year the public can participate in daily Mass, in all-night vigils and prayer services, and join in the religious celebrations on saints' Feast Days.

♱ Sunday Mass 0800 & 1015 *(times may change)*.
The Friars, Ayelsford.

❧ **The Friar's Tea Room** is located in a 17th-century, thatched-roofed barn and is open until late afternoon. An adjacent gift shop sells books, religious and non-religious articles, including a cheap, useful, eco-friendly hessian carry bag emblazoned on one side with the words 'Aylesford Priory' which is large enough to hold a stockpile of books and souvenirs.

❧ **Canterbury** in Kent was once a Celtic sacred place. When the Romans arrived, they introduced pagan laws which remained in place until the 6th century when **St Augustine** (d. 604) established the iconic **Canterbury Cathedral** and became its first archbishop. Over the centuries the cathedral has been added to and sections rebuilt. Some 600 years after the cathedral was founded, **Thomas Becket** (1118–1170), Chancellor of All England and Archbishop of Canterbury, was slain on the orders of the then king, **Henry II** (1133–1189). Becket's martyrdom and the subsequent destruction of his shrine by **Henry VIII** (1491–1547) was the catalyst for the cathedral becoming such an eminent place of Christian worship and pilgrimage. The location of the shrine, in the cathedral's **Trinity Chapel**, is marked by a burning candle.

♱ Sunday Services 0800, 0930 & 1100.
Canterbury Cathedral, The Precincts.

❧ The **Canterbury Cathedral** gift shop at 25 Burgate sells an eclectic selection of T-shirts, food items, scarves, jewellery, books, religious items and souvenirs.

Lancashire

❡ **The Ladyewell Shrine** (or Shrine of
Our Lady of the Well) is in **Fernyhalgh**,
along an isolated rural laneway
(Fernyhalgh Lane) 4 miles north-east
of **Preston**. The origins of the shrine
date back to the 11th century. Each
year scores of pilgrims visit the well
which is said to be linked to miraculous
healings. Numerous liturgical
celebrations take place in the church
here, including pilgrimages, Benediction
and Mass (both in the church and
outdoors). Relics, said to be those of
St Thomas Becket who was murdered at
Canterbury Cathedral, are kept here.

✝ Sunday Mass 1000 & 1500.

Church of St Mary of Fernyhalgh and Ladyewell.

❡ The locals say **Preston** has the best
markets in Lancashire; a vast indoor
fair is held in the town's **Market Hall**
every day except Sunday and an outdoor
market takes place each Monday,
Wednesday, Friday and Saturday.
An annual **Pot Fair** is usually held the
first week in September when potters
and artists come from far and wide to
sell their wares.

Norfolk

❡ A 60-mile-long medieval pilgrims'
route leads from **Ely Cathedral** in
Cambridgeshire to **Walsingham**
in Norfolk and is known as the
Walsingham Way. From Ely the trail
leads to **Swaffham** (a bustling market is
held in the town square each Saturday),
then on to the village of **Helhoughton**,
past the ruins of **Castle Acre Priory** (the
first Clunaic monastery in England) and
finally to the ruins of an Augustinian
monastery where a 12th-century
Holy House (a replica of the house in
which the Holy Family is said to have
lived in Nazareth) once held a much-
revered shrine (pre-Henry VIII). For
centuries a place of pilgrimage, the
monks established a chapel 1 mile from
the village; this became known as the
'Slipper Chapel' as it was customary for
pilgrims to walk this last 'Holy Mile'
barefoot.

❦ The Anglican Church has also established a Shrine to **Our Lady of Walsingham**, much frequented by pilgrims, and a separate 'Holy House' which contains a shrine modelled after the original. Both Catholic and Anglican churches conduct varied programs of pilgrimage (pilgrimage season is Easter to October) and daily liturgical services; both offer accommodation (*see* page 241).

☦ Sunday Services. *Times vary and are dependent on the number of pilgrims in residence.*
Anglican Shrine of Our Lady of Walsingham.

☦ Sunday Mass 1200. *Times may vary.*
Chapel of Reconciliation *or the* Slipper Chapel, Catholic Shrine of Our Lady of Walsingham.

❦ Pilgrims of all religious denominations join in the annual **Student Cross Pilgrimage** to Walsingham over the Easter long weekend. Participants walk to Walsingham, leaving from a number of different locations including London, Oxford, Leicester, Colchester and Nottingham. Accommodation is pre-arranged and after a hard day's march many pilgrims find a cosy pub where they can talk and relax over a quiet drink. Each group finally meets up in **Walsingham** to celebrate not only the Easter religious traditions but the social traditions as well, especially the 'pilgrims' party' held on Easter Saturday evening. The Student Cross Pilgrimage was first established in 1948 and many of the participants are happy returnees.

❦ The area's farmers sell only the freshest fruit and vegetables from their outlet in Guild Street in the centre of **Little Walsingham**. Other locally produced goods are also available. Try Mrs Temple's Walsingham cheese or tasty Norfolk Dapple (cheddar) from the nearby Ferndale Farm; or pack a picnic of home-made meat pies, Norfolk ham, locally baked bread and refreshing Norfolk cider.

Northumberland

❦ The Holy Island of **Lindisfarne** has been a place of pilgrimage for people of all religious views and persuasions ever since Irish monks, led by **St Aidan** (d. 651), settled here in 635. The monks came from a monastery on the **Isle of Iona** on the west coast of Scotland. St Aiden's monks wrote the *Lindisfarne Gospels*, an irreplaceable illuminated book of Latin manuscripts, which is now safely deposited in the British Library in London. A copy of the Gospels, thought to have been written in honour of **St Cuthbert**, a 7th-century Prior of Lindisfarne Priory, are stored in the Treasury of **Durham Cathedral**. Each Easter, the **Northern Cross Pilgrimage** departs from various towns and villages in northern England and Scotland in time to reach Lindisfarne Abbey on Holy Island by Good Friday. The route from the border town of **Melrose** departs from the 12th-century **Melrose Abbey** (St Cuthbert was prior of the original Melrose Abbey, which was established nearby), trails along the River Tweed, and navigates around the Eildon Hills and across the rolling curves of the Cheviots to **Holy Island** 65 miles away. The average time taken by most pilgrims is 5 days.

❦ From some miles away pilgrims will glimpse the 16th-century **Lindisfarne Castle** which stands out clearly on the peak of the island. The ruins of the 11th-century **Lindisfarne Priory** are nearby. The island is connected to the mainland by a 3-mile causeway, and visits to and from Lindisfarne are only possible at low tide.

❦ Throughout the year pilgrims and visitors are invited to participate in retreats and quiet days conducted by various church groups on the island or to spend some time in a spiritual sanctuary. Most formal retreats include a visit to the **Gospel Garden**s in tiny **Lindisfarne Village**. The gardens are designed in patterns similar to those depicted in the illuminated, 7th-century manuscripts.

❦ At the local **Lindisfarne Winery** in the centre of the village, pilgrims can sample the local mead, an alcoholic concoction of honey, herbs and local water, which according to taste may or may not complement the other island speciality—fresh crab sandwiches.

Somerset

❧ A place of folklore, legend and myth, **Glastonbury** has for over 2 millennia been considered a significant place of Christian spirituality. Indeed, it is often referred to as 'the cradle of English Christianity'. Some believe Jesus himself visited Glastonbury. To discover more about Glastonbury and its rich Christian heritage you could pick up a map from the local tourist information centre at 9 High Street and follow a self-guided walking trail around the town. The trail commences at the site of the ruins of **Glastonbury Abbey**. Along the way pilgrims can stop for refreshment in the Pilgrims' Bar of **The George**, also known as The George and Pilgrims' Inn, a 15th-century pub in High Street established by a one-time Abbot of Glastonbury, **John de Selwood** (abbot from 1456–1493), to provide accommodation for visiting pilgrims. Some believe an underground tunnel links the abbey with the pub, where to this day there's still a monk's cell and a confessional.

❧ The annual **Glastonbury Anglican Pilgrimage** is held on a Saturday each June and the Catholic Pilgrimage on a Sunday in the same month. The Anglican Pilgrimage commences at 1000 with an outdoor service among the abbey ruins which is followed by a procession led by clergy carrying a statue of the Blessed Virgin. The pilgrimage concludes with an afternoon prayer service at 1530. People of all religious denominations and beliefs are welcome to join in.

☩ Sunday Services 0800 & 0930. *No 0930 service on a 5th Sunday of the month.*

St John's Church, High Street, Glastonbury.

❧ The **Glastonbury Catholic Pilgrimage** has been an annual event since 1924 and commences with a church service at 1800 on the previous Saturday evening. The following morning the pilgrims walk to a sacred hill overlooking Glastonbury Abbey called the **Tor**, site of the martyrdom of the last Abbot of Glastonbury, the Blessed **Richard Whiting**, and his fellow monks in 1539. The pilgrimage continues through the town and back to the abbey ruins for Mass at 1530.

☩ Sunday Mass 0830 & 1000.

Latin Mass at **1215** *on the 3rd Sunday of the month.*

Church of St Mary, opposite the Abbey ruins.

❧ **Chalice Well,** one of the oldest holy wells in the country, lies at the base of the **Glastonbury Tor**. Pilgrims have been coming to the well for centuries to drink the water, said to have healing properties, to walk in the surrounding gardens and to simply withdraw from the pressures of daily life.

Pilgrimages
England

Sussex

❦ Each year the parishioners of **Arundel Cathedral** on England's south coast take part in preparing a colourful, artistic and unique display of flowers which they use to decorate the main aisle of the church, following a tradition which was pioneered by the **Duke of Norfolk** in 1877. The Carpet of Flowers is on public display for the 2 days leading up to the Feast of the Body and Blood of Christ, more commonly known as the *Feast of Corpus Christi*. The annual Corpus Christi procession commences with an early evening Mass in the cathedral, followed by a procession to **Arundel Castle** for a religious service. The procession then returns to the cathedral for a closing ceremony. The Feast of Corpus Christi falls on the Thursday after Trinity Sunday, which is 8 weeks after Easter Sunday. However, for practical reasons the celebrations take place on the Sunday following the actual Feast Day.

✝ Sunday Mass 0930 & 1115.

Arundel Cathedral.

❦ You could pop next door to the **St Mary's Gate Hotel** for lunch, or relax over a cup of tea and a snack at **Belinda's Tea Room** in Tarrant Street, which has a pretty rear garden area for outdoor dining.

Yorkshire

❡ The **York Minster Walking Group** meets on the first Saturday of each month. Walks range between 3 and 10 miles in length and most commence at **York Minster**. Some of the walks are to raise money for cathedral projects.

❡ **Pope Paul VI** (Pope from 1963–1978) presided over the canonisation of a new English saint in October 1970. In the 16th century, former Yorkshire butcher's wife and mother of three, **Margaret Clitheroe** (1556–1586), was charged with providing shelter to Catholic priests in her family home in York and also with allowing Mass to be celebrated there. When her activities were discovered she was put on trial and found guilty of the crime of protecting Catholic priests. Her punishment was death by crushing, which was carried out by placing enormous rocks on her back until she suffocated. When Margaret Clitheroe was canonised by Pope Paul VI he referred to her as 'the pearl of York'. A shrine was erected in the house where she and her husband and children once lived at 35 The Shambles, a narrow, cobblestoned medieval lane in the centre of the city. A relic of St Margaret Clitheroe is kept in York's **Bar Convent Museum.**

✝ Saturday Mass 1000. 35 The Shambles.

❡ These days **The Shambles** is a much friendlier place to visit and the street is lined on both sides with a wide choice of shops and eating places. One of the nicest is the charming **Earl Grey Tea Rooms** at number 15 where tea and coffee can be selected from an extensive menu and sipped in a cosy alcove or in the back garden, weather permitting.

❡ A traditional Boxing Day pilgrimage is held in North Yorkshire every year. Commencing at **Ripon Cathedral**, it moves along a 4-mile route to the ruins of the former Cistercian and now World Heritage listed **Fountains Abbey**, following a path once trodden by medieval monks. The pilgrimage concludes with a short service of prayer and thanksgiving. The Ripon Cathedral shop sells not only religious articles but also, surprisingly, jewellery, cosmetics, ceramics and confectionery.

✝ Sunday Services 0930 & 1230. Ripon Cathedral.

Pilgrimages
Northern Ireland

County Armagh

❧ **Armagh**, one of Ireland's oldest settlements, is often referred to as the ecclesiastical capital of the nation. **St Patrick** was once Bishop here (around 444) and both the heads of the Catholic and Anglican churches in Ireland are based in Armagh. In 2007 Catholic Archbishop **Dr Seán Brady** (b. 1939) was promoted to the status of Cardinal by **Pope Benedict XXIII**. **Archbishop Alan Harper** OBE (b. 1944) is the Church of Ireland Archbishop of Armagh and Primate of All Ireland.

❧ Both the Catholic and Anglican churches conduct pilgrimages in and around Armagh to sites linked to **St Patrick** which are also much visited by tourists and pilgrimage groups from other countries.

❧ It may be a myth that **St Patrick** planted the first apple tree in Northern Ireland (said to be at **Ceangoba**, east of Armagh city) but there is no doubt Armagh is still famous for its apples—particularly the Bramley cooking apple, although other varieties with tempting names like Angel Bites and Strawberry Cheeks are great for eating. The local apple cider is said to have sustained the Protestant **King William III** (of Orange; 1650–1702) and his troops before they fought and won the Battle of the Boyne in 1690 against the Catholic **King James II** (1633–1701).

County Down

❧ The (new) **St Patrick's Church** in **Saul** is built on the site of a 5th-century church where it is believed St Patrick preached his first homily. Each year, close to the anniversary of St Patrick's death on 17 March, a pilgrimage commences in the Saul Church and makes its way to the Church of Ireland's **Down Cathedral** in **Downpatrick**, 2 miles away, where St Patrick is buried along with Irish saints **Brigid** and **Columcille**.

♰ Sunday Mass 0930. St Patrick's Church, Saul.

♰ Sunday Service 1130. Down Cathedral.

❧ In nearby **St Ruell Wells**, 1.5 miles east of **Downpatrick**, four ancient wells said to have been blessed by St Patrick draw pilgrims and followers of the saint. It is claimed the waters have healing properties.

❧ In 2009, the Irish musical group **The Priests** made the *Guinness Book of Records* for having the 'Fastest-Selling UK Debut for a Classical Act', with their very first album called *No 5 Debut Album* which was recorded in Ireland and at the Vatican. In 2009 the album made the top 5 of the UK music charts with rock bands Guns N' Roses and The Killers just ahead. If you would like to attend a Mass conducted by one of the stars of The Priests—who in real life are unpretentious parish priests—Mass times at their parish churches are as follows—and with a little luck some singing might just take place.

👤 Very Rev Eugene D. O'Hagan PP

✉ Sacred Heart Church
Doagh Road
Ballyclare
County Down

♰ Sunday Mass 1100

👤 Very Rev Martin O'Hagan PP

✉ St Patrick's Church
Cushendun
County Antrim

♰ Sunday Mass 1200

👤 Very Rev David Delargy PP

✉ St Joseph's Church
Hannahstown Hill
Belfast
County Antrim

♰ Sunday Mass 1100

Pilgrimages
Scotland

East Lothian

¶ The Scottish leg of the **Northern Cross Pilgrimage** (*see* Northumberland) commences in **Haddington**, southeast of Edinburgh, and passes through **Dunbar**, said to be the town with the most sun in Scotland, on to **Coldingham** and the ruins of a priory which was home at various times to **St Cuthbert** (634–687) and **St Etheldreda** (636–679), and finally to the border town of **Berwick-Upon-Tweed**, just 5 miles from **Holy Island**. The route covers 60 miles which most pilgrims walk in an average of 4–5 days.

Argyll

¶ On the opposite side of Scotland, in 563 AD **St Columba** (*Columcille*, 521–593), along with a handful of Irish monks, established a monastery on the **Isle of Iona** which soon became a celebrated centre of spirituality, art and literature. It was here that *The Book of Kells* was created. However, the threat of a Viking invasion forced the monks to leave for a monastery in **Kells** in County Meath, Ireland. Today the island of Iona is a peaceful, spiritual place, where a program of retreats and pilgrimages are conducted throughout the year for people of any or no religious affiliation. Accommodation is provided in a wide choice of guesthouses (*see* page 247).

¶ Visitors to Iona won't go hungry. A most scenically located restaurant and bar on the pier at **Martyr's Bay** is open for meals, snacks and drinks and the Iona Community have tea rooms in the abbey. The **Argyll** and **Columba Hotels** both have restaurants and the **Iona Heritage Centre** runs a garden tea room in the Old Manse. Some restaurants close in December and January.

Dumfries & Galloway

Orkney

❦ **Whithorn Priory** in the region of Dumfries and Galloway in south-west Scotland was founded in the 5th century by **St Ninian** (c. 360–432) and was the first Christian church established in the country. St Ninian was legendary for his healing powers and after his death pilgrims flocked to the shrine where the saint's relics were kept. Pilgrims still come today and many visit **St Ninian's Cave** on the south coast of the Machars of Galloway, 3 miles south-west of Whithorn, where it has been suggested that St Ninian came to rest and meditate. The local diocese conducts a formal pilgrimage to the cave on the last Sunday in August. There is much to interest the tourist and the pilgrim here, including coastal walks, a museum, a new chapel and the original crypts under the remains of the priory.

☦ Sunday Mass 1200.

Church of St Martin and St Ninian, Whithorn.

❦ A book festival is held each September in **Wigtown**, 10 miles north of Whithorn, known as Scotland's 'book' town. Around **Whithorn** fresh scallops are the local culinary speciality, and crab and lobster are freely available in the local restaurants. Those who live here say the 9-hole **St Medan's Golf Course** on the coast west of Whithorn is the most picturesque in the world—and they could be right!

❦ In the midst of green, fertile farmland, on the main island of the **Orkney Isles**, further north of the Scottish mainland's most northerly point, **John O'Groats**, lie the remains of a church built in Viking times and known as the **Orphir Round Church** or the Church of St Nicholas. The church is believed to have been modelled on the Church of the Holy Sepulchre in Jerusalem, which is said to contain the tomb of Jesus. It is within walking distance of the hamlet of **Houton**, midway between the towns of **Stromness** and **Kirkwell** and where the South Isles Ferry Terminus is located. Information on the Vikings and their settlements on Orkney can be found at the **Orkneyinga Saga Centre** near the Orphir ruins.

❦ The Orkney brand of food products is well known through the UK and many are exported to other countries. If it's picnic weather you could dine alfresco and assemble a gourmet hamper of local Orkney oysters, cheese, crab pâté and smoked salmon and a packet or two of dry, crisp Orkney Bere biscuits spread with rich, creamy Orkney butter. If you prefer to make your own Bere biscuits the meal base is on sale in take-home bags from the **Barony Mills** near Earl's Palace, where it is produced.

Pembrokeshire

❦ The remains of a 6th-century monastic city stand near **St David's Cathedral** in the little enclave of the same name. **St David** (487–589) is the Patron Saint of Wales who died shortly after founding his monastery. In the 14th century the monastery was enclosed by a high stone wall, some of which still stands. Since medieval times, pilgrims have been visiting the cathedral to pray before the shrine of St David, which is believed to hold his relics. The remains of **Non's Chapel** (named after St David's mother), where it said St David was born, and a Holy Well (**Non's Well**) are within walking distance.

❦ Throughout the year the local bishop conducts day programs of 'Refreshment for the Soul'; all are welcome to participate.

❦ The cathedral restaurant overlooks the estate's gardens and full meals are served.

✞ Sunday Service 0800. St David's Cathedral.

❦ May is a good time to visit the city of St David's, not only for the warmer weather but for the **St David's Cathedral Festival of Classic Music** which is held over a 9-day period near the end of the month. St David's is the smallest city in the United Kingdom.

❦ Cistercian monks live, work and pray on the monastic island of **Caldey**, a mile and a bit off the southern coast of Pembrokeshire. The monks own the island and during the summer run a busy guesthouse. Visitors are invited to participate with them in the spiritual activities of the monastery. The monks manufacture a variety of fragrances and soaps and a bracing men's aftershave, all of which are sold here along with Abbot's Kitchen brand chocolate and shortbread, also made by the monks. Boats sail to the island from **Tenby Harbour** between Easter and October (the island is closed to visitors each Sunday and between November and Easter). The journey takes approximately 20 minutes.

✞ Daily Mass 1445. Caldey Abbey.

❡ **Nevern** in Pembrokeshire was once a medieval place of pilgrimage, the village's 5th-century **St Brynach's Church** being the destination. Pilgrims followed a path lined on either side with yew trees some hundreds of years old. One of the yew trees 'bleeds' a red-coloured liquid and is known as the 'bleeding yew'. The legends surrounding this tree are many and involve royalty, a hanging from the tree, wronged individuals, world peace and even Christ Himself. A 4-metre-high Celtic Cross stands in the churchyard amidst ancient gravestones and has a legend of its own. It is said that the first cuckoo bird of the summer perches on the cross on St Brynach's Day each 7 April and loudly announces his appearance to all and sundry. Nevern is on the old pilgrim path to St David's, 15 miles away; the trail can still be followed today. The path is part of the way-marked, **Pembrokeshire Coastal Walking Path** (180 miles).

✝ Sunday Service 1100 *(may change)*.

St Brynach's Church, Nevern.

Additional
Accommodation
England

London

♣ LONDON

ⓣ Adoratrices Convent Hostel

✉ 38 Kensington Square
Kensington, London W8 5HP

☎ +44 (0) 20 7937 4582

✉ adornoluk@hotmail.com

☞ Tube: High Street Kensington

♟ Open to women. Students only.

ⓢⓣ Allen Hall Seminary

✉ 28 Beaufort Street
Chelsea, London SW3 5AA

☎ +44 (0) 20 7349 5600

✉ maryaldridge@rcdow.org.uk
✉ www.allenhall.org.uk

🔲 Open during summer only

☞ Tube: Sloane Square

♛ Groups only. Open to men &
women.

ⓣ Capitanio Sisters Hostel

✉ Sister of the Child Mary
Nile Lodge, Queens Walk
Ealing, London W5 1TJ

☎ +44 (0) 20 8997 3933

✉ capitanio.sisters@virgin.net
✉ stbc.sisters@virgin.net

☞ Tube: Ealing Common

♟ Open to women. Students only.

ⓣ Carmelite Missionaries

✉ 189 Gloucester Place
Westminster,
London NW1 6BU

☎ +44 (0) 20 7262 4737
☎ +44 (0) 20 7723 5517

✉ cmldn@yahoo.com

🔲 Open to female students
year-round; open to all women
during summer holidays

☞ Tube: Marlebone or Baker
Street

♟ Open to women only

ⓣ City University London

✉ Finsbury Residences
15 Bastwick Street
Islington, London EC1V 3PE

☎ +44 (0) 20 7040 8811
☎ +44 (0) 20 7040 8037
☎ +44 (0) 20 7040 8592

✉ finsbury@city.ac.uk
✉ www.city.ac.uk/ems/
accommodation/guest_rooms.
html

☞ Tube: Barbican

🔲 Available year-round

♛ Open to men, women & groups

ⓣ City University London

✉ Peartree Court
15 Bastwick St
Islington, London EC1V 3PE

☎ +44 (0) 20 7040 8037
☎ +44 (0) 20 7040 8592

✉ events@city.ac.uk
✉ www.city.ac.uk/ems/
accommodation/guest_rooms.
html

🔲 Open during summer only

☞ Tube: Barbican

♛ Open to groups of 4 or more
only. Both men & women
may stay.

ⓣ Claredale House

✉ Claredale Street
Tower Hamlets,
London E2 6PE

☎ +44 (0) 20 7739 7440
☎ +44 (0) 20 7729 5570

✉ claredale@cassandclaredale.co.uk
✉ www.cassandclaredale.co.uk

☞ Rail: Bethnal Green Tube or
Cambridge Heath Rail.

🔲 Open during summer only

♛ Open to men, women & groups

ⓢ Ealing Abbey

✉ Charlbury Grove
Ealing London W5 2DY

☎ +44 (0) 20 8862 2100
☎ +44 (0) 20 8862 2206

✉ ealingmonk@aol.com
✉ www.ealingabbey.org.uk

☞ Tube: Ealing Broadway

♞ Open to men only

ⓣ Finnish Church Hostel

✉ 33 Albion Street
Rotherhithe
London SE16 7HZ

☎ +44 (0) 20 7237 4668

✉ lontoo@merimieskirkko.fi
✉ www.finnishchurch.org.uk

☞ Tube: Canada Water

♛ Open to both men & women

ⓣ Goodenough Club

✉ 23 Mecklenburgh Square
Camden, London WC1N 2AD

☎ +44 (0) 20 7769 4727

✉ reservations@goodenough.ac.uk
✉ www.club.goodenough.ac.uk

☞ Tube: Russell Square

♛ Open to men, women & groups

🏨 Great Dover Street Apartments

✉ 165 Great Dover Street
Southwark, London SE1 4XA

📞 +44 (0) 20 7407 0068
📠 +44 (0) 20 7378 7973

✉ stopover@kcl.ac.uk
🖥 www.kcl.ac.uk/kcvb

🛏 Open during summer only

🚇 Tube: Borough

👥 Open to men, women & groups

🏨 Guy Chester Centre

✉ Chester House
Pages Lane, Muswell Hill
London N10 1PR

📞 +44 (0) 20 8883 8204
📠 +44 (0) 20 8883 0843

✉ office@chesterhouse.org.uk
🖥 www.chesterhouse.org.uk

🚇 Tube: Muswell Hill

👥 Open to men, women & groups

🏨 International Lutheran Student Centre

✉ 30 Thanet Street
Camden, London WC1H 9QH

📞 +44 (0) 20 7388 4044
📠 +44 (0) 20 7383 5915

✉ ilscaccomm@lutheran.org.uk
🖥 www.lutheran.org.uk

🛏 Open during university holidays only

🚇 Tube: Euston, King's Cross-St Pancras or Russell Square

👥 Open to men, women & groups

🏨 International Students' House

✉ 229 Great Portland Street
Westminster
London W1W 5PN

📞 +44 (0) 20 7631 8310

✉ accom@ish.org.uk
🖥 www.ish.org.uk

🚇 Tube: Great Portland Street

👥 Open to both men & women

🏨 Lee Abbey

✉ 57-67 Lexham Gardens
Kensington, London W8 6JJ

📞 +44 (0) 20 7373 7242

✉ accommodation@leeabbeylondon.com
🖥 www.leeabbeylondon.com

🚇 Tube: Earl's Court

🛏 Open during summer only

👥 Open to both men & women

🏨 London School of Economics and Political Science

✉ Bankside House
24 Sumner Street
Southwark, London SE1 9JA

📞 +44 (0) 20 7107 5750

✉ bankside@lse.ac.uk
🖥 www.lsetopfloor.co.uk/banksideRooms.htm

🚇 Tube: Southwark

👥 Open to both men & women

✉ Grosvenor House Apartments
Grosvenor House
141-143 Drury Lane
Westminster
London WC2B 5TD

📞 +44 (0) 20 7107 5950

✉ grosvenor@lse.ac.uk
🖥 www.lsetopfloor.co.uk/grosvenor.htm

🚇 Tube: Covent Garden or Holborn

👥 Open to both men & women

✉ Northumberland House
Edward VII Rooms
8a Northumberland Avenue
Westminster
London WC2N 5BY

📞 +44 (0) 20 7107 5603

✉ northumberland@lse.ac.uk
🖥 www.lsetopfloor.co.uk/northumberland.htm

🚇 Tube: Charing Cross or Embankment

👥 Open to both men & women

Additional
Accommodation
England

London

ⓣ Methodist Chaplaincy House

✉ 58A Birkenhead Street
Camden, London WC1H 8BW

📞 +44 (0) 20 7278 2535

✉ m.tullett@ic.ac.uk
🖥 www.misw.org.uk

🚇 Tube: King's Cross-St Pancras

👥 Students only. Open to both men & women.

ⓣ Penn Club

✉ 21-23 Bedford Place
Camden, London WC1B 5JJ

📞 +44 (0) 20 7636 4718

✉ office@pennclub.co.uk
🖥 www.pennclub.co.uk

🚇 Tube: Russell Square

♿ Discuss access when you book

👥 Open to men, women & groups

ⓣ Queen Mary, University of London

✉ Mile End Road
Tower Hamlets
London E1 4NS

📞 +44 (0) 20 7882 8174
📞 +44 (0) 20 7882 7055

✉ conference@qmul.ac.uk
🖥 www.ccrs.qmul.ac.uk/
conferences/

🚇 Tube: Mile End or Stepney Green

👥 Groups only. Open to men & women.

ⓣ Religious of Mary Immaculate Hostel

✉ 16 Southwell Gardens
Kensington London SW7 4RL

📞 +44 (0) 20 7373 3869
📞 +44 (0) 20 7373 6086

✉ southwellgardens15@yahoo.co.uk

🚇 Tube: Gloucester Road

👤 Open to young women

ⓣ Royal Foundation of St Katharine

✉ 2 Butcher Row
Tower Hamlets
London E14 8DS

📞 +44 (0) 845 409 0130
✉ info@rfsk.org.uk

🖥 www.stkatharine.org.uk

🚇 Nearest Rail: Limehouse (Rail)

👥 Open to men, women & groups

ⓣ Sir John Cass Hall

✉ 150 Well Street
Hackney, London E9 7LQ

📞 +44 (0) 20 8533 2529
📞 +44 (0) 20 8525 0633

✉ cass@cassandclaredale.co.uk
🖥 www.cassandclaredale.co.uk

📷 Open during summer only

🚇 Tube: Hackney Central or Homerton

👥 Open to men, women & groups

ⓣ Sisters of St Dorothy

✉ Frognal House
99 Frognal
Hampstead
London NW3 6XR

📞 +44 (0) 20 7794 6893
📞 +44 (0) 20 7435 0724

✉ st.dorothy@virgin.net
🖥 www.st.dorothys.talktalk.net/
home/home.htm

🚇 Tube: Hampstead

👤 Open to young women

ⓣ Stamford Street Apartments

✉ King's College
127 Stamford Street
The Borough
London SE1 9NQ

📞 +44 (0) 20 7633 9506
📞 +44 (0) 20 7633 2184

✉ stopover@kcl.ac.uk
🖥 www.kcl.ac.uk/kcvb

👥 Open to men, women & groups

ⓣ St Matthew's House

✉ 20 Great Peter Street
Westminster
London SW1P 2BU

📞 +44 (0) 20 7222 3704
📞 +44 (0) 20 7233 0255

✉ office@stmw.org
🖥 www.stmw.org

🚇 Tube: St James's Park

👥 Open to both men & women

Bedfordshire

S St Michael's Anglican Convent

✉ 56 Ham Common
Richmond
London TW10 7JH

☎ +44 (0) 20 8940 8711

✉ hospitality@sistersofthechurch.org.uk
🖰 www.sistersofthechurch.org.uk

☞ Tube: Twickenham or Teddington

⚭ Open to both men & women

S St Peter's Bourne

✉ 40 Oakleigh Park South
Oakleigh Park
Barnet, London N20 9JL

☎ +44 (0) 20 8445 5535
☎ +44 (0) 20 8445 5535

✉ warden1@tiscali.co.uk
🖰 www.stpetersbourne.com

☞ Tube: Totteridge and Whetstone

⚭ Open to both men & women

T Swedish Seaman's Church Hostel

✉ 120 Lower Road
Rotherhithe
London SE16 2UB

☎ +44 (0) 20 7237 1644

✉ gasthem@swedishchurch.com
🖰 www.swedishchurch.com

☞ Tube: Canada Water

⚭ Open to Swedish men & women only

T University of Westminster Vacations

✉ 35 Marylebone Road
Westminster
London NW1 5LS

☎ +44 (0) 20 7911 5181
☎ +44 (0) 20 7911 5037

✉ uniletvacations@westminster.ac.uk
🖰 www.wmin.ac.uk/page-5198

☞ Tube: Baker Street

🛏 Accommodation is available in the university's residential halls over the university holidays. Halls are located in Victoria, the West End, Southbank, in the City and in Harrow and Highgate.

⚭ Open to both men & women

T Young Women's Christian Association of Great Britain

✉ Head Office
6-8 Kemplay Road
Camden London NW3 1SY

☎ +44 (0) 20 7435 5730

🖰 www.ywca-gb.org.uk

☞ Tube: Hampstead

♀ Open to women only

The YWCA has 13 centres in England and Wales

🏛 TURVEY

S Monastery of Christ Our Saviour

✉ Jacks Lane
Turvey MK43 8DH

☎ +44 (0) 1234 881 211

✉ turveymonks@yahoo.co.uk
🖰 www.turveyabbey.org.uk

⚭ Open to both men & women

S Priory of Our Lady of Peace

✉ Turvey Abbey
Turvey MK43 8DE

☎ +44 (0) 1234 881 432

✉ courses-retreats257@turveyabbey.org.uk
🖰 www.turveyabbey.org.uk

⚭ Open to both men & women

**Additional
Accommodation**
England

Berkshire

🍀 ASCOT

Ⓢ Ascot Priory

☞ Priory Road
Ascot SL5 8RT

📞+44 (0) 1344 882 067

📧 warden@ascotpriory.org.uk
🖥 www.ascotpriory.org.uk

💒 Open to both men & women

🍀 MAIDENHEAD

Ⓢ Burnham Abbey

✉ Lake End Road
Taplow, Maidenhead SL6 0PW

📞+44 (0) 1628 604 080
📠+44 (0) 1628 604 080

📧 burnhamabbey@btinternet.com
🖥 www.burnhamabbey.org

💒 Open to both men & women

🍀 READING

ⓢⓣ Douai Abbey

✉ Upper Woolhampton
Reading RG7 5TQ

📞+44 (0) 118 9715 399

📧 guestmaster@douaiabbey.org.uk
🖥 www.douaiabbey.org.uk

💒 Open to both men & women

Buckinghamshire

🍀 IVER HEATH

ⓢⓣ Bridgettine Guesthouse

✉ Fulmer Common Road
Iver Heath SL0 0NR

📞+44 (0) 1753 662 073
📠+44 (0) 1753 662 172

📧 brigittae@iverconvent.fsnet.
co.uk
🖥 www.bridgettineguesthouse.
co.uk/iver_heath.html

💒 Open to both men & women

Cambridgeshire

🍀 ELY

ⓢⓣ Bishop Woodford House

✉ Barton Road
Ely CB7 4DX

📞+44 (0) 1353 663 039
📠+44 (0) 1353 665 305

📧 bwh@ely.anglican.org
🖥 www.bwh.org.uk

💒 Open to both men & women

🍀 HUNTINGDON

Ⓢ St Francis' House

✉ Hemingford Grey
Huntingdon PE28 9BJ

📞+44 (0) 1480 462 185

📧 hemingford@mirfield.org.uk
🖥 www.mirfieldcommunity.org.uk/
retreat_hemingford.php

♿ Discuss access when you book

💒 Open to both men & women

🍀 ST NEOTS

Ⓣ Claret Centre

✉ The Towers
High St
Buckden
St Neots PE19 5TA

📞+44 (0) 1480 810 344

📧 claret_centre@claret.org.uk
🖥 www.buckden-towers.org.uk

♿ Discuss access when you book

💒 Open to both men & women

Channel Islands

JERSEY

The Biarritz Hotel

✉ St Brelade's Bay
Jersey JE3 8EA

☎ +44 (0) 1534 742 239

✍ info@biarritzhotel.co.uk
✍ www.biarritzhotel.co.uk

☺ Open to men, women & groups

Cumbria

AMBLESIDE

Rydal Hall

✉ Rydal, Ambleside LA22 9LX

☎ +44 (0) 1539 432 050

✍ mail@rydalhall.org
✍ www.rydalhall.org

☺ Open to men, women & groups

GRANGE-OVER-SANDS

Abbot Hall Hotel

✉ Kents Bank
Grange-over-Sands LA11 7BG

☎ +44 (0) 1539 532 896
☎ +44 (0) 1539 535 200

✍ abbot@christianguild.co.uk
✍ www.christianguild.co.uk/
abbothall/index.php

♿ Discuss access when you book

☺ Open to men, women & groups

Boarbank Hall

✉ Alithwaite
Grange-over-Sands LA11 7NH

☎ +44 (0) 1539 532 288
☎ +44 (0) 1539 535 386

✍ mail@boarbankhall.org.uk
✍ www.boarbankhall.org.uk

☺ Open to both men & women

Yew Tree Farm Cottage

✉ c/- Boarbank Hall, Alithwaite
Grange-over-Sands LA11 7NH

✍ mail@boarbankhall.org.uk
✍ www.boarbankhall.org.uk

☺ Open to both men & women

ULVERSTON

Swarthmoor Hall
(Quaker establishment)

✉ Swarthmoor Hall Lane
Ulverston LA12 0JQ

☎ +44 (0) 1229 583 204

✍ info@swarthmoorhall.co.uk
✍ www.swarthmoorhall.co.uk

☺ Open to both men & women

Cornwall

ST IVES

Treloyhan Manor Hotel

✉ St Ives TR26 2AL

☎ +44 (0) 1736 796 240
☎ +44 (0) 1736 798 377

✍ treloyhan@christianguild.co.uk
✍ www.christianguild.co.uk/
treloyhan/index.php

♿ Discuss access when you book

☺ Open to both men & women

Derbyshire

MATLOCK

Willersley Castle Hotel

✉ Cromford, Matlock DE4 5JH

☎ +44 (0) 1629 582 270
☎ +44 (0) 1629 582 329

✍ willersley@christianguild.co.uk
✍ www.christianguild.co.uk/
willersley

♿ Discuss access when you book

☺ Open to men, women & groups

**Additional
Accommodation**
England

Devon

🐾 EXETER

Ⓢ The Sheldon Centre

✉ Society of Mary and Martha
Dunsford, Exeter EX6 7LE

📞 +44 (0) 1647 252 752
📠 +44 (0) 1647 253 900

🖘 smm@sheldon.uk.com
🖘 www.sheldon.uk.com

♿ Discuss access when you book

🐾 Open to men, women & groups

🐾 LYNTON

Ⓢ Lee Abbey

✉ Lynton
North Devon EX35 6JJ

📞 +44 (0) 1598 752 621
📠 +44 (0) 1598 752 619

🖘 relax@leeabbey.org.uk
🖘 www.leeabbey.org.uk

♿ Discuss access when you book

🐾 Open to men, women & groups

Dorset

🐾 BOURNEMOUTH

**Ⓣ Daybreak Christian
Guesthouse**

✉ 6 Herbert Road
Alum Chine
Bournemouth BH4 8HD

📞 +44 (0) 1202 761 055

🖘 info@daybreakguesthouse.co.uk
🖘 www.daybreakguesthouse.co.uk

🐾 Open to both men & women

🐾 PAIGNTON

Ⓣ Park Hotel

✉ Esplanade Road
Paignton TQ4 6BQ

📞 +44 (0) 1803 557 856
📠 +44 (0) 1803 555 626

🖘 stay@parkhotel.me.uk
🖘 www.theparkhotel.net

♿ Discuss access when you book

🐾 Open to men, women & groups

🐾 SIDMOUTH

Ⓣ Sidholme Hotel

✉ Elysian Fields
Sidmouth EX10 8UJ

📞 +44 (0) 1395 515 104
📠 +44 (0) 1395 579 321

🖘 sidholme@christianguild.co.uk
🖘 www.christianguild.co.uk/
sidholme

♿ Discuss access when you book

🐾 Open to men, women & groups

🐾 DORCHESTER

Ⓢ The Friary

✉ Hilfield, Dorchester DT2 7BE

📞 +44 (0) 1300 342 314

🖘 hilfieldproject@franciscans.
org.uk
🖘 www.hilfieldproject.co.uk/
jumpoff.htm

♿ Discuss access when you book

🐾 Open to both men & women

Durham

🐾 DURHAM

Ⓣ St Chad's College

✉ The College Secretary
St Chad's College
18 North Bailey
Durham DH1 3RH

📞 +44 (0) 1913 343 358
📠 +44 (0) 1913 343 371

🖘 chads@durham.ac.uk
🖘 www.dur.ac.uk/StChads

🐾 Open to men, women & groups

Essex

BRADWELL-ON-SEA

Ⓢ Othona Community

✉ East Hall Farm
East End Road
Bradwell-on-Sea CM0 7PN

📞 +44 (0) 1621 776 564
📠 +44 (0) 1621 776 207

🖘 bradwell@othona.org
🖘 www.othona.org

♿ Discuss access when you book

🐾 Open to both men & women

🐾 CHELMSFORD

**Ⓢ Chelmsford Diocesan
House of Retreat**

✉ The Street
Pleshey, Chelmsford CM3 1HA

📞 +44 (0) 1245 237 251
📠 +44 (0) 1245 237 594

🖘 info@retreathousepleshey.com
🖘 www.retreathousepleshey.com

♿ Discuss access when you book

🐾 Open to both men & women

Gloucestershire

🍀 GLOUCESTER

ⓢ Prinknash Abbey

✉ Cranham
Gloucester GL4 8EX

📞 +44 (0) 1452 812455
📠 +44 (0) 1452 814 187

✉ guestsprinknash@waitrose.com
✉ www.prinknashabbey.org

⚥ Open to men only

🍀 LYDNEY

ⓣ Lindors Country House Hotel

✉ The Fence
St Briavels
Lydney GL15 6RB

📞 +44 (0) 1594 530 283
📠 +44 (0) 1594 530 559

✉ lindors@christianguild.co.uk
✉ www.lindors.co.uk

♿ Discuss access when you book

🎗 Open to men, women & groups

Herefordshire

🍀 WEOBLEY

ⓣ Mellington House

✉ Weobley HR4 8SA

📞 +44 (0) 1544 318 537

✉ ann@mellingtonhouse.co.uk
✉ www.mellingtonhouse.co.uk

🎗 Open to both men & women

Hampshire

🍀 FARNBOROUGH

ⓢ St Michael's (Farnborough) Abbey

✉ Farnborough GU14 7NQ

📞 +44 (0) 1252 546 105
📠 +44 (0) 1252 372 822

✉ guestmaster@farnboroughabbey.org
✉ www.farnboroughabbey.org

🎗 Open to both men & women

🍀 LYMINGTON

ⓢ St Dominic's Priory

✉ Shirley Holms Road
Lymington SO41 8NH

📞 +44 (0) 1590 681 874
📠 +44 (0) 1590 681 875

✉ dominican.sisters@talk21.com
✉ www.dominicansrs.co.uk

🎗 Open to both men & women

Hertfordshire

🍀 ST ALBANS

ⓢⓣ All Saints Pastoral Centre

✉ Shenley Lane
London Colney
St Albans AL2 1AG

📞 +44 (0) 1727 829 306
📠 +44 (0) 1727 822 880

✉ conf.office@allsaintspc.org.uk
✉ www.allsaintspc.org.uk

♿ Discuss access when you book

🎗 Groups only. Open to men & women.

**Additional
Accommodation**
England

Isle of Wight

🛏 RYDE

Ⓢ St Cecilia's Abbey

✉ The Garth
Ryde PO33 1LH

☎ +44 (0) 1983 652 602
📠 +44 (0) 1983 652 602

✍ info@stceciliasabbey.org.uk
✍ www.stceciliasabbey.org.uk

👤 Open to women only

Kent

🛏 CANTERBURY

Ⓣ Canterbury Cathedral Lodge

✉ The Precincts
Canterbury CT1 2EH

☎ +44 (0) 1227 865 350

✍ stay@canterbury-cathedral.org
✍ www.canterburycathedrallodge.
org

♿ Discuss access when you book

🏖 Open to men, women & groups

🛏 MINSTER

Ⓢ Minster Abbey

✉ Minster
nr Ramsgate CT12 4HF

✍ www.minsterabbeynuns.org

👤 Open to women only

🏠 During summer, families may
also stay here

Lancashire

🛏 BLACKPOOL

Ⓣ Lochinvar Christian Guesthouse

✉ Lochinvar
14 Chatsworth Avenue
Norbreck
Blackpool FY2 9AN

☎ +44 (0) 1253 351 761

✍ www.lochinvar-christianholidays.
co.uk

🏖 Open to men, women & groups

🛏 CARNFORTH

Ⓣ Capernwray Hall

✉ Carnforth LA6 1AG

☎ +44 (0) 1524 733 908
📠 +44 (0) 1524 736 681

✍ holidays@capernwray.org.uk
✍ www.capernwray.org.uk

🏖 Open to men, women & groups

🛏 LYTHAM ST ANNES

Ⓣ Ad Astra Fairtrade Guesthouse

✉ 39 Derbe Road
Lytham St Annes FY8 1N

☎ +44 (0) 1253 721 897

✍ info@adastra.me.uk
✍ www.adastra.me.uk

🏖 Open to both men & women

🛏 PRESTON

Ⓢ Tabor Carmelite Retreat House

✉ 169 Sharoe Green Lane
Fulwood, Preston PR2 8HE

☎ +44 (0) 1772 717 122
📠 +44 (0) 1772 787 674

✍ tabor@carmelite.net
✍ www.tabor-preston.org

🏖 Open to both men & women

🛏 WHALLEY

Ⓢ Whalley Abbey

✉ The Sands
Whalley Clitheroe BB7 9SS

☎ +44 (0) 1254 828 400

✍ office@whalleyabbey.org
✍ www.whalleyabbey.co.uk

🏖 Open to men, women & groups

Leicestershire

🐾 EAST NORTON

Ⓢ Launde Abbey

✉ East Norton LE7 9XB

📞 +44 (0) 1572 717 254
📠 +44 (0) 1572 717 454

✉ laundeabbey@leicester.anglican.
org
🌐 www.launde.org.uk

🐾 Open to men, women & groups

Norfolk

🐾 DITCHINGHAM

Ⓣ The Community of All Hallows

✉ Belsey Bridge Road
Ditchingham NR35 2DT

📞 +44 (0) 1986 892 749

✉ info@all-hallows.org
🌐 www.all-hallows.org

♿ Discuss access when you book

🐾 Open to men, women & groups

🐾 WALSINGHAM

Ⓢⓣ Anglican Hospitality Office

✉ The Milner Wing
The Shrine of Our Lady of
Walsingham
Common Place
Walsingham NR22 6BP

📞 +44 (0) 1328 820 239
📠 +44 (0) 1328 824 206

✉ accom@olw-shrine.org.uk
🌐 www.walsinghamanglican.org.uk

♿ Discuss access when you book

🐾 Open to men, women & groups

Ⓢⓣ Catholic Pilgrim's Bureau

✉ Elmham House
Friday Market Place
Walsingham NR22 6DB

📞 +44 (0) 1328 820 217

✉ elmhamhouse@walsingham.
org.uk
🌐 www.walsingham.org.uk/
romancatholic/

♿ Discuss access when you book

🐾 Open to men, women & groups

**Additional
Accommodation**
England

Northumberland

**🐚 HOLY ISLAND
(LINDISFARNE)**

Ⓢ **Marygate House**

✉ Holy Island
Berwick-upon-Tweed
TD15 2SD

📞 +44 (0) 1289 389 246
📠 +44 (0) 1289 389 246

✍ ian@marygateho.freeserve.co.uk
✍ www.marygatehouse.org.uk

🎗 Open to both men & women

🐚 RIDING MILL

Ⓢ **Shepherds Dene**

✉ Riding Mill NE44 6AF

📞 +44 (0) 1434 682 212

✍ enquiry@shepherdsdene.co.uk
✍ www.shepherdsdene.co.uk

🎗 Open to men, women & groups

Shropshire

🐚 SHREWSBURY

Ⓢ **Hawkstone Hall**

✉ Marchamley
Shrewsbury SY4 5LG

📞 +44 (0) 1630 685 242
📠 +44 (0) 1630 685 565

✍ hawkhall@aol.com
✍ www.hawkstone-hall.com

🎗 Open to men, women & groups

Somerset

🐚 MINEHEAD

Ⓣ **Baptist Holiday
Apartments**

✉ 1 The Esplanade
Minehead TA24 6DY

📞 +44 (0) 1643 703 473

✍ info@baptistholidayapartments.
org
✍ www.baptistholidayapartments.
org

🎗 Open to men, women & groups

🐚 RADSTOCK

Ⓢ Ⓣ **The Ammerdown
Centre**

✉ Ammerdown Park
Radstock BA3 5SW

📞 +44 (0) 1761 433 709
📠 +44 (0) 1761 433 094

✍ centre@ammerdown.org
✍ www.ammerdown.org

♿ Discuss access when you book

🎗 Open to men, women & groups

🐚 SOUTH PETHERTON

Ⓢ **The Community of
St Francis**

✉ Compton Durville
South Petherton TA13 5ES

📞 +44 (0) 1460 240 473
📠 +44 (0) 1460 242 360

✍ comptondurvillecsf@franciscans.
org.uk
✍ www.franciscans.org.uk/Page34.
htm

🎗 Open to both men & women

Suffolk

STRATTON-ON-THE-FOSSE

S **Downside Abbey**

✉ Stratton on the Fosse
Radstock BA3 4RH

☎ +44 (0) 1761 235 153
📠 +44 (0) 1761 235 124

✉ dommartin@downside.co.uk
🖥 www.downside.co.uk

⚥ Open to men only

WELLS

T **Vicars' Close Holiday House**

✉ Wells Cathedral Office
Chain Gate, Cathedral Green
Wells BA5 2UE

☎ +44 (0) 1749 674 483
📠 +44 (0) 1749 832 210

✉ visits@wellscathedral.uk.net
🖥 www.wellscathedral.org.uk

⚥ Open to men, women & groups

Surrey

WOKING

S **St Columba's House**

✉ Maybury Hill
Woking GU22 8AB

☎ +44 (0) 1483 766 498
📠 +44 (0) 1483 740 411

✉ retreats@stcolumbashouse.
org.uk
🖥 www.stcolumbashouse.org.uk

♿ Discuss access when you book

⚥ Open to both men & women

Suffolk

SUDBURY

S **Clare Priory**

✉ Ashen Road
Clare, Sudbury CO10 8NX

☎ +44 (0) 1787 277 326
📠 +44 (0) 1787 278 688

✉ clare.priory@virgin.net
🖥 www.clarepriory.org.uk

⚥ Open to both men & women

Sussex

BATTLE

S **Ashburnham Place**

✉ Battle
East Sussex TN33 9NF

☎ +44 (0) 1424 892 244
📠 +44 (0) 1424 894 200

✉ mail@ashburnham.org.uk
🖥 www.ashburnham.org.uk

⚥ Open to men, women & groups

COOLHAM

ST **St Cuthman's**

✉ Cowfold Road
Coolham
West Sussex RH13 8QL

☎ +44 (0) 1403 741 220
📠 +44 (0) 1403 741 026

✉ stcuthmans@dabnet.org
🖥 www.dabnet.org/stcuthmans

♿ Discuss access when you book

⚥ Open to both men & women

PENSHURST

S **Penhurst Retreat Centre**

✉ The Manor House
Penhurst nr Battle
East Sussex TN33 9QP

☎ +44 (0) 1424 892 088

✉ info@penhurst.org.uk
🖥 www.penhurst.org.uk

⚥ Open to both men & women

**Additional
Accommodation
England**

Warwickshire

🍀 **LEAMINGTON SPA**

🆂 **Offa House**

✉ Village Street
Offchurch
Leamington Spa CV33 9AS

📞 +44 (0) 1926 423 309

📧 offahouse@btconnect.com
🌐 www.offahouseretreat.co.uk

🎗 Open to men, women & groups

West Midlands

🍀 **BIRMINGHAM**

🆂 **St Bridget's Convent**

✉ Maryvale Institute
Old Oscott Hill, Kingstanding
Birmingham B44 9AG

📞 +44 (0) 121 3252405
📞 +44 (0) 121 3252 411

📧 bridgettine.maryvale@dsl.
pipex.com
🌐 www.brigidine.org/
Brigidine/350/352/Birmingham.
html

🎗 Open to both men & women

🆂 **Woodbrooke**

✉ 1046 Bristol Road
Birmingham B29 6LJ

📞 +44 (0) 121 472 5171
📞 +44 (0) 121 472 5173

📧 enquiries@woodbrooke.org.uk
🌐 www.woodbrooke.org.uk

♿ Discuss access when you book

🎗 Groups only. Open to men &
women.

Wiltshire

🍀 **SALISBURY**

🆃 **Sarum College
Hospitality Centre**

✉ 19 Cathedral Close
Salisbury SP1 2EE

📞 +44 (0) 1722 424 800
📞 +44 (0) 1722 338 508

🌐 www.sarum.ac.uk

🎗 Open to both men & women

🍀 **WARMINSTER**

🆂 **Ivy House: St Denys
Retreat Centre**

✉ 2-3 Church Street
Warminster BA12 8PG

📞 +44 (0) 1985 214 824

📧 stdenys@ivyhouse.org
🌐 www.ivyhouse.org

🎗 Open to both men & women

Worcestershire

🌸 PERSHORE

Ⓢ Holland House

✉ Main Street
Cropthorne
Pershore WR10 3NB

📞 +44 (0) 1386 860 330
📠 +44 (0) 1386 861 208

✉ enquiries@hollandhouse.org
✉ www.hollandhouse.org

🍀 Groups only. Open to men &
women.

Yorkshire

🌸 HUDDERSFIELD

Ⓢ Westwood Christian Centre

✉ Westwood Edge Road
Nr Golcar
Huddersfield HD7 4JY

📞 +44 (0) 1484 845 042

✉ westwoodcc@tiscali.co.uk
✉ www.westwood-centre.org.uk

♿ Discuss access when you book

🍀 Open to men, women & group

🌸 MIRFIELD

Ⓢ Community of the Resurrection

✉ Stocksbank Road
Mirfield WF14 0BW

📞 +44 (0) 1924 494 318
📠 +44 (0) 1924 490 489

✉ pnichols@mirfield.org.uk
✉ www.mirfieldcommunity.org.uk

🍀 Open to both men & women

🌸 SCARBOROUGH

Ⓣ Alexandra House

✉ 21 West Street
South Cliff
Scarborough YO11 2QR

📞 +44 (0) 1723 503 205

✉ info@scarborough-alexandra.co.uk
✉ www.scarborough-alexandra.co.uk

🍀 Open to both men & women

Ⓢ Wydale Hall

✉ Brompton by Sawdon
Scarborough YO13 9DG

📞 +44 (0) 1723 859 270

✉ admin@wydale.org
✉ www.wydale.org

🍀 Open to men, women & groups

🌸 SHEFFIELD

Ⓢ Whirlow Grange

✉ Ecclesall Road South
Sheffield S11 9PZ

📞 +44 (0) 114 236 3173
📠 +44 (0) 114 262 0717

✉ info@whirlowgrange.co.uk
✉ www.whirlowgrange.co.uk

♿ Discuss access when you book

🍀 Groups only. Open to men &
women.

🌸 SKIPTON

Ⓢ Parcevall Hall

✉ Appletreewick
Skipton BD23 6DG

📞 +44 (0) 1756 720 213
📠 +44 (0) 1756 720 656

✉ www.parcevall.bradford.anglican.org/index.html

🍀 Open to men, women & groups

**Additional
Accommodation
England**

**Additional
Accommodation
Northern Ireland**

Yorkshire

County Antrim

County Down

🐾 WASS

🅣 Crief Lodges

✉ Stanbrook Abbey
   Crief Farm
   Wass YO61 4AY

📞 +44 (0) 1347 868 207

💻 crieflodges@stanbrookabbey.
   org.uk
💻 www.stanbrookabbeyfriends.
   org/Crief-Lodges

♻ Open to both men & women

🐾 WHITBY

🅣 Moorlands Hotel

✉ 16 North Promenade
   Whitby YO21 3JX

📞 +44 (0) 1947 603 584
📱 +44 (0) 1947 821 668

💻 moorlands@christianguild.co.uk
💻 www.christianguild.co.uk/
   moorlands/index.php

♻ Open to both men & women

🆂🆃 Sneaton Castle Centre

✉ Whitby YO21 3QN

📞 +44 (0) 1947 600 051
📱 +44 (0) 1947 603 490

💻 sneaton@globalnet.co.uk
💻 www.sneatoncastle.co.uk

♿ Discuss access when you book

♻ Open to men, women & groups

🐾 YORK

🆂 Ampleforth Abbey

✉ Hospitality & Pastoral Office
   Ampleforth YO62 4EN

📞 +44 (0) 1439 766 889
📱 +44 (0) 1439 766 755

💻 pastoral@ampleforth.org.uk
💻 www.ampleforth.org.uk

♿ Discuss access when you book

♻ Open to men, women & groups

🐾 BELFAST

🅣 The Queen's University

✉ University Road
   Belfast BT7 1NN

📞 +44 (0) 28 9097 4403
📱 +44 (0) 28 9097 4489

💻 accommodation@qub.ac.uk
💻 www.stayatqueens.com

♻ Open to men, women & groups

🐾 PORTGLENONE

🆂 Bethlehem Abbey

✉ 11 Ballymena Road
   Portglenone BT44 8AF

📞 +44 (0) 28 2582 1211
📱 +44 (0) 28 2582 2795

💻 kelly@unite.net
💻 www.bethlehem-abbey.org.uk

♻ Open to both men & women

🐾 ROSTREVOR

🆂 Christian Renewal
Centre

✉ Rostrevor
   Newry BT35 8DL

📞 +44 (0) 28 4173 8492
📱 +44 (0) 28 4173 8996

💻 crc-rostrevor@lineone.net
💻 www.crc-rostrevor.org

♿ Discuss access when you book

♻ Open to both men & women

Ulster County

☗ ULSTER

Ⓣ University of Ulster

🔲 Open during summer only

✉ Coleraine Campus
Cromore Road
Coleraine BT52 1SA

📞 +44 (0) 28 7032 4665
📠 +44 (0) 28 7032 4948

⌨ c.scott@ulster.ac.uk
⌨ www.accommodation.ulster.
ac.uk/casuallet.html

✉ Derry Campus
Northland Road
Londonderry BT48 7JL

📞 +44 (0) 28 7137 5611
📠 +44 (0) 28 7037 5629

⌨ a.mullan@ulster.ac.uk
⌨ www.accommodation.ulster.
ac.uk/casuallet.html

✉ Jordanstown Campus
Jordanstown
Newtownabbey BT37 0QB

📞 +44 (0) 28 9036 6924
📠 +44 (0) 28 9036 6862

⌨ gr.campbell@ulster.ac.uk
⌨ www.accommodation.ulster.
ac.uk/casuallet.html

👥 Open to men, women & groups

Argyll

☗ ISLE OF IONA

Ⓢ Bishop's House

✉ Isle of Iona PA76 6SJ

📞 +44 (0) 1681 700 111
📠 +44 (0) 1681 700 801

⌨ bhiona@argyll.anglican.org
⌨ www.argyllandtheisles.org.uk/
retreats.html

👥 Open to both men & women

Ⓢ Cnoc a' Chalmain

✉ Catholic House of Prayer
Isle of Iona PA76 6SP

📞 +44 (0) 1681 700 369

⌨ mail@catholic-iona.com
⌨ www.catholic-iona.com/

👥 Open to both men & women

ⓈⓉ Iona Community

✉ Bookings Office
Isle of Iona PA76 6SN

📞 +44 (0) 1681 700 404

⌨ abbey.bookings@iona.org.uk
or ionacomm@iona.org.uk
⌨ www.iona.org.uk

👥 Open to both men & women

East Lothian

☗ HADDINGTON

Ⓢ Sancta Maria Abbey

✉ Nunraw
Haddington EH41 4LW

📞 +44 (0) 1620 830 228
📠 +44 (0) 1620 830 304

⌨ www.nunraw.org.uk

👥 Open to both men & women

Glasgow

☗ GLASGOW

Ⓣ Adelaide's Guesthouse

✉ 2098 Bath Street
Glasgow G2 4HZ

📞 +44 (0) 141 2484 970
📠 +44 (0) 141 2264 247

⌨ reservations@adelaides.co.uk
⌨ www.adelaides.co.uk

👥 Open to both men & women

Ayrshire

☗ LARGS

Ⓢ Benedictine Monastery

✉ 5 Mackerston Place
Largs KA30 8BY

📞 +44 (0) 1475 687 320

⌨ www.tyburnconvent.org.uk

👤 Open to women only

Morayshire

☗ ELGIN

Ⓢ Pluscarden Abbey

✉ St Benedict's &
St Scholastica's Retreat
Elgin IV30 8UA

📞 +44 (0) 1343 890 258

⌨ www.pluscardenabbey.org

♿ Discuss access when you book

👥 Open to both men & women

**Additional
Accommodation
Scotland**

**Additional
Accommodation
Wales**

Perthshire

🔸 **PERTH**

ⓢ **Kinnoull Monastery**

✉ Hatton Road
Kinnoull Perth PH2 7BP

📞+44 (0) 1738 624 075
📠+44 (0) 1738 442 071

💻 copiosa@kinnoullmonastery.org
💻 www.kinnoullmonastery.org

🕊 Open to both men & women

Roxburghshire

🔸 **HAWICK**

ⓢ **Whitchester Christian
Guest House**

✉ Borthaugh
Hawick TD9 7LN

📞+44 (0) 1450 377 477
📠+44 (0) 1450 371 080

💻 enquiries@whitchester.org.uk
💻 www.whitchester.org.uk

♿ Discuss access when you book

🕊 Open to both men & women

Conwy

🔸 **LLANDUDNO**

ⓢ **Loreto Centre**

✉ Abbey Road
Llandudno LL30 2EL

📞+44 (0) 41492 878 031
for group bookings
📞+44 (0) 41492 878 542
for retreats and self catering

💻 loretocentre@yahoo.co.uk
💻 www.loretollno.org.uk

🕊 Open to men, women & groups

Flintshire

🔸 **HAWARDEN**

ⓣ **St Deiniol's Library**

✉ Church Lane
Hawarden CH5 3DF

📞+44 (0) 1244 532 350
📠+44 (0) 1244 520 643

💻 enquiries@st-deiniols.org
💻 www.st-deiniols.com

🕊 Open to men, women & groups

🔸 **HOLYWELL**

ⓢ **St Winefride's Guest
House**

✉ 20 New Road
Holywell CH8 7LS

📞+44 (0) 1352 714 073
📠+44 (0) 1352 712 925

💻 stwinefrides@bridgettine.org
💻 www.saintwinefrideswell.com

🕊 Open to both men & women

Monmouthshire

🌸 MONMOUTH

ⓢ The Society of the Sacred Cross

☞ Tymawr Convent
Lydart
Monmouth NP25 4RN

📞 +44 (0) 1600 860 244

✉ tymawrconvent@btinternet.com
🖰 www.churchinwales.org.
uk/~tymawr

⚘ Open to both men & women

Powys

🌸 BRECON

ⓢ Society of the Sacred Heart

✉ Llannerchwen
Llandefaelog Fach
Brecon LD3 9PP

📞 +44 (0) 1874 622 902

✉ llannerchwen@aol.com
🖰 www.societysacredheart.org.uk

⚘ Open to both men & women

Pembrokeshire

🌸 CALDEY ISLAND

ⓢⓣ Caldey Abbey

✉ The Guestmaster
St Philomena's Guesthouse
Caldey Abbey
Caldey Island SA70 7UJ

📞 +44 (0) 1834 844 453

✉ info@caldey-island.co.uk
🖰 www.caldey-island.co.uk

⚘ Open to both men & women

🌸 ST DAVID'S

ⓢ St Non's Retreat Centre

✉ St David's
Pembrokeshire
West Wales SA62 6BN

📞 +44 (0) 1437 720 224
📠 +44 (0) 1437 720 161

✉ stmonsretreat@aol.com
🖰 www.stnonsretreat.org.uk

⚘ Open to both men & women

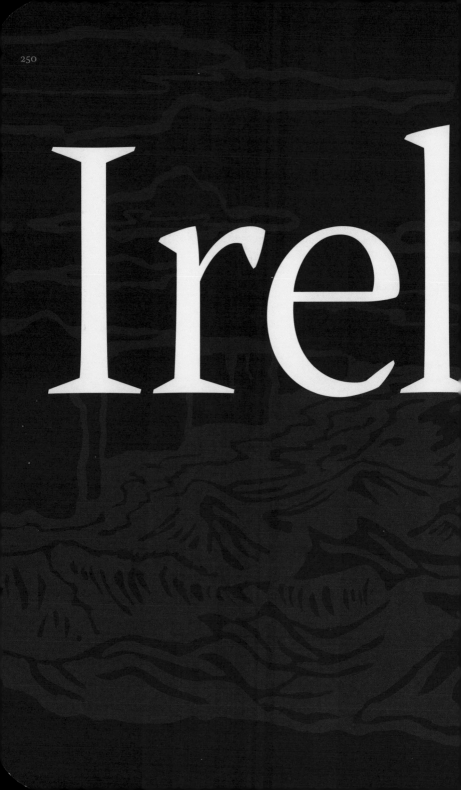

Irel

and

PROBABLY THE SAINTS IN HEAVEN
don't spend too much time boasting
of their achievements. But if they
do, I suspect the saints can bear
no more bragging from St Patrick.
For no nation has ever lived up more
fully to the virtues of its patron
saint than Ireland.

PRESIDENT BILL CLINTON
DUNDALK, 2000

ULSTER

N

CONNACHT

DONEGAL

Inishowen

Dundrean

DERRY

ANTRIM

Belfast

Donegal

Lough Derg

Rossnowlagh

Mullaghmore

TYRONE

DOWN

Enniskillen

FERMANAGH

ARMACH

Skreen

Sligo

Sligo

MONAGHAN

Ballina

SLIGO

LEITRIM

CAVAN

LOUTH

Collon

MAYO

Knock

Drogheda

Ballintubber

ROSCOMMON

LONGFORD

MEATH

Swords

GALWAY

Athlone

WESTMEATH

Dublin

Galway

Athenry

Maynooth

OFFALY

KILDARE

DUBLIN

Portarlington

Kildare

Glendalough

Brockagh

Ballymore Eustace

Donard

Wicklow

CLARE

LAOIS

WICKLOW

Glenmalure

Shannon

Roscrea

Kiltegan

Murroe

Limerick

KILKENNY

CARLOW

LEINSTER

Limerick

TIPPERARY

Ferns

LIMERICK

Kilkenny

WEXFORD

Tipperary

Blackwater

Tralee

Clonmel

Ballyvaloo

Annascaul

Wexford

Dingle

KERRY

WATERFORD

Killarney

Cappoquin

Skelling
Michael

Waterford

Cork

CORK

Blarney

Cobh

Kinsale

Leap

MUNSTER

IRELAND

HILE SNAKES, SHAMROCKS AND SHILLELAGHS have all been linked to St Patrick, the high-spirited shenanigans of St Patrick's Day each 17 March are yet another enduring legacy of the affection the Irish have for this much loved saint.

Many a myth or legendary folktale—perhaps just a touch embellished over time—has endured in Ireland across the centuries. What's more, the irrepressible spirit of the Irish is bound to ensure that the traditions of Celtic lore and the sophistications of modern-day Ireland are at one. But whether we can thank St Patrick for it or not, given its lush green countryside Ireland will probably always be known as the Emerald Isle.

However, since the times of St Patrick and St Brigid—for long the two most revered of Irish saints and who, via the Celtic faith, introduced Christianity to Ireland during the 5th and 6th centuries—Irish Christianity has seldom looked back, despite later periods of conflict and religious struggles.

Religion remains close to many an Irish heart. For centuries convents and monasteries across Ireland have been the focus of spirituality for pilgrims and now prestigious Christian Irish universities are opening their ancient doors to tourists of all denominations looking for affordable holiday accommodation.

And rest assured, the reputation of Irish folk for being genuinely warm and friendly is as strong as it always was outside the walls of the cloisters too. As they say in Ireland, *Céad míle Fáilte*—One hundred thousand welcomes!

County Dublin

HE DASHING RIVER LIFFEY surges through the centre of Dublin, neatly dividing Ireland's handsome, Georgian capital into north and south. This lively, cultured capital is the culmination of at least 1,000 years of development, growth and progress.

Renowned for its eager nurturing of the literary and theatrical arts, Dublin has been home to such cultural treasures as William Butler Yeats, James Joyce, Oscar Wilde and Jonathan Swift. The works of these poets and writers will never be allowed to fade from Irish memory, especially if the well-credentialled local intelligentsia has anything to do with it. Nor is it likely that Irish dance and folk music will ever fade in popularity.

Medieval landmarks are scattered throughout the county, with those in Dublin easily explored on foot. Modern-day sports lovers won't have far to go to work out the intricacies of Gaelic football or hurling; and the big name shops lining Dublin's pedestrianised Grafton Street are sure to keep any fussy fashionista amused.

Eating establishments reflect County Dublin's contemporary face, with modern restaurants dishing up eclectic fare and rubbing shoulders with cheery, traditional pubs which are just the place to down a jar of Guinness or sample an Irish coffee.

Reflecting a worldwide trend, Irish seminaries are no longer as full as they once were, even though the country has a devout, predominantly Catholic population. Even so, over the years thousands of pilgrims and travellers have found spiritual enrichment through the programs conducted by priests and nuns in Dublin's convents and retreat houses. Over 20 religious orders are represented in the county and all, in various ways, devote their time to the service of others.

01

Mercy International Centre

The **Mercy International Centre** is run by the Catholic order of the Sisters of Mercy, probably one of the best-known religious orders in the world, and which has its foundations in Dublin. Dubliner **Catherine McAuley** (1778–1841) built the house with money received from an inheritance in 1827 and set about using it as a centre to care for the disadvantaged. Four years later, in this house in Baggot Street she founded the worldwide religious order many of us are familiar with, and where the Sisters of Mercy continue to live their lives of service to others. In this place of hospitality and retreat, a life-sized statue of Sister Catherine stands outside the front door, welcoming guests.

❡ The convent's single and twin guestrooms cover two floors of the building and are cosy and comfortable, though small. Bathrooms are shared. There is a guests' lounge for relaxing and a small television room. Continental breakfast is available each day, and tea and coffee making facilities are provided at other times. Rooms of varying sizes are available for conferences and meetings. In 1994, the building was restored, including the chapel and St Catherine's room. The centre has been built roughly in a 'U' shape and some guestrooms overlook the garden.

❡ Throughout the year the sisters conduct programs of prayer and retreat, linked to the life of Catherine McAuley. Some take in guided walks and prayer stops to places in Dublin frequented by Sister Catherine. The sisters also run larger programs of pilgrimages to Mercy destinations throughout the world.

✉ 64A Lower Baggot Street
Dublin 2

💶 €35.00–40.00 pp, including light breakfast.

📞 +353 (0) 1 661 8061
📠 +353 (0) 1 676 5486

✉ bookings@mercyinternational.ie

🌐 www.mercyinternational.ie

☞ The Mercy International Centre is a short taxi ride from the centre of Dublin or approximately 30 minutes on foot. The number 10 bus from O'Connell Street stops at the centre; bus numbers 10A, 15X, 18, 25X, 49X, 51X, 66X, 67X and 77X stop in Baggot Street. The Landsdowne Road DART Station is a 10-minute walk from the centre.

✝ **Sunday Mass**
0700, 1000 & 1200
(Irish Mass)
Our Lady's Oratory
89 Lower Leeson Street

⛪ Open to both men & women

Open Houses
County Dublin Dublin

PLACES OF INTEREST ❧ **Catherine McAuley** is buried in a vault in the 'Sacred Garden' at the rear of the centre. In 1990 **Pope John Paul II** honoured her with the title 'Venerable', the first of three steps which the sisters believe will eventually lead to her sainthood.

❧ The 'Lower' was added to this section of **Baggot Street** in 1839. The street was formerly called Gallows Hill, as public executions were carried out here. Dublin also had a 'Misery Hill' on the site of the **Grand Canal Square**, where lepers were forced to spend their lives.

❧ The 4th lock of the **Grand Canal** is at the bottom of Lower Baggot Street and forms part of the 114-kilometre **Grand Canal Way**, along which run scenic and (mostly) well-maintained and signposted pathways, popular with the locals for walking dogs. It's possible to walk the entire route from **Dublin** to **Shannon** in County Clare, if you are so inclined.

❧ Not far from the Mercy Centre, at 85–86 St Stephen's Green, the elaborate interiors of **Newman House**, once part of the Catholic University, are open during the summer for guided tours. These include a visit to the classroom where writer **James Joyce** (1882–1941) studied and to the room of the Professor of Classics, Jesuit poet and Englishman **Gerard Manley Hopkins** (1844–1889). Prior to university James Joyce attended the Jesuit schools Clogowes Wood in County Kildare and Belvedere College in Dublin.

❧ For almost 23 years, playwright **Oscar Wilde** (1854–1900) and his family lived at 1 Merrion Square. The house is full of memorabilia and open to visitors in summer. A relaxed-looking Oscar, a distinguished alumnus of Trinity College, sprawls on a large rock in **Merrion Square Park**, which is also known as Archbishop Ryan Park.

❡ **Dermot Ryan** was a former Archbishop of Dublin (1972–1984). Before he died suddenly in 1985 at the age of 60, it was commonly thought that Archbishop Ryan would be appointed Cardinal. The land named after him was once owned by the Dublin Catholic Diocese which intended to build a cathedral. However, a cathedral never eventuated and the current Catholic Archbishop uses **St Mary's Pro** (interim) **Cathedral** as his headquarters.

✝ Sunday Mass 1000, 1100, 1245, & 1830.

❡ The **Merrion Square Art Gallery** is the retail outlet for hundreds of local artists who exhibit their work on the wrought iron fences each Sunday between 1000 and 1830. Somewhat more illustrious (and expensive) artwork can be inspected at the **Irish National Gallery**, also in Merrion Square.

❡ If it's that time of the year, stock up on exquisite, hand-painted Christmas cards from **The Card Company** at 14 Merrion Square. The designs are by Irish artists and range from the traditional to the more contemporary.

❡ To explore further afield, the red 'hop on hop off' bus makes three stops around Merrion Square and pulls up every 20 minutes.

FOOD AND DRINK Near the Mercy International Centre you will find **Larry Murphy's Pub** where you can enjoy a reasonably priced meal and a wide choice of good wine. You can eat outside in the summer.

✉ 43 Lower Baggot Street

☎ +353 (0)1 662 4561   €–€€

❡ If your savings on accommodation mean you can lash out on some fine dining, then Dublin has a number of Michelin-starred restaurants, including the 2-star French **Restaurant Patrick Guilbaud** in the Merrion Hotel and **L'Ecrívain** in Lower Baggot Street. Both serve classic, imaginative Gallic cuisine which can be tasted in a multi-course sample menu.

✉ Restaurant Patrick Guilbaud
   21 Upper Merrion Street

☎ +353 (0)1 676 4192   €€€€€

✉ L'Ecrivain, 109a Lower Baggot Street

☎ +353 (0)1 661 1919   €€€€€

❡ Cruise the Grand Canal on the floating (French) restaurant, the barge **La Peniche**. Anchors aweigh at 1800 and 2100 Tuesday to Sunday.

✉ *On the Grand Canal,* Mespil Road, *opp. Mespil Hotel.*

☎ +353 (0)87 790 0077   €–€€

02

Marino Institute of Education (MIE)

The **Marino Institute of Education** is located in the suburb of **Marino**, a residential area on the northern side of Dublin, just 3 kilometres from the city centre. It was established as an educational facility by the Blessed **Edmund Rice** (1762–1844), founder of the Congregation of the Christian Brothers, a Catholic religious order, and is now a teacher training college. Blessed Edmund is buried in the chapel of the Christian Brother's International Heritage Centre, in Mount Sion, County Waterford.

❧ Gracious old buildings are a feature of the establishment which is open to overnight guests all year round. It's also a popular venue for conferences and functions. Guests can come and go as they please, and relax or wander in the rambling gardens, designed by one of the brothers, which combine fountains and statuary with plants and shrubs from all over the world.

❧ The guestrooms, all single or twin, are furnished simply, in the style of student accommodation. Guestrooms are not en suite, although each has a hand basin; share bathrooms are located on each floor. There is an on-site restaurant where all meals can be taken, a guests' lounge/TV room, telephones, a laundry, tea and coffee making facilities on each floor, and plenty of parking. Internet, telephone and fax facilities are available and credit cards are accepted.

❧ The headquarters of the Christian Brothers is in nearby Marino House.

✉ Griffith Avenue
Marino
Dublin 9

🛏 from €40.00 pp (single room), including full Irish breakfast.

📞 +353 (0) 1 805 7760
📞 +353 (0) 1 833 5290

✉ info@mie.ie

✉ www.mie.ie

☞ From Dublin city centre take the number 123 bus from the bridge end of O'Connell Street to the Marino Institute. Buses 27c, 29a and 42a which depart from Connolly Station also stop near the centre.

✝ **Sunday Mass**
0930, 1100, 1230 & 1930.
Church of St Vincent de Paul
Griffith Avenue.

👥 Open to men, women & groups

PLACES OF INTEREST ❦ **Trinity College** old boy **Bram** (Abraham) **Stoker** (1847–1912), the creator of the legendary vampire *Dracula*, lived at 15 The Crescent, Marino. In 1878, in St Anne's Church in Dublin, Stoker married a former mistress of **Oscar Wilde**, **Florence Balcombe** (1858–1937). The couple moved to London, where he later died. His ashes are at the **Golders Green Crematorium** where his only son, **Irving Noel Thornley** (1879–1961), rests with him.

❦ A monumental 'white elephant' in the area is the old, misnamed **casino** in Cherrymount Crescent. The 'casino' was never destined for gamblers but rather as a lavish, 18th-century 'getaway'. Built by Irish statesman **James Caulfield**, the 1st Earl of Charlemont (1728–1799), the building has been referred to as 'the greatest piece of architecture in Ireland'. Land occupied by the MIE was once part of the Earl's estate.

❦ **Gaelic football** is Ireland's number one sport and is believed to have its roots in the 14th century. **Croke Park**, in St Joseph's Avenue, 1 kilometre from MIE, is the headquarters of the game. The history of Gaelic football is portrayed in the museum beneath the grandstand where there is also a gift shop.

❦ The national sport of **hurling**, an incredibly fast version of hockey, is also played here. Each year in **Croke Park Stadium**, the Archbishop of Cashel starts off the All-Ireland Hurling and Gaelic Football Finals with a throw. This tradition dates back to the early 1800s when Croke Park was named after His Grace the Most Rev. Dr **Thomas William Croke** (1824–1902), Archbishop of Cashel and Emly, the first Patron of the GAA (Gaelic Athletic Association). The honour was once bestowed on Irish Patriot **Michael Collins** (1890–1922). It seems that both patriot and archbishop managed to keep their digits intact!

Open Houses
County Dublin Dublin

❦ A 16th-century black oak statue, the Shrine of Our Lady of Dublin, stands in the **Whitefriar Street Church** (Our Lady of Mt Carmel), which is attached to a Carmelite monastery, in Aungier Street. The church's busiest day of the year is the Feast Day of Our Lady of Dublin on 8 September, although there is some competition on 14 February from St Valentine whose relics are also kept here.

✝ Sunday Mass 0800, 0930, 1030, 1130 (sung), 1230, 1600 & 1900.

❦ In the year 563, Irish monks were attached to the **Monastery of Iona** in the Scottish Hebrides, which was founded by **St Columba** (521–597), its first abbot. The monks were responsible for writing the acclaimed, illustrated manuscripts *The Book of Kells*. However, they lived in constant fear of Viking attacks and were forced to move their precious tome to a monastery in **Kells**, in County Meath, 55 kilometres north-west of Dublin. A detailed copy of *The Book of Kells* can be seen at the town's heritage centre.

FOOD AND DRINK ❦ The **Marino** area has some great eating places. The award-winning **Washerwoman's Hill Restaurant** (the building was once the local laundromat) is on Glasnevin Hill not far from the National Botanic Gardens. The cuisine leans towards Mediterranean and an early evening dining session (kids at special prices) attracts families and theatregoers.

✉ 60 Glasnevin Hill

☎ +353 (0) 1 837 9199 €€€

❦ Snacks and light meals are available every day at **Anderson's Food Hall and Café** in Glasnevin. In a previous life the premises was the local butcher shop. The deli sells a tempting array of picnic-type food and wines, and a busy café serves Italian coffee and international wines by the glass.

✉ 3 The Rise (off Griffith Avenue)

☎ +353 (0) 1 837 8394 €€–€€€

❦ Not far from Anderson's is the family-owned **Kavanagh's** public house. Less formally known as Grave Diggers' Pub because it is next to the entrance of the sprawling Glasnevin Cemetery, it has been serving traditional bar food and what is claimed to be the best 'jar' in Dublin, since 1833.

✉ Prospect Square

☎ +353 (0) 1 830 7978 €

03

Trinity College

Visitors to Dublin would be hard-pressed to find a more central or historic place to stay than **Trinity College**. Founded by Queen Elizabeth I in the 16th century, and established on the site of the (dissolved) Augustinian Monastery of All Hallows, Trinity College is the oldest university in Ireland. It is in a prime location in the centre of Dublin, and comfortable accommodation is offered to tourists and visitors during the summer and to groups all year round.

❧ Guests stay within short walking distance of both the famous Trinity Library in the college's 'Long Room' and the illustrated manuscripts of the medieval *Book of Kells*. During the warmer months (April to September) students conduct 30-minute guided tours of the 40-acre college campus. The tours leave from inside the College Green entrance every 40 minutes on weekdays, from 1015.

❧ Accommodation ranges from single and twin or double rooms to family-sized apartments accommodating up to eight people. Almost all have en suite facilities. Standard rooms are available on a share bathroom basis. All guestrooms are serviced daily and complimentary tea and coffee making facilities are provided. The complex has an on-site restaurant, bar and guest laundry. A number of car parks (pay) are in the vicinity of the college, which provides parking for bicycles only. Credit cards are accepted.

✉ Accommodation Office
West Chapel
Trinity College
College Green
Dublin 2

🛏 from €33.00 pp, including continental breakfast. Full Irish breakfast €5.00 pp. Discount rates are often available.

📞 +353 (0) 1 896 1177

✉ *reservations@tcd.ie*

🔗 *https://accommodation.tcd.ie*

☞ Trinity College is in the centre of Dublin. The Pearse Street DART Station is at the eastern end of Trinity College.

✝ **Sunday Mass**
1215 *except during July and August.*
Trinity College Chapel.

✝ **Sunday Service**
1045 *Choral Eucharist during term time only*
Trinity College Chapel.

❧ Open to men, women & groups

Open Houses
County Dublin Dublin

PLACES OF INTEREST ✤ *The Book of Kells*, a priceless, hand-written volume of the Gospels in Latin, and said to be one of the oldest books in the world, lies open, safe under a thick cover of glass, in the Trinity College library. Every day, a page in each of the two volumes of this precious manuscript is turned. Upstairs, in the library's Long Room, 200,000 volumes of rare, academic texts line the lofty walls from floor to ceiling. The Trinity College library shop sells a range of gifts, clothing and souvenirs, particularly in relation to *The Book of Kells*.

❡ **Trinity College** has produced many eminent old boys, including author **Jonathan Swift** (1667–1745) who graduated in 1686 and later wrote the entertaining satire *Gulliver's Travels*. Swift went on to become the Dean of **St Patrick's Cathedral** in Dublin (1713–1745). He was laid to rest in St Patrick's near 'Stella', his dear friend and past student Hester Johnson (1681–1728), to whom he dedicated his *Journal to Stella*.

✟ Sunday Services

0830 *(in the Lady Chapel)*, 1115 & 1515.

❡ If the weather misbehaves and you have left your umbrella at home, pop into **Campelli's** in Scarlet Row, Temple Bar for a classic, made-to-measure Mackintosh. If the rain just won't let up, you could take shelter at the **Guinness Storehouse** at St James Gate, 2 kilometres west of the city centre. Take the Guinness brewery tour then sit back and contemplate the meteorological conditions over a free pint at the **Gravity Bar**, the highest bar in Ireland.

❡ Dublin's **Christ Church Cathedral** has been attracting tourists and pilgrims for over 1,000 years and many come to pray before a medieval reliquary of **St Laurence O'Toole** (1128–1180), patron saint of Dublin and the city's first Irish bishop.

✟ Sunday Services 1100 & 1530.

❡ Dublin's **Halfpenny Bridge**, an iconic cast-iron pedestrian bridge, forms a gentle arch over the **River Liffey** between Bachelor's Walk and Temple Bar Square. The bridge was completed in 1821 and a halfpenny toll charged for pedestrians crossing the bridge.

❡ Discover the Dublin that existed pre-16th century at **Dublinia**, opposite Christ Church Cathedral at St Michael's Hill.

❦ **St Michan's Church of Ireland** in Church Street Dublin is not for the squeamish. The crypt houses long-dead bodies which have not completely decomposed on account of the quality of the air inside the chamber; they lie in a rather random, untidy, mummified state. The crypt is closed during church services. Tours of the crypt take place on most days for a small charge.

✝ Sunday Services

2nd & 4th Sundays at 1000

❦ Meet some of Ireland's most talented designers at the **Designer Mart** at Cow's Lane each Saturday from 1000 in **Temple Bar**. A vast array of clothing, craft and jewellery is on sale. A book market is held each weekend from 1100 on Temple Bar Square.

❦ **Temple Bar** is the home of the **Irish Film Institute** in Eustace Street and the location of the city's only arthouse cinema. Irish film producers screen their latest works here and an hour or two could be spent watching one of the daily feature movies. A film shop, bar and a restaurant are open every day. When travelling around Ireland keep an eye out for the travelling cinema or **Cinemoblie**, a specially adapted semi-trailer which converts to a 100-seat private theatre.

FOOD AND DRINK ❦ Brush up on your Gaelic over a coffee and a bite to eat at **Connolly Books and Café** in Temple Bar. Practice conversation sessions in Gaelic are held here each Friday between 1300 and 1400, and Irish and English language books are on sale. The annual **Irish Language Week** is held throughout Ireland in March each year. Dabble in a bit of Karl Marx—Connolly Books has been appointed the official bookshop of the Communist Party in Ireland.

✉ 43 East Essex Street, Temple Bar

☎ +353 (0)1 670 8707   €€

❦ At the **Winding Stair Bookshop** and rather up-market café in Temple Bar, the cappuccinos come with a view over the Halfpenny Bridge.

✉ 40 Ormond Quay, Temple Bar

☎ +353 (0)1 872 7320   €€–€€€

❦ **Mulligan's Pub**, behind Trinity College, was once a favourite drinking place of writer James Joyce.

✉ Poolberg Street, Temple Bar

☎ +353 (0)1 677 5582   €

❦ More cafés, pubs and eating places can be found in the city centre. There are also informal cafés, wine bars and more than a sprinkling of pubs and restaurants in the nearby **St Stephen's Green** area.

04

University College Dublin (UCD)

Once known as the Catholic University of Ireland, the **University College Dublin** is tucked away in 140 hectares of gardens and green space, just 5 kilometres south of the city centre. In 1960 a lack of space forced the university out of central Dublin to new headquarters in Belfield. UCD is now Ireland's largest university.

❡ The original college was first established near St Stephen's Green in the heart of Dublin, with learned advocate of higher education, **John Henry** (later Cardinal) **Newman** (1801–1890) appointed the first rector in 1854, a position he held until 1858. His residence, **Newman House** on St Stephen's Green, has been retained by the university. In 1859 the future Cardinal Newman established the Birmingham Oratory School, an English Catholic public school for boys, which has now moved to Woodcote, near Reading on the outskirts of London.

❡ Every year from early June to late August, the university rents its student rooms and apartments to tourists, students and groups visiting Dublin. Each separate apartment has four single guestrooms and is totally self-contained with two bathrooms, a kitchen and a sitting room. Guests are requested to bring their own bath towel. Bed linen is provided. Separate guestrooms which have en suite facilities are also available.

❡ The resources of the large UCD campus include Internet access, cafés, restaurants, bars, a mini-market and sports facilities. There are also ATMs, an on-site laundry, a pharmacy and a post office. The complex is so large it resembles a mini city in itself.

✉ Merville Reception
Belfield
Dublin 4

🛏 from €40.00 pp (single room).

☎ +353 (0) 1 716 1046
☎ +353 (0) 1 269 7111
📠 +353 (0) 1 269 7704

✍ reception@ucdvillage.ie

✍ www.ucdvillage.ie

☞ From O'Connell Street in the city centre take bus number 10, which will let you off inside the campus.

✝ Sunday Mass
1130 & 2100.
Campus Oratory,
University College
Dublin.

⚥ Open to men, women & groups

PLACES OF INTEREST ❦ The 15th-century **Rathfarnham Castle**, a few kilometres west of **Belfield**, was once the residence of the Archbishop of Dublin and later owned by the Society of Jesuits. In 1916 resident priest **Father William O'Leary** (1868–1939) constructed a sophisticated seismograph in the castle grounds which was used to detect earth tremors. The castle is open to the public.

❦ Formerly **Rathfarnham House**, the landmark Georgian buildings of the old **Loreto Abbey** once housed a prestigious girls' school run by the Sisters of the Institute of the Blessed Virgin Mary (IBVM), which closed in 1999. The founder of the order, **Mother Frances (Fanny) Ball** (1794–1861), died at the Loreto Abbey in Dalkey and is buried in Rathfarnham. **Mother Teresa of Calcutta** entered the IBVM at the age of 18 and lived at the Loreto Abbey in 1928 before founding the Missionaries of Charity and commencing her evangelical work in India.

❦ Further south, near the port of **Dun Laoghaire**, is the heritage town of **Dalkey**, home to many rich and famous, some of whom have houses on exclusive Sorrento or Vico Roads. Playwright **George Bernard Shaw** (1856–1950) once lived in Dalkey, author **Maeve Binchy** still does, and **Bono** of U2 fame has property in the district. Take the DART (Dublin Area Rapid Transport) to Dalkey for a scenic day trip from Dublin. The picturesque journey down the Irish coast takes around half an hour.

❦ It is a 30-minute walk from Dalkey along the coast to the town of **Killiney**. **Manderley Castle** in Victoria Road, Killiney is owned by Irish singer **Enya** (b. 1961). The controversial Irish singer **Sinead O'Connor** (b. 1966)—in 1992 she spectacularly ripped up a photo of the late Pope John Paul II on the American television show *Saturday Night Live*—lives in the coastal town of Bray.

Open Houses
County Dublin Dublin

One of the city's best produce markets is held on Saturdays in **Marlay Park** from 1000. The stallholders set up behind **Marlay House**, a stately Georgian mansion dating from the 13th century and named after Elizabeth, the daughter of the Rev. **George Marlay** (d. 1763), Protestant Bishop of Dromore in County Down. Combine a visit to the markets with a tour of the estate's walled ornamental gardens. Visitors can rest a while in the coffee shop in the old gardener's cottage. The **Wicklow Way** walking trail from Dublin to Glendalough officially commences at Marlay Park.

The **Dublin Bay Sea Tour** departs from the **Poolbeg Marina** in the heart of Dublin and heads down the River Liffey into Dublin Bay and on down to Dalkey and Dun Laoghaire before returning to the city. Places of interest are pointed out along the way, including the historic Mariner's Church in Dun Laoghaire, which now serves as the **Irish National Maritime Museum**. On display is the *Great Eastern*, the world's largest passenger ship when it was built in the year 1857. The ship weighed 32,000 tons and held 4000 passengers.

FOOD AND DRINK After investigating the attractions of **Rathfarnham Castle**, enjoy an Irish banquet and a night of traditional Irish music and dancing at **The Merry Ploughboy**, an award-winning Irish music pub.

✉ Edmondstown Road, Rockbrook, Rathfarnham
☎ +353 (0)1 493 1495   €€

The popular early evening menu is an economical option at **Dali's Restaurant** in the seaside village of **Blackrock**. A local favourite, it's a small, good-looking restaurant with a relaxed ambience, serving dishes prepared from quality seasonal ingredients, grown locally.

✉ 63 Main Street, Blackrock
☎ +353 (0)1 278 0660   €€€€

The home of the Australian Ambassador to Ireland is in the classy little waterside town of **Dalkey**. If the ambassador ever gets homesick he could take a genteel stroll down to one of the half a dozen pubs in Castle Street, most of which cater for Aussie tastes with Foster's on tap, Australian wines and sometimes traditional Australian fare.

Dalkey's produce market is held each Friday. The sisters of the **Dominican Ecology Centre** in Wicklow sell their organic produce here and also at the market in Bray each Saturday. Every Sunday, the **People's Park** in **Dun Laoghaire** is the attractive setting for a weekly food and bric-a-brac market.

County Kildare

SQUASHED AS IT IS between the counties of Dublin and Wicklow, County Kildare has no coastline. Its capital, Kildare (town), is just 50 kilometres west of Dublin. The county is a favourite destination for day-trippers from the Irish capital on account of its lush, grassy pastures, equine facilities and heritage towns.

Probably best known as Ireland's equestrian county, Kildare is famed for horse breeding; its studs and racecourses are internationally renowned. The Irish National Stud at Tully breeds the thoroughbreds that win so many of the world's major races. The Curragh, a legend in horseracing and steeplechasing, plays host to the Irish Derby; Punchestown is the home of the National Hunt.

Horseracing aside, the patroness of Ireland, St Brigid, has become a prime attraction for tourists travelling to Kildare. Brigid was quite a woman. An early role model for women's rights, she was the first abbess of the Order of Brigidines which was founded in 470 AD when she established the first Brigidine convent in the town. Today, St Brigid's Flame burns permanently in Kildare town's main square and the Brigidine Order has spread internationally.

For some Irish good fortune you might like to take home an Irish pewter 'good luck' spoon from Timolin. Like many places in Ireland there is a saint in the background here, dating to when St Moling (Mullins) founded a monastery nearby. The monastery's mill is now the Irish Pewter Mill.

05

National University
of Ireland (NUI)

The picturesque little town of **Maynooth** is part of the
Catholic Archdiocese of Dublin and home to the imposing
National University of Ireland, which incorporates
St Patrick's College Seminary, Ireland's National Seminary
and Pontifical University. The seminary is Ireland's
training centre for priests; in 2008, almost 70 men
were studying here for the priesthood and in 2009,
6 seminarians became ordained priests. Pope John Paul II
celebrated Mass in the chapel of Maynooth College when
he visited Ireland in 1979. The National Science Museum
is also on site. Maynooth is 24 kilometres west of Dublin.
❧ On-campus accommodation is available all year round
to tourists, students and holidaymakers; extra rooms
are made available during the summer holiday period.
The total complex can accommodate over 1,000 guests.
Accommodation ranges from self-catering apartments to
standard guestrooms on a share bathroom basis (on the
same floor) to en suite guestrooms for one or two people.
Rooms without a bathroom are fitted with a wash basin.
Upscale accommodation consisting of twin and double en
suite guestrooms, some with a sitting room, is available all
year round in the university's Stoyte House.
❧ The remains of the 12th-century **Geraldine** (Maynooth)
Castle, once home to the Earls of Kildare, are near the
university entrance. In 1983 the castle was used for scenes
in the film *Educating Rita*, starring British actors Michael
Caine (b. 1933) and Julie Walters (b. 1950).
❧ Much of the university was designed by English
architect **A. W.** (Augustus Welby) **Pugin** (1812–1852)
whose legacy includes numerous churches and stately
buildings (including Windsor Castle.)

✉ Maynooth
County Kildare

🛏 from €25.00 pp,
breakfast from
€8.00 pp.

☎ +353 (0) 1 708 3533
📠 +353 (0) 1 708 3534

✎ reservations@
maynoothcampus.com

✉ www.maynoothcampus.
com

☞ Take the train from
Dublin's Pearse, Tara
or Connolly stations
for the 30-minute
(express) journey
to Maynooth. The
university is a pleasant
10 minutes' walk from
the station. Express
buses 66x and 67x
depart from Pearse
Street Station for
Maynooth.

✝ **Sunday Mass**
0900, 1015, 1130,
1245 & 1800.
St Mary's Church
Main Street
Maynooth.

⚭ Open to men, women
& groups

PLACES OF INTEREST ❧ The university is situated along the **Royal Canal**. It is possible to walk the level towpath all the way from **Maynooth** to the town of **Kilcock**, a distance of 7 kilometres. For a more strenuous walk, play one of the Arnold Palmer-designed championship golf courses at the к **Club** in Straffan, 10 kilometres south of Maynooth.

❦ Families could visit the **Larchill Arcadian Garden** in **Phepotstown**, near Kilcock, west of Maynooth. The gardens were first laid in the 18th century and the design seen today remains true to the original, with wooded lakeside trails, statues, a lake and a landscaped park which is home to a variety of rare animals. The wife of **Robert Watson** (1822–1908), a former owner of Larchill, was once buried in the gardens here. However, a subsequent owner removed her remains and placed them in a churchyard. Not happy with this state of affairs, Mrs Watson's ghost has quite rightfully come back to haunt the place.

❦ **Castletown House** in **Celbridge** was built in 1722 for Irish MP **William Conolly** (1662–1729). Its grand classical architecture is said to have been the inspiration for the design of the White House in Washington. At the other end of the architectural scale is the **Wonderful Barn**, a carafe-shaped granary with an outdoor spiral staircase, located on the Castletown House Estate.

❦ The walking tracks of the **Donadea Forest** (on the Kilcock–Naas road) are of varying lengths. The 6-kilometre **Aylmer Slí na Sláinte** walk leads past a small replica of New York's Twin Towers, which was erected as a memorial to those who lost their lives in the attack on 11 September 2001. A fire fighter from Donadea was among the victims. Donadea is 8 kilometres south of Maynooth.

❦ The **Bog of Allen Nature Centre** in **Rathangan** is the largest peat bog in Ireland and the focus of a major conservation effort. Peat was once a source of cheap fuel and much of the bog has been utilised by turf cutters. According to legend a section of the bog called **Lullymore Island** is where St Patrick established his first monastery and a footprint set in stone is said to belong to him.

Open Houses
County Kildare Maynooth

❡ **The Lullymore Heritage Park**
near **Rathangan**, 10 kilometres north
of Kildare is dedicated to the local
environment and a place where learning
is fun. The centre caters especially for
families and a natty road train makes
visiting the farm, the gardens, the Bog of
Allen and the children's play areas easy.
The local area can be explored on any of
the themed walking trails and a cafe is
open for meals and snacks.

❡ History buffs and tourists on four
wheels could follow the **South Kildare
Heritage Trail**, a return driving route
to castles, churches and other historical
sites in Kildare through the villages
of Athy, Kilkea, Castledermot, Moone,
Timolin, Ballitore, Crookstown and
Ardscull. The trail can be joined at any
of these villages.

❡ If in search of a bargain visit the
Kildare Shopping Outlet Village in
Nurney Road, Kildare town. A bus
leaves from Dublin at 1000 from outside
the Dublin Tourism Office on O'Connell
Street. **The Kildare Heritage Centre**
opposite St Brigid's Cathedral keeps
a collection of limited edition books
and publications written by local
Irish authors.

FOOD AND DRINK ❦ Being a university
town there is no shortage of pubs and
restaurants in the area. One of the most
popular is **The Roost** where visitors can
mix with the locals in any of the seven
bars or in the beer garden. Reasonably
priced bar food is available. Restaurants
and more pubs can be found along
Main Street.

✉ Main Street, Maynooth
☎ +353 (0)1 628 9843   €

❡ The **Leinster Arms** in the centre
of Maynooth is said to be the hotel
where leader of the United Irishmen
(The political group responsible for
the Irish Rebellion) **Theobald Wolfe
Tone** spent his honeymoon in 1786.
The pub serves cheap, home-cooked
meals and is popular with the local
university students.

✉ Main Street, Maynooth
☎ +353 (0)1 628 6323   €€

❡ On the **Grand Canal**, 15 kilometres
north of Kildare, the little village of
Robertstown was once a stop on an
old Irish trading and barge route. The
pretty little village has a couple of quiet,
rustic pubs where meals and drinks are
served, including the aptly named **Barge
Inn**. Any over-indulgence can be walked
off on one of the towpath trails leading
from the village.

County Limerick

 OSTLY RURAL AND CLAD IN VARYING SHADES of sparkling emerald, County Limerick is the address of the most picturesque village in Ireland, the much-visited tourist magnet, Adare. The village embraces neat and trim thatched cottages, medieval churches, an excellent golf club, three longstanding priories and a number of handsome pubs and shops. The Gift Box, in the main street, keeps a collection of Limerick lace, the making of which was introduced to Ireland by nuns over a century ago.

Once inhabited by the Vikings, the county is rich in history and natural beauty. Ruins, medieval castles and more modern edifices—such as the 19th-century castle, Adare Manor and the Benedictine-owned Glenstal Abbey in Murroe (*Muroe*)—have helped preserve the character of the county. Glenstal, the country's best-known abbey, is run by a large community of Benedictine monks, who have achieved fame through their recordings of Gregorian chants and for the views of some of the unabashed, outspoken residents of the community. The monks are also well known for compiling a prayer book, *The Glenstal Book of Prayer,* which became a national best-seller in 2001; it is still available. Construction of a new abbey guesthouse at Glenstal was completed in 2006 and it is now open to receive guests. A homely B&B on the edge of the estate houses the overflow.

Open Houses
County Limerick Murroe

06

Glenstal Abbey Monastic Guesthouse

Glenstal Abbey was once the grand abode of the Barringtons, an aristocratic Limerick family who founded the tiny village in the mid-19th century. They built an impressive home, resembling a Normanesque castle, complete with massive stone towers, walls and gates. In 1927 the Benedictine Order took over ownership and established the renowned Glenstal Abbey and boarding school for boys. Most of the original architectural features have been preserved. The abbey sits on the edge of the village in 500 acres of woods laced with much-used walking trails. **Adare** village, the **Rock of Cashel** and the **Cliffs of Mohr** are all within easy driving distance.

⁋ The Benedictine monks of Glenstal Abbey run a busy, modern guesthouse, newly established in 2008 with 12 rooms, all en suite. While not strictly a tourist facility, like-minded people who want to explore the area, as well as those who wish to spend some quiet time in self-guided retreat, are welcome here. Meals are available; a number of pubs and restaurants are within 10 minutes' drive. The monks meet in the abbey church five times each day and visitors may attend these prayer services.

⁋ The monks of Glenstal Abbey continue to play an important role in Ireland's religious music scene. In 2003 they worked with Dublin-born singer Marie-Bernadette O'Connor—otherwise known as Sinead—to produce an album titled *Biscantorat: The Sound of the Spirit from Glenstal Abbey*. The monks run an eclectic gift shop stocked with their CDs and books and numerous other souvenirs.

✉ Murroe
County Limerick

🛏 from €60.00 pp (single room), including all meals.

📞 +353 (0) 61 386 103
📠 +353 (0) 61 386 328

✉ guestmaster@glenstal.org

🖥 www.glenstal.org

☞ Take the train to Limerick Station (not to Limerick Junction). Murroe is 16 kilometres east of Limerick on the Limerick line. Via the Limerick–Cappomore Road, Murroe is 20 kilometres east of Limerick. A bus departs from the station to Murroe once each day. Please check time before departure.

✝ **Sunday Mass** 1000.
Abbey of Glenstal, Murroe.

⚤ Open to both men & women

PLACES OF INTEREST ❧ One of Glenstal's best-known monastics, the author, philosopher and former headmaster previously known as **Brother Mark Patrick Hederman** OSB (b. 1936), created a minor controversy when he wrote the book *Tarot: Talisman or Taboo* (2003), revealing that on occasions he had used tarot cards to guide people on their spiritual journey. He later appeared on *Would You Believe—The Devil's Pack*, an RTÉ (Radio Telefís Éireann) top-rating religious television series and pointed out that tarot cards have their basis in Christianity, only becoming associated with the occult in more recent times. Brother Mark was elected abbot of the Glenstal community in 2008 and made history by first being ordained a priest before being installed as abbot by the Archbishop of Cashel and Emly, **Dr Dermot Clifford**, in 2009. Abbot Hederman has written numerous books including *The Haunted Inkwell* in 2001, *Walkabout* in 2005 and *Symbolism: The Glory of Escutcheoned Doors* in 2007.

❡ While the monks have found worldwide fame with their numerous releases, also renowned in the Irish music industry is harpist **Dr Janet Harbison**. From **The Irish Harp Centre**, in the Old Schoolhouse in **Castleconnell**, she conducts summer courses and weekend workshops for beginners of all ages.

❡ New York-born author **Frank McCourt** (1930–2009) is perhaps best known for his tremendously successful memoir, *Angela's Ashes*. Visitors to Limerick can re-live the McCourt story by taking a guided tour which visits the places associated with the book. **The Angela's Ashes Walking Tour** departs from the Limerick tourist office in Arthur's Quay at 1430 (check days). The McCourt family moved from the USA to **Limerick**, Ireland in 1934. Fifteen years later Frank McCourt returned to New York to find employment. He enlisted in the army. When he was discharged he enrolled at Brooklyn College from where he obtained his Master's Degree in teaching in 1967. He taught in local high schools for 30 years. In 1997 he won the Pulitzer Prize for *Angela's Ashes*.

Open Houses
County Limerick Murroe

❧ The signposted walk along the **Slieve Felim Way** is popular with keen ramblers. It commences near the abbey in Murroe and ends 35 kilometres further on in the village of **Silvermines** in County Cork. This scenic trail can be undertaken in short stages, as it leads through a host of charming hamlets and villages, with cosy, hospitable country pubs offering rest and refreshment.

❧ **The River Maigue**, which runs through the heart of **Adare**, attracts anglers for salmon and trout fishing during the season, which commences in mid-February. In 2008 the **Irish Open Golf Championship** was held at the **Adare Manor Golf and Country Club** which straddles the River Maigue. English golfer **Richard Finch** won the title after famously falling into the river after slipping on his approach shot to the 18th green.

❧ Further west of Adare, along the coast from Limerick, the Tarbert–Killimer car ferry crosses the **Shannon Estuary** between **Tarbert** in County Kerry and **Kilrush** in County Clare, a journey of 20 minutes.

❧ Take home a piece of Irish porcelain from the **Irish Dresden** factory on the Limerick–Cork border in the village of **Dromcolliher**, an offshoot of the Dresden factory in Germany, where elegant figurines, often outfitted with hand-made lace, are meticulously handcrafted. **Colman O'Kelly**'s antique shop in The Square is also worth a visit.

❧ If visiting **Foynes** for the **Irish Coffee Festival** you could call in to the **Flying Boat Museum**, housed in the original terminal building. Here, on account of the freezing weather conditions, the first Irish coffee was created in the winter of 1942 for passengers numbed by the cold after being turned back on an attempted Atlantic crossing.

❧ Foynes was the focus of the aviation world in 1939 when American airline **Pan Am**'s luxury flying boat, the *Yankee Clipper* completed the first commercial passenger flight between **New York** in the USA and **Foynes** in Ireland. A full scale replica of the Yankee Clipper is on display at the **Foynes Flying Boat Museum**.

A tavern in the village of **Croom** on the River Maigue is thought by many literary historians to be the meeting place of a small group of 18th century writers known as **The Maigue Poets**, who are said to have been responsible for inventing the often amusing **Limerick** verse. Others believe English author **Edward Lear** (1812–1888) who wrote *The Book of Nonsense* in 1861 which was full of amusing limericks was responsible. Lear's book was last reprinted by Echo Publishing in 2009.

The Foynes Yacht Club Marina is the departure point for a fast moving open boat trip down the **Shannon Estuary** to **Limerick**. The boat follows the coastline and points of interest include wildlife, Celtic ruins and **Scattery Island** off the town of Kilrush, the site of a 6th century monastic settlement establishment by **St Senan**. Warm, waterproof parkas and life jackets are provided.

FOOD AND DRINK Until recently the village of **Murroe** was a one-pub town. **The Valley Inn** in the main street was protected by an old law set down by a former English landlord, which stated that the village could only have one pub. Recently this law expired and, with the addition of a new housing estate outside the town, Murroe can now claim two pubs.

✉ The Valley Inn, Main Street, Murroe
☎ +353 (0) 61 386 300 €
✉ Croker's Bar & Restaurant, Main Street, Murroe
☎ +353 (0) 61 386 418 €€€

An exquisite culinary experience can be had in the **Oakroom Fine Dining Restaurant** in the 5-star **Adare Manor**—a pleasant and indulgent way to lighten the wallet. A traditional Irish afternoon tea by the massive fireplace in the drawing room is also an unforgettable—although less costly—experience.

✉ Limerick Road, Adare
☎ +353 (0) 61 605 200 €€€€€

On the Limerick–Cork road the tidy town of **Bruff** lazes on the banks of the **Morning Star River**. One of the area's most popular, family-style restaurants, **The Old Bakehouse** is in the town's main street.

✉ Main Street Lower, Bruff
☎ +353 (0) 61 382 797 €€

Spiritual Retreats
County Dublin Dublin

07

Dominican Retreat Centre

The Dominican Retreat Centre is situated in the grounds of St Mary's Priory, once the site of the 14th-century **Tallaght Castle** and home to the Archbishops of Dublin until 1822. Tallaght Castle was later sold to a private buyer and in 1856 was purchased by the Dominican Order. The order was founded by **St Dominic** (1170–1221) in the 13th century and is also known as the Order of Preachers. Not a great deal of the original castle remains, except for the tower which has been incorporated into the newer priory buildings and forms part of the retreat house. The original Friar's Walk, (a long, wide avenue lined with yew trees) and a 300 year old walnut (known as St Maelruain's tree and named after the founder of the original monastery), remain on the estate.

❡ St Mary's Priory is a leading centre of theological studies. Throughout the year, the Dominican friars who live and work here conduct days of reflection as well as weekend and weekly retreats, open to people of all beliefs and faiths. Accommodation is modest and each single (only) guestroom is simply furnished. Rooms contain a hand basin and share bathrooms are located on each floor. There is a lift to all floors and all meals are served.

❡ The priory is in extensive grounds which include an 18th-century walled garden conducive to meditation, silence, reflection and relaxation. There is plenty of on-site parking and the centre is handy to the local shopping centre.

SPIRITUAL RETREAT

✉ Tallaght Village
Tallaght
Dublin 24

💶 price on application.

📞 +353 (0) 1 404 8189
📠 +353 (0) 1 459 6080

✉ retreats@
dominicanstallaght.org

🖰 www.goodnews.ie/
tallaghthome

☞ Tallaght Village
is approximately
10 kilometres south of
the Dublin CBD. Bus
numbers 65, 77 and
77A leave from Eden
Quay in Dublin to
Tallaght.

✝ **Sunday Mass**
0900, 1030, 1145
& 1830.
Church of St Dominic
St Dominic's Road
Tallaght.

⚥ Open to men, women
& groups

PLACES OF INTEREST ❦ **Tallaght** is 10 kilometres south-west of Dublin, in the foothills of the mountains which form the border between County Dublin and County Wicklow. Depending on which side you are on, the mountains are known as the Dublin Mountains or the Wicklow Mountains.

❧ Tallaght is synonymous with **The Square** (near St Mary's Priory), one of the largest shopping complexes in Ireland, boasting almost 200 stores and restaurants. Other Irish megamalls are the **Dundrum Town Centre**, not too far away in **Dún Laoghaire**, and the **Blanchardstown Shopping Complex** near **Phoenix Park** in Dublin's north-west.

❧ **St Maelruain's Church of Ireland** stands across the road from the Catholic Priory of St Mary. St Maelruain's parish church was established in 1829 on the site of Tallaght's first monastery, which was founded by **St Maelruain** in 769. In its time the Monastery of St Maelruain was a leading centre of spirituality where monks followed a strict regimen of prayer and penance.

♱ Sunday Services 0830 & 1100.

❧ To seriously test your fitness, head for the **Wicklow Way**, a long-distance walking trail from **Marley Park** on the southern outskirts of Dublin, which passes through **Glendalough** and **Shillelagh** to **Clonegal** in County Carlow. The 120-kilometre-long trail leads through picturesque countryside and rolling mountain scenery, and is suitable for most people of average fitness. The cycle superstore in The Square hires bikes if you wish to explore the mountains on two wheels.

❧ Summer or winter, the artificial snow slopes in **Kilternan** are open for skiing or snow-boarding lessons. The not-for-profit centre is run by the Ski Club of Ireland and is in the grounds of **Kilternan Golf Club**. With four 'slopes' of varying difficulty, it is a perfect place to learn the ropes before tackling the real thing. Kilternan is 7 kilometres south-east of Tallaght.

Spiritual Retreats
County Dublin Dublin

❧ **Áras Chrónáin** (the Irish Cultural Centre) in Orchard Road, Clondalkin near Tallaght promotes Irish culture, music and dance through social evenings and other events. Visitors are welcome to come along and join in. And if you want to learn spoken Gaelic this is the place to be. **Clondalkin** is known as a centre for the Irish language and Áras Chrónáin offers a number of language classes at various levels throughout the year.

❧ If driving through Clondalkin, it's difficult to miss the town's **Medieval Round Tower**. This ancient monument was once part of a Celtic monastic complex which was raided by the Vikings in the 8th century. The tower is the only part of the original monastery still standing.

❧ **The Hazel Grove Golf Club**, in **Jobstown** in the west of Tallaght, was designed by Dublin-born golf course architect **Eddie Hackett** (1910–1996). It is said to be one of the friendliest golf clubs in Ireland.

FOOD AND DRINK ❧ The priory is in the centre of town with pubs, restaurants, shops and cafés in close proximity. However, if you are not feeling overly virtuous after your spiritual retreat you could always pop into **The Foxes Covert**, the pub opposite the Priory in Tallaght Village, for a pint of the black stuff. *Sláinte*!

✉ Main Street, Tallaght

✆ +353 (0) 1 451 5183   €

❧ One of the country's oldest pubs, the 18th-century **Johnny Fox's** in the suburb of **Glencullen** also has a claim to fame as the highest pub in Ireland. Weather permitting, sit outside and take in the views of the Wicklow Mountains in the distance. Irish music is played seven nights a week and a traditional Irish 'hooley night' of feasting, fun, dancing and music is held once a week. A helipad is thoughtfully provided.

✉ Glencullen

✆ +353 (0) 1 295 5647   €€€

❧ The **Captain Americas Cookhouse** chain has opened a relaxed family restaurant at Tallaght Cross serving kid-friendly food such as burgers, chips and garlic bread—but only in man-sized portions. Licensed.

✉ Tallaght Cross

✆ +353 (0) 1 414 1426   €€

SPIRITUAL RETREAT

08

Monastery of St Alphonsus

The Monastery of St Alphonsus was established in 1858 for sisters of the Redemptorist Order (also known as the Red Nuns because of the unusual colour of their habits). It is situated on a large allotment on the northern side of the River Liffey, 2 kilometres from the centre of Dublin. The sisters belong to an enclosed, contemplative community of religious women known as the Redemptoristines. Over the years the sisters sold off much of their estate to a property developer and in 2002 moved into a new, modern monastery established next to the site of the old one.

❡ Part of the new monastery includes the **Ruah Retreat Centre** which caters for groups holding meetings and retreats as well as for individuals. However, there is no interaction between guests and the sisters, and retreats and meditations are of a personal nature. Overnight accommodation with self-catering facilities is provided in the sisters' new retreat house which is attached to the monastery. The minimum stay is 2 nights and guests may join the nuns (and quite a few locals) in the chapel for prayer and liturgical services, if they wish.

❡ Being an enclosed community hasn't stopped the sisters from keeping pace with modern technology. The sisters have installed a web camera in the new monastery church and Mass, religious services and professions are often broadcast live to the monastery website. The sisters also have a 'blog' page on the site.

✉ St Alphonsus Road
Drumcondra
Dublin 9

🛏 from €28.00 pp
(single room), including
breakfast

☎ +353 (0) 1 860 3915

✉ ruah.retreat@
redemptorists.ie

🖰 www.rednuns.com

☞ Take the train to
Drumcondra Station
and walk the short
distance to the
convent.

✝ **Sunday Mass
0900.**
Monastery of
St Alphonsus,
St Aphonsus Road,
Drumcondra.

👤 Open to women only

Spiritual Retreats
County Dublin Dublin

PLACES OF INTEREST ❦ Dublin's **Writers' Museum** at 18 Parnell Square (near St Mary's Abbey) is a monument to the country's literary heroes and heroines, including Irish women writers: **Norah Hoult** (1898–1984), novelist and short story writer; **Lady Isabella Augusta Gregory** (1852–1932), playwright and co-founder of Dublin's **Abbey Theatre** with poet **William Butler Yeats** (1865–1939); and **Katharine Tynan** (1861–1931), poet and novelist. The museum's exhibits include first editions, original manuscripts, memorabilia and a multitude of portraits. A separate section of the museum has been set aside as a reading room for young readers and aspiring authors.

❧ Ireland's musical heritage is kept alive through performances of the **Comhaltas Ceoltóirí Éireann** (pronounced *coal-tus kyol-tory air-un*), an international establishment formed to promote traditional Irish music and dance. For something slightly less authentic but nevertheless lots of fun, keep an eye out for the Irish dance performances (Jury's Irish Cabaret) at **Jury's Ballsbridge Hotel** and at the **Burlington Hotel** in Upper Leeson Street.

❧ Visitors to Ireland can always take part in *céilí* **dancing** where participants are taught enough fancy footwork to rival *Riverdance*, with toe-tapping line and round dances set to music. A **Céilí Festival** is held in Dublin each St Patrick's Day (17 March).

❧ The **Irish National Botanic Gardens**, adjacent to Glasnevin Cemetery, were established in 1795 alongside the River Tolka. Art exhibitions and musical events are held in the gardens during the summer when it is eminently suitable for relaxed perambulation.

❧ During the summer months tours of the vast **Glasnevin Cemetery** are conducted by knowledgeable guides. Along the way the guides relate stories and anecdotes and little known items of interest as the cemetery is the last resting place of politicians and revolutionaries, the rich and the famous and over one million Dubliners.

In some hundreds of hectares of lush green parkland and sports fields, 2 kilometres to the west of Dublin city, **Phoenix Park** provides Dubliners with a peaceful escape from the hustle and bustle of the city. The park is the official residence of the President of Ireland and, it seems, hundreds of flighty, fallow deer. A large cross on a mound in Phoenix Park commemorates a Mass celebrated by **Pope John Paul II** in 1979 and attended by 1.25 million people. Africa is on full display at **Dublin Zoo** which is situated in the grounds of Phoenix Park.

If you're interested in bargain hunting, the all-day Saturday craft market in **Wolfe Tone Park** in Mary Street is a good place to start. Gourmet foods are on sale at the food market held in the park each Friday from 1000. The park is named after Trinity College old boy and Irish Nationalist **Theobold Wolfe Tone** (1791–1828), who fought for the passing of the Catholic Relief Bill in 1793.

For more up-market shopping, browse the range of hand-crafted Celtic jewellery at **Dickson and Dickson** in Lower O'Connell Street. Or inspect a hand-knitted Aran sweater at the **Blarney Woollen Mills** in Nassau Street. The street (opposite Trinity College) is lined with shops selling souvenirs and all things Irish.

FOOD AND DRINK If you are lucky enough to score a table you could relax in the basement restaurant of The Dublin Writer's Museum. Appropriately named **Chapter One**, it is one of the city's best. Bookings are recommended.

✉ 18–19 Parnell Square

✆ +353 (0)1 873 2266 €€€€€

Fagans Pub in Drumcondra was the former Irish *Taoiseach* (prime minister) **Bertie Ahern**'s local watering hole. Bill and Hillary Clinton have also dropped by for a pint.

✉ 146 Lower Drumcondra Road

✆ +353 (0)1 837 5309 €€

Bewley's Café in Grafton Street has long been the favoured haunt of Dublin literati and theatre buffs, along with everyday coffee-shop philosophers. An established eating place in Dublin since 1800, the historical cafe closed its doors in 2005. However, as a result of the public outcry, a new and more modern Bewley's has emerged, serving its famous coffee and Irish fare Monday to Saturday and at breakfast time on Sundays.

✉ Grafton Street

✆ +353 (0)1 672 7720 €€–€€€

County Cork

ORK, IRELAND'S LARGEST COUNTY, takes in the sheltered, deep waters of Cobh Harbour (pronounced *'cove'*), the second largest natural harbour in the world (Sydney's magnificent, sheltered harbour being the largest). Cobh is situated on an island in Cork Harbour and connected to the mainland via bridges to Fota Island. The town was the last port of call of the British passenger liner the *Titanic* on its maiden and tragically final voyage in 1912.

There are over 600 kilometres of craggy Cork coastline and the waters hum with boating activity, especially in summer. The county brews its own varieties of stout—Murphy's and Beamish—both of which are said by the locals to taste even better than the more common variety. The county's 'stone-kissing' legends are played out daily at Blarney Castle by way of rather inelegant, ritualistic close contact with a slab of very hard rock. Every summer weekend, one festival or another is held somewhere in County Cork, including Gaelic festivals which are held frequently in the west of the county, one of the remaining 'Gaeltacht' (Irish-speaking) areas in Ireland.

Thirteen centuries ago, St Finbarr (c. 550–623), the Patron Saint of Cork, founded a school and monastery from which the city of Cork eventually grew. Until the 16th century, St Fin Barre's was the heart of the city, a hallowed centre of prayer and learning. Cork's statuesque, Gothic St Fin Barre's Cathedral is said to have been built on the original site of the monastery.

Today, a diversity of religious orders have established convents and monasteries in the county and many, following in the tradition of their eminent predecessor, conduct spiritual retreats and days of prayer.

09

St Benedict's Priory

St Benedict's Priory, a sister of the Tyburn Convent in London, is located overlooking **Cobh Harbour** in an historical building which was once Cork's Admiralty House. Today the building is a convent where an enclosed contemplative congregation of nuns, the Adorers of the Sacred Heart of Jesus of Montmartre, live and work. The sisters follow the Rule of St Benedict.

❧ The sisters do not conduct formal retreats or offer spiritual guidance as such. However, accommodation is available to groups or individuals who wish to make a self-guided retreat or have some private time of reflection in the tranquil surrounds of this spiritual haven. Visitors who prefer to make a single-day retreat are also welcome. Guests can join with the community in celebrating Mass and other liturgical services, including the Liturgy of the Hours. Holy Hours are conducted weekly, in the convent church, for the general public between 2000 and 2100.

❧ Decades of inspired effort have been put into the priory's landscaped gardens which are designed around the shape of a cross. Sections include an interpretation of the biblical Garden of Gethsemane and the Pool of Solomon, both named after the sacred gardens of old. There is also a large memorial garden and pond dedicated to those who have lost a child. The gardens are open to the public.

❧ The sisters run the **Oasis** gift shop and a café serving home-made cakes and snacks, sometimes baked by the nuns themselves.

✉ The Mount
Cobh
County Cork

💷 suggested offering around €45.00 pp, including all meals.

📞 +353 (0) 21 481 1354

🖥 www.tyburnconvent.org.uk/monasteries/ireland/ireland.html

☞ Trains depart from Cork's Kent Station in Lower Glanmire Road every half an hour for Cobh, which is 20 kilometres south-east of Cork. The journey takes almost 25 minutes. Cobh station is located next to the Cobh Heritage Centre. From there it is a short taxi ride to the priory or a stiff uphill walk.

✝ **Sunday Mass** 0800, 1000, 1200 & 1900. St Colman's Cathedral Cobh.

♀ Open to women only

Spiritual Retreats
County Cork Cobh

PLACES OF INTEREST ❦ **Cobh**, once called Queenstown, was the last port of call for the Belfast-built luxury liner the *Titanic* before it sailed on its fateful journey to New York on 11 April 1912.

❦ Seventeen-year-old Cork girl **Annie Moore** (1877–1924) a passenger on the *Titanic*, was the first person to pass through New York's **Ellis Island** immigrant processing facility; she has been honoured with bronze statues of herself and her two younger brothers in both Cobh and New York.

❦ The town also has ties to the great ocean liner the *Lusitania* which was sailing to Cobh when it was struck and sunk by a German U-boat off the coast of **Kinsale** in 1915. The Lusitania departed from New York on 1st May 1915, 10 days after the German Embassy in Washington issued this warning.

Travellers intending to embark on the Atlantic voyage are reminded that a state of war exists between Germany and her allies and Great Britain and her allies; that the zone of war includes the waters adjacent to the British Isles; that, in accordance with formal notice given by the Imperial German Government, vessels flying the flag of Great Britain, or any of her allies, are liable to destruction in those waters and that travellers sailing in the war zone on the ships of Great Britain or her allies do so at their own risk.

❦ The journeys of the *Titanic* and *Lusitania* can be followed in a guided tour called The Queenstown Story, presented by the **Cobh Heritage Centre** which is located in a restored railway station on **Deepwater Quay**.

❦ One of the best views in town is from the restored, heritage-listed **St Colman's Cathedral**, which with 49 bells has the largest carillon in Europe. Bell-ringing recitals take place in the cathedral between May and September. In 1953 comedy duo **Laurel and Hardy** sailed into Cobh and were taken aback to hear the carillon playing their theme song. Admission is free— tune in from anywhere in Cobh.

❦ While not terribly large, **Fota Island** in Cork Harbour has room for a zoo and a wildlife park which is the home and breeding place of cheetahs, giraffes, zebras and other exotic species. The island is still big enough for a par-71 championship golf course. The island is connected by bridge to the mainland and a ferry service operates from Ringaskiddy. Another island in Cobh Harbour, **Spike Island**, was once the 'Irish Alcatraz'; not connected to the mainland, it was the site of the county prison which closed in 2004. **Haulbowline Island** is the headquarters of the Irish Navy.

❡ The annual **Cobh People's Regatta** is held in mid-August. As well as activities on the harbour, wheelbarrow races, parades, fireworks and the all-important crowning of the Regatta Queen take place.

❡ Take in spectacular views over the **Irish Sea** on a walk along the scenic **Ballycotton** coastline. The 14-kilometre round trip takes you from Ballycotton to Ballytrasna and Ballyandreen, a section of the **East Cork Way** (for walkers) and a sanctuary for nature lovers and birdwatchers.

❡ The national memorial to Irish revolutionary **Michael Collins** (1890–1922) is located in Emmet Square, **Clonakilty**, 60 kilometres south-west of Cobh. **The Michael Collins Memorial Centre** has been established on the site of the Collins' family home at Woodfield on the outskirts of the town. A roadside memorial has been erected in **Béal na mBláth**, west of Cork, at the site of the ambush where Michael Collins was fatally wounded.

FOOD AND DRINK ❧ There are plenty of pubs in Cobh, many with a nautical connection. However, **Gilmore's Bar**—formerly called Mansworths—is the only pub in the town which was in business the day the *Titanic* sailed; quite likely it played host to departing passengers and their families.

✉ 4 Middleton Street

✆ +353 (0) 21 481 1965   €€

❡ The best water views in **Ballycotton** are from the **Bayview Hotel** which is situated high on the cliffs of the town. The hotel's chefs only have to wander down to the harbour below to meet the fishing boats and their 'catch of the day'.

✉ Ballycotton

✆ +353 (0) 21 464 6746   €€€

❡ **Aherne's Seafood Restaurant** in nearby **Youghal** is one of the county's best-known seafood restaurants. The decor is sophisticated and stylish and the daily menu is always a surprise; it is based on what the local fishermen happen to have caught overnight. Youghal is a 40-minute drive north-east of Cork.

✉ 163 North Main Street

✆ +353 (0) 24 92 424   €€€€

Spiritual Retreats
County Cork Montenotte, Cork

10

St Dominic's Retreat House

Dominican Friars first arrived in Cork in 1229. They founded a priory and church near **St Fin Barre's Cathedral**. Known as St Mary's (*Mairies*) of the Isle it was later seized by Henry VIII. In the late 18th century, the order established a new priory in the centre of the town and constructed the present-day church of St Mary's of the Isle. In 1952 the order purchased a second property, '**Ennismore**' from a local Irish family. Today Ennismore is a busy centre for retreats being in an ideal location for quiet contemplation and prayer.

⸡ With views of Lough Mahon and set in hectares of rambling, established gardens, the house is run by Irish Dominican friars who conduct retreats regularly throughout the year—on a daily basis, over a weekend or for up to 6 days. At various times retreats are based around relaxation and stress, and meditation and yoga are often incorporated into the program.

⸡ The type of accommodation available at Ennismore varies. There is a modern retreat house which caters comfortably for up to 40 people, in single and twin guestrooms. All guestrooms share bathrooms on the same floor but are equipped with a wash basin. A second building caters for up to 20 guests with similar facilities. All meals are available. Also on the property is a small, self-catering house, The Lodge, which one or two people can use if they prefer to make a private, self-guided retreat. However, all guests are welcome to join in liturgical services with the community.

⸡ A number of meeting rooms are within the complex.

✉ Colmcille Avenue
Montenotte
Cork
County Cork

🛏 from €45.00 pp,
including all meals.

☎ +353 (0) 21 450 2520
📠 +353 (0) 21 450 2712

📧 ennismore@eircom.net

🌐 www.ennismore.ie

☞ Bus number 8 from Patrick Street in Cork stops near St Dominic's. The retreat house is 4 kilometres from the city centre.

✝ **Sunday Mass**
0830, 1030 & 1200.
Cathedral of St Mary and St Anne, Roman Street, Cork.

✝ **Sunday Services**
0800, 1115 & 1900.
St Fin Barre's Cathedral, Cork.

⚭ Open to men, women & groups

PLACES OF INTEREST ❧ **Blarney Castle** and the mythical **Blarney Stone** are situated a few kilometres north of Cork, in the lovely village of Blarney. Legend has it that all who desire the 'gift of the gab' will be granted such upon kissing the stone, which is a feat in itself, requiring physical agility and a head for heights. The village is pretty, but understandably quite touristy. However, the barn-like **Blarney Woollen Mills** makes for an interesting visit; it retails everything from cable-knitted cashmere and Aran sweaters, mohair throws and Irish linen to Irish fragrances and Celtic jewellery.

❧ Anyone with a weakness for crystal will find it hard to resist the **Kinsale Crystal Factory** in Market Street, Kinsale. Each piece is hand-cut and signed by the creator. Authentic Kinsale Crystal is only available from this shop. Around the corner in Pearse Street, the **Kinsale Silver Shop** and factory create exclusive hand-crafted jewellery in sterling silver. Many of the designs have a Celtic origin. Boland's **Kinsale Craft Shop** sells locally made handcrafts, including clothing, jewellery and ceramics.

❧ A memorial to the passengers of the *Lusitania* has been erected at the **Old Head of Kinsale** on the outskirts of the town. From here you can look out to sea towards where the wreck of the ship lies, some 18 kilometres off the coast.

❧ Woodturning has always been an archetypal Irish craft and at **Dunbogue Wood Design** in Dunbogue, 25 kilometres south-west of Cork, day courses are conducted. Only naturally felled trees are used.

❧ **Cork** town, a centre for the arts in Ireland, hosts an annual **Jazz Festival** each October. One of the country's most celebrated events, it attracts jazz musicians from all over the world. The **Cork Film Festival** is also held in October and features the works of Irish and international film-makers.

❧ The ruins of **Bridgetown Abbey** near **Castletownroche**, north of Cork, are well worth a visit. The ruins were once an Augustinian priory, established in 1224 by the once-powerful Irish Roche family, many of whom are buried in the abbey graveyard.

Spiritual Retreats
County Cork Montenotte, Cork

❦ Lace-making was introduced into Ireland in the 19th century by Poor Clare nuns. Pieces worked to the nuns' original patterns can be purchased at the **Kenmare Lace and Design Centre** in The Square in Kenmare, where classes in lace-making are also conducted.

❦ **The Tubrid Holy Well** in Mill Street is a pilgrimage site honouring the Madonna. It is said to be a place of healing, particularly during the month of May (known as Mary's Month). **St John's Well**, with its healing waters reputed to cure warts, and known locally as *Tobar na Faith*, is in **Mushera** near **Kilcorney**.

❦ And if the kids haven't spotted a leprechaun yet, then get over to **Leahy's Open Farm** on the outskirts of **Dungourney Village** on the Tallow Road and check out the Leprechauns' Cave.

FOOD AND DRINK ❦ If you have some time to spare consider a visit to Cork's year-round permanent indoor **English Market** in Grand Parade. Open Monday to Saturday, the county's farmers and growers parade their wares. You could sample some local specialities, including *drisheen*, a traditional dish of sheep's organs blended into a delicious black pudding, a unique gustatory experience in itself. Pop upstairs and dine in comfort at the **Farmgate Café**.

✉ Old English Market, Princes Street

☎ +353 (0) 21 427 8134　　　　　€€–€€€

❦ Sweet local oysters, lobster from the tank, and rib-sticking seafood chowder are usually on the menu at the **Jim Edwards** pub and seafood restaurant on the Quay in Kinsale.

✉ Market Quay

☎ +353 (0) 21 477 2541　　　　　€€€

❦ Even less formal is the breezy **Fishy Fishy Café** down by Kinsale Harbour. Its 'fishing trawler fresh' menu is ever changing. The doors open 7 days a week in summer—just don't ask for a T-bone.

✉ Crowley's Quay

☎ +353 (0) 21 470 0415　　　　　€€€

❦ **Kinsale** is said to have more restaurants and cafés than any other area in Ireland. Visit in October, if you can, when the annual **Gourmet Festival** is held.

County Louth

HE SMALLEST COUNTY IN IRELAND, Louth is one
of the gateways to the Irish Republic. Belfast can be
visited in a day trip from here.

Celtic gods, mythical giants and tyrannical rulers
are all part of Louth's cultural inheritance, along with
Monasterboice, the first religious settlement in the county, founded
near Drogheda in the 5th century by St Buite, the monastery's first
abbot. The round tower, once used by monks as a hiding place in
times of danger, and three ancient, ornate Celtic high crosses still
stand on the site.

In 1979 some 300,000 people made the pilgrimage to a parcel of
land on Tullyesker Hill in Killineer, on the outskirts of Drogheda, to
attend an outdoor Mass celebrated by Pope John Paul II. The Pope
was assisted by 2,000 priests and a 6,000-strong choir. The Papal
Cross was erected as a permanent memorial, and when the Pope
died in April 2005 the site was visited by throngs of people lighting
candles and paying their respects.

A few kilometres away are the evocative, 12th-century remains of
the Mellifont Cistercian Abbey, founded by St Malachy in 1142 and
once Ireland's pre-eminent abbey. The ruins lie scattered alongside
the more contemporary Mellifont monastery, where the monks of
the Cistercian Order of Strict Observance follow the Benedictine
Rule of Hospitality.

11

Monastery of St Catherine of Siena

The Dominican Sisters of St Catherine of Siena have had a presence in **Drogheda** since 1722 when Irish-born nun Mother Catherine Plunkett was transferred from Brussels to set up a congregational house suitable for a community of Dominican women. The original premises have long gone and today the Domincan sisters live in a large, modern-looking convent overlooking the town.

❧ The sisters run a small retreat house where guests come to make their own private retreat in silence. However, guests may attend liturgical services with the nuns, including the Liturgy of the Hours and the Divine Office.

❧ The newly refurbished, self-catering guest section is comfortably furnished, with four en suite guestrooms, all of which have Internet access. A laundry with washing and drying facilities is available. Guests can take advantage of a quiet, private garden area and the River Boyne is not far away. A communal kitchen is provided for the use of guests. Groups who wish to undertake a day retreat are welcome.

❧ An amusing anecdote relates to **Mother Catherine Plunkett**. She 'had come from Brussels to act as first prioress of the Convent. The members of the community always wore secular dress, but a rumour spread that they were Popish nuns and an official was sent to make inquiries. He interviewed the prioress, being of course quite unaware that she was a nun, and told her of the report that there were nuns in the house. "Sir," she replied, "I can assure you the ladies of this establishment are as much nuns as I am." He apologized and went away satisfied.' (Dónal O'Sullivan, Carolan *The Life, Times and Music of an Irish Harper*, 2001)

✉ The Twenties
Drogheda
County Louth

💷 price to be negotiated.

✎ sienamonastery@
eircom.net

🖰 www.dominicans.ie

☞ Take the train to Drogheda. The monastery is on the northern outskirts of the town, a short taxi ride from Drogheda Station. Drogheda is 55 kilometres north of Dublin.

✝ **Sunday Mass**
0900.
Monastery of
St Catherine of Siena,
The Twenties,
Drogheda.

👤 Open to women only

PLACES OF INTEREST ❧ **Drogheda** is one of Ireland's oldest towns, as can be seen in the ruins of medieval abbeys and the 13th-century St Laurence's gate that was once part of the town wall. The Franciscan religious order established an early presence in Drogheda, but after 800 years of service the friary and the High Lane Church were closed in 1999. The church and friary were donated by the order to the Drogheda community and now form part of an art gallery and café. The few friars who remain in the town take an active role in the running of the two businesses.

❧ **Louth** is the land of legends and if spending some time in the county you will most likely hear the story of the **Jumping Church of Kildemock**. Once officially called the Millockstown Church, it is now in ruins, just south of **Ardee**. The story suggests that some 3 centuries ago a side wall of the church 'jumped' inside to exclude the grave of a lapsed Catholic who was buried within. True or not, the wall is clearly askew.

❧ Drogheda has two churches called **St Peter**—one Church of Ireland and the other Catholic. St Peter's Church of Ireland was destroyed by British political leader **Oliver Cromwell** in 1649 and later rebuilt.

✝ Sunday Services St Peter's Church of Ireland, Peter Street, Drogheda. 0830 & 1100.

✝ Sunday Mass Church of St Peter, West Street, Drogheda. 0800, 1100 & 1215.

❧ A Dominican priory was founded in Drogheda in the early 13th century. The only part of the building still standing is the **Magdalene Tower**, in Magdalene Street on the northern side of the river.

❧ A shrine in **St Peter's Catholic Church** displays a glass reliquary containing the severed head of Jesuit priest and saint **Oliver Plunkett** (1629–1681) who was hung, drawn and quartered on the Tyburn Gallows in London to become the last Catholic martyr to die at the hands of an English monarch. Oliver Plunkett was canonised in 1975 by Pope Paul VI.

Spiritual Retreats
County Louth Drogheda

❡ Not far from Drogheda a monastery was established at **Monasterboice** by **St Buite** (died c. 521), around the year 500. The ruins include a High Cross erected in the 9th century and known as **Muiredach's Cross**. The cross is said to be the finest example of a High Cross in the country. Some centuries later (1142) monks from the **Abbey of Clairvaux** in Ville-sous-la-Ferté, in Champagne's Aube department in France, established a Cistercian monastery (Mellifont) nearby, with the help of **St Malachy O'More** (1094–1148), Bishop of Armagh. St Malachy's former student **Christian O'Conarchy** (c. 1100–1186) was elected first abbot of the new monastery which remained occupied by Cistercian monks until the dissolution in 1539. Both the old and the new Mellifont (1938) are located near each other.

❡ The **Oriel Driving Trail** provides an excellent opportunity to see some of rural County Louth. The signposted trail is 150 kilometres long and leads through picturesque countryside and medieval villages, and past numerous historical sights. The trail starts and finishes at Drogheda. Maps are available from the local tourist office.

FOOD AND DRINK ❡ If you fancy cooking as well as eating, the talented chefs at the **Ghan House Cookery School** in Carlingford host cooking classes from the luxury of a restored Georgian mansion in the centre of the town. The pubs and shops of Carlingford are only steps away.

✉ Greenore Road

☏ +353 (0) 42 937 3682

❡ **County Down** in Northern Ireland is on the other side of **Carlingford Bay**. If you happen to be in Carlingford in August you could catch the **Carlingford Oyster Festival**, a highlight for residents and tourists alike. If you miss out there is no better place to sample the local produce than at **The Anchor Bar**, otherwise known as PJ's Pub, in medieval Tholsel Street. Near the Tholsel (Street)Archway, PJ's is one of the oldest and most popular pubs in Carlingford and a rather magical place as the genuine leprechaun bones by the front door testify.

✉ Tholsel Street

☏ +353 (0) 42 937 3106   €€

❡ Food is presented with style and flair at the contemporary **Rosso Restaurant** in **Dundalk** where the chef's high standards have been rewarded with numerous culinary awards.

✉ 5 Roden Place

☏ +353 (0) 42 935 6502   €€€€

County Waterford

DATING BACK TO THE TIME when Vikings occupied Ireland, the bustling coastal capital of Waterford is the country's oldest city. The Vikings landed here some time during the 10th century and soon came face to face with the Christian faith. In medieval times monasteries were established, firstly by St Declan who founded a monastic city at Ardmore on the coast south of Waterford in the year 416. This was followed in the 6th century by St Maelanfaid's Molana Abbey, established on a small island in the River Blackwater, and by the Augustinians' Mothel Abbey near Rathgormack. Today's monastic descendants are well settled in the county in more modern ecclesiastical abodes.

Waterford may be the home of a famous crystal factory, but the county's cultural agenda is jam-packed with concerts and artistic events, parades and festivals, some catering for special interests such as travel writing, gardens, walking, and even oysters and mussels. The Spraoi Festival each August is said to be the biggest weekend street carnival in Ireland; the *Feile Na nDeise* festival held in Dungarvan each May, celebrates traditional Irish music, dance and culture. And culture and heritage have never been more evident than at the Ring Gaeltacht area on the southern end of Dungarvan Harbour, where Gaelic (the Irish language) is used in daily life in preference to English.

Enjoy the *craic*! Good times, good company!

Spiritual Retreats
County Waterford Cappoquin

12

Mount Melleray Abbey

In an idyllic location, nestled midst rugged mountainous terrain a few kilometres from the riverside town of **Cappoquin**, stands Ireland's oldest working Cistercian (Trappist) abbey. **The Abbey of Mount Melleray** was founded in 1832 by monks from the Abbey of Melleray in Brittany, France. They had been expelled from their abbey during the French Revolution and their search for suitable property for a new abbey led them to a location at the foot of the Knockmealdown Mountains in rural County Waterford. The monks worked diligently to construct a monastery and church and lived off the land they had acquired. Today the monks continue to work the land, running a thriving dairy farm which helps provide for the needs of the locals.

❧ The monks' morning begins at 0400 with prayer in the chapel, followed by six more scheduled prayer times during the day. Guests have always been welcome and these days the Cistercians share their daily lives with day visitors and pilgrims who come to pray, meditate and spend time in a monastic atmosphere. Retreats are self-guided but guests can join the monks in liturgical services.

❧ Guests, male and female, are accommodated in the abbey guesthouse in simple single, double or triple rooms, all of which have a wash basin. Bathrooms are on a share basis.

❧ The monks manage a gift shop where books and religious articles can be purchased. There is also a heritage centre and a café where visitors can enjoy a drink and a bite to eat under the Irish sun, with some luck.

✉ Cappoquin
County Waterford

💷 price to be negotiated.

📞 +353 (0) 58 54404
📠 +353 (0) 58 52140

✉ guestmaster@
mountmellerayabbey.org

🖥 www.
mountmellerayabbey.org

☞ Mount Melleray Abbey is located 6 kilometres from the village of Cappoquin. It's a bit off the beaten track, however, and there is no public transport. Taxis are not always easy to find in either Cappoquin or nearby Lismore, 8 kilometres west. Ideally, the abbey is accessed by car.

♱ **Sunday Mass**
1000 (sung).
Abbey of Mount Melleray,
Cappoquin.

⚥ Open to both men & women

PLACES OF INTEREST ❧ A long row of neat, grey brick houses near the entrance to **Mt Melleray Abbey** once accommodated boarders who were students of the former Mt Melleray College. The houses are still used as accommodation as they are now owned by the Catholic Boy Scouts of Ireland who conduct outdoor activity programs for young people. **The National Scout Museum** is on-site.

❧ On the road from **Cappoquin** to **Mt Melleray** a shrine and roadside grotto (known as the Melleray Grotto) is dedicated to the Virgin Mary, who is said to have appeared frequently at this spot during a 3-week period in August 1985. A number of locals witnessed the apparitions and relayed the messages to the Irish people that Our Lady is said to have given them. The appearances sparked quite a deal of controversy and some locals are still keen to voice their opinion when given the opportunity. The shrine is a much-visited place of pilgrimage, with Masses and prayer vigils held regularly. Plastic bottles are provided for pilgrims to fill with 'blessed' water from a well.

❧ **St Mary's Abbey** (or Glencairn Abbey) near **Lismore**, on the shores of the Blackwater River, a local salmon fishing hotspot, is the home of Cistercian nuns who live a devout Christian lifestyle in the only female Cistercian abbey in Ireland. The abbey was established in 1932. The sisters follow a schedule of prayer seven times daily in the abbey church; visitors and passers-by can join in. The sisters have released a CD titled *In Praise of Mary*, produced by Irish singer **Nóirín Ní Riain** (b. 1951). It was recorded in the abbey church to commemorate the 75th anniversary of Cistercian life in Ireland.
✝ Sunday Mass 1100.

❧ A scenic, circular driving route, the **West Waterford Monastic Trail**, leads to important Christian sites in and around the Cappoquin area. Glencairn Abbey and Mt Melleray are suggested stops, along with cathedrals, churches, ruined abbeys and the **Carmelite Monastery of Saint Joseph** in Tallow, which was established in 1839. During the Irish Potato Famine in 1847 the nuns' lace-making school offered employment to the local girls in making Tallow Lace. The nuns left Tallow in 1910 and handed over the monastery and school to the local diocese.

Spiritual Retreats
County Waterford Cappoquin

From Cappoquin the signs on the Glenshelane walking path point towards historic **Lismore Castle**, the Irish home of the Duke and Duchess of Devonshire. The castle's Jacobean-style gardens, thought to be among the oldest in Ireland, can be explored between Easter and October. This is a most scenic area of Ireland, and walking and motoring maps are available from the Heritage Centre in Lismore. The centre's craft shop sells a large range of souvenirs, Irish knitwear and jewellery.

Despite troubling economic times the world-renowned **Waterford Crystal Factory** in Cork Road, Waterford, a mere 70 kilometres east of Cappoquin, is well worth a visit. Call beforehand to check tour availability and retail store hours.

☎ +353 (0) 51 332 500

Local artists display their creations at the **Ardmore Pottery and Craft Gallery** in the town of Ardmore, on the coast south of Waterford. Or learn how to do it yourself at the **Glencairn Pottery School** which conducts weekend courses for beginners.

FOOD AND DRINK The **Pastis Bistro**, an award-winning French restaurant run by Irishwoman Fiona Tricot and her French husband Stéphane, is situated close to Glencairn Abbey, 4 kilometres west of Lismore. Would-be Francophiles can indulge in country-style pâté, *cassoulet*, steak and '*frites*', and classic *tarte tatin*.

✉ Glencairn Inn

☎ +353 (0) 58 56232   €€€–€€€€

The Cloisters Tea Rooms at the abbey serve home-made soup, snacks and tasty toasted sandwiches. Opening hours are from 1200, and through each afternoon except Monday.

✉ Mount Melleray Abbey

☎ +353 (0) 58 54404   €

Next to the entrance to Mt Melleray the **Pilgrim's Rest Hotel** specialises in traditional Irish cream teas. The tea rooms are also open for all meals.

✉ Mount Melleray

☎ +353 (0) 58 52917   €

A picnic on the Blackwater can be easily prepared as the shops in Cappoquin do a brisk trade in the local Knockalara cheese and Crinnaghtaun apple juice. **Barrons**, the town bakery and a fixture in Cappoquin since 1885, can supply the home-baked bread. Mary McGrath's traditional home-made jams are a delicious accompaniment.

County Wicklow

IDED BY A GENEROUS MOTHER NATURE, Wicklow is often referred to as 'the garden of Ireland'. Tourists are attracted to the county as it is close to Dublin and offers much of interest for those with limited time.

The county is also known for its significant religious heritage. The Wicklow Way Walking Trail leads from Rathfarnham in Dublin's south through some of Ireland's most captivating landscapes and on to the newly restored pilgrim's trail, St Kevin's Way. This 30-kilometre walk will take you through the Wicklow Hills and the mountain-high village of Hollywood and on to the haunting remains of the monastic city of Glendalough. If travelling by car, Glendalough is about an hour's drive south of Dublin.

St Kevin established a monastic and spiritual sanctuary in Glendalough during the 6th century and even today religious orders run houses of retreat from where numerous pilgrimages depart. The ruins of the monastic city are spread over a 3-kilometre area; scenic walking trails lead to sites of religious significance, including places where St Kevin lived and worshipped.

And while the television series *Ballykissangel* may have brought fame to the tiny town of Avoca, many other villages of the county are equally picturesque—and possibly somewhat less over-run with fans!

WICKLOW was one of the most violent sectors in Ireland during the Rebellion of 1798. No county sent more of its natives to the harsh penal colony of New South Wales, Australia.

DR RUAN O'DONNELL, *THE REBELLION IN WICKLOW 1798*

Spiritual Retreats
County Wicklow Brockagh

13

Tearmann Spirituality Centre

The St Patrick's Missionary Society, an international order of Catholic priests founded in Ireland in 1930, runs a refuge of prayer, peace and renewal in **Brockagh**, a tiny hamlet between the villages of Glendalough and Laragh. Retreats of varying lengths are conducted— anything from a weekend, 6 days, 1 month or up to 3 months (by prior agreement). During the summer months retreats are often based on the Celtic spiritual heritage. Accommodation is in well-equipped, self-catering apartments overlooking the Glendalough Valley. The apartments each consist of en suite bedrooms, a fully equipped kitchen, lounge room and dining area. Laundry facilities are available.

¶ Day groups are also welcome to visit St Patrick's and take part in guided walkabouts through rural Wicklow and the spectacular Glendalough valley to places of spiritual and religious significance. These guided walks are conducted by prior arrangement. Guests of St Patrick's are encouraged to explore the valley as part of their spiritual journey. The monastic city is within walking distance of the Tearmann Centre.

¶ The headquarters of the St Patrick's Missionary Society is in Kiltegan, south-west of Brockagh, where the Society runs another retreat house.

¶ Father Michael Rodgers, who established the Tearmann Centre, wrote the book *A Celtic Pilgrimage* (Moorehouse Publishing) with co-author the Rev Marcus Losack of Glendalough, the founder of *Ceile De*, an Irish network promoting pilgrimages in Celtic spirituality. Father Rodgers is the director of the Tearmann Centre and lives on site.

✉ St Patrick's Missionary Society Brockagh Glendalough County Wicklow

🏨 from €45.00 pp per day (single room). No meals provided.

☎ +353 (0) 404 45208
☎ +353 (0) 404 45639
📠 +353 (0) 404 45208

✉ micr@eircom.net

✉ www.tearmann.ie

☞ Take the St Kevin's express bus from the bus stop at the Nassau Street end of Dawson Street, Dublin to Glendalough which is adjacent to Brockagh. The bus departs Dublin at 1130 daily. Times may change. Glendalough is 47 kilometres south of Dublin.

✝ Sunday Mass
1130.
Church of St Laurence O'Toole, Roundwood

⚥ Open to both men & women

PLACES OF INTEREST ❧ Panoramic views of the **Wicklow Valley** are the reward for those who hike through the Brockagh Forest, toughing it out over Brockagh Mountain and trekking down to the marked St Kevin's Way walking track and into Glendalough.

For maps and information on the **Wicklow National Park,** the National Park Information Office is based at the Upper Lake in Glendalough. There are nine marked walking trails of varying lengths weaving through the park. Watch out for lizards, but courtesy of St Patrick there are no snakes here.

Andrea Webb, Head Guide, Wicklow Mountains National Park advises:

Please be aware that many of the walking tracks in Ireland are not signposted or maintained. Walking in Ireland is an enjoyable, but often damp experience. To enjoy it safely come prepared with rain gear, good walking boots and use a map and a compass the further you explore.

The **Wicklow Mountains** have provided the scenic backdrop for a number of Hollywood movies. Scenes from *Excalibur, Braveheart* and *Michael Collins* were all filmed here. Scenic, well signposted film trails have been established for each movie and maps (for motorists) are available from local tourist offices or from the County Wicklow Film Commission in Station Road, Wicklow. The trails lead through the areas where these movies were shot.

During summer the **Brockagh Resource Centre** stages a popular organic food and craft market on the second Sunday of the month between 1100 and 1800, and a car boot sale once every month. The sisters from the **Dominican Farm and Ecology Centre** near Wicklow sell their organic produce at this market alongside local growers selling fresh fruit and vegetables, flowers and home-made items. Close to the centre is a cycle hire outlet where mountain bikes can be rented for the day.

Spiritual Retreats
County Wicklow Brockagh

From Brockagh and Glendalough, the road back to Dublin leads through the picturesque village of **Roundwood**, snuggled in to the Wicklow Hills; locals claim it is the highest village in Ireland and tourists can enjoy some wonderful views. However, visitors often find the charming, rustic houses and the cosy ambience of at least three excellent eating places even more of an attraction.

If travelling north to Roundwood, approximately 8 kilometres from Glendalough, you could journey by **Lough Tay**, also known as *Guinness Lake*, where with a little imagination you can make out a Guinness-shaped glass, dark waters and the white sandy beach resembling froth.

The Victoria's Way Sculpture Park, a Buddhist meditation centre on the outskirts of Roundwood is an oasis of tranquillity with kilometres of walking paths and plenty of private spaces. Along the paths oriental-style sculptures from India contribute to the sense of calm.

If you have a head for heights you could take the **Greystones** to **Bray** cliff walk, a wriggly, scenic 8-kilometre path along the coast with views to Wales (on a clear day).

FOOD AND DRINK The attractive village of Roundwood is an accessible out-of-town getaway for Dubliners, some of whom drive down for Sunday lunch. **The Roundwood Inn**'s claim to fame is as recent winner of the prestigious 'Pub of The Year' award. Cosy up by the roaring log fire and try a traditional Irish stew.

✉ Main Street

☎ +353 (0) 1 281 8107 €€–€€€

The Coach House claims the best Irish music in Roundwood and the place gets pretty busy each weekend. Traditional Irish fare is served and a blazing log fire adds to the atmosphere.

✉ Main Street

☎ +353 (0) 1 281 8157 €€–€€€

Further along the road to Dublin, **The Hungry Monk** restaurant and wine bar in the seaside resort town of **Greystones** (just south of Bray) will settle any hunger pangs. Home-grown Irish beef and fresh seafood is a speciality; friendly looking monks watch over proceedings agreeably from the walls.

✉ Church Road

☎ +353 (0) 1 287 5759 €€€

Bray is a bustling little town with plenty of cafés and restaurants. However, for a cheap treat pick up some fish and chips and find somewhere to sit along the seafront promenade.

Spiritual Retreats
County Wicklow Glendalough

14

An Clochán Spirituality Centre

An Clochán is a retreat and pilgrimage centre located on the Old Pilgrim Way to the historic monastic city of **Glendalough**. Run by Catholic nuns attached to the religious order the Dominican Sisters of Cabra, the large, comfortable guesthouse has views over the Glendalough Valley. It is just a short walk from An Clochán into Glendalough itself and shops and cafes can be easily accessed on foot. The Dominican Sisters first established a house in Ireland in Galway in 1644. In 1718, the sisters established a house in Cabra, north of Dublin. Since then their order has continued to spread thoughout the country and the world.

❦ The sisters conduct guided retreats but, if preferred, guests may make a private retreat with little interaction with the nuns. However, all guests are encouraged to take a pilgrim walk through the monastic city led by one of the sisters. Day-long mini-retreats for groups are also conducted. The house has a large lounge room (no television), a reading room and a small kitchen.

❦ Particular attention is paid to serving healthy meals, a feature of the Dominican lifestyle in Ireland. A sister convent and farm in Wicklow is run by Dominican nuns as an ecology centre, raising awareness about the importance of caring for the environment and living in harmony with the whole community of life on planet earth.

✉ Wicklow Gap Road
Glendalough,
County Wicklow

🛏 private retreat,
€40.00 pp per day,
including meals.

🛏 weekend retreat,
€250.00 pp, including
meals.

☏ +353 (0) 404 45137
☏ +353 (0) 404 45962

✉ anclochan@eircom.net

☞ Take the St Kevin's
express bus from the
Nassau Street end of
Dawson Street, Dublin
to Glendalough. The
bus departs Dublin at
1130 daily. Times may
change. It is a short
walk to An Clochán.

✝ **Sunday Mass**
1130.
St Mary's and
St Michael's
Rathdrum.

👤 Open to women only

Spiritual Retreats
County Wicklow Glendalough

PLACES OF INTEREST ❧ **Hollywood** is in Ireland! The village is situated in the **Wicklow Mountains** and marks the beginning of the ancient pilgrimage trail (St Kevin's Way) to Glendalough.

❦ **The Glendalough Valley** is an area of great beauty. It is a paradise for ramblers, history lovers and for those interested in matters ecclesiastical. There are walking trails, ruins, old gravestones, deer and in summer loads of tourists. All vastly different to the time when **St Kevin** (497–617 AD) chose to live in the uninhabited, isolated valley as a retreat from the world.

❦ **The Wicklow Mountains' Spring Walking Festival** is held each April/ May with guided, day and overnight walks leaving from a different village each year. In the evenings enjoy Irish music, dance, much merriment and just a little fanciful storytelling. Of course, if you would rather tour the mountains in comfort, **The Wicklow Mountaineer** train departs Dublin's Connolly Station for **Arklow** to link with a coach for further travel in the region.

❦ High in the heart of the **Wicklow Mountains** is the town of **Rathdrum**, the location of the movie *Michael Collins*, starring Irish actor **Liam Neeson** (born in Ballymena in 1952) in the leading role and **Julia Roberts** (b. 1967) as Collins's fiancée Kitty Kiernan. The BBC television series *Ballykissangel* was filmed in Avoca, a few kilometres further on. **Fitzgerald's Pub** is usually open for a drink; the Church of Sts Mary and Patrick is nearby. Both locations were used in the series.

✝ Sunday Mass 1100.

❦ Irish poet **Thomas Moore** (1759–1852) found inspiration in the Avoca area and refers to it in his poem '*The Meeting of the Waters*' (the Avonmore and Avonbeg Rivers).

❦ **Newtownmountkennedy**, between the coastal towns of **Greystones** and **Wicklow**, is the village with the longest name in Ireland. It is home to **Druids Glen** and **Druids Heath**, two of the most scenic (and difficult) golf courses in Ireland. There's a history of pagan priests worshipping in this area, and a druid surveys the 12th hole on the Glen from the elevated vantage point of an ancient stone altar. A few kilometres north-east, near **Kilcoole**, is the **Glenroe Open Farm**, the location for the popular television series *Glenroe*.

❧ The Dominican sisters' Farm and Ecology Centre, **An Tairseach** (*The Threshold*), is situated near the town of Wicklow. Organic fruit, meat and home-grown vegetables can be purchased here. There are nature trails to explore and the sisters lead guided walks around the estate on set days during summer. They also run 10-week, live-in Sabbatical programs, which in their words are for 'Exploring Spirituality in the Context of an Evolving Universe, an Endangered Earth and the Christian Tradition'.

❧ The scent of Ireland is packaged and ready to take home at **Fragrances of Ireland** in **Kilmacanogue**, where perfumes and soaps are reminiscent of the aromas of the Irish countryside.

FOOD AND DRINK ❧ Take a tour of the woollen mill, the oldest in Ireland, and afterwards, indulge in some scones and raspberry jam with a smothering of Irish clotted cream in the café of the **Avoca Handweavers** in **Avoca**. Meals are served daily. You could always take home some pure woollen yarn or maybe a copy of the *Avoca Café Cookbook*.

✉ The Mill, Avoca Village

☎ +353 (0) 402 35105 €€€

❧ **The Hollywood Inn** has been around since the late 1700s and, being at the start of the Pilgrim's Way, has most likely provided food and other sustenance to many a flagging traveller on the way to the monastic city. The inn serves great pub food, including burgers, a hearty Irish stew, and even a simple Wicklow ham sandwich. Always popular on a clear day, as the rear courtyard is a wonderful sun trap.

✉ Hollywood

☎ +353 (0) 45 864 846 €€

❧ Living up to its name, **Tutty's of Hollywood** was the pub where Michael Collins (played by Liam Neeson) had his last drink in the movie *Michael Collins*.

✉ Hollywood

☎ +353 (0) 45 864 108 €€

❧ **The Square Steakhouse** in Wicklow town claims to serve the best steak in the country—and it's locally grown!

✉ Market Square

☎ +353 (0) 404 66422 €€€

Spiritual Retreats
County Wicklow Glendalough

15

Glendalough Hermitage

The monastic city founded by **St Kevin** in the 6th century is set in a fertile valley among the **Wicklow Mountains** in an area of remarkable beauty. The hospitable nuns and priests of the parish conduct single-day retreats and lead guided pilgrimages along marked routes to places frequented by St Kevin. Although St Kevin's parish church in **Glendalough** was established in 1847 the hermitages were constructed on the estate much later.

❦ The hermitage accommodation (single and twin) consists of self-catering cabins or *'cillíns'* (hermitages) situated in the grounds of St Kevin's Parish Church. Each cabin has a small kitchen and bathroom and is centrally heated. The cabins are simple and unpretentious, with an open fire, and are stocked with religious literature. Tea and coffee as well as fuel for the fire are provided. There are no eating facilities on the property and meals must be taken elsewhere. However, the centre is within a few minutes walking distance of shops, pubs and restaurants.

❦ Groups often arrive in Glendalough by the busload to take a pre-arranged pilgrimage to the monastic city and past 'stations' for prayer and reflection. Sister Kathleen from St Kevin's Parish says that 'the beauty of the surroundings and the faith heritage of Glendalough speak to people'.

❦ According to Father Kevin Doran, who is attached to St Kevin's in Glendalough, 'Many people think of Glendalough as a place to come in the summer. And it can be very pleasant in the winter months—the *'cillíns'* are well heated.'

✉ St Kevin's Catholic Church
Glendalough
County Wicklow

🛏 Single hermitage from €45.00 pp, not including meals. Double hermitage from €35.00 pp, not including meals. Special winter rate available on application from November to the end of February.

☎ +353 (0) 404 45777
📠 +353 (0) 404 45777

✉ glendalough2007@eircom.net

🖥 www.glendalough.dublindiocese.ie

☞ Take the St Kevin's express bus from Dawson Street, Dublin to Glendalough. The bus departs Dublin at 1130 daily. Times may change. To reach the hermitage, get off outside the post office in Laragh. The monastic city is less than 2 kilometres west of Laragh.

✝ Sunday Mass
0930 & 1130.
St Kevin's Church, Glendalough

⚥ Open to both men & women

PLACES OF INTEREST ❦ The gardens of **St Kevin**'s in Glendalough have evolved over the years and are particularly conducive to meditation. But there are a few surprises. A re-creation of St Kevin's 'cell' (the place where St Kevin came to pray and meditate) has been constructed in the style of the original, and a monument of the Twin Towers in memory of the September 11 tragedy is a recent addition. The garden project is ongoing and donations are always gratefully received.

❧ During the summer months a boat can be taken to the site of St Kevin's 'bed', the narrow cave where the saint is said to have slept and which is difficult to access by land. From the shoreline, a few steps lead up to the ruins of an ancient church called **Temple-na-Skellig** (*Church of the Rock*), below the location of the cave. St Kevin's 'cell', however, is in a quite different, elevated but very scenic area on the same side of the lake; it can be reached on foot. St Kevin's 'bed' can also be safely seen from across the lake along the Miners' Road.

❧ A legend relates that St Kevin once had an ardent admirer, a young girl called Kathleen. According to poet **Thomas Moore** in his ballad 'By that Lake, whose Gloomy Shore', Kathleen had 'eyes of most unholy blue'. It is said that one night she turned up at the cave where St Kevin was sleeping and, appalled by her behaviour, he thrashed her with stinging nettles. Kathleen later regretted her actions, apologised and is said to have become an extremely devout woman. In his poem Thomas Moore sees things from a different angle and says that St Kevin 'Hurls her from the beetling rock / Glendalough, thy gloomy wave / Soon was gentle Kathleen's grave!'—which is most unlikely behaviour for a saint.

❧ Among the monastic ruins is a 30-metre high, 1,000-year-old **Round Tour**. Possibly established as a place of hiding and retreat from Viking invaders, it is near a still-standing 8th-century Celtic cross.

❧ The St Kevin's Celtic cross also comes in necklace form and can be purchased in many of the shops in the **Glendalough** area, along with jewellery in other ancient Celtic designs.

Spiritual Retreats
County Wicklow Glendalough

❦ In **Glendalough** itself, the **Wool and Craft Shop** (behind the Glendalough Hotel) has a range of products if you're on the lookout for a local souvenir. Locals hand-knit garments and craft items for the shop. Or take home a *Bodhran* (an ancient Celtic drum said to have been played by St Kevin himself) from the **Irish Music Visitor Centre** on the outskirts of **Laragh**, near **Glendalough**.

❦ The **Blue Glass Studio** on the Laragh—Glenmalure road specialises in stained glass and glassware and **The Celtic Craft Shop** in **Laragh** is yet another Irish knitwear and craft shop specialising in Celtic designs.

❦ **Glendalough** and the surrounding area are major tourist attractions and during the warm, summer months traffic can be a headache on the narrow, hilly roads as motorists compete with cyclists and the numerous charter buses out of Dublin. To beat the traffic plan ahead and leave early.

FOOD AND DRINK ❦ The **Glendasan River Restaurant** in the Glendalough Hotel is the closest restaurant to the monastic city. Full meals are available here. Bar food and light snacks are served and a roaring open fire provides warmth and ambience in cooler weather.

✉ Glendalough

☎ +353 (0) 404 45135   €€–€€€

❦ Near the entrance to the **Glendalough Hotel** are a number of stalls selling take-away food and drinks. A kilometre away in **Laragh**, **Lynham's Pub**, a popular watering hole along the Wicklow Way, caters to mountain walkers' hearty appetites; Irish bands play on the weekends.

✉ Laragh

☎ +353 (0) 404 45345   €€

❦ The **Wicklow Heather Restaurant** in Laragh is one of the best in the area with a reputation for serving good food. Dine *al fresco*, in the smart dining room or surrounded by learned tomes in the Writers' Room. The restaurant opens for breakfast at 0800 followed by snacks and meals into late evening.

✉ Glendalough Road, Laragh

☎ +353 (0) 404 45157   €€€

❦ **Rathdrum**, a short drive south of Glendalough, is well endowed with pubs, most serving meals or bar food. **The Glenmalure Golf Club** dining room is open to visitors for lunch.

✉ Greenane, Rathdrum

☎ +353 (0) 404 46679   €

16

Slí an Chroí

As well as having a guesthouse in **Brockagh** the St Patrick's Missionary Society has another facility, a retreat house called **Slí an Chroí**, on the outskirts of the village of Kiltegan, near the Carlow and Kildare borders. Kiltegan nestles in a picturesque rural setting at the foot of the Wicklow Mountains, 65 kilometres south of Dublin. It has been the headquarters of the St Patrick's Fathers since 1930 when the missionary order was first established in Ireland. Today the order is active in the Sudan, other parts of Africa and the West Indies.

❡ The St Patrick's centre in Kitegan is in an area well known for hill walking, trail riding and rambling through the Wicklow woods. The accommodation at Slí an Chroí (*the Way of the Heart*) is in simple guestrooms, each with a wash basin; shared bathroom facilities are on each floor. Many of the 16 large, but modestly-furnished single or twin guestrooms look out over rolling green pastures. Groups, families and those travelling alone are welcome to spend time here. Guests are required to bring their own towels and as accommodation is offered on a self-catering basis, no meals are provided. Facilities are available to prepare snacks and drinks. Pubs and cafés can be found in the surrounding villages. The centre has plenty of parking.

❡ Day groups are welcome to take part in guided walkabouts through rural Wicklow and the spectacular Glendalough valley, as well as to places of spiritual and religious significance. The valley is within the Wicklow National Park and has a network of marked walking trails.

✉ St Patrick's Missionary Society
Kiltegan
County Wicklow

💷 price to be negotiated.

✆ +353 (0) 59 647 3488
✆ +353 (0) 59 647 3622

✉ spsgen@iol.ie

🖰 www.spms.org/
stpatricksmissionarysociety/
Main/CRA_Sli.htm

☞ There is scant public transport in the area so it is best to access the monastery by car. Follow the signs in Kiltegan village to St Patrick's. There is no public transport between Kiltegan and Glendalough, which is approximately 22 kilometres away.

✟ **Sunday Mass**
1000.
Church of the Assumption, Tynock, nr Kiltegan, Co Wicklow.

⚭ Open to men, women & groups

Spiritual Retreats
County Wicklow Kiltegan

PLACES OF INTEREST ❧ Grand and Gothic. the 19th-century **Humewood Castle** was built for a wealthy Irish politician, **The Right Honourable William Wentworth Fitzwilliam Hume-Dick**, MP (1805–1892), and is a major attraction in **Kiltegan** (named after an obscure Irish missionary, **St Tegan**, thought to have been a follower of St Patrick). Much of the castle has been handsomely restored and the property has facilities for polo, fishing, eventing and falconry. In 2008 Humewood Castle was purchased by a property development company which has a 3-year plan to convert the estate into a top-drawer golf and equestrian resort.

❧ If golf is where your interest lies, a few kilometres north of **Kiltegan**, the 18-hole championship **Rathsallagh Golf Course** near the village of **Dunlavin**, designed by **Peter McEvoy** OBE (British Amateur Golf Champion in 1977 and 1978) and **Christy O'Connor Jnr** (former Ryder Cup Great Britain and Ireland team member), is open to visitors. If it's the third weekend in June you will find plenty of entertainment in the village as the annual Arts Festival gets underway.

❧ The market town of **Baltinglass**, on the banks of the River Slaney near Kiltegan, has been designated a Heritage Town. The town is recognised for the remains of a 12th-century **Cistercian Abbey** and ancient forts in the nearby hills; the Stone Age hill fort, known as the **Brusselstown Ring**, is Europe's largest. Bronze Age burial chambers have also been discovered here. Horse stables are in the neighbourhood and riding trails climb up into the hills. The town's heritage centre is also the local tourist information office and is open during the summer months. The centre can provide a wealth of information on the history of the area.

❧ The relics of **Baltinglass Abbey**, including the abbey church, lie alongside the fast-flowing **River Slaney**, north of Baltinglass. The abbey was established for the Cistercian order in 1148 by **Dermot McMurrough**, King of Leinster, and flourished for centuries until it was closed down during the 16th-century Dissolution of the Monasteries.

❧ The stately 18th-century, Palladian-style **Russborough House** in **Blessington**, north of Kiltegan, has been fully restored to its former grandeur. The all-granite Irish manor took a decade to build; it was completed in 1751. Furnished with antiques and *objets d'art*, the house is said to be one of the most beautiful in the country.

❧ The village of **Shillelagh**, south of **Kiltegan**, is the home of the Irish 'shillelagh', a traditional wooden stick or club made famous by American singer Bing Crosby (1903–1977) in the song *'With a Shillelagh under My Arm'*. The village is near what remains of the **Tomnafinnoge Forest** which supplied the wood for the original shillelaghs. A *shillelagh* is made from a suitably shaped branch of a Blackthorn tree. Traditionally used as a means of self-protection, today a shillelagh more commonly refers to a walking stick. You can buy a shillelagh in Shillelagh at the **Olde Shillelagh Stick Makers** in Main Street.

FOOD AND DRINK ❧ **The Dying Cow**—so called after an unfortunate creature belonging to the pub's former licensee—is more formally known as **Tallon's Pub**. It's a welcoming, rural watering hole and resting place for walkers on the Wicklow Way. Irish music night is on Thursdays. According to **Paddy Dillon** in his book *The Irish Coast to Coast Walk*, the Dying Cow was so named after 'the police visited late one night, and the landlady at the time objected, saying she wasn't serving drinks after hours, but only providing refreshments to neighbours who were helping her with a dying cow!' (Paddy Dillon, *The Irish Coast to Coast Walk*, Cicerone Press 2005).

✉ Stranakelly Crossroads, Tinahely

☎ +353 (0) 40 238 224   €

❧ Back in **Kiltegan** at **Katie Lowe's Pub** you may be lucky enough to be entertained by local musicians playing the Irish *bodhrán* (a type of drum said to have been used by St Kevin). Snacks and bar food are served.

✉ Kiltegan Village

☎ +353 (0) 59 647 3207   €

❧ **Quinn's** pub in **Baltinglass** attracts the local equestrian and racing crowd, and is filled with punters on race days who could possibly spend their winnings at the pub's **McAllistairs Restaurant**.

✉ Main Street

☎ +353 (0) 59 648 1266   €–€€

County Dublin

❧ If you plan to drive from **Dublin** to **Galway** you could consider bypassing the main roads and following the quieter, more scenic route. **The Monastic Way** is an alternative route which takes in monastic sites, abbeys, medieval churches, heritage castles, holy wells and numerous sacred places and tourist attractions. The east–west 'way' is over the ancient, historical **King's Highway**, through the Irish Midland counties of **Kildare**, **Meath** and **Offaly**, leading from one side of the country to the other. It is approximately 220 kilometres from Dublin to Galway and on average should be about 3 hours' driving, not including stops. There are numerous ecclesiastical sites *en route*, including the first suggested stop out of Dublin at **Maynooth** in Kildare and the Irish Seminary of **St Patrick's College** which stands quite majestically alongside the substantial ruins of a 12th-century castle, almost in the centre of the town.

❧ Other possible stops include **Clonard** in **Meath** where **St Finian** (c. 470–550) established a monastery in the 6th century and where these days, the town's aptly named **Monastery Inn** provides a warm welcome. After Clonard are the labyrinth and gardens of the 15th-century **Grange Castle**, the remains of **Monasteroris**, a 14th-century Franciscan monastery, the Holy Wells of **Croghan** and **Kilclonfert**, the resident ghosts of the 18th-century **Charleville Castle** in Tullamore and, for therapeutic purposes, the **Tullamore Dew Distillery**. The way leads on to the ruined castles of **Lemanaghan** and **Doon**, to the 6th-century remains of the monastic city of **Clonmacnoise** and to the 19th-century **Cathedral of St Brendan** in **Loughrea** and its unique stained-glass windows of Celtic design.

County Clare

The town of **Ennis** has been closely associated with the Franciscan religious order for more than 800 years. Of the town's two Franciscan friaries, the oldest was founded in the 13th century and the most recent in 1854. The oldest friary is now an impressive ruin but was once home to 1,000 monks. The new, fully working friary stands nearby. The Sisters of the Order of the Poor Clares live in a separate monastery in the town.

† Sunday Mass

0745. Poor Clares Oratory.

0930, 1030 & 1200. Franciscan Friary.

The medieval town of **Ennis** lies on the River Fergus and can be easily explored on foot. Guided tours leave from opposite the tourist office in Arthur's Row every day at 1100 except Tuesday and Sunday. Ennis is a festival town and the **Fleadh Nua Irish Festival** is held each May with displays of traditional music and dance, street entertainment, parades and Irish dancing lessons taking over. An **Irish Music Festival** is held here in November. In September, those who are still looking for Mr or Mrs Right descend on **Lindoosfarna**, north of Ennis, for the annual month-long matchmaking festival.

Scattery (*Iniscathaig*) **Island** lies off the coast of **Kilrush** in the Shannon Estuary. It is a place of pilgrimage, being the ruins of a monastery and church established by **St Senan** (488–560), from which women were banned and where the Archangel Michael is said to have appeared to the saint in the 6th century. The Scattery Island Information Centre at Merchant's Quay in Kilrush has an exhibition on the history of the monastic settlement and a boat leaves for the island from the Kilrush marina.

The still-standing ruins of an ancient monastery, built by **St Caimin** (of Inis Cealtra), a compatriot of **St Senan** (d. c. 653) and now a place of pilgrimage, stands on **Holy Island** in Lough Derg (be aware that there is more than one Lough Derg in Ireland) in a picturesque part of the country north of **Limerick**. St Caimin is buried in the church named after him and pilgrims' trails crisscross the island.

County Clare

❧ In times past it was a tradition for pilgrims to visit the island on Good Friday and Whitsuntide to 'do penance by walking barefoot about the rough and rocky shore of the island' (Hugh Brigdall, 1962). Irish poet **Philip Dixon Hardy** (1794–1875) wrote of pilgrims in 1836: 'for this [pilgrimage] is performed on naked knees, through a heap of rugged stones. All must without assistance descend on the naked knees a step nearly a foot in depth. This is a most painful operation'. Legends associated with the island include some about the existence of the Lough Derg Monster. Another claims that if you see your reflection in the water, your sins are forgiven. Yet another insists that you can renew your marriage vows on an ancient '**ballaun stone**' or 'bargaining stone', traditionally the place where deals were sealed in the past. The Holy Island boat sails from the pretty **Mountshannon** harbour during the warmer months, though not in bad weather. A map of the island is available from the boat captain.

County Cork

❧ A 6th-century pilgrimage site lies on the southern outskirts of the town of **Ballyvourney** where **St Gobnait** (pronounced *'gawb net'*, which is Abigail or Deborah in English), the Patron Saint of Beekeepers, is buried (d. c 6th century). St Gobnait was the first abbess of a convent which she founded on this site with the help of another Irish saint, **St Abban of Murnevin** (570–620), the nephew of **St Kevin** (498–618). The site is quite spread out and pilgrims can make a 'pattern' (a type of pilgrimage, also called 'making the rounds') walking to various places of spiritual significance, including a shrine, a Holy Well and the remains of a medieval church. The saint was an avid beekeeper who used honey to cure her fellow sisters of minor illnesses and is said to have fought off invaders by letting loose her bees. A stone from the ruins of St Gobnait's Church has been set into the walls of the **Mt Mellerary Abbey Church** in Waterford. Her Feast Day is celebrated in Ireland on 11 February.

✝ Sunday Mass 0830 & 1130.

Church of St Gobnait, Ballyvourney.

County Donegal

Ballyvourney is in the Gaeltacht Mhúscraí (*Gaelic-speaking*) area of Cork. The Gaeltacht Mhúscraí areas are dedicated to the preservation of all things Irish—particularly music, dance and the Irish (Gaelic) language. Many of the local street signs in these areas are in Gaelic. This particular area is known for its artisans who work using traditional rural methods. **The Quilt Centre** in **Ballymakeera**, **The Woollen Market** and the **Keltic Leather** shop and **Coolavokig Pottery** in **Macroom** are all located near Ballyvourney.

Present-day pilgrims still visit the **Tubrid Holy Well** near **Millstreet**, between Mallow and Killarney, whose waters are said to have the power to heal. May is a traditional time to visit the well.

Pilgrims must travel by boat to reach **St Patrick's Island**. The pilgrimage site is situated on an island in Lough Derg, near the village of **Pettigo** and steeped in over 1,000 years of religious history. It is believed that **St Patrick** (385–461) once inhabited a cave on the island where he experienced visions of Purgatory and Hell. After this became known, medieval pilgrims began to flock here to view the 'entrance to Hell'. Hence the island came to be known as **St Patrick's Purgatory**.

Pilgrims access the island by small boat with many making the traditional, barefoot Lough Derg pilgrimage, which takes place over 3 days and is officially held during the pilgrimage season between 1 June and 15 August. The tradition is that on the first day of the pilgrimage, participants attend morning and evening Mass in **St Patrick's Basilica** (on the island) and then meditate and pray for a full 24 hours. Pilgrims have one meal each day, of dry toast or oatcakes and black tea/coffee or a special 'pilgrim soup' of hot water flavoured with salt and pepper. The total cost is approximately €45 which includes simple accommodation.

County Donegal

❡ A 1-day retreat with a light lunch
of sandwiches and a hot drink are
available to those who are unable to
make the 3-day pilgrimage or who have
health issues.

❡ During the pilgrimage season Mass is
celebrated in **St Patrick's Basilica** every
day at 0630 and 1830.

❡ During 1-day retreats, which are
conducted during May and the last
2 weeks of August and September, daily
Mass is celebrated at 1500.

❡ If you are heading for **Donegal** town,
sometimes called the 'tweed capital of
Ireland', the renowned Irish weavers
Magees sell from their factory shop in
The Diamond shopping centre in the
middle of town.

County Galway

❡ The ruins of the **Monastery of
Kilmacduagh** lie a few kilometres
south of the heritage town of **Gort**.
The monastery was founded in the 7th
century by **St Colman** whose remains
lie in a tiny burial ground here. Legends
abound about St Colman and the
Kilmacduagh monastery, one being that
no person or animal will ever be killed by
lightning in the Parish of Kilmacduagh.
According to the story, lightning once
struck a local villager with such force
that he was hoisted through the air and
landed (deceased) in the next county.

❡ **Kylemore Abbey** sits in splendid
grandeur on the banks of a placid
salmon lake in the rocky, mountain
wilderness of the Irish **Connemara** and
is occupied by nuns of the Benedictine
Order. From the shores of the lake even
the most amateur of photographers can
hardly fail to snap an impressive photo
of this breathtaking edifice. Sections of
the abbey are open to visitors and the
nuns' walled, botanical gardens, located
in a separate area, are also well worth
seeing. The abbey's **Mitchell Henry
Restaurant** caters for up to 200 guests
and much of the produce used in the
menu is grown in the abbey garden.
The nuns bake cakes and biscuits and
make jam to sell in the gift shop where
woollens, jewellery and the renowned
Kylemore pottery are on sale.

❦ The stately abbey was built in 1865 by Englishman, doctor and MP **Mitchell Henry** for his wife Margaret. Some decades after Margaret's unexpected death in 1875, the Benedictine Order purchased the castle. At the time the order needed an abbey for nuns who had been driven out of their convent in **Ypres** in Belgium after it was destroyed during World War I. The nuns established a prestigious boarding school, attracting the daughters of wealthy and influential European families. However, in recent times there was a drop in the number of boarders and the nuns made a decision to close the school. However, the sisters continue to live at the abbey. American actress **Angelica Huston** (b. 1951) is a former student of Kylemore Abbey; she later studied at Trinity College in Dublin. The Henrys are buried in a crypt in the abbey grounds.

❦ **St Brendan's Cathedral** in **Clonfert** is all that remains of a major medieval ecclesiastical settlement including a monastery, a cathedral and a school which were established by **St Brendan** (484–577) in the 6th century. All that remains of the original structure is the cathedral, which is noted for its decorative carvings and statuary and as the possible burial place of St Brendan. The saint is also known as St Brendan the Bold of Clonfert, St Brendan the Navigator or the Voyager, as he travelled widely to spread the word of Christianity. Along with St Christopher, St Brendan is known as the Patron Saint of Travellers.

✝ Sunday Service 0900.

County Kerry

❡ A 'Saint's Road', a 16-kilometre-long ancient pilgrimage route, trails up to the summit of **Mount Brandon** on the **Dingle Peninsula** which, it is said St Brendan climbed 'to see the Americas' before he set sail in the mid-6th century. These days the trail is considered too difficult and too dangerous to be used as a pilgrimage route. Mount Brandon is also called St Brendan's Mountain (*Cnoc Brennain*).

❡ One of the most scenic walks in Ireland is the 180-kilometre-long **Dingle Way**, which can usually be completed in around 10 days. One for experienced walkers, the way-marked route starts and finishes in **Tralee** and follows the coastline around the Dingle Peninsula. Trekkers pass through the tiny village of **Camp**, the scenically blessed **Dingle** area, **Ballycurrane** near Mount Brandon (where it is almost compulsory to stop for a drink at **The Bóthar Pub**) and on to the coastal village of **Castlegregory**. Accommodation options along the way range from basic (e.g. **Finnegan's Hostel** in Tralee from €14.00 pp per night) to 4-star (e.g. the **Dingle Skellig Hotel** from €150.00 pp for 2 nights). The routes between the larger towns are from 7 to 17 kilometres in length.

❡ A small stone structure on the Dingle Peninsula, known as the **Gallarus Oratory**, is believed to be the earliest Christian church constructed in Western Europe. The Oratory is still standing and is thought to be around 1,200 years old even though it looks quite new. Not far away are the ruins of the **Riasc** (*Reask*) monastic site, thought to be around the same age.

❡ Early Christian monks often disciplined themselves as a means of penance, and sometimes took suffering to extremes. Punishment certainly comes to mind when exploring the monastic settlement on desolate **Skellig Michael**, a tiny rocky island 12 kilometres off the coast of County Kerry. The original monastery is thought to have been founded by local Irish saint, **Fionan**, in the 6th century and was occupied by monks for the next 600 years. Even today it is a feat in itself just to reach the monastic site which is a climb of almost 700 steep steps to what remains of the monks' simple, stone beehive huts, churches, refectory and graveyard—and the best view in the county. The island is part of a World Heritage-listed site and can be accessed by licensed boat and only in good weather. Boats depart from the fishing village of **Portmagee** between Easter and October. The journey takes around 45 minutes.

County Kildare

❡ A tall, sculpted monument dedicated to **St Brigid** (c. 451–525) has stood in the centre of the town of **Kildare** since February 2006 and 'St Brigid's Flame' burns perpetually in Kildare's town square in the name of peace and justice and in honour of Brigid. The legend of the flame stems from the original St Brigid's Fire, first lit by Brigidine nuns in the 5th century and kept alight until the 16th century.

❡ **Kildare** is the site of a working monastery for Carmelite Friars and the ruins of two abbeys: the **Grey Abbey** established for the Franciscan Order in Kildare in 1260, and the 13th-century **Black Abbey**, established for the Knights Hospitaller (also known as the Knights of Malta), the ruins of which lie in the grounds of the **Irish National Stud**. The still functioning **White Abbey** is owned by the Carmelite Order and white-robed Carmelite Friars live and work here.

✝ Sunday Mass 1000 & 1200.

White Abbey Church, Kildare.

❡ The sisters of the Brigidine Order's **Solas Bhríde Centre** of Celtic spirituality, prayer and hospitality conduct pilgrimages which they call 'Following in the Footsteps of Brigid'. The pilgrimages commence at the centre and pilgrims visit sites relating to St Brigid, including the Fire Temple behind St Brigid's Cathedral, Holy Wells and prayer stones, and continue on to the rolling pastures of **The Curragh**. A special pilgrimage is held on the Feast Day of St Brigid, 1 February, the first day of the Irish Spring. This annual evening torchlight procession departs from the Solas Bhride Centre and continues on to **St Brigid's Well**, one of Ireland's Holy Wells and once part of what is thought to have been a double monastery where Brigid was abbess.

✝ Sunday Mass 0900, 1100 & 1900.

St Brigid's Church, Kildare.

✉ Solas Bhríde

14 Dara Park

Kildare, County Kildare

✆ +353 (0) 45 522 890

✐ solasbhride@eircom.net

✐ www.solasbhride.ie

County Kilkenny

❧ A restored medieval Cistercian Abbey stands in the centre of the riverside town of **Graiguenamanagh** (*Gráig na Manach*), pronounced '*Graig-na-Manna*' and meaning the 'Village of the Monks'. The town grew around the original **Duiske Abbey**, established for Cistercian monks in 1204 and it was once the largest abbey in Ireland.

☦ Sunday Mass 1100.

Duiske Abbey Church, Graiguenamanagh.

❧ This little waterside backwater on the River Barrow has 13 pubs, 19 bookshops and an 800-year-old heritage—something for everyone!

County Louth

❧ It is believed that **St Brigid** (*Brighid* or *Bríd*) was born in the hilltop village of **Fochard Muirtheimne** (*Faughart*) or on the northern outskirts of **Dundalk**, which has led the site to become a popular place of pilgrimage for her followers. Public pilgrimages are often conducted here, including a pilgrimage by torchlight on St Brigid's Feast Day, 1 February, to the shrine dedicated to the saint. A national pilgrimage is held on the first weekend in July. A small relic of St Brigid is kept in the shrine.

☦ Sunday Mass 0830 & 1100.

Church of St Brigid, Kilcurry (Faughart).

❧ The **Catholic Church of St Peter**, in the town of **Drogheda**, is the site of the National Shrine of **St Oliver Plunkett** (1625–1681), a former Archbishop of Armagh and Primate of All Ireland who was hanged, drawn and quartered from the Tyburn Tree in London on 1 July 1681. The shrine within the church houses the relic of St Oliver's head. Each year on his Feast Day a pilgrimage departs from the **Our Lady of Lourdes Church** on the outskirts of **Drogheda** for St Peter's Church. The pilgrimage culminates in a Mass dedicated to St Oliver Plunkett, a relation of Mother Catherine Plunkett, founder of the Dominican women's convent in Drogheda.

☦ Sunday Mass 0800, 1100 & 1215.

St Peter's Church, Drogheda.

County Mayo

❧ The shrine of **Our Lady of Knock**, who is also known as the Queen of Ireland and Queen of the Gael, is the country's most important Marian pilgrimage site and each year attracts more visitors than any other pilgrimage site in the country. Pilgrims have come to the shrine from far and wide since the reported appearance in 1879 of Our Lady, St Joseph and St John the Evangelist to 15 local people who were together at the time in the **Church of St John the Baptist**. The shrine is open to pilgrims all year round but the main pilgrimage 'season' is from the end of April to the beginning of October.

🕆 Sunday Mass Knock Shrine

Winter: 0900, 1100, 1200, 1500 & 1700

Summer: 0800, 0930, 1100, 1200, 1500 & 1900

❧ The **Foxford Woollen Mill**, on the Foxford to Ballina Road, was established in 1892 by a local nun, **Mother Agnes Morrogh Bernard** (1842–1932), of the Sisters of Charity to provide employment for villagers during the Irish Potato Famine. Today the still-active mill is quite a tourist attraction, for its guided tours and for the sheer variety of tweed, blankets, rugs and other woollen products on sale. The mill is situated 29 kilometres north of Knock.

❧ The 12th-century Augustinian Abbey of **Cong**, in a picturesque location in this lovely town, was once an esteemed monastery where the last King of Ireland, **Rory O'Connor**, died in 1198. An elaborately carved, oaken Gaelic Cross once used by the Augustinian monks is displayed in the National Museum of Dublin.

❧ The Hollywood movie *The Quiet Man*, starring American actor **John Wayne** (1907–1979) and Irish-born actress **Maureen O'Hara** (b. 1920), was filmed in the village of **Cong** in 1951. Cong is situated 1 kilometre from the shores of **Lough Corrib** (*Lake Corrib*) and an ideal way to see this most scenic part of the world is from a boat cruising on the lake. A cruise boat departs from the 13th-century **Ashford Castle** near Cong, now one of Europe's most luxurious hotels. Passengers can disembark at **Inchagoill Island** to see the restored church, **Teampall Na Naoimh** (*Church of All Saints*), said to have been built by St Patrick.

County Mayo

❧ **St Patrick** famously fasted for 40 days on the **Croagh Mountain** in 441 AD. On 'Reek Sunday', the last Sunday in July, hundreds of pilgrims visit the *Reek*, as Croagh Mountain is sometimes called. The route is approximately 12 kilometres in length. The pilgrimage is moderately difficult and only suitable to be taken by those in good health. The weather is usually more favourable for such a trek between May and October. Information and details of the pilgrimage trail can be obtained from the **Teach na Miasa** (*Croagh Patrick Visitor Centre*) in nearby **Murrisk** (near Westport) at the foot of the mountain near the beginning of the pilgrims' path and close to the 15th-century ruins of the Augustinian **Murrisk Abbey**.

❧ Another starting point is **Ballintubber Abbey** which sits at the edge of **Lough Carra** (*Lake Carra*) and where each June, July, August and December guided days of retreat as well as pilgrimages take place. The longest pilgrimage route is the 17-kilometre each way Tóchar Phádraig walk to Craogh Patrick, an ancient pilgrim trail established before the time of St Patrick. Spiritual retreats are held on peaceful Church Island, a short boat trip across Lough Carra (Lake Carra). A passion play is staged each Easter in the grounds of Ballintubber Abbey which is also known as the **Holy Trinity Abbey**.

✠ Sunday Mass 1130. Holy Trinity Abbey.

County Meath

❧ *The Book of Kells*, Ireland's most treasured, handwritten medieval manuscript, is thought to have been commenced in an abbey founded by Irish saint, **Columcille** on the **Island of Iona** in Scotland in the 6th century. When Viking invaders attacked the abbey some 300 years later the monks were forced to flee to Ireland, taking the precious documents to a monastery in **Kells**, north of Dublin for safekeeping. The monks completed their task and *The Book of Kells* was presented to Trinity College in 1661. Only the ruins of the monastery in Kells remain.

❧ The **Hill of Slane** is well known in Ireland's religious history as the place where **St Patrick** is said to have lit a Paschal fire in defiance of the Druids who at the same time were lighting a bonfire on the **Hill of Tara** to honour their pagan gods. A Franciscan monastery, now in ruins was built on the hill in the early 16th century. The Hill of Slane is also used as a viewing point for surveying the evergreen Irish countryside and attracts pilgrims and tourists alike.

County Offaly

❦ Actor **Pierce Brosnan** (b. 1953), a former 'James Bond', was born in Academy Street in **Navan**, Meath and educated during his early years at **Scoil Muire** (*School of Our Lady*), a primary school in Abbey Road run at the time by the De la Salle Brothers. In 2001 the actor married **Keely Shaye Smith** (b. 1953), at **Ballintubber Abbey** in County Mayo.

❦ The ruined monastery of **Clonmacnoise**, a name meaning '*the Meadow of the Sons of Nos*', was founded by the scholarly **St Ciarán** (*Kieran the Younger*) around 545 AD. It remained a centre of Christianity and learning until the 16th century. Over the centuries the monastery has been destroyed and rebuilt several times and today this scenic, still and most tranquil corner of **Offaly** continues to attract pilgrims and tourists. The busiest day of the year in Clonmacnoise is 9 September, St Ciarán's Feast Day, when crowds of pilgrims visit the ruins to take part in the celebration of an outdoor Mass. Clonmacnoise is on the Shannon River and moorings are provided for those travelling by boat.

❦ The history of the monastery is revealed in *The Annals of Clonmacnoise* by Conell Mageoghagan (Books LLC, 2009) which is available in bookstores and through online booksellers.

County Tipperary

On a hill on the outskirts of **Cashel** the impressive ruins of a legendary ancient monastery, the **Rock of Cashel** or St Patrick's Rock, loom large over the village below. From the 5th century this enormous stronghold was the seat of the Kings of Munster, who handed it to the Catholic Church in the early 12th century. The remains of a cathedral, an ancient round tower and the still-standing **Cormac's Chapel**, built by **King Cormac** a former king of Cashel (c. 836–908), mark the site. **The Cashel Folk Village** is located in the village and depicts the history of this famous edifice. 'Cashel' has lent its name to a classic design used on Waterford crystal. It is also famous for Cashel Blue, a strong, biting blue-veined cheese produced locally. **St Patrick** is thought to have visited Cashel in the 5th century.

Tipperary is home to the well-preserved **Holy Cross Abbey** on the outskirts of **Thurles**, a place of pilgrimage on account of a fragment of the true Cross being kept inside the church. The 14 Stations of the Cross have been established in the gardens of the Abbey in memory of Italian monk and saint, **Padre Pio de Pietrelcina** (1887–1968). An identical set of these Stations was given to **Pope John Paul II** as a gift when he visited Ireland in 1979. The Stations have been installed in the Vatican Gardens in Rome.

✞ Sunday Mass 0900, 1100 & 1600.

Holy Cross Abbey, Thurles.

The lovely Protestant **Church of St Mary** in Rathealty Road, Thurles is a fully functioning Church of Ireland as well as the site of a commemorative famine and war museum.

✞ Sunday Services Times vary.

The church opens to visitors each Sunday between 1330 & 1700.

County Waterford

❧ **St Declan** established the first monastic settlement in Ireland at **Ardmore** in County Waterford in 316 AD. Legend claims that Declan—who became the first Bishop of Ardmore—once possessed a sacred bell which he placed for safekeeping inside a large hollow rock. The rock floated away, so Declan followed it in a boat and was led to Ardmore on the Waterford coast where the rock was washed ashore. A large boulder on the southern end of Ardmore beach, known as St Declan's Rock is still visited by pilgrims. The scientific explanation for the presence of the rock states that it was washed from a glacier some kilometres away.

❧ **St Declan's Way** is a 95-kilometre-long pilgrim path which commences at the old monastic city in Ardmore. The route trails along the Blackwater River to **Cappoquin**, past the abbeys of Mt Melleray and Glencairn, on to the heritage town of **Lismore** and over the heather-cloaked **Knockmealdown Mountains** into County Tipperary, then along the uneven path known as the **Rian Bó Phadraig** (*Track of St Patrick's Cow*) and on to the **Rock of Cashel** in County Tipperary. The legend associated with St Patrick's Cow relates to a stolen calf which was shepherded over the Knockmealdown Mountains by a cattle rustler. When the cow discovered her calf missing she panicked and frantically used her horns to cut her way across the mountain and come to the rescue. The Track of St Patrick's Cow is the route the cow took.

❧ There is a shorter, 5-kilometre cliff walk around the **Ardmore** coast for pilgrims and tourists with less time. Maps are available from the local tourist offices.

County Wexford

❧ The tiny settlement known as **Our Lady's Island** is situated on an island of the same name, 20 kilometres south of the town of **Wexford**. The island is connected to the mainland by a causeway. It is thought that pilgrimages to this site were first established by **St Abban** (from Abingdon in England) in the 6th century. The official pilgrimage season commences on 15 August, the Feast of the Assumption of Our Lady, and concludes on 8 September, Our Lady's birthday. Each pilgrimage commences with the celebration of an outdoor Mass. This is followed by the recitation of the Rosary which takes place during a Eucharistic Procession around the island. Sunday Mass is celebrated in the parish church at 1100 and on each day of the pilgrimage season at 1500 and 2000. The Parish Church was designed by **Augustus Welby Pugin** (1812–1852), the architect who designed Trinity College in Dublin. Pugin was an acquaintance of the first Catholic Archbishop of New South Wales, Australia, **John Bede Polding** (1794–1877), who commissioned the architect to design a number of churches, including the still-standing **St Francis Xavier's Church** in the village of **Berrima** in the Southern Highlands of New South Wales and **St Stephen's Chapel** next to **St Stephen's Cathedral** in **Brisbane**, Queensland.

❧ With some luck your pilgrimage could be taken in blissful weather. **Wexford** is the sunniest place in Ireland and averages almost 5 hours of sunshine each day—although this is somewhat disputed by the folks over at **Malin Head** in **Donegal**. Maybe this is one of the reasons **St Muirdealach** chose to live in a cave in Donegal, known as the **Wee House of Malin**. An old legend maintains that there was no limit on the number of people the cave could hold— it just kept on getting roomier. And well-fed cave dwellers they must have been as crab, lobster and salmon are prolific in the local waters.

County Wicklow

❦ Pilgrims can follow a 29-kilometre pilgrims' trail known as **St Kevin's Path** which leads from the village of Hollywood through the **Wicklow Mountains** and on to the ancient Christian religious settlement of **Glendalough**. The path mirrors the trail St Kevin used when he walked from **Hollywood** (in Wicklow) to establish a monastic city. Situated near two picturesque lakes in a naturally beautiful part of Ireland, the 6th-century monastic city is a place of retreat, peace and pilgrimage as it was in the days when St Kevin lived here. Formal retreats and pilgrimages are run by the local parish all through the year or pilgrims can make a self-guided pilgrimage to St Kevin's favourite places. The local visitors' centre in **Glendalough** is situated on the edge of the monastic site and can provide maps and information.

✝ Sunday Mass 0930 & 1130
St Kevin's Church, Glendalough

Additional Accommodation

County Dublin

🍀 DUBLIN

Ⓢ Avila Carmelite Centre

✉ Bloomfield Avenue and
Morehampton Road
Dublin 4

📞 +353 (0) 1 6430 200

✍ avila@ocd.ie
✍ www.ocd.ie

🐝 Open to both men & women

Ⓣ Dublin City University

✉ Campus Residences Ltd
Dublin City University
Accommodation
Glasnevin
Dublin 9

📞 +353 (0) 1 7005 736

✍ www.summeraccommodation.
dcu.ie

🏠 Open during summer only

Ⓣ Mercer Court

✉ Lower Mercer Street
Dublin 2

📞 +353 (0) 1 4744 120
📞 +353 (0) 1 6729 926

✍ info@mercercourt.ie
✍ www.mercercourt.ie

🏠 Open during summer only

🐝 Open to men, women & groups

Ⓣ National College of Ireland

✉ Mayor Street
Dublin 1

📞 +353 (0) 1 4498 500
📞 +353 (0) 1 4972 200

✍ info@ncirl.ie
✍ www.ncirl.ie

☞ DART: Connolly Train Station

🏠 Open during summer only

🐝 Open to men, women & groups

Ⓢ Orlagh Retreat Centre

✉ Old Court Road
Rathfarnam
Dublin 16

📞 +353 (0) 1 4958 190

✍ info@orlagh.ie
✍ www.orlagh.ie

🐝 Open to men, women & groups

🍀 SWORDS

Ⓢⓣ Emmaus Accommodation and Retreat Centre

✉ Ennis Lane
Lissenhall
Swords

📞 +353 (0) 1 8700 050
📞 +353 (0) 1 8408 248

✍ emmauscentre@emmauscentre.ie
✍ www.emmauscentre.ie

🐝 Open to men, women & groups

County Cork

🍀 CORK

Ⓣ University College Campus Accommodation

🐝 Open to men, women & groups

🏠 Open during summer only

✉ University Hall
Victoria Cross
Cork

📞 +353 (0) 21 4818 455
📞 +353 (0) 21 4818 448

✍ universityhall@ucc.ie
✍ www.ucccampusaccommodation.
com

✉ Victoria Lodge
Victoria Cross
Cork

📞 +353 (0) 21 4941 200
📞 +353 (0) 21 4941 299

✍ victorialodge@ucc.ie
✍ www.ucccampusaccommodation.
com

✉ Castlewhite Apartments
Western Road
Cork

📞 +353 (0) 21 4902 867
📞 +353 (0) 21 4341 473

✍ castlewhite@ucc.ie
✍ www.ucccampusaccommodation.
com

🍀 LEAP

Ⓢ Myross Wood House Retreat Centre

🐝 Myross Wood

✉ Leap
Skibbereen
West Cork

📞 +353 (0) 28 33 118

✍ mscmyross@eircom.net
✍ www.mscireland.com

🐝 Open to men, women & groups

County Donegal

✤ DUNDREAN

Ⓢ St Anthony's Retreat Centre

✉ Dundrean
Burnfoot

☎ +353 (0) 74 9368 370

✉ sarce@eircom.net
✉ www.columbacommunity.
homestead.com/StAnthonys.html

✤ Open to men, women & groups

✤ INISHOWEN

Ⓢ Loreto House

✉ Centre for Peace and
Reconciliation
Linsfort
Buncrana
Inishowen

☎ +353 (0) 74 9362 204

✉ info@loretolinsfort.com
✉ www.loretolinsfort.com

✤ Open to both men & women

✤ LOUGH DERG

Ⓢ St Patrick's Purgatory

✉ Station Island
Lough Derg
Pettigo

☎ +353 (0) 71 9861 518
☎ +353 (0) 71 9861 518

✉ info@loughderg.ie
✉ www.loughderg.ie

✤ Open to men, women & groups

✤ ROSSNOWLAGH

Ⓢ La Verna Retreat House

✉ Franciscan Friary
Rossnowlagh

☎ +353 (0) 71 9851 342
☎ +353 (0) 71 9852 206

✉ franciscanfriary@eircom.net
✉ www.geocities.com/
friaryrossnowlagh/

✤ Open to both men & women

County Galway

✤ ATHENRY

Ⓢ Esker Monastery and Retreat House

✉ Esker
Athenry

☎ +353 (0) 91 844 549
☎ +353 (0) 91 845 698

✉ eskerret@indigo.ie
✉ www.eskercommunity.net

✤ Open to men, women & groups

✤ GALWAY

Ⓣ National University of Ireland

✉ University Road
Galway

☎ +353 (0) 91 492 264
☎ +353 (0) 91 494 512

✉ conference@nuigalway.ie
✉ www.conference.ie

🔒 Open during summer only

✤ Open to men & women.
Groups only.

**Additional
Accommodation**

County Kerry

🏠 ANNASCAUL

🅂 Lios Dána Lodge

✉ Inch, Annascaul

📞 +353 (0) 66 9158 223
📠 +353 (0) 66 9258 223

✉ liosdana@eircom.net
🖥 www.liosdanalodge.com

👥 Open to both men & women

County Kildare

🏠 BALLYMORE EUSTACE

🅂 Avelin Celtic Retreat Centre

✉ Bishopsland
   Ballymore Eustace

📞 +353 (0) 45 864 524

✉ begg@iol.ie
🖥 www.avelin.hitsplc.com

👥 Open to both men & women

County Laois

🏠 PORTARLINGTON

🆂 Mount St. Anne's

✉ Killenard
   Portarlington

📞 +353 (0) 57 8626 153
📠 +353 (0) 57 8626 700

✉ msannes@eircom.net
🖥 www.mountstannes.com

👥 Open to men, women & groups

County Limerick

🏠 LIMERICK

🆃 University of Limerick

✉ Campus Life Services
   University of Limerick
   Limerick

📞 +353 (0) 61 202 433

✉ pcc@ul.ie
🖥 www.ul.ie/campuslife

👥 Open to men, women & groups

🏠 MURROE

🆃 Rinnaknock B&B

✉ Glenstal
   Murroe (Moroe)

📞 +353 (0) 61 386 189

✉ walshseaver@eircom.net
🖥 www.homepage.eircom.
   net/~rinnaknock/

👥 Open to both men & women

County Louth

🏠 COLLON

🆂 Mellifont Abbey

✉ Collon

📞 +353 (0) 41 9826 103

✉ info@mellifontabbey.ie
🖥 www.mellifontabbey.ie

👥 Open to both men & women

County Mayo

🏠 BALLINTUBBER

🆂 Ballintubber Abbey Retreats

✉ Ballintubber
   Claremorris

📞 +353 (0) 94 9030 934
📠 +353 (0) 94 9030 018

✉ btubabbey1@eircom.net
🖥 www.ballintubberabbey.ie

✝ Day retreats only

👥 Open to men, women & groups

🏠 KNOCK

🆂 Knock House Hotel

✉ Ballyhaunis Road
   Knock

📞 +353 (0) 94 9388 088
📠 +353 (0) 94 9388 044

✉ info@knockhousehotel.ie
🖥 www.knockhousehotel.ie

👥 Open to men, women & groups

County Sligo

🍀 MULLAGHMORE

🛂 Star of The Sea Centre

✉ Mullaghmore

📞 +353 (0) 71 9176 722

✍ mercymullaghmore@eircom.net
✍ www.staroftheseacentre.ie

🎗 Open to men, women & groups

🍀 SKREEN

Ⓢ Holy Hill Hermitage

✉ Skreen

📞 +353 (0) 71 9166 021
📞 +353 (0) 71 9166 954

✍ holyhill@eircom.net
✍ www.spirituallifeinstitute.org

🎗 Open to both men & women

County Tipperary

🍀 CLONMEL

Ⓢ Glencomeragh House

✉ Kilsheelan
Clonmel

📞 +353 (0) 52 6133 181
📞 +353 (0) 52 6133 636

✍ info@glencomeragh.ie
✍ www.glencomeragh.ie

🎗 Open to both men & women

🍀 ROSCREA

Ⓢ Mount St Joseph Abbey

✉ Roscrea

📞 +353 (0) 50 521 711
📞 +353 (0) 50 522 198

✍ info@msjroscrea.ie
✍ www.msjroscrea.ie

🎗 Open to both men & women

County Waterford

🍀 WATERFORD

Ⓢ Grace Dieu Manor

✉ Tramore Road
Waterford

📞 +353 (0) 51 374 417
📞 +353 (0) 51 874 536

✍ gracedieu@ireland.com
✍ www.homepage.eircom.
net/~gracedieu/

♿ Discuss access when you book

🎗 Open to men, women & groups

County Wexford

🍀 BLACKWATER

🛂 St John of God Retreat and Holiday Centre

✉ Ballyvaloo
Blackwater

📞 +353 (0) 53 37160
📞 +353 (0) 53 37501

✍ ballyvalooretreatcentre1@
eircom.net
✍ www.ssjg.ie/what_we_do/
ballyvaloo-retreat.html

🎗 Open to men, women & groups

🍀 FERNS

Ⓢ St Aidan's Monastery

✉ Ferns
Enniscorthy

📞 +353 (0) 53 9366 634

✍ staidansferns@eircom.net
✍ www.staidans-ferns.org

🎗 Open to both men & women

County Wicklow

🍀 DONARD

Ⓢ Chrysalis Retreat Centre

✉ Donard

📞 +353 (0) 404 4540 4713
📞 +353 (0) 404 4540 4713

✍ peace@chrysalis.ie
✍ www.chrysalis.ie

🎗 Open to both men & women

🍀 GLENMALURE

Ⓢ Shekina Sculpture Garden

✉ Glenmalure

📞 +353 (0) 404 1283 8711
📞 +353 (0) 404 1283 8711

✍ cmccann@gofree.indigo.ie
✍ www.shekinasculpturegarden.
com

✝ Self-guided day retreat only

🎗 Open to men, women & groups

Sister Ita's Sultana Scones

Preparation time	20 minutes
Cooking time	15–20 minutes
Oven	200°C / 400°F / Gas 6

Sieve the flour, baking powder and the salt into a bowl, and rub in the margarine. Add the sugar, fruit and the peel, if using. Mix well.

❧ Beat the eggs and mix with the milk, reserving a little to brush over the scones. Make a well in the centre of the flour, add the eggs and milk and mix to a soft dough.

❧ Turn out on to a floured board and roll out to about 2½ cm / 1 inch thick. Cut into rounds, using a 6.3 cm / 2½ inch fluted cutter. Brush over with some beaten egg.

❧ Put on to a greased baking sheet and bake in a preheated hot oven (200°C / 400°F / Gas 6) for 15–20 minutes. Turn out on to a wire tray to cool.

- 450 g / 1 lb / 4 cups flour
- 1½ tsp baking powder
- 1½ tsp salt
- 55 g / 2 oz / 4 tbsp margarine
- 55 g / 2 oz / 4 tbsp sugar
- 110 g / 4 oz / ⅔ cup sultanas (USA golden raisins)
- 15 g / ½ oz mixed peel (USA candied citrus peel) (optional)
- 2 eggs
- 280 ml / ½ pint / 1¼ cups milk

From the *Kylemore Abbey Cookbook* and reprinted with the kind permission of Sister Maire Hickey OSB, Kylemore Abbey, Ireland.

From the days of the Abbey Guest House of the 1950s to the tour buses of the 1990s, and right up to her retirement a few years ago at the age of 90, Sister Ita's scones were legendary in the Connemara. She is sadly missed by visitors, drivers and guides who fondly recall her friendship and warm hospitality.

The *Kylemore Abbey Cookbook* is available from *amazon.com* or *amazon.co.uk*.

With thanks to

Tony Clark
Kathleen
Tom
Lucy
Bree
Jim

Tom & Maureen
Tom Jnr

...reviewers, advisers
and all who offered
ideas, encouragement
and assistance.

Monsignor Tony Doherty
Father Brian Gleeson CP
Father Michael Kelly SJ
Father Pius Mary OSB
Frere Columban OCIST
Sister Pat Malone SOSJ
Tim Fischer AO
   *Australian Ambassador
   to the Vatican*

Duncan Beale
Philippa Beeston
Simon Brady
Katharine T. Carroll
Jenny Clements
Christine Ferretti
Maureen Gibson
Geoff Girvan
Pat Grady
Mary and Michael Happ
Lauren Knapmann
Naomi Kneeshaw
Peter Lancaster
Peter Long
Jacqui MacCarthy
Paul McMahon
Wendy Miller
Lloyd and Sally Ryan
Pam Stinson-Bell
Judy Temple
Skye Wentworth
Warren Wickman
Karen Williams
Ve Wood
Dennis Woollam
Nowel Zaarour

I SOMETIMES
THINK THAT
THOMAS COOK
should be
numbered among
the secular saints.
He took travel
from the privileged
and gave it to the
common people.

ROBERT RUNCIE
ARCHBISHOP OF
CANTERBURY,
1980–1991

A SPECIAL THANKS TO

French Government
Tourist Office
franceguide.com

Ireland Tourist Board
discoverireland.com

British National
Tourism Agency
visitbritain.com

a–g

h–st

FR France
UK United Kingdom
IE Ireland

st–z